Conventions and Structures in Economic Organization

NEW HORIZONS IN INSTITUTIONAL AND EVOLUTIONARY ECONOMICS

Series Editor: Geoffrey M. Hodgson
Research Professor, University of Hertfordshire Business School, UK

Economics today is at a crossroads. New ideas and approaches are challenging the largely static and equilibrium-oriented models that used to dominate mainstream economics. The study of economic institutions – long neglected in the economics textbooks – has returned to the forefront of theoretical and empirical investigation.

This challenging and interdisciplinary series publishes leading works at the forefront of institutional and evolutionary theory and focuses on cutting-edge analyses of modern socio-economic systems. The aim is to understand both the institutional structures of modern economies and the processes of economic evolution and development. Contributions will be from all forms of evolutionary and institutional economics, as well as from Post-Keynesian, Austrian and other schools. The overriding aim is to understand the processes of institutional transformation and economic change.

Titles in the series include:

Employment Relations and National Culture
Continuity and Change in the Age of Globalization
Ferrie Pot

Institutions and the Role of the State
Edited by Leonardo Burlamaqui, Ana Celia Castro and Ha-Joon Chang

Marx, Veblen and Contemporary Institutional Political Economy
Principles and Unstable Dynamics of Capitalism
Phillip Anthony O'Hara

The New Evolutionary Microeconomics
Complexity, Competence and Adaptive Behaviour
Jason D. Potts

National Competitiveness and Economic Growth
The Changing Determinants of Economic Performance in the World Economy
Timo J. Hämäläinen

Conventions and Structures in Economic Organization
Markets, Networks and Hierarchies
Edited by Olivier Favereau and Emmanuel Lazega

Conventions and Structures in Economic Organization

Markets, Networks and Hierarchies

Edited by
Olivier Favereau

University of Paris X, Nanterre, France

Emmanuel Lazega

University of Lille I, France

Published with the support of the University
of Paris X, Nanterre

NEW HORIZONS IN INSTITUTIONAL AND EVOLUTIONARY
ECONOMICS

Edward Elgar
Cheltenham, UK • Northampton, MA, USA

Published by
Edward Elgar Publishing Limited
Glensanda House
Montpellier Parade
Cheltenham
Glos GL50 1UA
UK

Edward Elgar Publishing, Inc.
136 West Street
Suite 202
Northampton
Massachusetts 01060
USA

A catalogue record for this book
is available from the British Library

Library of Congress Cataloguing in Publication Data

Conventions and structures in economic organization: markets, networks, and hierarchies/edited by Olivier Favereau and Emmanuel Lazega.

p. cm.—(New horizons in institutional and evolutionary economics series)

'Published with the support of the University of Paris X, Nanterre'.

Includes bibliographical references and index.

1. Institutional economics. 2. Evolutionary economics. 3. Economics—Sociological aspects. 4. Economics. I. Favereau, Olivier. II. Lazega, Emmanuel, 1956– III. New Horizons in institutional and evolutionary economics

HB99.5 .C655 2003
330—dc21

2002072171

ISBN 1 84064 510 5

Typeset by Cambrian Typesetters, Frimley, Surrey
Printed and bound in Great Britain by MPG Books Ltd, Bodmin, Cornwall

Contents

Acknowledgments

This book came out of the Cnrs summer school 'Organizations and markets' (Paris, Maison Suger, 20–24 July 1998) that was organized by Alain Degenne, Olivier Favereau and Emmanuel Lazega. We are grateful to the participants of this summer school who cared to contribute to this volume and to Jean-Luc Lory, Director of the Maison Suger, who hosted it.

Support for the production of this book was provided by several research centres: Lasmas-Cnrs in Paris and in Caen, Forum at the University of Paris 10, and Clersé-Cnrs at the University of Lille 1. We are particularly grateful for help in the production of the manuscript to Lise Mounier, as well as to Annick Degenne and Daniel Urrutiaguer.

Contributors

David N. Barron, professor, Jesus College, Oxford University

Christian Bessy, research officer, Centre d'études de l'emploi, Paris

Olivier Biencourt, professor, University of Maine, France

Didier Chabaud, professor, University of Paris I

Alain Degenne, research officer, Lasmas-CNRS, Caen

François Eymard-Duvernay, professor, University of Paris X

Olivier Favereau, professor, University of Paris X

Henk Flap, professor, Utrecht University

Emmanuel Lazega, professor, University of Lille I

Siegwart Lindenberg, professor, University of Groningen

Lise Mounier, research assistant, Lasmas-CNRS, Paris

Stéphane Saussier, professor, University of Paris I

Daniel Urrutiaguer, University of Paris X

Harrison C. White, professor, Columbia University

Introduction

Emmanuel Lazega and Olivier Favereau[1]

This book asserts that economists and sociologists need the combined concepts of conventions and structures to deal with markets and organizations. We argue that there is room for cooperation between the two disciplines when economists take into account conventions, and sociologists structures and flows of resources. *Conventions* refer to values, rules and representations that influence economic behaviour.[2] *Structures* refer to patterns of interests and relationships reflecting resource interdependencies among members of any social system.

At first sight, the relationship between conventions and structures is obvious. On the one hand, for example, the principle of reciprocity (as described by sociologists such as Mauss or Gouldner) can be conceived of as a convention. This convention may influence, for example, whom members of an organization approach for advice. In effect, one might think that members approach others with the most expertise, but very often this is not what happens: because they probably cannot give anything in return (or because they do not want to recognize these others' status, or because they do not want to be perceived as inexperienced), they often approach people who are at a similar level, who may not know more about this special subject than they do, but for whom, at some point in the future, they will be able to return the favour. The rule of reciprocity will informally determine in part the shape of advice flows in the organization, and thus the structural opportunities and constraints weighing on members' productive abilities. On the other hand, structural features of a collective actor also influence the assertion or definition of rules. The shape of interdependence among members, especially asymmetric interdependence called status or power, also defines members' capacity to decide what is fair and what is unfair in the distribution of efforts and allocation of rewards.

However, the relationship between these two dimensions of economic activity (whether production or exchange) is not really spelled out in current social sciences. Both mainstream economics and new institutional economics feel rather uneasy about rules and values, because of their strong notion of instrumental rationality (either optimizing or bounded); symmetrically structuralist sociology is at pains to give a high analytical status to individual and collective representations, because of a traditional holistic bias.

The project of this book is to study whether it is not only possible but indispensable to combine some sort of structural sociology (in terms of networks) and some sort of institutional economics (in terms of conventions) in order to improve our understanding of coordination, be it organization-like, network-like or market-like. This study, in spite of its systematic character, is still only a challenge. For it to be successful, and to prevent amateurism on both sides, real affinities between these research programmes should lead to statements about covariance between changes in structures and changes in conventions. Empirical progress resulting from this convergence being still virtual, exchanges will remain at the theory level. We have first to introduce our views of structural sociology and institutional economics, before surveying the content of each chapter, in two steps: didactic, then exploratory.

HOW ARE CONVENTIONS AND STRUCTURES RELATED IN A BROADLY CONCEIVED STRUCTURAL SOCIOLOGY?

What is a Broadly Conceived Structural Sociology?

A broadly conceived structural approach to social life can be summarized by five characteristics.[3] The *first* is that it combines an understanding of the interests of actors themselves with that of their organization as a whole, thus bridging the levels of individual and collective action. It does so by looking at the organization as a small political community.[4] Information on interactions and relationships between members is used as information on their resource interdependencies, derived power relationships and coordination efforts. The *second characteristic*, one that separates it from earlier and narrower forms of structuralism, is its capacity to look jointly at economic and symbolic activities. Saying that actors use their resource interdependencies as a source of power presupposes a form of rationality that includes cost–benefit calculations, but also symbolic activity such as appropriateness judgments (based on previous investments in relationships, recognition of identities, identifications to reference groups and the use of various forms of authority arguments) allowing individuals to politicize their exchanges and controls. Actors' politicization has two combined but potentially conflicting dimensions: niche seeking and status competition, both based on selections of, or investments in, relationships. A member's social niche can be defined as a relational context, or subset of other members in the organization, with whom this member commits him/herself to exchange many different types of resources at a relatively lower cost, an advantage that can be called 'bounded solidarity'. As strategic and interdependent entrepreneurs, these individuals also compete for status: they try to concentrate resources in their own individual hands so as to benefit from a position of strength when negotiating terms of exchange (that is, bartering) within and outside their quasi-groups.

These (realistic) assumptions about members' strategic rationality lead to a *third characteristic* of a broadly conceived structural approach. As mentioned above, it bridges the individual and collective levels of action by thinking in terms of multi-level social mechanisms. Examples of such mechanisms provided in previous research include generalized exchange (a form of bounded solidarity based on the existence of cycles of indirect reciprocity among selected colleagues), lateral control (a form of early monitoring and sanctioning of deviant conduct that both spreads and concentrates the costs of control) and regulatory change (a form of 'constitutional' redefinition of the rules of the game that is driven by members with multiple forms of status). By taking such social mechanisms into consideration, this approach combines both individual cost–benefit reasoning and explanations of stable participation in collective action, or cooperation. The *fourth characteristic* of this approach is its use of network analysis as a method for looking at the relational dimensions of these social mechanisms, at their consequences, at the ways in which niche seeking and status competition are combined, managed or prevented from getting out of hand. As suggested by standard definitions of multiplexity, cooperation and coordination are not understandable without complex social relationships and interdependencies as components of such processes. Network analysis is particularly well suited here, because it analyses systematically the ways in which members politicize their exchanges and controls; that is, the ways in which they select their partners when they transfer and exchange many types of production-related resources, and resulting interdependencies.

Finally, the *fifth characteristic* of a broadly conceived structural theory – one that is more to the point for the purpose of this book – is its account of collective actors' built-in dependence on cultural, that is, normative, processes. Saying that status provides a position of strength to define terms of exchanges is equivalent to saying that it helps define or select the values, norms and rules from which such terms are consciously or unconsciously derived. In early structural sociology, the conceptual relationship between relational structures, on the one hand, and rules, norms and values, on the other hand, has been elusive. In narrow structural approaches, resource interdependencies, more than norms, were considered the only principle of social order. Our approach, however, aligns itself with a more Weberian (1920; see also Swedberg, 1998) and institutional perspective when it emphasizes the interpenetration of the interactional and normative realms in order to explain social change or stability. Institutional theories of action have long stressed organizational values, norms and rules as restraints on grabbing economic behaviour and brutal exercise of power. Such values are debated, contested and permanently redefined by members. Organizations change in part because they can redefine their formal and informal rules (Reynaud, 1989). This institutional level of organization was explicitly formulated by many sociologists (Merton, 1959; Parsons, 1956) and by studies of political or micropolitical efforts, by competing interests, to change the rules. Such efforts may or may not be successful, and social arrangements are often stable enough to hide such underlying contests. But structural analysis can help in identifying them.

Specifically, two notions combine a structural and an institutional perspective: Selznick's idea (1957) of 'precarious values' and the notion of 'multi-status oligarchs'. A value is precarious because it is always in danger of losing its flag carriers and representatives; that is, the active support by organized interest groups and elites that help preserve it as a candidate for top priority on the list of all competing values. 'Multi-status oligarchs' are precisely the members of a collective with enough status to redefine priorities between precarious values and derived policy options. Indeed, regulatory changes need the support of members with several forms of status. These oligarchs must have the capacity to promote regulatory changes and deal with the negative effects of broken promises induced by social change. Particularly when differences in power are not huge among members, this capacity often rests on sacrifice of resources by such multi-status oligarchs, and on the legitimacy obtained from such sacrifices. Those who can afford to give up resources for the common good while not losing power are people who have several inconsistent forms of status. Thanks to this inconsistency, or loose coupling, losing one form of status does not entail losing another. Multi-status oligarchs can thus drive change (the redefinition of rules) while staying in power.

In effect, the connection between structure and culture as theorized by Selznick (1957) through the notion of precarious value is useful because any regulatory process – or process of redefinition of rules governing the collective – is a form of change that involves broken promises in the redistribution of resources (Reynaud and Reynaud, 1996). When the rules of the game are changed, some parties come out as losing resources and others as winning resources compared to the ex ante distribution. This is why, in organizations as in any political community, regulatory changes need the support of members with both power and legitimacy to push for these changes. Specific members, those with multiple and loosely connected forms of status, are the key in such changes, because they can use such dependencies and legitimacy in the regulatory process.

Structural Sociology, Social Exchange and Barter

Values count for economic actors, not simply through moral virtue but through politicized negotiation of the terms of exchanges. This means that conventions (a term that could easily – perhaps too easily – be used by sociologists as a synonym for rules) are connected to structures not only through the concepts of precarious value and multi-status oligarchs, but also through other underlying concepts. It is true that Selznick's approach is indispensable, in our view, to any structural understanding of social life and exchanges. However, it does not encompass the whole of the relationships between structures and conventions. Analytically speaking, upstream of Selznick's approach, an underlying theory of strategic rationality is available as a bridge. In effect, since actors politicize their exchanges by using their resource dependencies and identity criteria, rules and conventions are linked to relational structures in several ways.

Recall that social niches are subsets of actors that are able to share identity criteria, to exchange multiple resources without general equivalence and to suspend short-term opportunism. This reminds us that the theory of action on which structural sociologists rely is necessarily an interactionist theory of social exchange, to be distinguished from market exchange. Social life can be identified with a set of particularistic exchange systems handling multiple resources between heterogeneous actors, while allowing social mechanisms that are necessary for their reproduction. The basic notions here are those of multiplexity and barter, which allow for exchanges that are different from market exchanges. The latter relies on general equivalence introduced by accounting and monetary measures which make it possible to evaluate and compare goods. It pretends to ignore the heterogeneity of actors involved in the exchange in order to reach a form of universalism that does not need social structures. But for structural sociology, the notions of multiplexity and barter are precisely the notions that bring a symbolic dimension into social exchanges (and thus the notions of identity, authority and hierarchy of allegiances).

This theory of action was recently developed in different directions: first, as an interactionist theory of 'coorientation' through 'appropriateness judgments' that are necessary for members of any collective to define the situation and to politicize allocation of resources; second, as a theory of the management of multiplex resources explaining the possibility of 'generic' social mechanisms identified above, such as bounded solidarity, control and regulation. This, in our view, is equivalent to saying that conventions (understood both in Lewis's narrow sense and in Favereau's more general sense) are needed as follows in structural economic sociology.

First, norms and rules are necessary to structuralist understanding of social life because they are needed for cognitive coorientation: there is no definition of the situation without legitimate authority and without deference towards members who can wield authority arguments in the process of (re)defining the situation. Conventions are minimally needed as signals of symbolic recognition of membership and of authority. Second, norms are also needed for social exchange and the constitution of social niches and the bounded solidarity that characterizes them. In effect, norms help create relationships (that are then necessary for generic social mechanisms). Others are often selected as exchange partners or third parties so as to conform to the rules, or because they are thought to be able to share one's values, the same rules of the game. For example, convergent social expectations (such as normative expectations expressed by colleagues) reduce individual costs of social control by triggering lateral control interventions at the triadic level (Lazega, 2000; Lazega and Lebeaux, 1995; Lazega and Krackhardt, 2000); they also create the role of multi-target lever. The dynamics of structure are intextricably intertwined with the normative realm. Third, without norms, there is no connection between the micro and the macro levels of analysis. For example, indirect and postponed reciprocity, also identified here as generalized exchange or bounded solidarity, is a meso-level social mechanism that is not conceivable outside a social niche and without common normative ground. Similarly, without norms, there can be no management of status competition since, in any society, social values define acceptable forms of status (in)consistency. To come back to the example of control as a social mechanism, costs of control of others increase dramatically when norms concerning avoidance of conflict escalation are weak, because the second-order free-rider problem (that is, 'who will monitor and sanction deviant behaviour?') becomes unmanageable. Finally, norms are also necessary for driving endogenous change: procedural rules organize constitutional or regulatory deliberations in any group: learning of new behaviour by the collective.

In turn, relational structures are necessary not only for efficient formulation and interpretation of rules and conventions (which otherwise would be endless), but also for change and evolution of rules. Recall that, since any such change means broken promises, it positions members who were called 'multi-status oligarchs' favourably to redefine priorities between precarious values and derived policy options. Regulatory changes, and indeed social change in general, need the leadership and support of members with several inconsistent forms of status. Thus, in our view, conventions and structures are inextricably related in broadly conceived structuralist approaches to social and economic life.

HOW ARE CONVENTIONS AND STRUCTURES RELATED IN THE CONVENTIONALIST BROADENING OF THE INDIVIDUALIST RESEARCH PROGRAMME IN ECONOMICS?

Our broadly conceived institutional approach to economic life can be summarized by five characteristics, which are very close to the five characteristics defining the structural approach to social life, *mutatis mutandis*.[5]

The *first* is that the rational individuals exhibited by economic theorizing are interested not only in personal direct sources of satisfaction but also in collective indirect ones. More precisely, the arguments of the utility function, beside consumption and leisure, should include an evaluation of the 'quality' of the collective entities to which the individual belongs: it is a trivial fact of economic life that individuals had rather work in firms reputed for their equity, invest in a democratic peaceful society, make business with an administration not infested with corruption, and so on. Of course the quality of the collective entities just mentioned will eventually exert a first-order impact upon the private arguments of the utility function but the point is that the evaluation of the collective entity cannot be reduced to its material consequences, except for highly peculiar periods (crisis probably). It could be shown that qualifiying the collective entity is a very convenient shorthand for an economic agent who has to fill in the blanks of incomplete contracting due to radical uncertainty in an interactive context. Such a practice, typical of procedural rationality and obviously of high evolutionary efficiency, should be backed by a new theory of identity for homo economicus, like the theory of 'social identity' (Turner, 1987; Haslam, 2001). Ultimately, that first characteristic, the most basic one, is the economic application of the Aristotelian postulate: man is a political animal.

The *second characteristic* specifies conventionalist economics within the non-standard components of economic theory making use of bounded rationality. Homo economicus has neither the cognitive abilities nor the necessary information to remain the relentless optimizer modelled by mainstream economics. But if he is less rational, he is also more intelligent: one aspect of his intelligence regained consists in the appearance of an interpretive form of rationality, in excess of its computational form, which is the only one available to the mainstream homo economicus. The interpretive ability of the new homo economicus comes from necessity: questions of rationality could no longer be dealt with apart from questions of coordination, as is supposed in the distinct axiomatics of decision theory (Von Neumann and Morgenstern, 1944, Savage, 1954) and of general equilibrium theory (Arrow and Debreu, 1954). The semantic capacities of individual agents are required even in isolation, for instance when the choice problem implies a quality judgment (usually multicriteria) – but their use must be generalized, when dealing with others. It is manifest in contexts of incomplete contracting, since agents have to make a mental representation about the type of collective entity associated with a satisfactory functioning of contractual exchanges. That representation is endowed with all the formal properties usually attributed to conventions, according to their most common meaning: tacitness, unknown source, absence of authorized sanctions, and so on.

The conversion to cognitive realism at both levels, psychological and sociological, has already laid several stepstones, on the way to building a bridge from individual to collective planes. The *third characteristic* brings to the fore the theme of coordination by means of rules, as a generalization of coordination by market prices, privileged by mainstream economics, since . . . Adam Smith. For conventionalist economics, it is simply impossible to speak about economy without speaking about organizations, and to speak about organizations without speaking about rules – and we have just seen that it is impossible to speak about (interpretation of) rules without speaking about conventions. The whole field of organizational structures and mechanisms is on the research agenda of conventionalist economics. What has already been seriously investigated is the role of objects (so strangely neglected in the analysis of coordination) and also the authority relationship through the labour contract.

In order to study those subjects, the 'economics of conventions' – and this will be the *fourth characteristic* of a broadly conceived institutional approach to economic life – makes use of some specific tools (beside the traditional ones used by economists). First, attention is directed towards the verbal arguments produced by the agents themselves, in case of conflict, to justify their attitude and the situations where all the agents are led to agree about the relative strength of their respective arguments (the interested reader is invited to refer to Boltanski and Thévenot, 1991, while keeping in mind the following methodological principle: coordination of economic behaviours must include, in our view of homo economicus, coordination of judgments about economic behaviours); second, research is centred on the rules followed by economic agents, but the rules should be understandable by the agents themselves (as in participant observation recommended by Piore, 1974), which means that the researcher tries to be faithful to the variety of the systems of interpretation, in which economic agents are trained, from their childhood. It comes as no surprise that one of the favourite tools of the conventionalist approach is the typology, notwithstanding the obligation of supplying the unique 'grammar' supposed to generate the different types.

Let us conclude with the *fifth characteristic*, the interdependence between structures and values in the account of the collective order, especially with respect to its dynamic aspects. It is less difficult than it may seem at first sight to study dynamics in an analytic framework stressing rules (and behind rules, conventions), because rules in a world marked by overwhelming problems of interpretation should be considered as a heuristics, more than ready-made solutions. Indeed, our broadly conceived institutional economics, at least at the level of organizations, reduces the problem of collective change to a problem of organizational learning, for instance along the lines of the model built by Argyris and Schön (1978). Although it is a drastic simplification, it nonetheless offers deep insights on the hidden contradiction between values and the dynamics of structures (the contradiction between values and the content of structures is well known). Argyris and Schön (1978) differenciate single loop learning (SLL), which confirms the existing set of rules, and double loop learning (DLL), which requires a move in the set of governing variables. Now their most important result is negative: spontaneous DLL is impossible, because the perspective of leaving the ancient governing variables and entering an unknown game frightens nearly all the actors, accustomed to the existing 'rapports de force', and triggers multiple 'defensive routines'. Only fiat or extreme crisis can countervene those endogeneous obstacles to DLL (Argyris, 1988). And it will be so as long as the managers of an organization do not accept the falsifiability of their criteria (in a quasi-Popperian mood) when they discuss with their subordinates: the worst contradiction lies between values and changes in structures, if not in the structures themselves.

We can now ask the question which is at the heart of this introduction, because it is at the heart of this book.

What is the Degree of Proximity between such Broadly Conceived Institutional Economics and Structural Sociology?

The first point to be noticed is the remarkable similarity (with some significant differences) between the five characteristics in the two programmes. The first and the second are almost identical; the third and the fifth suggest complementarity rather than identity; difference is logically at its maximum with the fourth one, devoted to methods. It is obvious that structural sociology is better equipped to model precise organizational mechanisms, thanks to its practice of network analysis, whereas institutional economics has a comparative advantage to integrate moral values within coordinating devices, through its ability to deal with social representations and models of personal identity.

The best insight on the content of what we call the 'proximity' between the two research programmes may be given by the notion of 'social niches',[6] defined in the (broad) structuralist programme as subsets of actors where short-term opportunism is suspended (Lazega, 2001). In the (broad) institutionalist dictionary, no item dubbed 'social niche' can be found. Nevertheless, the conventionalist approach is not ignorant of the phenomenon and it has much to say on its cognitive/psychological implications at the level of individual rationality. The problem of social niche has simply to be correlated with the problem of incomplete contracting: how is it possible that a rational non-altruistic individual agent agrees to the terms of an incomplete contract (that is, a contract unable to specify a rule of conduct in any conceivable state of nature?). Indeed, this seemingly technical problem is no less than the major theoretical problem of the foundations of cooperation in a world of non-cooperative rationality.

On a strictly inter-individual basis, the solution can be found in rereading the acceptance of an incomplete contract by a non-altruistic agent as a credible signal of his intention to cooperate. The signal is credible, because it is costly: the agent becomes the 'hostage' of his partner, in the event of an unforeseen contingency (Williamson, 1996, ch. 5 ; Favereau, 1997). Note that the efficiency of the signal is not only preserved but paradoxically, reinforced by the non-altruism of the agent: it is his long-term interest to suspend his short-term interest.

The inter-individual face of the solution has to be supplemented by the collective face, already evoked to introduce the broad acception of conventions: we have proved it is not irrational to suspend short-term opportunism. It remains to be understood why/when a rational agent decides to do so. Let us recall the conventionalist solution: the rational agent thinks his contractual relationship will give him access to a satisfactory 'common world', together with all the members of the relevant collective. What objective elements of the organization under scrutiny enables him to think so? Here is the place where the structural analysis of 'social niches' becomes an indispensable ally to allow the conventionalist analysis to overcome its weaknesses and answer its own most difficult questions. We will have some more to say on this point in the next paragraph (see also note 4).

The second point to be noticed may be enunciated concisely: the four reasons listed above (pp. 5–6) to explain why norms/rules/conventions are needed in structural economic sociology are completely coherent with the spirit of the conventionalist trend within the institutional economics. The first two reasons (on the role of rules, respectively, as cognitive guidelines and as normative foundation of social niches) are most apparent in the conventionalist model of organizational learning. The last two reasons (on the role of rules, respectively, in the micro–macro link and in the process of collective learning) would need a significant addition of new conventionalist stuff, at the higher level of the whole society, such as the work of Boltanski and Chiappello (1999) but the general line of the argument would be the same: the capitalist system cannot but provoke resistance, objections, criticism, conflicts, struggles . . . Therefore holders of power find it simultaneously necessary and productive to absorb part of the criticism by revising work organizations in a way which is more congruent with some selective set of values. We may summarize the point by making the remark that the conventionalist approach and the structural approach meet about the question of legitimacy (even if both rarely use this vocabulary).

The family resemblance is strong enough to raise the question of its primary source. Let us risk a conjecture. The central issue in social science is the connexion between representations and structures. The new ('broad') structural sociology proceeds from the discovery that, in a human world, structures are neither completely nor correctly analysed without the representations about the structures, whereas, in a social world, the new ('conventionalist') institutional economics proceeds from the discovery that representations are neither completely nor correctly analysed without the context of their surrounding structures: indeed, in a perfecly homogeneous world, mental representations are either devoid of any analytical interest or overcrowded with artificial problems and theoretical artefacts (such as common knowledge, in game theory). A corollary of this conjecture is that cooperation between ('broad') structural sociology and ('conventionalist') institutional economics will be most productive in the field of socioeconomic change: it is highly plausible that true dynamics come from interplay between (change in) representations and (change in) structures.[7]

To end this section on a more cautious note, 'family resemblance' is not synonymous with perfect likeness. Structural sociology and institutional economics, even broadly conceived, are not two labels for the same merchandise. The difference is still there: the first approach starts from the social exchange (beautifully re-evaluating barter) and shows the market exchange as a very special case; the second approach is only concerned with market exchange but has found it is mistakenly modelled, when it is done with the sole help of the traditional tools of mainstream economics (whose hard core is rational choice theory).[8] Good economics has now to borrow some good sociology to do its own job. That means that economics needs an exteriority; and therefore sociology too.

This book provides mainly theoretical contributions that help in the effort to mind and fill the gap between the two disciplines. To frame this dialogue between economists and sociologists, the texts offered here are considered to be either didactic in the sense that they lead to the necessity of such a combined research programme, or exploratory in the sense that they deal in one way or another with this complementarity.

A DIDACTIC PART

The first series of chapters provide the current landscape of theories that bring together sociological and economic approaches, while not yet combining the notions of conventions and structures in economics and sociology of markets and organizations.

Typical of an approach that builds on structural insights and pushes towards a general theory of action *without referring to conventions* is the theory of social capital by Henk Flap. In the first chapter, he presents the elusive link between rational choice approaches and structures as defined by networks analysts. Someone's social relations can be interpreted as his social capital since they are instrumental for goal attainment. Rational actors invest and disinvest in relationships depending on the present value of future help. Their social capital has four dimensions: the number of persons prepared to help, the strength of the relationships, the resources to which these relationships give access, and the degree to which these others have alternatives to dealing with ego. This key idea is meant to explain the effects of social networks as well as the emergence of networks. Structural effects are especially identified with organizational conditions influencing the returns on social capital. This production–investment argument is supported by findings in labour market research and research on primary relations. Major themes within the research programme are the constraints of places ('foci') and numbers ('the supply side') as well as technological and organizational conditioning of returns of social capital (for example, weak ties are a liability in communist societies, so people have smaller networks with a small, dense niche of strong ties to the few whom they trust). Recent developments within the programme concern the goal specificity of social capital as well as the social capital of corporate actors.

Contrary to Coleman's approach (1990), rules are ruled out here as a form of social capital because the latter concept would then, it is argued, lose its specificity. This theory aims at closing a theory gap in network research and explaining why the neostructuralist claim of pure structural effects is wrong. It does so by compounding all the resources that circulate under the same abstract category of social capital. Resources brought by social capital are left deliberately general and vague; they are any form of help. It is unclear, however, how norms would influence the value of social capital. Members are instrumentally rational in their investments and disinvestments in ties. There is little collective action in this approach. There are no formal structures and rules in this chapter's reasoning on social capital. Henk Flap starts with rational choice and networks, not with production and collective action. Measurements of social capital are looking for a stable unit which might be a dyadic tie, although a tie associated with many conditions. This raises the issue of the existence of networks that do not lean on institutional and organizational structures, without specific collective goals, from which actors are able to extract resources 'in general'.

Two schools in economics that bring rules into their thinking are then represented and discussed. First, 'Économie des Conventions' is characterized by its importing of elements from the sociology of organizations into economics.

Building on the understanding of convention described above, François Eymard-Duvernay describes the conventionalist approach to organizations (who find themselves at the intersection of various markets), including a statement about pluralities of rules and of rationalities. In his view, coordination is not only in the calculations of rational actors, it is based on judgments and conventions about quality. He observes that there is a wide variety of enterprises within a single sector. The strength of the market theory is that it fits all these activities into the same framework of calculation. But that is also its weakness. Organizations as such have an important and underestimated role in coordinating various markets.[9] Recognition of the coordination role played by firms involves an investigation of their variety, which corresponds to a variety of forms of coordination, and the development of a comparative approach. Eymard-Duvernay presents a theoretical and empirical comparative approach of 'corporate models'. Each model corresponds to a coherent conception of what the quality of a product and of work is (quality convention). There is no single best way of evaluating quality, and this uncertainty complicates coordination within activities. The concept of convention orients the analysis of institutions in a particular direction. It indicates that there is a plurality of conventions and that the problem is choosing between different possible conventions. He presents examples of this kind of arbitration by managers: between what he calls complete contract and close ties; between market and network. He also explores the question of the dynamics of conventions.

In other words, Eymard-Duvernay joins sociologists who assert that actors are not just parts of structures. They act on them in a plurality of ways. His is a position that is close to negotiated order theory (Strauss, 1978). Is the relationship with structures absent from his work, as is often the case with this latter theory? Identifying an action regime on which the firm operates is vital for the firm. Although structures may be assumed in his approach, there is no description of interdependencies of actors in their interpretation work. What Eymard-Duvernay is interested in is the means that actors use to renegotiate an order, even if it is not predictable through their interactions. Conventions are the means that guide interpretation in the situation. This is where learning and apprenticeship are brought in. Contract incompleteness leads to learning and interpretation is problematic. This approach offers leads for understanding the relationship between conventions and structures in a very crude way: for example, a domestic action regime is only compatible with small units including only a few actors. But bringing out resource interdependencies among different types of actors in a multilateral situation is not the main focus. Thus, in several ways, the question of this book challenges Eymard-Duvernay's approach to enlarge what it means by resources[10] and to take into account such differences as vertical versus horizontal coordination.

Economics of Conventions is not alone in the study of rules in economics. The second school, New Institutional Economics, emphasizes the role played by institutions considered as patterns of interactions between actors, in the sense of rules that constrain their behaviour. In his contribution, Christian Bessy specifies the differences between the above-mentioned and North's (1990) definition of rules. He looks at the convergence between New

Institutional Economics (NIE) and the Economics of Conventions (EC). Certain developments in NIE over the past few years have created areas of overlap with the EC on the question of the institutional anchorage of economic exchange and the organization. Since the work of Williamson (if not of Coase), the comparison between different coordination mechanisms or organizational forms, depending on the characteristics of the institutional environment, and, more analytically, the hypothesis of 'bounded' rationality, have constituted research perspectives common to both approaches. Certain developments in NIE over the past few years have created areas of overlap with the French EC school of thinking on the question of the institutional embeddedness of economic exchange and its type of organization. Bessy's chapter identifies these similarities (beyond the divergences), taken from the most recent work of North on cognitive processes, for NIE, and certain representatives of EC. In the first part he considers the plurality of institutions, with a particular focus on the problems of analytical coherence facing both approaches. In the second part he analyses more precisely the interdependence between cognitive processes and institutions. Both parts highlight problems of empirical investigation and validation of analyses. It is worth keeping in mind that, in his work on institutional change, North's interest in the part played by 'informal' institutions (conventions, behavioural norms and so on) caused him to move further away from neoclassical economics. More recently, the emphasis on the articulation between cognitive processes and institutions (Knight and North, 1997) has brought him even closer to the research programme of the EC. Bessy notes that observation constraints characterizing a research programme common to both approaches, as defined here with reference to ties between cognition and institutions, are very costly, especially as validation constraints based on statistical proof.[11] But in terms of combining instrumental and axiological rationalities, NIE and EC face the same challenges.

In our view, two more approaches attempt to bring together insights from economics and sociology. The first is transaction cost economics (TCE), the second organizational ecology (OE). In the first, a protostructural approach to markets and organizations is offered that stops short of actually looking into how they operate. The second eliminates agency altogether. Before moving to more limited, but deeper, attempts, these approaches are also presented.

Chabaud and Saussier present a summary of TCE basics in which the institutional environment is assumed. TCE understand organizations as coordination devices that are not reducible to the price mechanism. Their coordination of collective action is based on contracts dealing with moral hazard and opportunistic behaviour. But contracts and property rights are not sufficient to coordinate; they are incomplete and they fail, among other things because of asset specificities involved, for example when these assets are intangible and personal. They are difficult to contractualize and to enforce, so TCE studies governance structures built to deal with failing contracts. An institutional environment structures transactions and production by favouring specific contractual arrangements plus collective governance devices, incentive intensity, modalities of control and modalities of adaptation. This is where TCE agrees in principle to bring in a form of social discipline, thus a more structural approach. The authors are more transaction cost economists, expanding on Williamson's perspective via Claude Ménard's (1997, 2000) approach. In their chapter they illustrate the weaknesses and recent improvements of the theory, focusing more especially on the analysis of inter-firm agreements and intra-firm organization. In TCE, the notion of governance structure implies that actors choose their constraints the mechanisms that will safeguard their contracts, and make their mutual commitments credible. Partners' characteristics, for example their level of asset specificity, may or may not encourage the creation of an economic tie. This insight, however, is not pushed towards its true structural implications, that is, a true understanding of resource interdependencies among actors. Governance structures are understood as formal devices that help actors reach such credible commitments to each other and overcome their respective opportunism. Individuals can compute what kind of governance structure is more adapted to the transaction. Another aspect is that, when the specificity of assets and therefore interdependence between agents increase, this introduces a dynamic dimension. This becomes a way to endogenize the assets. And the dynamic aspect is more difficult to integrate with standard tools.

Specifying the relationship between TCE and structural analysis, on the one hand, and 'économie des conventions', on the other, is important here. First, in many ways, Chabaud and Saussier are structuralists, but the structures that they look at remain formal and legal. In effect, for Williamson, there is no need for conventions. Actors only calculate. They ask: what is the governance structure that minimizes transaction costs? There is nothing left to interpret. Structures of governance are legal constraints: market, hierarchy, hybrid. One of these governance structures, hierarchy, has a great variety. But resource interdependencies do not lead to new structures in Williamson's reasoning, although nothing serious prevents this theory from adding them. Second, the distinction between calculation and interpretation mentioned above is practical for differentiating TCE and EC, with North's NIE standing in between. For TCE, all can be boiled down to calculation (transaction costs, even metaphorically speaking). NIE stands in between because it considers part of the institutional environment as informal. Institution is not simply a set of vague and remote constraints (TCE), but a model of interaction between agents (EC and NIE). Thus the institution is the structure, but not in the sense of a pattern of resource interdependencies. Hierarchies of rules are added to such structural constraints (with informal rules being the most inert, and thus difficult to change).

Finally, organization ecology also represents an attempt to bring together economics and sociology. It is based on the assumption that agency also may have limits. David Barron looks at the way OE helps in the definition of opportunities and constraints for organizations, then at the combination of legitimacy and density in OE, and at the articulation of structural analysis and OE. Reviews of organizational ecology usually start by making reference to Hannan and Freeman's (1977) article, which was the foundation for the large body of research that has developed over the past twenty years or so. The central question posed by Hannan and Freeman was 'Why are there so many kinds of organizations?' Although little, if any, empirical research has sought to answer this question directly, ecologists are always concerned with explaining how 'social economic, and political conditions affect the relative abundance and diversity of organizations and attempt to account for their changing composition over time' (Baum, 1996, p.77). To this end, most empirical research in this tradition has concentrated on explaining the rates at which new organizations are founded and/or the rate at which existing organizations disband, a sub-branch of organizational ecology that is sometimes called organizational demography. The other main sub-branch of the field has been concerned with changes in individual organizations. This sub-branch has developed out of the work of another American sociologist, Miller McPherson (1983). Recently, a few scholars have been attempting to combine some of the features of these two sub-branches of ecological research. The encapsulation of the concerns of ecological researchers quoted above summarizes some of the key characteristics of ecological research. First, it is concerned with the effect of the *environment* on organizations. In this sense, it is an example of what Scott (1991) calls an open systems theory. Second, it seeks to explain characteristics of *collections* of organizations: populations.

After presenting this ecological and dynamic approach to organizational survival, David Barron tries to combine concepts that ring a bell mainly with structural approaches (not much with conventionalist ones). The concepts are those of niches, legitimacy and organizations. Reasoning here begins with organizations in need of resources, and moves to the demographics of organizational forms (small/large, specialized/generalists), foundings, growth rates and mortality, by thinking in terms of density, various forms of legitimacy and competition. Here Barron reaches more structural forms of reasoning when discussing the structuring of organizational populations, particularly with the concept of niche, niche width and niche overlap. He compares his definition with what Harrison White (1981a) and others call a niche in network terms. Specifically, he explores four areas where ecological and structural theories have been drawn together: (a) the use of network concepts and data to define and identify population niches (and hence organizational forms) (Burt, 1982; Burt and Talmud, 1993); (b) the diffusion of organizational forms via social networks (Barron, 1998); (c) the role played by networks in organizational dynamics (McPherson and Ranger-Moore, 1991); (d) technology networks and organizational niches (Podolny *et al.*, 1996).

With OE, we changed the level of analysis. What organization ecologists want to explain is organizational diversity, what differentiates firms, not markets. Their research is about the dynamics within a market. We are looking at and comparing populations of organizations. Organization ecologists think of themselves as different from contingency theories in that they do not study individual organizations: this is how they want to be a bridge between economics and sociology. Compared to approaches which look at the emergence or social construction of markets and their boundaries, this theory takes markets as a given. It is much more about organizational survival in given markets than about markets themselves. The main thrust of the theory has been to understand, given a grouping of organizations that evolves over time in a complex world made of markets, governments and so on, what are the chances of survival for various categories of organizations. OE thus introduces a key dependent variable for many processes examined above, but does not contribute to explaining its results from an actor-oriented perspective, be it instrumental or axiological. One might think that organization sociologists should cut across standard economists' technologically driven definition of market instead of assuming it.

In their chapter, Emmanuel Lazega and Lise Mounier summarize the contribution of early structural analyses of markets and organizations. They then look at new structural approaches that combine structural analyses with richer behavioural assumptions. This leads to an understanding of resource interdependencies as a basis for the emergence of social mechanisms such as bounded solidarity (based on generalized exchange) and control, with their influence on members' returns on investments (in effort, in resources and in relations). The notion of multiplexity and the study of barter of different types of resources are used to think of organizations or even whole industries (Granovetter, 1994) as structured and constraining exchange systems. In general, it is recognized that networks help members get access to the resources they need; but they are a sort of jungle. Collective actors need rules and conventions to distribute and allocate those resources in ways less dependent on personal ties. Networks are made of pairwise relations that are put together by actors who commit themselves to each other. They are not only concatenations or pairwise ties in the eye of the observer. In order to look at the way collective actors solve problems of coordination, one has to look not only at the exchanges that they reflect, but also at the ways in which their members manage and politicize these exchanges. For this, it is important to bring in a whole series of concepts (rules, values and fairness judgments) that the notion of convention encompasses. This distinction between an old and a new structural approach to markets and organizations is meant to illustrate the coming together of perspectives combining instrumental and axiological forms of rationality (Ferrand and Shijders, 1997). The next section presents contributions that come closer to that goal.

THE EXPLORATORY PART: ATTEMPTS TO COMBINE CONVENTIONS AND STRUCTURES

Explicit attempts to combine conventionalist and structural approaches to opportunity and constraint first include Alain Degenne's theory (Chapter 7) of how economic relationships are regulated ; Favereau, Biencourt and Eymard-Duvernay address the issue of structure and interdependencies in their criticism of Harrison White's model. Emmanuel Lazega and Lise Mounier look at the way structural characteristics of members constrain the process of (re)defining formal and informal rules. Siegwart Lindenberg attempts to combine structural and normative approaches in a theory of solidarity. In order for a link to exist between the two disciplines, there is a need for a theory of individual action and a contextualization. Do we find them in all the texts that claim to combine them? Recall that *structure* is defined as regularities in multiple resource interdependencies among actors in place; interdependencies are always multiplex (defined for several resources) and multilateral. *Conventions* are defined as rules or quasi-rules that help in the coordination with others through consent or quasi-consent.

Combining conventions and structures can be done by beginning to look at the relationship between labour markets and organizations. For example, labour market studies show that, with the diversification of goods, firms cannot plan their work well ahead of time, so there is a flexible labour contract and a specific labour market for a specific good production. Regardless of this, the process of hiring is a kind of blindspot in standard economic theory, which does not need any particular theory of recruitment: every worker has his/her own 'marginal productivity' and the only problem, for the recruiting firm, is to compare it with a wage level. Indeed, in such a world, there is only a market for labour. Organization appears (and recruitment becomes a practical and a theoretical issue) as soon as this 'marginal productivity' becomes unclear. In this context, Alain Degenne offers a view of labour markets that looks at types of trajectories of persons at entry level. He combines the perspective of employers with that of employees (or prospective employees) to capture the 'match' between them. He shows that we need detailed analysis of the employer–employee relationship, its forms of regulation, its variety, its multiplexity, in order to understand what is a labour market. New trends in the hiring of youth and substantial recent research interest in this population both indicate that these new hiring policies are now being applied to other categories of job seekers. Subsidized jobs, temping and their forms of precarious employment are not incompatible with the establishment of stable employer–employee relationships. Precarious employment is a complex phenomenon that cannot be boiled down to a by-product of economic recessions. There is no evidence that a sustained return to high growth will sweep away established behaviour patterns, especially when they are the result of a process of repositioning a company in its market.

In Degenne's broad structural approach, labour markets have two interconnected dimensions: wages and relations between partners; what is being negotiated is rarely wages, it is rather the relationship. He has a typology of forms of trust between employer and employee and his language is sometimes close to that of transaction costs economics (costs of maintaining the relationship and so on). He writes about a 'match', not really about a 'market'. He insists on the diversity of contracts. In his typology of contracts, some relations are long-term (as opposed to spot transactions). This burgeoning structural approach to labour markets focuses on the multiplex employer–employee tie and two of its dimensions. Such ties are the building blocks of wider structures; constraints (and macroeconomic consequences for unemployment) could therefore be derived from this exploratory approach. One limitation, however, is that it is less 'organizational' than it could be from its own point of view, mainly owing to the lack of proper data. One can observe labour markets and behaviour in them (for example, testing hypotheses on the relationship between wages and commitment, since the latter are also meant to reduce opportunism), but this is rarely done. So there is still a whole part of reality missing from this presentation, mainly because the right data sets are not available (that is, there is the problem of combining employers' and employees' perspectives in the same data set). As long as we do not have data about the circulation of personnel between firms (which need personnel but do not have time to train them and cannot afford to give them long-term contracts), we do not evaluate theories about an organizational approach to the labour market.

Nevertheless, Degenne's view opens up an avenue for combining rules and resources. The circulation of the resource that the employer wants most (worker's goodwill) needs a context of trust that they must build together in very different ways that are not yet spelled out. Specific combinations of ways characterize entire segments of the labour market. The scientific goal here being to redefine the structure of the labour market, this is work in progress that does not yet reach that stage. It is a form of neo-institutionalist reasoning, or perhaps a transaction costs reasoning applied to (mainly informal) labour markets – but without calculation of transaction costs. From the perspective of this book, it is important to see that Degenne does include conventions in his model since his analysis rests on an agreement between employers and employees, if not on common representations, that is, on a basic ingredient of the idea of convention. He is looking for a structure that would emerge from the trajectories of actors involved in these different types of conventions in the employment relationships. As for Henk Flap's approach, the main (and only) resource here is the other's goodwill.

Harrison White's (1981b, 2001) model of markets is another theory showing the complementarity of economic and sociological approaches allowing for combination of conventions and structures. In 1981, Harrison White extended and simplified his theory of relational structures in order to devise an entirely new model of markets for manufactured goods, founded on the variance of business firm choices in a quality/price space. He looks at product markets through the issue of the quality of goods. Differences in organizational structures in firms are connected to the nature of the goods produced and to the quality of these goods. The combination of the two approaches in this type of market is offered in the juxtaposition of goods markets and interorganizational structures. In this perspective, Olivier Favereau, François Eymard-Duvernay and Olivier Biencourt present their reading of the $W(y)$ model with its basic components (networks of producers watching each other, uncertainties and judgments about the quality of goods, the subsequent creation of niches, and the typology of sustainable markets). They show that White's typology of viable markets could be connected with the existence of quality conventions, on which consumers and producers must agree, if competition is to produce some kind of order. In other words, they combine this model in broad strokes with types of firms, quality conventions and contexts of exchange (merchant, industrial and domestic). Finally, they argue that this connection should be considered an opportunity for improvement of both theories: theory of relational structures and theory of conventions.

The connection between quality conventions and $W(y)$ deserves more scrutiny so as to identify their commonalities. The market schedule $W(y)$ supposes a dispersion of firms on a quality array on which the firm must place itself. This approach is thus close to conventions because, in White's model, a specular phenomenon produces an order, through a mixture of calculation and interpretation. An underlying structure of interdependencies is assumed behind every quality convention, but, as in Alain Degenne's approach, it is not necessarily explicitly described and conceptualized. The main resource here is an actor's aptitude to produce in a way slightly different from that of others, that is, in a way that makes him or her different.

Olivier Biencourt and Daniel Urrutiaguer offer two case studies to illustrate this approach. For them, market profiles help to formalize producer and customer networks' logics. In the road transport case, economic deregulation led to a resistance to commercial contracts. Either relationships between hauliers and customers are constructed on the basis of personal trust, as in a 'paradox' market, or there is a pressure on industrial attestation, as in a 'crowded' profile. White's typology shows the way to classify organization performances by the comparison of consumers' tastes and producers' costs with changes in volume and quality of products. The quantitative valuation method of theatrical institutions which are interpreted as a market organized by the director–programme planner has proved adequately operational in this way. For empirical studies the main limit of White's model is its vertical differentiation of products. So quality is assessed by consensus while in the quality order of theatre, judgments exhibit the opposition between media renown embodied by drama critics and institutional attestation of programme planners. Intermediaries are ignored while playing a key part in the networks formation for theatre and road haulage.

Another attempt to look at the relationship between conventions and structures can be credited to 'framing theory' of solidarity. In his chapter, Siegwart Lindenberg theorizes the coming together of economics and sociology since the 1960s; he aims to answer three questions left open by previous theories of solidarity (including rational choice theories of solidarity and social capital). What kind of behaviour constitutes solidarities? Under what conditions is solidarity supposed to arise and why? What makes solidarity precarious and how is this precariousness resolved? Part of the chapter deals with the inadequacy of other theories. After criticizing Durkheim's approach, Lindenberg presents his version of a rational choice approach to solidarity, especially by asserting hypotheses about how actors sustain a farsighted rationality that puts restraints on maximizing behaviour. Lindenberg thus provides new microfoundations for solidarity. His theory is that framing, a cognitive process that adjusts situationally the marginal utility of goods, is the crucial phenomenon underlying solidarity and sharing groups. Frames and rules are thus very strongly interdependent.

He then addresses the issue of how sharing groups maintain frame stability, especially through relational signalling. This theory allows him to differentiate weak and strong solidarity in society at large. Lindenberg's approach is easily connected to convention theory (through relational signalling that is based on language and metacommunication). But there is more difficulty in connecting this approach with a structural perspective, because Lindenberg's approach assumes that just making small signals is enough to restore cooperation. It is a very strongly situational theory that emphasizes the precariousness of cooperative endeavours; perhaps structures come in via the stabilization of the frames as an organizational process, and the creation of a long-term rationality also as an organizational process. Nevertheless, structural constraints and power relationships that express them are simplified to such an extent that many social processes characterizing collective action in organizations or coordination in markets may not be easily derived from this original combination of actor's instrumental and axiological rationalities accounting for solidarity.

The variety of approaches to economic action described above leads to many possible syntheses. In our view, it is worth narrowing this set of possible syntheses down to a comparison between a broadly conceived structural approach and a broadly conceived 'économie des conventions'. This comparison is provided next.

CONCLUSION

To summarize, contributions to this book promote research programmes that are important for attempts to combine conventions and structures, axiological or value-oriented and instrumental rationalities. Economics of conventions assumes that members think about their economic activity, and that economics should take such representations and reflexivity into account. This approch is entirely compatible with a Weberian sociological perspective in which actors' interpretive work helps them sort out their interests. Economic sociology considers the intertwining of instrumentally and normatively rational actions in equally close ways. Norms and values count for economic actors, not simply through moral virtue but often through politicized social exchange and derived relational structures.

If bringing together the two perspectives is somewhat suprising and innovative, it is because structural sociology used to start from a holistic, anti-individualistic approach, while institutional economics in terms of conventions proceeded from an individualist methodology, although of a type admitting collective objects (see Dupuy *et al.*, 1989, introduction). For heterodox economists, this rapprochement helps in combining the individualistic tradition of economics with themes such as relational structures, inequalities and power, in order to analyse more accurately the content and consequences of agents' decisions, whether individual or collective, or both. For structural sociologists, it is an opportunity to think about ways to combine analyses of multiplex social exchanges and that of market exchanges when accounting for individual and collective actions.

Finally, it is worth reflecting on the possible use of even closer ties between conventions and structures for a research programme that would be useful to both economists and sociologists. Such closer ties emerge in the enmeshed dynamics of conventions and structures. For sociologists, efforts to reshape one's opportunity structure take the form of redefinition of rules (either for the management of exchanges or for the selection of exchange partners). This is consistent with basic assumptions of the French school of economics of conventions (Dupuy *et al.*, 1989; Favereau, 1997, 2001b; Salais and Storper,

1993). As already mentioned members interpret their economic activity, and that economics should take such representations and reflexivity into account in order to theorize coordination in production. Similarly in the Weberian tradition, economic sociology wants to show the intertwining of instrumentally rational actions and normatively rational actions. Norms and values count for economic actors, through the negotiation of the terms of exchanges and selection of exchange partners.

Conventions thus include rules to which members refer to conduct production-related exchanges. With regard to economic behaviour, particularly barter, conforming to customary rules is helpful in that it makes exchanges predictable in a context in which pure cost–benefit calculation is suspended, given the conditions under which barter is possible. As seen above, identification with others in the niche is used to understand how members deal with multiplex ties and barter. With identification come attached a series of rules concerning the management of multiplex resources.[12] Others are often chosen as exchange partners, bystanders or third parties so as to confirm the rules. The latter thus reach a certain stability that helps economic actors coordinate production and distribution. This definition has strong normative extensions: it helps identify what to expect legitimately in terms of commitments and solidarity in exchanges of resources. Institutionalized definitions of the situations always conflict with less institutionalized ones, but they nevertheless often overlap sufficiently to help in handling exchanges of multiple resources.

This normative realm includes conventions, understood either as informal rules or as interpretive keys to formal rules that help in the coordination with others through consent (agreement) or quasi-consent. For the French representatives of 'économie des conventions', convention refers to many more aspects of social and economic life than rules, although the latter are included in the former. Conventions are often agreements about how one should coordinate with others, but grounded on interpretation as much as on calculation. But to the extent that they are rules, they do not determine behaviour mechanically because they have to be interpreted and applied. They are sometimes resources, sometimes constraints, depending on the situation and on where the individual is in the structure. This is why actors have to have an idea of the social collective associated with the correct functioning of these rules, that is, in which they want to coordinate with others (see Favereau, Biencourt and Eymard-Duvernay's chapter below). Underneath every kind of rule, there is a conventional representation of the collective. We referred to one such collective as a social niche. Thus, if conventions can be construed as a set of rules of the game based on precarious values in organizations, 'économie des conventions' can be easily connected with a structural approach, even more easily if actors are not allowed to get rid of the problem of conflicts of interpretation of the rules. Here, structure is defined by roles and status (or multiple forms of status) as a concentration of various types of resources in oligarchs, that is, notables multiplying elective charges to 'read' social norms have a real regulatory power as intermediaries holding together the different parts or constituencies of a system, but they also agitate symbols of legitimacy. The link between structure and convention is provided by the process of selection of multi-status oligarchs for the renegotiation of rules of the game. Social mechanisms also contribute heavily to governance, especially when all members tend to take part in regulatory activities, that is in the reformulation of formal or informal rules and conventions.

This means that 'convention' cannot be equated only with 'rule' in order to create a narrow bridge between structural sociology and 'économie des conventions'. This reduction is only an analytical 'moment' in the use of the concept of convention by sociologists trying to understand the coexistence of multiplex social exchange and market exchange. The notion of convention shows how actors, even competitors, meet and organize their cooperation. But conventions develop in a context that is relationally and symbolically structured. Existing conventions thus need to be differentiated from creation of new conventions. Dynamics of structures play a role in this differentiation.

Therefore there is a need to differentiate between new conventions (endogenous rules, for example) and old conventions (embedded norms, for example). In effect, relational structures are also the product of multiple and symbolic determinations (old, exogenous and embedded norms as well as new and endogenous rules) that coexist in these structures in spite of their heterogeneity. It would be unfortunate to hide this heterogeneity under the label of 'institution' or 'convention', not only because of the fact of normative ambiguities and of multiplexities, but also because this heterogeneity creates room for structural dynamics.

A dynamic approach to conventions and structures needs to leave behind a narrow form of interactionism that does not take into account the multilateral, multiplex and multi-level dimensions of relational structures. This leads to the necessity to distinguish rules as the product of the aggregation and combination of ties into a multiplex structure from rules that create ties and structures. Regulating interactions creates structures and in such structures actors elaborate further, 'second order', rules and conventions. This is compatible with an approach that looks at multi-level social mechanisms. Generalized exchange, lateral control and other mechanisms can be derived from relational investments that themselves use opinions, ideas, representations and norms: they have an institutional dimension. But their multi-level character indicates that they also emerge from an aggregation of elementary structures that pre-exist: dyadic and triadic ties. They are thus second order institutions, products of actors confronted by this specific structure combining primary elementary substructures.

In many ways, a relationship is not only a conduit for resources, but already an expression of values that it 'represents' or of 'first order' rules and conventions that it enacts. In that sense, the connection between relational structures and convention is more direct than a connection that only depends on the notions of precarious values and multi-status oligarchs. This can be taken into account even if structural sociologists concerned with collective action may be more interested in focusing on 'second order' rules and conventions because they are the product of politicized behaviour of members who are confronted by the relational structure that emerged (at least partly) from their previous interactions.

Conventions and institutions on which economists focus both emerge from and produce relational environments that are themselves the product of previous conventions and institutions, for example exogenous norms. These relational environments are multiplex, multilateral, and they produce multi-level social processes that are necessary for collective action. In effect, interdependent actors participate in and corner themselves by participating in (re)constructing constraining structures and then take advantage of opportunities offered by these constraining structures. Structural sociology becomes a sociology of change that is able to focus on second order conventions iteratively (but not mechanically) generating new cycles of structuration based on conventions. Behind social mechanisms, there are actions and investments in relationships, social niche building and status competition that produce new structures embedded in older and mature ones.

'Economie des conventions' is a theory that helps combine social and market exchange. In effect, conventions need multilateral and multiplex relational structures in which they become appropriate. Much more remains to be done, however, in order to exploit this rapprochement. Both conventions and structures change, and it is ultimately in the evolution of organizations and markets that their combination makes most sense.

NOTES

1. We thank Lise Mounier and Sébastien Delarre for suggestions made on a first draft of this text.
2. Our emphasis on conventions comes from the fact they are at the same time one kind of rule (informal, and so on) thoroughly studied by Lewis (1969) and an interpretive component of all kinds of rule, the importance of which is stressed in the research programme of 'économie des conventions' (see Favereau, 1999, 2001b).
3. This text summarizes and simplifies ideas and examples relevant to this topic that can be found in previous work (Lazega 1992, 2001).
4. There is, however, disagreement among structural sociologists about the extent to which a formal organizational structure has to exist for networks of ties to be able to help generate collective action.
5. For developments of the ideas sketched in the next two paragraphs, see Favereau (1999, 2001b).

6. The notion of 'multi-status oligarch' is also quite interesting, from the point of view of joint research in the two paradigms, because it stresses the role of certain individuals, occupying certain situations, in alleviating the obstacles to the process of organizational learning.
7. For instance, conventionalist economics is currently trying to grasp 'coordination failures' and 'reproduction failures' in a common framework (see Favereau, 2001a): network models would have much to bring, in order to put concrete flesh on these conceptual bones.
8. Thus the interpretation of internal labour markets as an intertemporal exchange of promises suggested by Doeringer (1986), after Akerlof (1982) and extended by conventionalist economics (see Favereau, 1999) is a striking example of interpenetration of barter exchange and market exchange.
9. Eymard-Duvernay insists more on judgments and conventions about quality. There may be a general problem with having the same vocabulary to cover all forms of coordinations: most relations are not contractual ex ante because the contract often emerges in the interaction. But this vocabulary is nevertheless used because it is understood by economists.
10. Rather, resources are seen through distributed cognition. The environment is full of resources; but one does not need to know everything about them to act in an efficient way. One needs to know how to rely on knowledge dispersed in the environment. But there is no attention here to the structure as a pattern of resource interdependencies allowing for vertical or horizontal coordination.
11. Differences remain nevertheless. North uses only one sense of the word 'convention', that of informal rules. He does not believe that formal rules create problems of interpretation. His is a very macro vision of coordination; the actor never actually shows up, never actually negotiates the rules of the game, and we do not know where his dynamics come from, while 'Economy of Conventions' starts closer to actors.
12. This approach is consistent with the theory of appropriateness judgments sketched above. Members manage their resources through choices of exchange partners and interactively elaborate appropriate information as well as a supposedly shared, legitimate and validated 'definition of the situation' (Lazega, 1990, 1992). Judgment of appropriateness and relational structure are linked by the concepts of identity, status and authority. Sociocultural conventions from which to construct solutions to economic problems must be transmitted, and validated by others. Conventions are rooted in authority relationships, as well as in routines.

REFERENCES

Akerlof, George A. (1982), 'Labor contracts as partial gift exchange', *Quarterly Journal of Economics*, 97, November, 543–69.

Argyris, Chris (1988), 'Problems in producing usable knowledge for implementing liberating alternatives', in David E. Bell, Howard Raiffa and Amos Tversky (eds), *Decision making*, Cambridge: Cambridge University Press, pp. 540–61.

Argyris, Chris and Donald A. Schön (1978), *Organizational learning: a theory of action perspective*, Reading, MA: Addison-Wesley.

Arrow, Kenneth J. and G. Debreu (1954), 'Existence of an equilibrium for competitive economy', *Econometrica*, July, 265–90.

Barron, David N. (1998), 'Pathways to legitimacy among consumer loan providers in New York City, 1914–34', *Organization Studies*, 19 (2), 207–33.

Baum, Joël A.C. (1996), 'Dynamics of organizational responses to competition', *Social Forces*, 74: 1261–97.

Baum, Joel A.C. and Jitendra V. Singh (1996), 'Dynamics of organizational responses to competition', *Social Forces*, 74, 1261–97.

Boltanski, Luc and Eve Chiappello (1999), *Le nouvel esprit du capitalisme*, Paris: Gallimard.

Boltanski, Luc and Laurent Thévenot (1991), *De la justification: les économies de la grandeur*, Paris: Gallimard.
Burt, Ronald S. (1982), *Toward a Structural Theory of Action*, New York: Academic Press.
Burt, Ronald S. and Talmud, I. (1993), 'Market niche', *Social Networks*, 8, 97–117.
Coleman, James S. (1990), *Foundations of Social Theory*, Cambridge: Harvard University Press.
Doeringer, Peter B. (1986), 'Internal Labor Market and Non Competing Groups', *American Economic Review*, May, 48–52.
Dupuy, Jean-Pierre *et al.* (1989), 'L'économie des conventions', *Revue Economique*, 40(2).
Favereau, Olivier (1997), 'L'incomplétude n'est pas le problème, c'est la solution', in B.Reynaud (ed.), *Les limites de la rationalité (tome 2): Les figures du collectif*, Paris: La Découverte, pp. 219–33.
Favereau, Olivier (1999), 'Salaire, emploi et Economie des Conventions', *Cahiers d'Economie Politique*, Printemps, 163–94.
Favereau, Olivier (2001a), 'L'économie du sociologue ou penser (l'orthodoxie) à partir de pierre Bourdieu', in B.Lahire (ed.), *Le travail sociologique de Pierre Bourdieu: dettes et critiques*, Paris : La Découverte, pp. 255–14.
Favereau, Olivier (2001b), 'Theory of Information: from Bounded Rationality to Interpretative Rationality', in P. Petit (ed.), *Economics and Information*, Dordrecht : Kluwer, pp. 93–120.
Ferrand, A. and T. Snijders (1997), 'Social networks and normative tensions', in L. - Van Campenhoudt, M. Cohen, G. Guizzardi and D. Hauser (eds), *Sexual interactions and HIV risk: new conceptual perspectives in European research*, London: Taylor & Francis, pp. 6–21.
Granovetter, Mark (1994), 'Business Groups', in Neil Smelser and Richard Swedberg (eds), *Handbook of economic sociology,* Princeton, NJ: Russell Sage Foundation.
Hannan, Michael T. and John Freeman. (1977), 'The population ecology of organizations', *American Journal of Sociology*, 56, 929–64.
Haslam, S.Alexander (2001), *Psychology in organizations: the social identity approach*, London: Sage.
Knight, J. and D. North (1997), 'Explaining economic change: the interplay between cognition and institutions', *Legal Theory*, 3, 211–26.
Lazega, Emmanuel (1990), 'Internal Politics and the Interactive Elaboration of Information in Workgroups: An Exploratory Study', *Human Relations*, 43, 87–101.
Lazega, Emmanuel (1992), *The Micro-politics of Knowledge*, New York: Aldine de Gruyter.
Lazega, Emmanuel (2000), 'Rule enforcement among peers: A lateral control regime', *Organisational Studies*, 21: 193–214.
Lazega, Emmanuel (2001), *The Collegial Phenomenon*, Oxford: Oxford University Press.
Lazega, Emmanuel and David Krackhardt (2000), 'Spreading and shifting costs of lateral control in a law partnership, a structural analysis at the individual level', *Quality and Quantity*, 34, 153–75.
Lazega, Emmanuel and Marie-Odile Lebeaux (1995), 'Capital social et contrainte latérale', *Revue Française de Sociologie*', 36, 759–77.
Lewis, David K.(1969), *Convention: a philosophical study*, Cambridge: Harvard University Press.
McPherson, J. Miller (1983), 'An ecology of affiliation', *American Sociological Review*, 48, 519–35.

McPherson, J. Miller and James R. Ranger-Moore (1991), 'Evolution on a dancing landscape: organizations and networks in dynamic Blau Space', *Social Forces*, 70, 19–42.

Ménard, Claude (1997), 'Internal characteristics of formal organizations', in C. Ménard (ed.), *Transaction Cost Economics: Recent Developments*, Cheltenham, UK and Lyme, US: Edward Elgar, pp. 30–58.

Ménard, Claude (2000), 'The enforcement of contractual arrangements', in C. Ménard (ed.), *Institutions, Contracts and Organizations. Perspectives from New Institutional Economics*, Cheltenham, UK and Northampton, MA, USA: Edward Elgar, pp. 234–54.

Merton, R.K. (1959), *Social theory and social structure*, Glencoe: The Free Press.

North, Douglas (1990), *Institutions, institutional change and economic performance*, Cambridge: Cambridge University Press.

Parsons, Talcott (1956), 'A sociological approach to the theory of organization', *Administrative Quarterly*, 1, 63–85.

Piore, Michael (1974), 'Comment and Discussion', *Brookings Papers on Economic Activity*, no. 3, 684–8.

Podolny, Joel M., Toby E. Stuart and Michael T. Hannan (1996), 'Networks, knowledge and niches, competition in the worldwide semiconductor industry, 1984–1991', *American Journal of Sociology*, 102, 659–89.

Reynaud, Jean-Daniel (1989), *Les Règles du jeu*, Paris: Armand Colin.

Reynaud, Jean-Daniel and E. Reynaud (1996), 'La régulation des marchés internes du travail', *Revue Française de sociolo*gie, 37, 337–68.

Salais, R. and M. Storper (1993), *Les mondes de production*, Paris: Editions de l'Ecole des Hautes Etudes en Sciences Sociales.

Savage, Leonard J. (1954), *Foundation of Statistics*, New York: Wiley; 2nd edn, 1972, New York: Dover.

Scott, John (1991), *Social network analysis: a handbook*, London: Sage.

Selznick, Ph. (1957), *Leadership in Administration*, Evanston, IL: Row, Peterson & Co.

Strauss, Anselm (1978), *Negotiations: Varieties, Contexts, Processes and Social Order*, San Francisco: Jossey-Bass.

Swedberg, R. (1998), *Max Weber and the Idea of Economic Sociology*, Princeton: Princeton University Press.

Turner, John C. (1987), *Rediscovering the social group : a self-categorization theory*, Oxford : Basil Blackwell.

Von Neumann, J. and O. Morgenstern (1944), *Theory of Games and Economic Behavior*, Princeton: Princeton University Press; 2nd edn, 1947, 3rd edn, 1953.

Weber, Max (1920/1978 edn), *Economy and Society*, edited by Guenther Roth and Claus Wittich, Berkeley: University of California Press.

White, Harrison C. (1981a), 'Production markets as induced role structures', in S.L. Leinhardt (ed.), *Sociological Methodology*, San Francisco: Jossey-Bass, pp. 1–57.

White, Harrison C. (1981b), 'Where do markets come from ?', *American Journal of Sociology*, 87, 517–47.

White, Harrison C.(2001), *Markets from Networks*, Princeton: Princeton University Press.

Williamson, Oliver E. (1996), *The Mechanisms of Governance*, New York: Oxford University Press, pp. 120–44.

1. No man is an island: the research programme of a social capital theory

Henk Flap[1]

THE THEORY GAP IN NETWORK ANALYSIS

The study of social networks has gained momentum since the 1960s. It produced impressive findings, such as that persons who are more integrated into their networks have a better life expectancy (Berkman and Syme, 1979). Judged by the number of publications and its various fields of application one can only conclude that network research is flowering. Milestones in the development of this research tradition are Granovetter's 1973 article on 'The strength of weak ties' and his 1974 book on *Getting a Job*. Unjustly neglected, however, is his 1979 essay on 'The theory gap in social network analysis', in which he laments the empirical and methodological bias of network research and its lack of theoretical integration and explanatory depth. Stinchcombe (1989) added that there is not much cross-fertilization among fields of application. Furthermore, existing studies would oversee that network effects are conditional upon certain social and institutional circumstances.

Social network studies have mainly been kept together by the orienting notion that all network structures have some effect on the actions of the actors enmeshed in these networks. This notion provides for an underlying unity, but it also makes network research somewhat akin to the search for the dependent variable, known from the earlier status-inconsistency literature. In sociological research it has become a kind of routine to include network factors in the analysis as a kind of turbo-chaser to boost explained variance.

The prospects for more general theories in network research are, however, not as dim as one might think while reading Granovetter's criticism. There are a number of developments that hold promise for the future. One is the articulation of a structuralist view, the other is the development of the social capital theory. Both take the idea of a goal-directed, rational acting man as their point of departure, the former uses its alleged atomism to define its own position, the latter uses it to create a new research programme by adding new auxiliary assumptions on networks.

STRUCTURALISM

The structuralist stance claims that social networks are so restrictive that, to explain people's actions, you only have to know the structure of the social network these actors are part of: 'Give me the network and I will tell you what they will do.' Although this branch of network studies did not deliver a general integrative theory, it produced numerous valuable theoretical insights, which are partly empirically corroborated, and which will be part and parcel of more general theories.[2] An example is the 'strength of weak ties' argument: although news travels more quickly through strong ties, they will barely ever bring you news that is really new, because friends of friends will be friends. Only a weak tie and no strong tie will be a bridge to interesting other social worlds.

Actual research by the structuralists is less far removed from rational choice sociology than one would imagine while reading programmatic statements (Berkowitz, 1982; Wellman and Berkowitz, 1988). Close reading reveals that structuralists make assumptions as to why individuals act as they do. They have to, to make sense of where networks come from, how they change and how network effects feed back into the networks. For example, in re-analysing the data of Coleman *et al.*'s *Medical Innovation*, Burt (1987) explains the influence of others on the people's decisions as a way to resolve their uncertainty about risky choices by comparing themselves to others who are similarly placed within the social network at large, that is, who are structurally equivalent. Or take the analysis of product markets by Leifer and White (1988). They assume that producers jockey for status positions and profit, and that they decide upon what prices to set for their products, not by looking at the actual demand by buyers, but by reference to what similar other producers are doing. Burt, White and Leifer in fact use a signalling argument: in case of uncertainty, people use signals to decide what is in their best interest. Or, take 'the strength of weak ties'. This effect is supposedly the outcome of a cognitive strain towards balance: people want their friends to be friends. This causes in-breeding and destroys local bridges.[3] So it is not so much the unrealistic nature of their assumptions about rationality but the alleged failure of rational choice sociology to incorporate social structure in its accounts of economic and other human actions that sets structuralism apart from rational choice sociology.

The kernel of the structuralist view can be rephrased, in that all social, including economic, phenomena are embedded in social networks (Granovetter, 1985, 1992). The strongest selling point of structuralism is that it tries to beat neoclassical economics on its own home turf, the analysis of the economic world (Zukin and DiMaggio, 1990). All markets are socially organized through networks (White, 1981). This applies to conventional markets, like labour markets (Granovetter, 1974), consumer markets (Frenzen and

Davis, 1990), product markets (Leifer and White, 1988), housing markets (Grieco, 1987) and stock markets (Baker, 1984a, 1984b), but also to unfamiliar markets like those for culture (Faulkner, 1983; Powell, 1985), legal assistance (Heinz and Laumann, 1981) or illegal services such as abortion (Lee, 1969) or providing cocaine (Snijders *et al.*, 1995).

Rational choice theory, in its most renowned form, that is, the received view of neoclassical economics, does not take social structure into account and assumes society to consist of social atoms, fully informed, where prices are written in the sky, and without transaction or enforcement costs, without institutions actually. But there is nothing in the idea of rational choice that makes it impossible to include social networks among the constraints under which actors have to act or to use rational choice ideas in explaining structural effects – especially not, and this is Granovetter's second criticism, if one relaxes the assumption that profit, especially money, is the only goal people strive for. People also long for esteem, status, companionship and eternal bliss. Moreover these preferences are influenced by social conditions. Rational choice can even level a third criticism, that the historical development of institutions is neither arbitrary nor chosen freely at will. Granovetter criticizes slick rational choice explanations of institutional change with efficiency arguments. Path dependency of consecutive choices locks people in as well as their creations, like organizations, in historically evolved institutional arrangements that are hard to alter without great transaction costs (McGuire *et al.*, 1993). The evolution of networks itself is strongly path dependent as well (Doreian and Stokman, 1997). The three notions (embedded economic markets, socially conditioned preferences and path dependent social construction of institutions) constitute what has been called the 'new economic sociology'. This is the sociological alternative to the received view in economics about organizations and markets, and its more recent branches of 'new institutional economics', like transaction cost economics (Swedberg, 1997).

Yet there is something amiss with the embeddedness argument in its strong version. No general assumption on effects of network structures seems to hold empirically. Disturbing factors forever seem to pop up, making for '*A* not leading to *B*'. Granovetter, for example, assumed that weak ties make for quick dissemination of relevant information on job vacancies. However, his own research evidence is not that strong. Others could not confirm the idea either in research on the job-finding process of different occupational groups in western industrial societies (Lin *et al.*, 1981b; Bridges and Villemez, 1986; Grieco, 1987; Preisendörfer and Voss, 1988; Forsé, 1999; Flap and Boxman, 1999), non-western industrial societies (Völker and Flap, 1999) and non-western agrarian societies (Bian, 1997). The suggestion that informal contacts lead to better jobs also is not unconditionally true. There is no clear relation between size of the personal networks and frequency of informal job finding. For example, in western societies, ethnic minorities and people from the lower classes generally find their job more often through informal contacts, although they usually do have smaller personal social networks. Job-finding methods do not bear a relation to the prestige of the job that is found. Placement via social networks seldom results in higher prestige jobs and often negatively affects income. Differences between societies in the job-finding process suggest that institutional conditions influence the effects of networks on the occupational career. People did find their job through an informal contact more often in the United States than in the Netherlands. The actual contact person also has a larger impact on occupational success in the United States (De Graaf and Flap, 1988). The discussion on the conditions under which social contacts do promote occupational achievement is not yet decided, but it is clear that the use of informal contacts does not produce a better job, unless the contact person has good resources himself.

There always seem to be societal factors that complicate or interfere with structural effects. Why do structuralist law-like ideas about systematic network effects always meet with exceptions? One inroad to these theoretical questions might be starting off from a constraints-driven rational choice perspective on social networks which conceives of networks as social resources. Some social anthropologists (Kapferer, 1972; Boissevain, 1974) and sociologists (Fischer, 1982; Fischer *et al.*, 1977) took this perspective in the 1970s. The argument has been taken a few steps further lately by sociologists who came to conceive of social networks as social capital. They are rational choice sociologists who, inspired by the achievements of human capital theory, apply an utilitarian, rational choice point of view to social networks. Or they are neo-Marxist and neo-Weberian sociologists who apply an interest-driven account of human action to social networks. All stress the productive and investment side to social networks (Bourdieu, 1973; Loury, 1977; Coleman, 1988; Flap, 1988; Burt, 1992; Lin, 2001). The social capital idea holds a promise to integrate a large part of the research literature on social networks.

In the remainder of this chapter I will provide a sketch of the research programme of a theory of social capital, its core, its main questions and some tentative answers, and explain why the structuralist claim of pure structural effects will be refuted (once this claim is thoroughly studied on its truth value in capital research); there will be exeptions to the claim because of institutional and technological conditioning of the instrumental value of social networks. Finally I cite some research evidence that shows that the programme works and discuss a number of theoretically inspired promising, as yet unresolved, questions.

SOCIAL CAPITAL THEORY

The way out of this unsatisfying situation in network research may be to concentrate on the assumptions regarding man, or put otherwise, regarding human nature. Why not make arguments more accessible and liable to criticism and start with more explicit assumptions on what makes individuals act? Of course, one should stick to the original explanatory problem as to why there are exceptions to structural effects. So, although the theoretical primacy is sought at the individual level, the analytic primacy remains at the structural level.[4]

How to proceed next? Something should be known about the goals people care for. One can try to establish them empirically in each situation. More informative and thought efficient is to assume that basic preferences do not change drastically; human nature is the same through the ages and in different places, meaning that people have the same fundamental needs, the same general goals. These goals can be summarized as the wish to improve one's life chances, or, according to Adam Smith (Lindenberg, 1990), one's physical welfare and status.

Such a proposal is not at odds with classical or present-day sociology: it may go against programmatic statements, but not against the grain of explanations actually delivered (Boudon, 1981). There is a common ground, between sociologists and economists, in the assumption that people act goal directed but under social constraints and frequently with unintended consequences (Lindenberg, 1990). Because often there are different courses of action to attain these goals and there are always constraints, if only of time, people have to choose.

This common view also holds that those with more resources will better succeed in reaching these goals. According to Smith, and this is an important assumption, there are typical means for different social groups to reach these goals. Under the constraints posed by capitalism in a free market society, man hardly has a choice but to specialize in some economic resource, since this is a means to most other 'goodies' man might want. Having economic capital (financial or human capital) proves to be the grand route to a good life, to success, well-being and status in western capitalistic societies. In the course of its development, economics specialized in the study of different economic means, specifically financial capital in a capitalist free market society.

This point seems somehow to have got lost in economics: it is not for the love of money, but simply because money is the key to many of the good things that people want out of life, that people strive for higher profits, income and wages. People's preferences or interests are socially conditioned; given their social situation, people can only achieve their more ulterior goal of having a good life by realizing these less general goals. The latter are instrumental goals, so to speak.[5] People produce their own subjective well-being by optimizing these instrumental goals. So they might also, if under particular restrictions achieving some goal is difficult, to some extent substitute one general or instrumental goal for the other (Ormel *et al.*, 1999). In many contexts social capital is part of the production function for status and physical well-being.

Sociology contributed at least three major insights to this common view of man. For one, next to economic means it studied several others that promote these goals. According to its neo-Weberian synthesis, there are three main types of resources to achieve a better living: economic resources (financial assets and capital goods, but also occupational knowledge and skills), political resources (voting rights, membership of political bodies such as parties) and symbolic resources (occupational prestige).

Secondly, sociology describes several other institutional conditions next to markets, in which man can find himself. Accordingly, sociology is not a science of leftovers from economics. Economics can perhaps better be named 'market sociology'. In traditional societies individual action is mainly influenced by traditions transmitted through the generations, whereas in modern societies individual behaviour is constrained by markets and organizations. A major sociological task is to specify how these institutional constraints influence the returns on the use of these three types of resources.

Thirdly, sociology stresses, more explicitly than economics, the unintended, often perverse, collective effects of individual goal-directed action.

How does this exercise help us to explain network effects? The logical thing to do is to interpret personal networks as resources, analogous to these other resources, to treat them as a sort of capital that is instrumental in reaching general goals. This ties in nicely with neo-Weberian thoughts on life chances being determined by one's economic, political and cultural resources. It seems natural to extend this series with social resources.

The idea is not new, though. 'To have friends is to have power: for they are strengths united'; these are the words of Thomas Hobbes in his famous *Leviathan* (1663). This assumption, however, is of great heuristic value in social network studies. It is the hard core of a budding research programme. It serves as a guide for where to look for explanations of network phenomena. In a nutshell, it presents a research programme in which personal social networks are treated as a specific resource, that is, as a social resource. Hobbes, of course, referred to its importance in the struggle for survival. Social resources are important not only for physical safety, but also for most other goals people have in life, such as companionship, social esteem and good health.

The core of social capital theory is formed by two simple propositions. One is the social resources hypothesis according to which people who are better equipped with social capital will be better able to attain their ends, and the second is the investment hypothesis stating that people will invest in social capital according to its instrumental value in producing their ends. Take note: social networks are not seen simply as yet another constraint in the choice process, but as social capital with which goals can be produced that would otherwise be impossible to attain.

These thoughts lead to some interesting, new questions. At least the following can be discerned:

1. What are the main constituents of social capital and how do the various effects of social capital depend on its main constituents?
2. Precisely what about a social network makes it productive?
3. How are social resources related to other resources? Specifically, does social capital increase the returns to human capital, and can they be substituted for each other?
4. Under what circumstances, particularly in what kinds of societies, are social resources most important?
5. How do people acquire social resources? How and when do persons invest and divest in others?
6. Why are social resources distributed unevenly?

This series of related questions articulates the contours of a research programme that is encompassed by the idea of ego-centred social networks as social resources. Such a programme systematizes the results of social network research, creating a system that was lacking before. By now, several theoretical and empirical contributions to this budding research programme can be discerned (Flap, 1999).

Scattered through the social sciences literature are attempts at providing answers to the questions. Lin (1981a, p. 1163) hinted at an answer to the first two questions. Social resources consist in 'the wealth, status, power, as well as the social ties, of those persons who are directly or indirectly linked to the individual'. The resources of affiliated individuals are substitutes for someone's own resources, that is why Boissevain (1974, pp. 158–63) called them 'second order resources'. An important aspect of the latter is the diversity of the second-order assets. The number of alters willing (apart from being 'able') to grant assistance enlarges ego's social capital, for which Coleman (1990, p. 306) introduced the image of *credit slips*.

In certain research areas, especially in studies on social support and health, it is taken for granted that the mere presence of other persons already promotes goal achievement. But what is at the other end of a tie is often all-important. A mother, for example, will usually be willing to help her child with his studies; however, if she did not receive much education herself, this help will be of no great avail. According to Coleman (1988) the American youth currently has a dim future because parents do not want to help their children as much as in earlier days, although parents do have more resources than their predecessors.

Social capital is made up of at least three elements: the number of others prepared or obliged to help ego when called upon to do so, the extent to which they are ready to help, and what is at the other end of the tie.[6]

One could include the structure of the network as a fourth dimension of the social capital concept. Bourdieu (1981) and Coleman (1990) hold that there is social capital in a dense social network. It is critical, for example, to school success: a rather tightly knit community network is an asset as parents will continuously observe each other's children and correct them should they go astray, or at least they will notify the parents of these children.

Dense networks not only lower the cost of information search, they also decrease the costs of the enforcement of norms. These arguments on the effects of dense networks are also forwarded by transaction cost economics. Coming to an agreement and enforcing it is easier in a closed social network. It spreads reputations for being trustworthy and thereby increases the chances of cooperation because people know that acts of opportunism will be uncovered, and probably sanctioned by others by the withdrawal of future help (Granovetter, 1985; Raub and Weesie, 1990). So trust will be higher in closed networks.

Burt (1992) proposes the opposite, that is, that the structural autonomy of a person within a network increases the readiness of others to provide help. If others do not have alternatives for you, and you do have alternatives for them, you are autonomous, which not only brings non-redundant information but also control benefits.[7] Being autonomous, of course, is an instance of having a favourable exchange rate in transactions with others. So being in the middle between other persons who are otherwise disconnected, having 'structural holes', can be seen as an aspect of social capital. This principle was earlier discovered in studies of patronage-ridden societies: the staying power of patronage derives partly from the particular network structure it implies, that is, an open triangle (Singelman,1975; Flap, 1989). Social psychological group experiments on exchanges in pre-given networks already pointed out that not the most central persons, but those who are in a brokerage position, profit most from exchanges (Marsden, 1982).

With respect to the third question, Bourdieu (1981, Bourdieu and de Saint-Martin, 1982), Coleman (1988) and Burt (1992) argue that a person's social capital increases the returns to his other resources. The productivity of social capital is coming from the opportunities brought to you by your network to make a profit on your other resources, especially your human and financial capital. Social capital adds to their value. In methodological terms this is an interaction effect of social and other resources. It is not clear to what extent people can substitute one kind of capital for the other or convert one kind in another type of capital.[8]

As to the second element of the hard core of the social capital programme, the investment decisions, if we interpret people's social networks as their available social capital and do not leave it at this metaphor, we are closer to an answer to the fifth question, that is how people acquire social capital, and the largely equivalent question of how and why social networks change. The idea of social capital implies that men spend their resources on others, not only for the efficacy of the moment, but also with an eye to the future. As early as 1923, Marcel Mauss, in his famous 'Essai sur le don, forme archaïque de l'échange', expounded on how people acquire social capital, viz. by giving and in that way indebting others to them.

Social capital is an entity, consisting of all expected future benefits derived, not from one's own labour, but from connections with other persons. It is sensible to view all of men's actions in this light. That is, every human action is equally an investment decision in which actors, whoever they may be, look into the future to justify current actions. However, people do not invest only in social capital, but also in economic, symbolic and political capital. They try to combine their investments in such a way that a package, a portfolio, results by which they hope to maximize their life conditions.

In their investment decisions people will always discount what they think future benefits will be and consider the value they have for them now. The importance of a relation is not only determined by past investments in it but also by the expectation of future help from it (Boissevain, 1974, p. 250). People will invest and divest in social capital according to the expected value of future support.[9]

There are a number of assumptions implied in the hard core of social capital theory. The importance of social capital in social life strongly relates to its being a case of non-simultaneous exchange of help (*delayed* or *generalized reciprocity*) which usually is, at the time it is given, considerably more valuable to the recipient than it is costly to the donor (Coleman, 1990). This means that it is required that there be some complementarity of the partners' fortunes. If they do not expect that there might be a reversal of fate, generalized reciprocity between two partners will not occur (Cosmides and Tooby, 1992; Litwak, 1985).

Furthermore, as time is involved there will be a discount rate to the value of future help (Taylor, 1974, p. 9). The faster the value of social capital has to be discounted, the smaller the expected value of support will be. Axelrod (1984, p. 12) catches the idea's meaning with the image of 'the shadow of tomorrow'. The value of social capital increases by enlarging the shadow of tomorrow. The future is less important than the present, for three reasons. The first is that players tend to value pay-offs less as the time of their obtainment recedes into the future. The second is that there is always some chance that the players will not meet again. A relationship may end when one or the other player moves away, changes jobs, dies or goes bankrupt (ibid.). Thirdly, together with the costs connected to any exchange, there is a risk that the other acts opportunistically and does not repay his debt. Because there is a time delay between investments and returns, one has to trust the other that he or she will repay the service delivered and not act opportunistically. Investing in others is similar to what game theory calls playing a trust game (Dasgupta, 1988). This risk adds to the expected costs of investing in others, thereby increasing the discount rate.

As to the costs of investments in others and of entertaining a particular tie, these have not been clearly envisioned in social capital research until now. They will be lowered notably if both partners to a tie are members of a pre-existing group (Lindenberg, 1998).

There is a way of acquiring social capital without having to mobilize one's resources, that is, through endowment, or more generally through ascription of rights to support by certain people. The major example, of course, is being born into a family. An important part of man's social capital develops without his own intervention, even without he himself being aware of it, like being born into a family. Or think of all the indirect ties created by the ties of one's colleagues, acquaintances, friends and kin. Direct ties too are not always consciously constructed: one's weak ties especially often grow 'at random', as a by-product of actions directed towards other goals. Yet one has to be cautious, since even within a family a person has to make choices regarding whom to interact with and how much (Foster, 1961).

The beauty of the programme is that we have one key-idea, explaining in principle effects of social networks as well as the emergence and change of social networks. Such an investment theory enables to explain why theories that are often used to explain personal relations, like exchange theory and cognitive balance theory, meet with refutations. Refutations are, for example, battered wives staying in a strained relationship with their husband or partners who are quite satisfied in their intimate relationship but who nevertheless make an end to it or sleep around with others (Rusbult *et al.*, 1991, Rusbult and Martz, 1995).

People invest and divest in social networks pending their expected value of future support. Together with the direct costs and rewards of entertaining a particular tie, the past investments in the tie ('the shadow of the past'), the shadow of the future, the quality of the available alternative relations and the cross-linkage between the personal networks of both partners in a relation are involved in the decision to invest or divest. The shadow of the past is important not only because one has learned about the trustworthiness of particular others or because they start to like one another in continuing relationships but also because investments in particular others are nearly always relation-specific (Lin, 2001, pp. 143–64). They are largely lost if one switches partners.

If a person's investments in others are more clustered in tightly interconnected others, it is more difficult to withdraw one's investment in a particular other because this will damage relations with others as well (Kapferer, 1972).

The answer to the sixth question, why social capital is unevenly distributed, is rather simple. People can produce more social capital, the more economic, symbolic and political resources they control, and since these are usually unevenly distributed, the same goes for social resources. Lin *et al.*, (1981a) stress that the social background of one's parents influences the social resources of the children. Combining the social resources and the investment hypothesis (the more social capital someone has, the better he can achieve his goals; and the more economic, symbolic and political resources someone has, the more social resources he can produce) leads one to expect reproduction and accumulation of social inequality. Social inequality will be perpetuated intragenerationally and intergenerationally by differences in access to and use of social capital (Bourdieu, 1973; Flap, 1991). Social closure through the selective employment of its social capital is a compensatory strategy that can be used by an elite at moments when its position is threatened, for example if leftist governments try to redistribute wealth from the rich to the poor or stimulate bright children from the lower classes to educate themselves in order to climb the social ladder (Bourdieu and de Saint Martin, 1982).

There is still one question to which an answer is awaited, that is the fourth question on how institutional arrangements influence the returns on social capital. It will turn out that this question is largely equivalent to the question as to why there are no pure structural effects. Below I will deal with conditions, such as level of technology and the kind of legal institutions, that confound structural effects by causing differences in returns of the same networks, that is, in its instrumental value as social capital. But before I come to that I will first discuss some necessary preconditions for any network effect, such as, numbers and places.

CONSTRAINTS

Places and Numbers

Without meeting there will be no mating (Verbrugge, 1977). This insight sank in only recently. Basic to meeting chances are kinds of people and numbers. The circumscriptive effect of numbers on chances to meet particular others was brought to the fore by Blau and Schwartz (1984) in their study on marriage patterns. Their point is summarized neatly in the one-liner: 'You can't marry an Eskimo, if no Eskimo is around'. They presented strong empirical evidence. This argument does not apply only to marriage ties, but to all kinds of relations, for example, in the United States it is far easier for a black person to have a white person for a friend than the other way round.

The most obvious condition influencing contact opportunities, apart from absolute numbers, is places and facilities. Feld (1981, 1984) noticed that social interaction is often tied to certain places offering foci for interaction with other people. Obvious examples of foci that can organize social ties are public places and facilities, like bars, shops, schools, discos, restaurants, libraries or public squares, but one can also think of work places, voluntary associations or other organizations. Places in which people are brought together for a particular goal offer an occasion to meet others. As a result their network becomes organized around such a focal point. Social ties emerging in such situations are a quasi by-product of other interactions and the relational demography of such foci strongly determines which ties are actually formed (Flap *et al.*, 1998a, pp. 117–18; Lindenberg, 1998; Kalmijn and Flap, 2001).

The above is a supply-side argument: the composition of people's social networks will reflect the composition of the pool of people that come together in the places that they visit, that is, the opportunity structure for selection of associates (Marsden, 1990, p. 397). This state of affairs can be described as easily in terms of opportunities as in terms of restraints. Structuralists emphasize the latter option as they call into question the voluntaristic assumption that ties exist because two members of a dyad want to interact with one another. In practice, many ties are involuntary in that they come as part of a network membership package. They may be ties to persons who must be dealt with at work or in the neighbourhood (Wellman, 1988b, p. 41).

The restraining influence of places and numbers shows, for example, in the desolation of the black underclass in the American inner cities. This is a result not of a culture of poverty, but of the lack of sustained contact with people who have a stable work history and live in more stable areas (Wilson, 1987, p. 61). The social isolation makes it much more difficult for those who are looking for jobs to be tied into the job network. Even if job vacancies become available in an industry near or within the inner-city neighbourhood, workers who live outside the inner-city may find out about these vacancies sooner than those who live near the industry because the latter are not tied into the job network.

Technology

Although some types of social capital are goal-specific (for example, it takes a strong man to carry an invalid), its major advantage is, not unlike money or human capital, that it is often a means to all ends. Litwak (1985) showed that support from informal networks is far more important in the sheer amount of services delivered than care provided by formal organizations. Informal relations can better master events and tasks with many contingencies, that are not easily subdivided or involve problems for which the time of their occurrence is hard to tell, that require continuous availability of certain others. That is why most everyday problems cannot be routinized or standardized. But when solutions can be routinized and standardized through technology or universal legal laws and rules, the value of social capital usually shrinks. Yet new highly developed technologies also produce new non-standard, non-routine exigencies because of all kinds of unforeseen tight couplings in technological and work processes (Perrow, 1986), which can only be mastered by resourceful people and through fine-tuning of social relations. Social networks generally seem to be more important in the service industry that in manufacturing because dealings with other people cannot easily be standardized.

Analyses of African stateless societies at a rather low level of technology, (horticulture and herding) show the strong impact of technology on what can and has to be done by social networks. In such a situation an extra premium is put upon the formation and maintenance of social capital since under subsistence conditions each family is too small to support itself (Gluckman, 1965, pp. 13–14). Moreover, since there are 'no cops and constables' in stateless societies, one had better have friends for personal protection (Flap, 1988, 1997). And as food and other goods are difficult to store or trade, the main investment available to man is in personal relationships with others. Generally, the value of social capital will increase in periods of economic contraction, even in industrial societies. During extreme emergencies, like a famine, catastrophe or war, social capital will indeed be indispensable to the preservation of life.

Institutions

Conceptualizing social networks as 'social capital' has advantages over seeing them as 'social resources', because the former focuses explicitly on discounting, returns on investments and the institutional conditioning of the value of social capital. The same relations will be more or less productive under differing institutional constraints.

Institutions and social technology, can provide universal standard routines that make particularistic solutions through mobilizing social capital more or less superfluous. The welfare state provided social rights, pre-empting much of the former value of social networks. But man does not live by bread alone; social prestige and an identity cannot be created through issuing social laws, although they might help. Particularistic solutions are called for and there will always be some minimum value in social relations with others.

The absence of a constitutional democratic state puts an extra premium upon the formation and maintenance of social capital. Extreme cases are concentration camps. As Primo Levi (1979, pp. 94–5) states, in his horrific autobiographical account of his time in Auschwitz:

> With the adaptable, the strong and the astute individuals, even the leaders willingly keep contact, sometimes even friendly contact, because they hope to perhaps derive some benefit. But with the musselmen, the men in decay, it is not even worth speaking, because one knows already that they will complain and will speak about what they used to eat at home. Even less worthwhile is it to make friends with them, because they have no distinguished acquaintances in camp, they do not gain any extra ration, they do not work in profitable Kommandos and they know no secret method of organizing. And in any case, one knows that they are only here on a visit, that in weeks nothing will remain of them but a handful of ashes in some near-by field and a crossed-out number on a register.

Sometime institutions obstruct people's goal attainment and they use social networks to circumvent these obstacles. Dutch history abounds with illustrations. During the Republic in the 17th and 18th centuries, certain families of regents managed to stay in power for decades by carefully managing their social capital. They succeeded by creating affinitive relationships with other powerful families and by so-called 'contracts of correspondence', written agreements between contending political factions to share power by way of rotation. In this manner they were able to circumvent laws and moral indictments against family government, while at the same time keeping conflicts and deceit to a minimum (van Dijk and Roorda, 1980).

The compensatory mechanisms mentioned by Bourdieu have already been described above. Elites in democratic societies will close their ranks to potential marriage partners from other social classes, guard their resources and compensate for egalitarian measures taken by social–democratic or socialist governments. It shows that social capital can be effective notwithstanding moral disapproval and legal prohibitions on the use of social connections, if relations are hidden from others through ignorance or secrecy (Bourdieu and de Saint Martin, 1982, p. 42).

A recent discussion, especially in the political sciences, revolves around the presumed erosion of social capital of western societies. Putnam (1993) examined why everything seems to go worse economically and politically in the Italian south than in the north. He argues that civic traditions in the north promote the growth of lateral social ties, voluntary organizations, norms and trust which in turn make possible good governance, legitimate democratic government and economic growth. According to Coleman (1993) there is an irrevocable loss of social capital in western industrial societies, caused by technological changes, the growth of the welfare state and the rising number of large organizations providing services that were once produced in the family and the neighbourhood. These developments devalue social ties to others and destroy the social capital in the family and local community. Parents, for example, will not take care of other parents' children. They will not even invest any more in their own children, because their need for them has decreased with the availability of old age pensions, and it is no longer shaming for a family to have a child that went astray. The images of 'bowling alone' and 'cheque book-writing organizations' summarize the discussion (Putnam, 1995a). We should note, however, that such trends as the decline in membership rates of voluntary associations are to be discerned in some western countries, but certainly not in all (Forsé, 1999).

The general point these authors seem to make is that the existence of alternative solutions to the question of how to achieve well-being might devalue social capital. A prime example is that, with television absorbing much leisure time, people do not need each other any more for company and entertainment (Putnam, 1995b) and that welfare provisions eliminate risks against which people formerly tried to insure themselves by engaging in family and community networks. Time-budget studies, indeed, show that there is less informal socializing nowadays than 20 years ago.

Institutions not only influence the general value of social connections, they also influence what type of relationship might be instrumental to a good life. A major example in our day is provided by the political turnover in Eastern Europe from a totalitarian one-party to a democratic multi-party political system and from a centrally controlled economy to a market economy. The institutional changes alter the returns of investments in social capital and they thereby affect the (di)investment of persons in one another, which implies that their social networks will change.

Research in the former German Democratic Republic (GDR) suggests, for example, that weak ties, quite unlike the situation in western societies, have perverse effects in communist societies as they pose a threat (Völker and Flap, 1995a, 1995b, 1997a, 1997b, 1999). One never could be sure whether state or party organs were not spying on one's private life, or whether third persons would not collect information that could prove to be dangerous upon disclosure. Although the regime did succeed in mixing neighbourhoods socially (the professor living next to the plumber or the pimp), people actually living next door to each other kept their dealings with each other to a minimum. The Marxist experiment that was meant to create social cohesion actually resulted in people having small personal social networks.

Although nowadays fear of weak ties is gone and one would expect networks to grow, years after the turnover people's networks are still small; in particular, the core networks have not changed much. People seem to cling to what they have, probably because they do not yet know what is in their best interest nowadays, let alone how specific social relations might serve these interests (Völker, 1995; Völker and Flap, 1995a, 1997a, 2001).

Organizational conditions also influence the value of social capital. Whenever the quality of services and products is hard to measure or the damage potential of a job is high, social networks come in and the value of social capital goes up, because people rely more on the opinion of others they trust. For example, for jobs with a high damage potential, employers and contacts want to be certain that they do not hire or recommend the wrong person, which they accomplish by recruitment through established informal channels (Flap *et al.*, 1998a; Flap and Boxman, 1999, 2001; Völker and Flap, 1999). In addition, strong ties also provide more leverage to ward off opportunistic acts.

Cultural differences in the way people look at the future, as indicated, for example, by financial saving rates (Oberhofer, 1989), may be responsible for more or less elaborate social networks. Differences between cultures in types of relations they value also might affect the relational pattern that emerges. Banfield (1958), for example, held the cultural ethos of amoral familialism among peasants responsible for the lack of cooperation beyond the family in southern Italy: there was no trust of other persons outside one's own family.

THE PROGRAMME WORKS

The social capital programme works, as can be seen from the results of empirical research on the emergence and effects of social networks that was inspired by the programme. It has produced a cumulative research effort, especially in the area of occupational attainment. Adding to what has already been said above, many a person finds his job through informal channels, even in modern industrial societies, a tendency that even seems to be increasing, at least as far as the Netherlands is concerned (Moerbeek *et al.*, 1995). The central finding is that, not so much the number of people prepared to lend a helping hand, nor the cohesion within the network, but the resources of the persons within one's network are critical social capital in achieving a good job. It was furthermore demonstrated (Lin *et al.*, 1981a; De Graaf and Flap, 1988) that part of the effect on occupational success originally attributed to human capital had to be attributed in fact to the employment of social resources, human capital being partly responsible for better social resources.

Tests of the investment hypothesis for the dissolving of romantic love relationships (Rusbult *et al.*, 1991, Rusbult and Martz, 1995) and for stability of informal relationships over a period of several years, while experiencing a number of other life events (Busschbach, 1996; Busschbach *et al.*, 1999), support the idea. These tests show that, apart from direct rewards and costs, especially the shadows of the past and of the future determine investment and stability in social relations. Busschbach showed that the embeddedness of ties contributes to their stability only in the short term. In addition, for an embedded instrumental tie to last, people have to invest more. Companionship and emotional ties that are embedded will last even when a person temporarily does not invest in them.

The programme produced new interpretations of well known facts in established fields of study, such as, stratification research. Part of the status attainment literature deals with the effect of a person's social capital as represented by the education and occupation of his father. The argument can be generalized to husbands, wives, siblings, uncles and so on. Another finding that can be better understood within a social capital framework is that in larger families children profit less from their parents' resources, probably because siblings have to compete for these resources (Downey, 1995). Not only can the whole of occupational achievement literature in a way be subsumed under the social capital argument, this argument also produces new predictions for such an established field, for example, the strength of the tie to the parents conditions the returns children will experience from their parents' resources in their educational as well as in their occupational career.

Social capital research has also opened up new research areas. Great impact was made by the study of Coleman and Hoffer (1987) on the differential school success of minorities in the United States, which was shown to be greater in Catholic schools. The presumed reason was the greater social capital located in the communities of parents surrounding these schools. Children achieve better educational results attending schools in which the parents of one child take care, on their own initiative, of the children of other parents. Especially, children of parents who do not have many personal resources themselves profit from such schools. Migration tends to destroy this kind of capital, which is detrimental to the educational and occupational chances of children unless the father and the mother have strong relations with their children (Hagan *et al.*, 1996).

Within the sociology of the family, McLanahan (1984) provided the start of research on the detrimental effects of single-parent families, especially of divorce, on the educational and occupational chances of the children. Children of one-parent families have lower educational achievements, a high school drop-out rate, lower earnings and occupational status, and a greater chance of becoming a welfare recipient. McLanahan interprets these effects as caused by loss of social capital within the family. A divorce seems to be more incisive than the death of a parent, probably because the death of a parent does not end the support delivered by the child's family of both parents, in contrast to the divorce which often puts an end to relations with at least part of the wider family. An uncle with a good social position, for example, might compensate for a deceased father (Tepperman, 1972).

Another new problem opened up by social capital research is the mutual influence of partners on each other's career. When spouses support one another, education is not only human capital, but also social capital. Bernasco *et al.* (1997) demonstrate such 'cross-effects'. There is a cumulation of advantages within a family, as partners well provided with educational and occupational resources establish coupled careers in which each partner promotes the career and income of the other. A similar argument can be made for the very employment of the spouse. Just being employed, for example, brings with it information, also to a person's partner, which is not available to others. Research shows that having a partner with a higher education promotes a partner's chances of being employed, of attaining a job with a higher prestige, and higher hourly wages (Ultee *et al.*, 1988).

Social capital theory also made an impact in the area of minorities research. We have already cited the network argument made by Wilson (1987) on the fate of black people in the urban ghetto. Borjas (1995) shows that, net of the resources that usually influence educational and income attainment and of neighbourhood poverty, there is a negative effect of living in a community of co-ethnics with few resources. Portes (1998) emphasizes that because of the relative lack of alternatives these minorities develop a bounded solidarity. The willingness among such minorities to help each other is probably greater than in other groups. Poor people, like many immigrants, are not isolated, as is often thought, but frequently are rather well connected (Fernandez-Kelly, 1994). However, they do not profit from their networks because there are only a few second-order resources being integrated. Ethnic entrepreneurs sometimes profit from this lack of alternatives of their co-ethnics by hiring them as cheap labour (Zimmer and Aldrich, 1987). Although ethnic entrepreneurs cannot compete with co-ethnic entrepreneurs that do have more educational and financial resources, they do better than co-ethnics with a similar education who are working as an employees (Bates, 1994).

Yet another application of the social capital argument can be found in the research on organizational success and failure (Aldrich *et al.*, 1987; Brüderl and Preisendörfer, 1997; Flap *et al.*, 1998b). Founders of new business enterprises with networks rich in social capital will be more successful, those without will sooner face financial failure. It is not so much an entrepreneur's ties to his family and other persons in his private sphere that matter, but especially his ties in the business world at large. The death of an organization also seems to be influenced by the ties of management (D'Aveni, 1990).

Programmatic differences notwithstanding, new economic sociology and new institutional economics merge in actual research of business transactions. While reading recent work by DiMaggio and Louch (1998) or Batenburg *et al.* (2002), it is hard to tell whether one is dealing with a study coming from the one or the other tradition, although judged by the references the former is more inspired by new economic sociology and the latter by new institutional economics. This recent research shows that social embeddedness of a transaction between organizations leads to repeated transactions that, in addition, require less management effort (Heide and Miner, 1992; Gulati, 1995; Blumberg, 1997; Buskens, 1999; Rooks *et al.*, 2000). The effects of the shadow of the past are stronger than those of the future, those of embeddedness in a network of similar others have the weakest effect. DiMaggio and Louch (1998) demonstrate something similar for private persons. Persons who buy products the quality of which is not clear, like a used car, prefer to buy from a relative or a friend rather than a dealer with whom they do not have a social relationship.

This kind of research comes up with interesting results that are congenial to a social capital theory of social relations, yet the investment in social ties is not spelled out as clearly in the social capital theory, although the implications are the same. In particular, Williamson's discussion of the choice of hybrid governance structures for transactions as an alternative to either market or hierarchy is pertinent (Williamson, 1996, p.108). A particularly interesting research result that showed up is an interaction between past and future: the length of the future does not matter to the management effort that much if there is already a large past (Batenburg *et al.*, 2002).

One bone of contention is left, that is, whether networks with holes or dense networks promote performance. It is my contention that Burt's idea only seemingly contradicts Bourdieu's and Coleman's idea on the positive value of integration of a group. The first idea refers to situations in which individuals can further their ends better by competing with others, whereas the latter idea refers to the situation in which individuals generally can better improve their fate by cooperation. There it is also the difference between competition between groups and competition between individuals.[10] Another manner in which to reconcile both views was recently presented by Uzzi (1999). He describes how firms that entertain strong ties to a particular bank, or, more precisely, an account manager at a bank, and also have ties at arm's length to other banks, get better deals in their dealings with the bank because they use their weak ties to evaluate the deals they make in their strong connections. In fact the bank also turns out to close a better deal, because it is far better informed about the characteristics of its client and the condition his firm is in (see Flap *et al.*, 1998a, pp.134–6).

The first surge of studies along the lines of the research programme has sharpened the theoretical formulations and produced interesting new theoretical questions. The first issue I want to discuss is that persons not only use their resources to attain their ends or invest in achieving other resources, they also defend their production functions, social capital included, if their life chances heavily depend on these (Kapferer, 1972, p.107). They place themselves in social situations, such as conflicts between persons they are involved with, in such a way as to safeguard their investments.

As the future is indeterminate in many respects, it is hard to conceive what a victory over others might mean, and it is because their own good life depends on continuing cooperation with others that people try to keep their options open. They try to stay in the game, rather than to outsmart others. Their objective is not to be caught on the wrong side, not so much aiming at keeping to a particular relationship, as keeping enough general and specific social capital to be reasonably sure not to be without support in the future.

Taking this argument one step further (this is my second point), people might also improve upon their present situation by attacking the production functions of others, by applying network surgery. Attacking the resource base of the others with whom one has to compete is another way to safeguard one's own life chances. For a particular person, this could mean, for example, driving a wedge between others who form a coalition against him (Lazega, 1992; Gargiulo, 1993).

Thirdly, a classic theme from cultural anthropology returns in network research among present-day western societies. People play out similar interests in each singular social relationship they entertain with others. This provides a twist to the investment idea, an indeterminacy to providing some kind of help to another person: is providing help to someone else an act of deference or of noblesse oblige? Is giving or receiving status-enhancing (Leifer, 1985)? Especially if people meet in social, relatively unstructured, situations, they try to strike a balance between giving and receiving. There is often a delicate balance between giving and receiving: people try to define their giving as an indication of prestige and not as a sign of growing indebtedness.

Fourthly, social networks matter most in social conditions that can be situated between a market type of situation and a monopoly. Leifer and White (1988) contend that most real-life markets have to be situated somewhere between a complete free market and a monopoly, since usually they contain between five and 12 'players'. In these situations the structure of social networks between producers matters more for the determination of prices, for investment decisions and the like. The returns on investment in social relations with other players are higher if the social situation is neither a free market nor a monopoly. Social capital is more critical to success the more competition is imperfect and the more abundant the financial and human capital to invest (Burt, 1992, p.10).

Fifth, quite unlike what arguments about erosion of social capital in modern society suggest, many people are normally up to their limits involved in social life, also in modern times. Maybe people have never been as free to choose with whom to 'hang out' as in our day. In the past, laws enforcing persons to provide help to their next of kin or to their neighbours were not created out of whim but were instigated because such assistance had been lacking. A case can be built that, as regards the question whether community is lost, saved or liberated, the latter is a better approximation of social life in present-day western societies (Wellman, 1979; Wellman *et al.*, 1988).

Yet, and this is my sixth point, social capital is like ether, it evaporates. It differs from other kinds of capital, such as cultural capital, in that it grows in use. Because social capital fades away if no action is undertaken, people often consciously try to create institutional carriers for informal networks, foci one might say, like fraternal or other voluntary organizations with signs communicating who is 'one of us'. People stabilize social production functions in which social resources are included by building institutional brickwork around it (Müller, 1986). Baron and Hannan (1994) suggest that internal labour markets are created by employers to bind employees with valuable human and social capital to the company, for example those with extensive ties to customers.

Seventh, Coleman (1990) notices that there is a collective good aspect to social capital, that could lead to an underinvestment in social capital: why should anyone contribute to keeping their common network in good shape? It is not a pure collective good, though: individuals do not provide information for nothing. There is also an argument to be made for the opposite statement: because people do not know their future and do not know whose help they might need, they do not want to be caught on the wrong side and invest in far more people than they will ever cash in on.

Eighth, social capital might help to account, not only for success, but also for failure, demotion or absence of mobility. Granovetter once drew attention to the peculiar fact that, although most sociological research on social mobility is concerned with change of position, in reality most people are not that mobile or not mobile at all. The real problem is to explain why so many people do not change jobs. An answer might be found in the absence of any sizeable social capital, or in the presence of sour capital, that is an individual having enemies, occupying a position within the organization that is decisive for his chances of promotion. The influence of foes in the occupational career would lead to unsuccessful attempts at upward mobility, instances of prolonged stability, and downward mobility over the whole occupational career. Do friends not only help in obtaining a higher occupational position but also help to foreclose demotion? And do enemies induce sociable demotion and do they bloc upward mobility? Persons who stay in their job for a long period of time probably are either persons without friends or foes, or persons who have friends on their job and on their own level. Moerbeek *et al.* (1995) found, in an analysis of data on occupational careers of a representative sample of Dutch respondents, that somebody who gets another job through an internal hiring gains 20 points of job prestige on Blau and Duncan's well-known occupational prestige scale (running from 0 to 100), compared to one who has to change jobs because of having troubles with colleagues.

The last issue is that social capital is not a one-dimensional all-purpose resource, but has distinguishable components that may be generally useful or goal-specific. For example, some types of support, such as emotional support and providing company, are more or less directly implied by a close relation plus the willingness and opportunity to be together, whereas other types of support, such as instrumental and information help, also invoke others' resources. Which forms of social capital have benefits in diverse life domains and which are especially valuable in specific life domains (for example, school performance, obtaining a job, doing one's work, lending money, advice for personal problems, health, housing and leisure)? How do the various effects of a person's social capital depend on its constituents? Trust, for example, relates to the strength of the ties and the structure of the network, whereas achieving instrumental goals is more directly dependent on what kind of resources are on the other side. Podolny and Baron (1997) and Völker and Flap (2001) assume and demonstrate that open networks of ties with instrumental contents as well as closed networks of identity-based ties do promote upward mobility in work organizations. Völker and Flap (2000) show something similar with respect to job satisfaction. Take note: this is yet another way to solve the seeming contradiction between the different structural interpretations of social capital.

CONCLUSION

Social capital theory is a research programme that might help to close the network gap in social network analysis. One key idea, social networks being social capital, explains the emergence as well as the effects of networks: a person's social capital promotes his goal achievement, and he will invest in it depending on its instrumental value. Although its popularity is rapidly growing, there is also some scepticism. For example, Baron and Hannan (1994) stated that its 'theoretical cutting edge is lost if attention is not called to investments, rates of return, opportunity costs, the future, and the ability to appropriate the returns from the investment.' However, the programme does not only bring unity to a formerly disintegrated research area; on top of that, it provides new predictions that work in empirical research.

It helps to understand why there are, contrary to the structuralist claim, no pure structural effects: structural effects meet with exceptions because the instrumental value of social capital is contingent upon existing institutions and available technology. Often the ends themselves change if institutions change, not the ultimate goal of making the best of one's life, but the instrumental goals. Institutional change may change the instrumental value of personal networks by providing an alternative means to the same goal. For example, psychological tests might also tell an employer what risks he runs by hiring a prospective employee, and he would not have to rely on personal relations any more.

Like social-capital theory, structuralism emphasizes norms less as a steering mechanism for individual action. Their ideas about man basically are not that different. Structuralism also implies in its implicit individualistic assumptions that individual action is driven by interests: to be specific, not to be caught on the wrong side. The difference is that structuralism does not make an issue of exceptions to the structuralist effects it theorizes about, and that it does not explicitly use individualistic assumptions to explain why there are exceptions to the predicted effects, probably because it would go against the grain of the programme of structurally induced social action to take into account the conditioning of these effects by institutional arrangements, for instance.

The size of different social groups determines the opportunities to meet and entertain relationships with people of such groups. Moreover, without available places and foci that offer opportunities to meet, nothing would come from the availability of others. The study of the influence of social contexts on the emergence of social networks has only just begun, and manipulating contexts offers a rare opportunity to steer the developments of social networks somewhat. Interesting research questions include whether there is any unbundling of contexts in our society, an unbundling that might be detrimental to the emergence and maintenance of social capital (Coleman, 1990). A potential revolutionizing idea is that people choose particular contexts instead of particular persons. If a person has a work-related problem he wants advice from somebody from the work context, preferably a friend (Feld, 1984). Some foci, like a bar or a dance hall are freely chosen by people instead of being forced upon them, as occurs in the case of being born into a particular family and neighbourhood. This problem shift might pull the rug from beneath existing research on interaction partners.

Our sketch of a social capital theory did not provide definitive answers (for other reviews, see Sandefur and Laumann, 1998; Portes, 1998; Flap, 1999; Burt, 2000; Lin, 2001). In particular, the question as to what 'really' is the mechanism behind the effects of networks did not receive a satisfactory answer. This is because saying that it is the instrumental value of a network as social capital shifts the question to what makes social capital productive. A cursory review of the literature suggests that there is not one particular mechanism that can be made responsible for the productiveness of social capital. The main mechanisms addressed are the following:

- provision of access to opportunities to apply one's human and financial capital;
- non-redundant information;
- referrals by others to third parties that signal one's capacities and quality;

- providing access or information about 'business opportunities' at the right timing;
- a lubricant in dealings with others, promoting trust in people, agreements or quality of products;
- obligation to help people based on services rendered in the past;
- help based on expected benefits in the future;
- affording help to jump a few places in a waiting queue of persons who want to be served;
- providing specific help with tasks with many contingencies, not easily subdivided, or to satisfy needs for which the time of their occurrance is hard to predict;
- provision of control benefits, a favourable exchange rate in dealings with others;
- enforcing agreements and norms of cooperation;
- providing standards of comparison of ways to decide in situations of risk or uncertainty.

Finding some common dominator among the mechanisms hinted at above is hard. The last mechanism is somewhat different from the others in that it helps to frame cognitively the social situation of the actor and to define what is in his interest, whereas the others are more directly instrumental in promoting his interest in some sense.

A major provision for the further development of the research programme is to take seriously the analogy with human capital, minding the commonalities as well as the differences, not leaving social capital as only a weak figure of speech, but using its theoretical cutting edge by calling attention to investments, rates of return, opportunity costs, the future, investing and divesting, discounting, portfolios of various types of capital, substitution and the ability to appropriate the returns from investments.

Our deliberations lay near that particularism is here to stay, therewith underlining the continuous importance of network research in general and the social capital programme in particular.

NOTES

1. The first draft of this chapter was written in 1990 during a stay at the Department of Sociology, Columbia University, New York. The author thanks Bonnie Ericson, Nan Lin and Beate Völker for comments on an earlier version of the chapter. An earlier version was presented at the Fifth European Social Network Conference, 6–10 July 1995, London, and at the workshop on 'Rational choice and social networks', 26–28 January 1995, at Nias, Wassenaar, the Netherlands, University of Utrecht.The main title is taken from a poem by John Donne.
2. Not at issue here are the great contributions of structuralism to social sciences in providing sophisticated methods for the measurement and analysis of network characteristics. For an early description, in network terms, of the structuralist group, see Mullins (1973).

3. Efforts to explain the emergence and changes in real-world networks while using balance theory were not very successful. For example, conflicting loyalties are stubbornly recreated, although they are hurtful to the mind and the heart (Granovetter, 1979). For a structural analysis of these effects from a social capital perspective, see Flap (1988, 1997).
4. A merger between rational choice ideas and structuralism also seems to be in the making by more lenient structuralists, such as Granovetter (1985) and Burt (1992, 2000). There are similar developments in social psychological exchange theory (Cook and Whitmeyer, 1992; Molm and Cook, 1995).
5. These facts of life are described in Marxist terms, as that human action is interest-driven and that the interests of people are largely determined by their place within the institutional arrangement, especially within existing property rights systems.
6. How to measure social capital is a problem we will not go into here. For a discussion on how to generalize social capital measures across alters, ties or second-order resources, see Snijders (1999).
7. Burt (1992, 2000) tested whether being autonomous is an asset in the career process by looking at the career pattern of top managers in a number of large firms and only confirms this hypothesis for male managers. They do not get ahead further, but faster. The hypothesis does not hold for female managers. Yet another pure structural effect gone astray.
8. Boxman, De Graaf and Flap, (1991) demonstrated that, for managers of large Dutch companies, social capital helps to achieve a higher income at any level of human capital, but human capital makes no difference at the highest levels of social capital.
9. An earlier version of the investment theory was proposed by Rusbult *et al.*, (1991), whose theory does not include expected future benefits and second-order resources.
10. The distinction between positively and negatively connected networks, as introduced by Cook *et al.* (1983) might also be relevant here.

REFERENCES

Aldrich, Howard, Ben Rosen and Bill Woodward (1987), 'The impact of social networks on business foundings and profit: a longitudinal study', in Neil Churchill *et al.* (eds), *Frontiers of Entrepreneurship Research*, Wellesley, MA: Center for Entrepreneurial Studies, pp. 154–68.

Axelrod, Robert (1984), *The Evolution of Co-operation*, New York: Basic Books.

Baker, Wayne E. (1984a), 'The social structure of a national securities market', *American Journal of Sociology*, 89, 775–811.

Baker, Wayne E. (1984b), 'Floor trading and crowd dynamics', in Patricia A. Adler and Peter Adler (eds), *The Social Dynamics of Financial Markets,* Greenwich: JAI Press, pp. 107–28.

Banfield, Edgar (1958), *The Moral Basis of a Backward Society*, Chicago: University of Chicago Press.

Baron, James N. and Michael T. Hannan (1994), 'The impact of economics on contemporary sociology', *Journal of Economic Literature,* 32, 1111–46.

Baron, James N., P.D. Jennings and Frank R. Dobbin (1988), 'Mission control? The development of personnel systems in U.S. industry', *American Sociological Review*, 53, 497–514.

Batenburg, Ronald S., Chris Snijders and Werner Raub (2002), 'Contacts and Contracts: Dyadic Embeddedness and the Contractual Behaviour of Firms', forthcoming in *Research in the Sociology of Organizations*, 16.

Bates, Timothy (1994), 'Social resources generated by group support networks may not be beneficial to Asian immigrant-owned small businesses', *Social Forces,* 72, 671–89.

Berkman, Lisa and Seymor Syme (1979), 'Social networks, host resistance and mortality', *American Journal of Epidemiology*, 109, 186–204.
Berkowitz, Steven D. (1982), *An Introduction to Structural Analysis*, Toronto: Butterworth.
Bernasco, Wim, Paul de Graaf and Wout Ultee (1997), 'Coupled careers', *European Sociological Review*, 14, 15–31.
Bian, Yanjie (1997), 'Bringing strong ties back in: indirect ties, network bridges and job searches in China', *American Sociological Review*, 62, 366–85.
Blau, Peter M. and Joseph Schwarz (1984), *Cross-Cutting Social Circles*, New York: Academic Press.
Blumberg, Boris F. (1997), *Das Management von Technologiekooperationen*, Amsterdam: Thesis Publishers.
Boissevain, Jeremy (1974), *Friends of Friends*, Oxford: Blackwell.
Borjas, George J. (1995), 'Ethnicity, neighborhoods and human-capital externalities', *American Economic Review*, 85, 365–90.
Boudon, Raymond (1981), *La logique du social*, Paris: Hachette.
Bourdieu, Pierre (1973), 'Cultural reproduction and social reproduction', in R. Brown (ed.), *Knowledge, Education and Cultural Change*, London: Tavistock, pp. 71–112.
Bourdieu, Pierre (1981), 'Le capital social', *Actes de la recherche en sciences sociales*, 31, 2–3.
Bourdieu, Pierre and Monique de Saint Martin (1982), 'Le patronat', *Actes de la recherche en sciences sociales*, 32, 3–82.
Boxman, Ed, Paul de Graaf and Henk Flap (1991), 'The impact of social and human capital on the income attainment of Dutch managers', *Social Networks*, 13, 51–73.
Bridges, William P. and Wayne J. Villemez (1986), 'Informal hiring and the labor market', *American Sociological Review*, 51, 574–82.
Brüderl, Jozef and Peter Preisendörfer (1997), 'Network support and the success of newly founded business', *Journal of Small Business Economic*, 9, 1–13.
Burt, Ronald S. (1987), 'Social contagion and innovation: cohesion versus structural equivalence', *American Journal of Sociology*, 92, 1287–1335.
Burt, Ronald S. (1992), *Structural Holes. The Social Structure of Competition*, Cambridge, MA: Harvard University Press.
Burt, Ronald S. (2000), 'The network structure of social capital', in Robert I. Sutton and Barry M. Straw (eds), *Research in Organizational Behaviour*, Greenwich, CT: JAI Press, pp. 345–423.
Buskens, Vincent (1999), *Social Networks and Trust*, Amsterdam: Thesis.
Busschbach, Jooske van (1996), 'Uit het oog, uit het hart?', Amsterdam: Thesis.
Busschbach, Jooske van, Henk Flap and Frans N. Stokman (1999), 'Stability and change in personal networks. A test of the investment theory', paper presented at the Sociologendagen, Utrecht, 29 May.
Coleman, James S. (1988), 'Social capital in the creation of human capital', *American Journal of Sociology*, 94, Supplement S95–S120.
Coleman, James S. (1990), *The Foundation of Social Theory*, Boston: Bellknap Press.
Coleman, James S. (1993), 'The rational reconstruction of society', *American Sociological Review*, 58, 1–15.
Coleman, James S. and Thomas Hoffer (1987), *Public and Private Schools: The Impact of Communities*, New York: Basic Books.
Cook, Karen S. and Joseph M. Whitmeyer (1992), 'Two approaches to social structure: exchange theory and network analysis', *Annual Review of Sociology*, 18, 109–27.
Cook, Karen S., Richard M. Emerson and Mary R. Gillmore (1983), 'The distribution

of power in exchange networks: theory and experimental results', *American Journal of Sociology*, 89, 275–305.

Cosmides, Leda and John Tooby (1992), 'Cognitive adaptations to social exchange', in J.H. Barkov, L. Cosmides and J. Tooby (eds), *The Adapted Mind*, Oxford: Oxford University Press, pp. 163–228.

D'Aveni, Richard (1990), 'Top management prestige and organizational bankruptcy', *Organization Science*, 1, 121–42.

Dasgupta, Partha (1988), 'Trust as a commodity', in Diego Gambetta (ed.), *Trust, Making and Breaking Cooperation*, Oxford: Oxford University Press, pp. 49–72.

De Graaf, Nan Dirk and Henk Flap (1988), 'With a little help from my friends', *Social Forces*, 67, 453–72.

Dijk, Jan van and Andries Roorda (1980), *Het patriciaat in Zierikzee onder de Republiek*, Middelburg: Historisch Genootschap.

DiMaggio, Paul and Hugh Louch (1998), 'Socially embedded consumer transactions', *American Sociological Review*, 63, 619–37.

Doreian, Patrick and Frans N. Stokman (eds) (1997), *Evolution of Social Networks*, Amsterdam: Gordon Breach.

Downey, Douglas B. (1995), 'When bigger is not better: family size, parental resources and children's educational performance', *American Sociological Review*, 60, 746–61.

Faulkner, Robert R. (1983), *Music on Demand*, New Brunswick: Transaction Books.

Feld, Scott (1981), 'The focused organization of social ties', *American Journal of Sociology*, 86, 1015–35.

Feld, Scott (1984), 'The structured use of personal associates', *Social Forces*, 62: 640-52.

Fernandez-Kelly, M. Patricia (1994), 'Social and cultural capital in the urban ghetto', in Alejandro Portes (ed.), *The Economic Sociology of Immigration*, New York: Free Press, pp. 213–47.

Fischer, Claude S. (1982), *To Dwell Among Friends*, Chicago: University of Chicago Press.

Fischer, Claude S, Robert Max Jackson, C. Ann Stuene, Kathryn Gerson, Lynne McAllister Jones with Mick Baldassare, (1977), *Networks and Places*, New York: Free Press.

Flap, Henk (1988), *Conflict, Loyalty and Violence*, Bern: Peter Lang.

Flap, Henk (1989), 'Patronage: an institution in its own right', in Michael Hechter, Karl-Dieter Opp and Reinhard Wippler (eds), *Social Institutions*, New York: Aldine de Gruyte, pp. 225–43.

Flap, Henk (1991), 'Social capital in the reproduction of inequality: a review', *Comparative Sociology of Family, Health and Education*, 20, 6179–6202.

Flap, Henk (1997), 'The conflicting loyalties theory', *L'Année sociologique*, 47, 183–216.

Flap, Henk (1999), 'Creation and returns of social capital', *La Revue Tocqueville*, 20, 5–26.

Flap, Henk and Ed Boxman (1999), 'Getting a job as a manager', in Roger Lenders and Shaul M. Gabbay (eds) *Corporate Social Capital and Liability*, Boston: Kluwer, pp. 197–216.

Flap, Henk and Ed Boxman (2001), 'Getting started', in Nan Lin, Karen Cook and Ron Burt (eds), *Social Capital: Theory and Research*, Chicago: Aldine. pp. 159–181.

Flap, Henk, Bert Bulder and Beate Völker (1998a), 'Intra-organizational networks and performance', *Computational and Mathematical Organization Theory*, 4, 109–47.

Flap, Henk, Patrick Fleracker and Frits van Uxem (1998b), 'The success of small business foundings in the Netherlands. Effects of financial, human and social capital and the liabilities of newness and smallness', paper presented at the EGOS Conference, Maastricht, 9–11 July.

Flap, Henk and Beate Völker (2001), 'Social capital at the workplace and job satisfaction. Goal-specific social capital.' *Social Networks*, 23, 297–320.

Forsé, Michel (1999), 'Social capital and status attainment', *La Revue Tocqueville*, 20, 59–81.

Foster, George M. (1961), 'The dyadic contract', *American Anthropologist*, 63, 1173–92.

Frenzen, Jonathan and Harry L. Davis (1990), 'Purchasing behaviour in embedded markets', *Journal of Consumer Research*, 17, 1–12.

Gargiulo, Martin (1993), 'Two-step leverage: managing constraint in organizational politics', *Administrative Science Quarterly*, 38, 1–19.

Gluckman, Max (1965), *Politics, Law, Ritual in Tribal Society*, Oxford: Blackwell.

Granovetter, Mark S. (1973), 'The strength of weak ties', *American Journal of Sociology*, 78, 1360–80.

Granovetter, Mark S. (1974) (rev. ed. 1995), *Getting a Job*, Cambridge, MA: Harvard University Press.

Granovetter, Mark S. (1979), 'The theory gap in social network analysis', in Paul W. Holland and Samuel Leinhardt (eds), *Perspectives on Social Network Research*, New York: Academic Press, pp. 501–18.

Granovetter, Mark (1985), 'Economic action and social structure: the problem of embeddedness', *American Journal of Sociology*, 91, 481–510.

Granovetter, Mark (1992), 'Economic institutions as social constructions', *Acta Sociologica*, 35, 3–11.

Grieco, Margaret (1987), *Keeping it in the Family*, London: Tavistock.

Gulati, Ranjay (1995), 'Does familiarity breed trust?', *Academy of Management Journal*, 38, 85–112.

Hagan, John, Ross MacMillan and Blair Wheaton (1996), 'New kid in town: social capital and the life course effects of family migration on children', *American Sociological Review*, 61, 368–85.

Heide, Jan B. and Anne S. Miner (1992), 'The shadow of the future: effects of anticipated interaction and frequency of contact on buyer–seller relations', *Academy of Management Journal*, 35, 265–91.

Heinz, John P. and Edward O. Laumann (1981), *Chicago Lawyers*, New York: Russell Sage.

Hobbes, Thomas (1663), *Leviathan*, London: Penguin.

Kalmijn, Matthijs and Henk Flap (2001), 'Assortative meeting and mating: unintended consequences of organized settings for partner choices'. *Social Forces*, 79, 1289–1312.

Kapferer, Bruce C. (1972), *Strategy and Transaction in an African Factory*, Manchester: Manchester University Press.

Lazega, Emmanuel (1992), 'Analyse de réseaux d'une organisation collegiale: les avocats d'affaires', *Revue francaise de sociologie*, 33, 559–89.

Lee, Nancy Howell (1969), *The Search for an Abortionist*, Chicago: University of Chicago Press.

Leifer, Eric (1985), 'Interaction preludes to role setting: exploratory local action', *American Sociological Review*, 53, 865–78.

Leifer, Eric M. and Harrison C. White (1988), 'A structural approach to markets', in Michael Schwartz and Mark Mizruchi (eds), *The Structural Analysis of Business*, New York: Cambridge University Press, pp. 85–108.

Levi, Primo (1979), *Is this a Man?*, London: Penguin, first published as 'Se questo è un uomo', 1958, Tarino.
Lin, Nan (2001), *Social Capital: A Theory of Social Structure and Action*, Cambridge: Cambridge University Press.
Lin, Nan, John C. Vaughn and Walter M. Ensel (1981a), 'Social resources and occupational attainment', *Social Forces*, 59, 1163–81.
Lin, Nan, John C. Vaughn and Walter M. Ensel (1981b), 'Social resources and strength of ties', *American Sociological Review*, 46, 393–405.
Lindenberg, Siegwart (1990), 'Homo socio-economicus', *Journal of Institutional and Theoretical Economics*, 146, 727–48.
Lindenberg, Siegwart (1998), 'Solidarity: its microfoundations and macro dependence. A framing approach', in Patrick Doreian and Thomas Fararo (eds), *The Problem of Solidarity. Theories and Models*, Amsterdam: Gordon Breach, pp. 61–111.
Litwak, Eugene (1985), *Helping the Elderly*, New York: Guilford Press.
Loury, Glenn (1977), 'A dynamic theory of racial income differences', in Phyllis A. Wallace and Annette M. LaMond (eds), *Women, Minorities, and Employment Discrimination*, Lexington, MA: Lexington Books, pp. 153–88.
McGuire, Patrick, Mark S. Granovetter and Michael Schwartz (1993), 'Thomas Edison and the social construction of the early electricity industry in America', in Richard Swedberg (ed.), *Explorations in Economic Sociology*, New York: Sage, pp. 213–46.
McLanahan, Sara (1984), 'Family structure and the reproduction of poverty', *American Journal of Sociology*, 90, 873–901.
Marsden, Peter V. (1982), 'Brokerage behavior in restricted exchange networks', in Peter V. Marsden and Nan Lin (eds), *Social Structure and Network Analysis*, Beverly Hills: Sage, pp. 201–19.
Marsden, Peter V. (1990), 'Network diversity, substructures and opportunities for contact', in Craig Calhoun, Marshall W. Meyer and W. Richard (eds), *Structures of Power and Constraint*, Cambridge: Cambridge University Press, pp. 397–410.
Mauss, Marcel (1923), 'Essai sur le don, forme achaïque de l'échange', *L'Année sociologique seconde série*, 1, 30–186.
Moerbeek, Hester, Henk Flap and Wout Ultee (1995), 'That's what friends are for', paper presented at the International Social Network Conference, London, 6–10 July.
Molm, Linda D. and Karen S. Cook (1995), 'Social exchange and social networks', in Karen S. Cook, Gary Alan Fine and James S. House (eds), *Sociological Perspectives in Social Psychology*, Boston: Allyn and Bacon, pp. 209–335.
Müller, Hans-Peter (1986), *Klassen, Kassifikationen und Lebensstile*, Mannheim: Universität der Bundeswehr.
Mullins, Nicholas C. (1973), *Theories and Theory Groups in American Sociology*, New York: Harper Row.
Oberhofer, Tom (1989), 'The changing cultural discount rate', *Review of Social Economy*, 47, 43–54.
Ormel, Johan, Siegwart Lindenberg, Nardi Steverdink and Lois M. Verbugge (1999), 'Subjective well-being and social production functions', *Social Indicators Research*, 46, 61–99.
Perrow, Charles (1986), *Complex Organizations*, New York: McGraw-Hill.
Podolny, Joel M. and James N. Baron (1997), 'Resources and relationships: social networks and mobility in the workplace', *American Sociological Review*, 62, 673–93.
Portes, Alejandro (1998), 'Social capital: its origins and applications in modern sociology', *Annual Review of Sociology*, 24, 1–24.

Powell, Walter W. (1985), *Getting into Print*, Chicago: University of Chicago Press.
Preisendörfer, Peter and Thomas Voss (1988), 'Arbeitsmarkt und soziale Netzwerke', *Soziale Welt*, 39, 104–19.
Putnam, Robert (1993), 'Social capital and institutional success', in *Making Democracy Work. Civic Traditions in Modern Italy*, Princeton: Princeton University Press, pp. 163–85.
Putnam, Robert (1995a), 'Tuning in, tuning out: the strange disappearance of social capital in America', *Political Science and Politics*, 28, 664–83.
Putnam, Robert (1995b), 'Bowling alone: America's declining social capital', *Journal of Democracy*, 6, 65–78.
Raub, Werner and Jeroen Weesie (1990), 'Reputation and efficiency in social interactions: an example of network effects', *American Journal of Sociology*, 96, 626–54.
Rooks, Gerrit, Werner Raub, Frits Tazelaar and Robert Selten (2000), 'How inter-firm cooperation depends on social embeddedness?', *Acta Sociologica*, 43 (2000) 123–137.
Rusbult, Caryl E. and J. Martz (1995), 'Remaining in an abusive relationship: an investment model analysis of nonvoluntary dependence', *Personality and Social Psychology Bulletin*, 21, 558–71.
Rusbult, Caryl E., Julie Verette, Gregory A. Whitney, Linda F. Slovik and Isaac Lipkus (1991), 'Accommodation processes in close relationships', *Journal of Personality and Social Psychology*, 60, 53–78.
Sandefur, Rebecca L. and Edward O. Laumann (1998), 'A paradigm for social capital', *Rationality and Society*, 10, 481–501.
Singelman, Peter (1975), 'The closing triangle', *Comparative Studies in Society and History*, 17, 389–409.
Snijders, Chris (1996), *Trust and Commitments*, Amsterdam: Thesis.
Snijders, Tom A.B., Marinus Spreen and Roel Zaagstra (1995). 'The use of multilevel modeling for analyzing personal networks: networks of cocaine uses in an urban area', *Journal of Quantitative Anthropology*, 5, 85–105.
Snijders, Tom A.B. (1999), 'Prologue to the measurement of social capital', *La Revue Tocqueville*, 20, 27–44.
Stinchcombe, Arthur (1989), 'An outsider's view of network analyses of power', in Robert Perrucci and Harry R. Potter (eds), *Networks of Power*, New York: Aldine de Gruyter, pp. 119–33.
Swedberg, Richard (1997), 'New economic sociology: what has been accomplished, what is ahead?', *Acta Sociologica*, 40, 161–82.
Taylor, Michael (1974), *Anarchy and Cooperation*, London: Wiley.
Tepperman, Lorne (1972), 'The natural disruption of dynasties', *Canadian Review of Sociology and Anthropology*, 9, 111–33.
Ultee, Wout, Jos Dessens and Wim Jansen (1988), 'Why does unemployment come in couples?', *European Sociological Review*, 4, 111–22.
Uzzi, Brian (1999) 'Embeddedness in the making of financial capital: how social relations and networks benefit firms seeking financing', *American Sociological Review*, 64, 481–505.
Verbrugge, Louis M. (1977), 'The structure of adult friendship choices', *Social Forces*, 56, 576–97.
Völker, Beate and Henk Flap (1995a), 'The effects of institutional transformation on personal networks. East Germany, Four years later', *Netherlands Journal of the Social Sciences*, 31, 87–109.
Völker, Beate and Henk Flap (1995b), 'Amitié et inimitié sous communisme d'État: Le cas de l'Allemagne de l'Est', *Revue française de sociologie*, 36, 629–54.

Völker, Beate and Henk Flap (1997a), 'The comrade's belief: intended and unintended consequences of communism for neighbourhood relations in the former GDR', *European Sociological Review,* 13, 241–65.
Völker, Beate and Henk Flap (1997b), 'The perverse effects of weak ties in a semi-totalitarian society', Paper presented at the conference on the Management of Durable Relations, Woudschoten, June.
Völker, Beate and Henk Flap (1999), 'Getting ahead in the GDR', *Acta Sociologica,* 43, 17–34.
Völker, Beate and Henk Flap (2001), 'Weak ties as a liability. The case of East Germany.' *Rationality and Society*, 13, 397–428.
Völker, Beate (1995), *Should Auld Acquaintance be forgot . . .?*, Amsterdam: Thesis.
Wellman, Barry (1979), 'The community question', *American Journal of Sociology*, 84, 1201–31.
Wellman, Barry and Steven D. Berkowitz (eds) (1988), *Social Structures,* Cambridge: Cambridge University Press.
Wellman, Barry, Peter J. Carrington and Alan Hall (1988), 'Networks as personal communities', in Barry Wellman and Steven D. Berkowitz (eds), *Social Structures. A Network Approach*, Cambridge: Cambridge University Press, pp. 130–84.
White, Harrison (1981), 'Where do markets come from?', *American Journal of Sociology*, 87, 517–47.
Williamson, Oliver E. (1996), *The Mechanisms of Governance*, New York: Oxford University Press.
Wilson, William Julius (1987), *The Truly Disadvantaged*, Chicago: University of Chicago Press.
Zimmer, Catherine and Howard Aldrich (1987), 'Resource mobilization through ethnic networks. Kinship and friendship ties of shopkeepers in England', *Sociological Perspectives*, 30, 422–45
Zukin, Sharon and Paul DiMaggio (eds) (1990), *Structures of Capital*, Cambridge: Cambridge University Press.

2. Conventionalist approaches to enterprise

François Eymard-Duvernay[1]

INTRODUCTION

The research programme on the economics of conventions was spawned by a combination of several disciplines and institutions. Economists wanting to develop a realistic approach to rational behaviour in organizations joined forces with specialists in other disciplines (sociology, philosophy, law, management) to account for modes of coordination involving rules, objects and interactions between people. This academic work overlapped with reflection at Insee[2] on the role of categories and the plurality of firms' investments in coordination. The present chapter reviews this research programme with regard to corporate studies, and compares it to other programmes with similar aims.

Paradoxically, until recently the firm received very little attention in economic analysis. The reasons are clear. Since the neoclassical turning point, economists have focused primarily on the consumer economy, neglecting the analysis of productive activity. In this approach, the firm is reduced to an entrepreneur acting in various markets, and to a productive function with technical constraints outside the model. Its importance is considered only in a negative mode, when it occupies a monopoly position that disturbs market mechanisms. The Keynesian current did nothing to enhance the microeconomic approach to business. Renewed interest in organizations during the past two decades stems from a set of complex causes. It was probably becoming increasingly obvious that the efficiency of an economy relied, to a large extent, on organizations. Economists could not continue to leave this area of investigation in the hands of management scholars. Moreover, it opened new fields for research, creating an extremely fertile dynamic. Thus the economics of information found in employer–employee relations a vast field for application.

Contract theory, the framework of this new research programme, has renewed the lessons of economics. Contracts are local balances, in specific informational contexts. The challenge is to find appropriate incentives for creating the most efficient balance possible, despite incomplete information.

This generic label covers several types of contract, depending on the information structures postulated. As a result, the discipline risks being fragmented, since the unifying framework of the market is undermined. On the other hand, it is possible to account for a wide variety of relationships, by modifying the informational context. The economist is thus in a position to understand relations which appear to be deviant compared to standard market models. For example, wage stability is explained by the assurance of employers who are supposed to have less aversion to risk than employees; wage increases linked to length of service are seen as a form of incentive, in situations where employees' efforts are difficult to gauge, and so on.

The renewal initiated by this research programme should not be underestimated. The introduction of uncertainty into the economic agent's environment is essential. It reveals new possibilities for dysfunctioning in the coordination of actions. Some studies, now classical, have shown that markets are likely to disappear in situations of asymmetrical information (Akerlof, 1970; Stiglitz, 1987; Orléan, 1991). Global imbalances in markets (the labour market as well as the commodity and financial markets) are explained by information-related problems, which is a new way of linking macroeconomics and microeconomics. Our critique concerns the fact that this potentially important opening is limited by the maintenance of the standard model of rationality. The problem of uncertainty is somewhat facilely solved by the calculation of probabilities, and that of the interdependence of strategies by unrealistic assumptions of common knowledge.

Our programme describes a far less transparent economic world than the one to which the standard approach of rationality inevitably leads. In it, agents learn without knowing beforehand what they are going to learn. They conclude agreements which do not foresee the complete course of transactions. It seems amazing that such proposals can be seen as 'heterodox' when they are, to say the least, trivial. Admittedly, the solutions to problems thus posed are not easy, and they call for significant shifts from the neoclassical programme.

Can the tools of economic analysis be adapted for use in explaining interactions in a truly uncertain world? H. Simon has extensively explored a model of rationality suited to this aim. We have summarized the main features as follows.

- Agents of organizations are part of a hierarchy which establishes the common values of the organization and sets up the apparatus facilitating the coordination of actions, oriented by these common values (Simon, 1960).
- This apparatus relieves the agents of calculations; they are 'cognitive simplifiers' which focus attention on certain tasks and make practical

behavioural norms routine. The division of labour favours such cognitive economy.

- Agents' calculations cannot be reduced to a universal formula (taking the optimum decision in relation to the objective), to be applied to everyone in all situations. These calculations implement strategies which have been learned and which vary according to the subject's experience. So-called 'intuitive' behaviour frequently results from the quasi-instantaneous activation of these memorized strategies (Simon, 1983).
- The essential problem of choice is not one of calculating the optimum decision, but of deciding on the best calculation procedure (Simon, 1976).
- The limits of rationality are irreducible. Agents' perceptions are not as objective as they are made out to be; they are partly formed (and deformed) by theories in people's minds, materialized in information systems. The induction made by agents and the theories they use to anticipate their environment, are based as much on beliefs as on rationality (Simon, 1983).

This model of rationality, summed up in the concept of bounded rationality, can lead to an evolutionary programme if applied rigidly. The 'short-sighted' agent is guided by her or his environment which selects the most suitable behavioural routines. The loop is looped if we assume that the environment is constituted by other agents, all just as 'short-sighted', since changes in the population are determined by the gains procured for everyone, depending on behaviours which may overlap (although totally randomly) (Boyer and Orléan, 1994).

The bounded rationality model does, however, have other applications which perpetuate the 'cognitive transition' initiated by the new economics of information (Favereau, 1997). These research programmes emphasize the ways in which agents can increase their cognitive capacities, through learning and the use of collective devices (Favereau, 1989, 1994). They focus more on values which are grounded in institutions and which orient actions (Boltanski and Thévenot, 1991). The choice of a decision-making procedure is not only a cognitive problem, for information devices are closely linked to orders of value. The idea of rules mobilized in these programmes links the cognitive approach (the rule spares the rationality) to values (the rule indicates how a value is attributed to the actions) (Reynaud, 1992).

In this chapter we stress the pluralistic approach to rules. This enables us to account for the cognitive indeterminacy of many situations: a single fact can be interpreted in different ways depending on the inference made and the form of information used to understand it. The plurality of rules is one way of taking into account the limits of rationality. It is also a way of taking into account the plurality in ways of attributing value to an action, itself a result of the plurality of institutions. This approach is based on the idea that, most of the time, agents do not have a single way of calculating, and that coordination is above all a problem of agreement on the way of calculating. The creation of markets has the effect of establishing a unified form of calculation, and their extension aims at propagating it to increasingly large areas of social life. But the firm is evidently a more complex environment in which several evaluation principles coexist.

This plurality of rationality complicates coordination. One could consider that, ideally, it is necessary to converge towards a unified economy, but we conclude differently, arguing in favour of pluralism which, in our view, is a condition of real economic democracy. The coherence of our approach is based on the maintenance of pluralism in the social sciences, contrary to attempts at universalization inherent in each research programme. This pluridisciplinarity is not a façade; it is a condition for the maintenance of debate on the forms of economic organization, at a corporate level and in society.

THE COMPARATIVE APPROACH TO FORMS OF COORDINATION

The Plurality of Institutions

Can intracorporate relations be reduced to a single form of coordination? Any social science is tempted to generalize a form of coordination as widely as possible. This tendency has been particularly marked during the past 20 years in economics where new tools for analysis allow basic market mechanisms to be applied as far afield as the family, politics or organizations. This imperialism of economists is also found in other disciplines: some currents close to sociology consider that the market and organizations are merely the result of power struggles between social groups, or that they are 'embedded' in social networks (Granovetter, 1985). The choice of a research strategy is crucial. The reduction of all transactions to contract, totally overlooks the institutions which, through the ages, shaped organizations as we know them today. The variety of cultures is also diminished by this reductionist strategy, whereas it has never been as visible as now, in this time of globalization of trade. Recognition of the plurality of institutions is an essential issue in research (Friedland and Robertson, 1990). The result is a plurality of values which are not freely transferrable from one institution to another. Behaviour is not the same in a family as in a market or an association. One of the agents' competencies consists of knowing how to identify the nature of their institutions, and of adopting the appropriate behaviour. Should one, for all that, endorse the rigid partitioning of institutions, with each one belonging to a specialized social science? The answer is obviously no. The challenge facing current interdisciplinary developments is to maintain the pluralism of institutions, while creating a common framework to account for movements between institutional devices, and for situations in which several institutional contexts tend to be involved. This type of framework of analysis is particularly well-suited to organization studies.

The observer of economic life is faced with a wide variety of enterprises within a single sector. The strength of the market theory is that it fits all these activities into the same framework of calculation. But that is also its weakness. Recognition of the coordination role played by firms involves an investigation of their variety, which corresponds to a variety of forms of coordination, and the development of a comparative approach. This approach is followed by several currents in economics (Aoki *et al.*, 1990) but remains in the minority. Moreover, even in these currents, institutions are reduced to informational contexts because of the wish to keep in line with the dominant economic approach. A.O. Hirschman (1986) is certainly one of the authors who has gone furthest in developing the comparative approach, by comparing two forms of action. One has been studied more extensively in political science (the voice) and the other in economics (the exit).

We have developed a theoretical and empirical comparative approach of 'corporate models'. Each model corresponds to a coherent conception of what the quality of a product and of work is. There is not only one way of evaluating quality, and this uncertainty complicates coordination within activities (Boisard and Letablier, 1987; Eymard-Duvernay, 1989). This approach links the work to the product in an original way, compared to the classical function of production. Coherence between inputs and outputs is not only quantitative but also qualitative. Hence the quality of work and raw materials is closely related to the quality of the product. These compatibility constraints exceed the limits of the firm (network of suppliers and distributors), creating areas of relations subjected to the same rule of quality assessment, called 'worlds of production' (Salais and Storper, 1993).

By using the 'Economies of Worth' model (Boltanski and Thévenot, 1991), we can consolidate the institutionalist basis of these approaches. The different 'quality conventions' (of the product and the work) are inscribed in more global conceptions of society. The rules which determine what a good product (or good work) is, are not 'internal' rules (and in this respect the notion of 'internal market' can lead to confusion); they are the result of institutional constructions which go beyond the framework of the firm (Marsden,1989). An enterprise is based on outside institutions, which may be the state (large organizations draw on public administrations to a large extent), the family (the paternalist movement aims to build the firm on the family model) or science (Taylor and Ford introduced methods from scientific laboratories into the firm). The greatest innovators in the field of corporate management usually had a societal project. Corporate rules are rooted in political philosophies, just as the market was constructed by the founders of economics as a political philosophy. The typology of societies in the 'Economies of Worth' model, which recapitulates these different political philosophies, helps to identify the institutions on which corporate rules are based.

The Plurality of Action Regimes

It is very difficult to incorporate these approaches into traditional economics, for they put the market among a plurality of economies. In this sense they border on interdisciplinarity, and traditional economics cannot assimilate such symmetry between alternative forms of coordination. Approaches which establish translations between disciplines are nevertheless possible. We can thus develop a comparative approach based on models which are more widely recognized in the economists' field (Favereau and Thévenot, 1996; de Larquier, 1997), with each model representing a form of coordination.

But another type of comparative approach, more closely linked to recent developments in economics, is also possible. As we have seen, the main thrust of current research in economics focuses on local forms of coordination and contracts. The market as a form of universal coordination is thus fragmented into a multitude of contracts, without it being possible to re-establish a unified representation at the level of an economy. Of note here is the fact that a parallel evolution is under way in sociology, with the development of interactionism and ethnomethodology, or approaches in terms of sociotechnological networks (Callon, 1986). This convergence facilitates original forms of discussion between the two disciplines (Chiappori and Orfali, 1997). Our approach consists of maintaining comparison, but basing it on local models of action (which we call action regimes) and not on comparisons between societies. Political philosophies are no longer the main foundation for representing the different action regimes. We replace them with more local social science models: models of organizations, and contracts. The term 'convention' enables us to mark this new position; it denotes more local forms of agreement than do rules, which usually refer to arrangements of highly institutionalized relations.

In this comparative approach a relationship based on a complete contract, as analysed by economists, is most often the point of anchorage of reflection. The aim is to show the efficiency of alternative forms of coordination. Two types of 'heterodox' relations are thus of particular interest: closeness (*relations de proximité*) and networks.

Contracts or Closeness?

Closeness between people plays an important part in corporate managers' reflection. Many organizations, both public and private, try to move closer to users or customers, which involves extensive reorganization (for example, decentralization, creation of new jobs). How can the nature of these relations be characterized precisely, to facilitate reflection on their efficiency? Two significant differences emerge, compared to complete contracts. First, closeness implies that the relations remain informal. Interaction is preferably verbal since written communication is affected by the fact that it could be used in court. Secondly, there is a time dynamics in close relations: exchange consists of a sequence of interactions. This sequence is seldom anticipated. The metaphor of conversation during which unexpected repartee occurs is still the most appropriate (Piore *et al.,* 1997). One could say that these relations involve specific resources. The notion of trust is also used frequently to explain them. But apart from the use of specific terms, it is important to rely on a model of coordination which adequately accounts for agents' forms of calculation in these relations, and the ways in which they are coordinated.

To analyse these forms of coordination we used a study carried out on an organization providing subsidized housing, which had adopted a decentralization policy (Eymard-Duvernay and Marchal, 1994). In this study, we compared two forms of coordination:

- a form in which relations between people are related to general rules;
- a form in which coordination between people is based on interactive engagement. In this coordination regime, the rules, qualifications and technical objects are incorporated in the interactions in a dynamic process. General rules are amended locally during these processes and new agreements are made. The operations carried out by the actors to mobilize others consist primarily of negotiation. The devices supporting these relations take into account the interests of the people that are to be mobilized, in the framework of a negotiation. If the coordination is unsuccessful, they must be amended so that the interests of the various actors coincide as far as possible.

Can such sequences of interaction be analysed in the formal frameworks developed by game theory? For example, a tenant owes the organization money. The cooperative solution consists of negotiating the debt, with both parties trying to reach an agreement. This is in the interests of all concerned (for example, if the owner tries to recover the entire debt by going to court, he could end up getting nothing). This situation could be translated into the same terms as the prisoner's dilemma. If the owner trusts the tenant, he does not take him to court and agrees to the payment of the debt in instalments. If, in this situation, the tenant honours this trust, he pays his debt (or a good part of it) late. This cooperative solution is not balanced, however, if both parties act rationally (Kreps, 1990). The owner therefore sues the tenant and recovers only part of the debt, late. The tenant is subjected to legal pressure and ends up having to pay the debt, albeit late.

Game theory models have a static nature. Even in repeated games, cooperation or defection are decided instantaneously and thought processes are immediate. Observation shows processes in which cooperation is renewed and maintained. Not everything is decided from the outset. The agents must maintain the cooperation through their actions. These temporal processes rely on external mediums which memorize past interactions and facilitate the sequence of self-reinforcing cooperation. People are not rigidly 'cooperative' or 'individualistic'; these characteristics are built up during interactions (Livet, 1994). We can identify the conditions in which mutual cooperation is promoted, for example: relations established on a long-term basis; qualified agents close to users; external mediums (including a decentralized information-processing system) used to memorize commitments and to establish them as information shared by several agents. All these investments have a cost.

Close relations are extremely fragile in organizations, because their efficiency is not clearly perceptible and, by nature, they cannot be formally recorded. In the case of pressure to cut costs they may be sacrificed more or less explicitly and the consequences perceived only much later, or not at all. The maintenance of close relations is of major importance for employment. Many redundancies result from processes of 'rationalization' which neglect the economies that these relations induce. The argument in favour of 'neighbourhood jobs' is not valid only for jobs in which services are provided to private individuals; in the most industrialized sectors these jobs may or may not be sacrificed.

Market or Network?

In order to expand on the comparative approach, we need to refine the map of action regimes, beyond dual oppositions. This will enable us to introduce a 'networked' action regime. We suggest organizing the debate between action regimes around two axes: the first opposes planned and negotiated action; the second contrasts individual and collective action (Eymard-Duvernay and Marchal, 1997). Complete contracts involve action which is planned (the commitment is in the form of the contract) and individual. A first series of 'heterodox' relations (as compared to the models of standard theory of rationality) is generated by doing away with the planned nature of the action (individuals engage in a process of interactions), while a second series is generated by framing the action with collective devices. We thus reveal four typical action regimes: the institution (collective and planned action); the network (collective and negotiated action); the market (individual and planned action); and interaction (individual and negotiated action). To draw up this map, we compared two areas of debate: that which takes place between managers, on the best ways of arranging organizations, and that in the social sciences, on the most relevant models for accounting for coordination. This map is used to clarify the arguments supporting the different action regimes, by means of comparison. It aims at simulating controversy between managers who systematically investigate different forms of organization. The advantage of drawing on the social sciences lies in the wide generality of the action regimes that they formalize. They thus constitute general classes of management tools. We have applied this approach to the study of recruitment apparatus and controversies on ways of evaluating people's skills.

In reflection on new forms of management, the concept of a network is used more and more often. 'Networked' organizations are clearly a new ideal form of management. The comparative approach of action regimes enables one to situate this form of coordination. It is particularly useful to clearly specify how it is distinguished from coordination by the market, to which it is frequently compared. Relations in a network are not based on a contract in the strict sense of the term; action emerges as relationships take shape, without being determined in advance by a contractual undertaking. Calculation is the work not of the agent but of the entire network, which means it is not an individual action. Thus agents' rationality is 'distributed' in their environment. These forms of action have been successfully analysed by sociologists of innovation networks (Akrich *et al.*, 1988) and by theoreticians of 'distributed artificial intelligence' (Hutchins, 1995). If we refer to the map of action regimes proposed above, the network is diametrically opposed to the market (individual and planned action). It is also useful to distinguish it from close relations which remain inter-individual.

If we revert to the example of the tenant owing rent to the housing council, these two actors can be linked by a network of relations. For example, the tenant's environment provides a more or less formal guarantee which allows the owner to trust him.

The comparative approach of action regimes is currently proving to be an extremely dynamic means of investigating new forms of action and new empirical ground (Dodier, 1995; Bessy and Chateauraynaud,1995; Corcuff, 1996; Boltanski, 1990; Thévenot, 1997).

VARIATIONS IN CONVENTIONS

How does one go from one convention to another? What are the dynamics of conventions? The exploration of these questions adds real value to pluralistic approaches to coordination. In a universalistic approach there is, by construction, no evolution in the framework of coordination. The only variations are conjunctural: they concern the restoration of equilibriums through modifications in the parameter of adjustment (the price, for economists). Structural variations in the framework of coordination are, by contrast, the main issue in pluralistic approaches: variations from one activity to another or one economy to another, as well as variations in the course of history.

We have to distinguish two scales of variation: long variations, in terms of historical duration or cultural gaps, and short variations which consist of differences between activities within a single economy, or changes in conventions in an organization, during interaction and so on. Can we hope for continuity in the analysis, from one scale to another? The answer is probably no. A unified paradigm necessarily switches either towards methodological holism ('macro' social structures determine 'micro' behaviours) or towards individualism ('macro' structures emerge from 'micro' behaviours). Our research programme aims at switching from one type of study to another, macroinstitutionalist and microinstitutionalist, by creating passages between the two, but without claiming to create a unified framework. In our view this 'sacrifice' is unavoidable.

Long Variations

The 'Economies of Worth' model is a sound analytical tool for large-scale institutional variations. We can parametrize changes in modes of coordination over long periods, for the different societies: development of the industrial society with Taylorism and Fordism, of civic society with collective negotiation, and of domestic society with paternalism. The 'post-Taylorian' period would, according to this analysis grid, be characterized by the strengthening of the market society at the expense of the industrial society (decline of mass production), the domestic society (decline in hierarchical forms of authority) and civic society (decline in trade unions and collective negotiation). This analysis grid is also suited to the comparative study of different economies, marked by specific histories. Apart from the static approach, what are the determinants of long variations? Explanations in terms of efficiency are hardly credible. Either they are tautological or they lack the most important determinants. Can the development of Taylorism be understood independently from the profound social and political changes related to the two world wars? Economic history shows us that it cannot. The emergence and development in the long term of markets as forms of organization are part of evolutions described by macrosocial and political approaches. Similarly, the understanding of differences between economies cannot disregard these determinants (see, for example, the study by Piore and Sabel, 1984, on the comparative evolution of forms of coordination in the United States and Italy).

The success of the French school of regulation can be ascribed to its articulation between historical and macroinstitutional approaches, on the one hand, and macroeconomics, on the other. Connections can be made with microeconomic approaches of forms of organization. The Fordist and Toyotist systems are thus linked to clearly identified modes of management (Boyer and Saillard, 1995). However, the analysis focuses primarily on macroeconomic aggregates, with local coordination receiving little attention. The comparative approach of action regimes aims at articulating the macro and micro scales of analysis better. Can one study local interactions in detail, with all their variety, without omitting the long-term dimension of variations? That is the challenge facing research today, in sociology and economics alike.

The evolutionary approach to these questions, currently mobilizing many research teams, does not satisfy us. The natural selection of routines cannot account for action in institutions. The strength of evolutionism is that it does without the other social sciences, but that is also its weakness. The paradigm of the contract is clearly open to criticism. But rather than getting round it from below, by drastically reducing the actors' competencies, we must set it into a broader institutional perspective. Actors do indeed have limited rationality, but they are capable of understanding the general principles of the functioning of a society, organization or interaction. This capacity, of a political order, shared by those with whom they act, enables them to move about in an uncertain environment. We shall now suggest some directions for a research programme of this type.

Two Levels of Action

Wanting to move closer to the natural sciences, economists observe the world from above. They model agents who react to their environment, and they are the only ones to concern themselves with the question of agreement in society. The agents in their model act in a far more 'short-sighted' way. While economists may endow these agents with a huge amount of information (sometimes excessive) on their environment, they do not endow them with a capacity for organization. They retain the monopoly over this capacity, by recommending forms of organization which ensure good coordination, even if by default (by stigmatizing any form of organization in order to allow free play between the agents). Our approach consists of endowing agents with this capacity for organization. This assumption, which enhances the agent, may, however, reduce the scholar. Since they can no longer occupy a position in which they observe the agents from above, scholars have to admit that their position is different from that of natural science researchers.

The agents' main problem becomes the choice between several forms of relationship. This type of decision can best be described in detail by distinguishing two levels of action. At level I, the agent decides on an action in a given organizational framework. At level II, the agent decides on an organizational framework. This distinction is artificial, for there is extensive interpenetration between these two levels, with level I actions helping to establish, consolidate or, on the contrary, undermine the organizational frameworks on level II. It is, however, useful from an analytical point of view. The crucial question is: how to account for the deformation of the organizational frameworks, that is, actions at level II?

An example, anecdotal but familiar to everyone who speaks the French language, enables us to situate different answers to this question, that is, the convention of saying 'tu' (the familiar form of 'you') or 'vous' (the formal form) to someone.

- For a structuralist, the decision results from long-term relations between the classes, actualized by the agents' ability to recognize these relations in a situation. The attempts by a manager to generalize the familiar form is, from this point of view, based on a strategic intention to disregard class differences.
- Economists will be tempted to see in this a problem of coordination. They may formalize it in a game of pure coordination, as in Lewis: the 'tu' and the 'vous' are conventional and once one of these terms has been established it becomes difficult to defy the convention. Coordination is a problem of information. It requires 'specular' behaviour in which each person tries to put him or herself in the other's position.
- For an evolutionist, the agent is endowed with behavioural routines. An individual used to saying 'tu' in an environment in which the valid convention is the 'vous' has a reduced benefit and therefore her/his behaviour is not reproduced.
- For Boltanski and Thévenot, each situation defines a society which induces the use of 'tu' or 'vous'. The agents are capable of interpreting the convention prevailing in a certain situation, and of changing it. If I am a friend of the president of France I can, on the same day, switch from one type of relationship to another, depending on the context (the situation). The uncertainty becomes critical when several conventions are likely to be activated in the same situation.
- If we consider short variations in conventions, we must account for the ways in which the situations are arranged, rather than taking them as given. Action at level II implies that the agent explores different frameworks of relationship (saying 'tu' or 'vous') and makes the appropriate adjustments. The agent's decision-making space is a sphere of conventions.

Difficulties of Moving on to Level II

Dysfunctioning in an action regime and criticism by certain important actors may require a change of regime. At level II, agents (reflexively) move away from the conventions which they usually follow, and compare several conventions. The shift to level II facilitates organizational learning (Favereau, 1994). On what conditions is it possible? Psychologists emphasize cognitive biases which cause agents to be stuck on an assumption (Hutchins, 1995) and the weight of action models which block the opening to alternative theories (Argyris and Schön, 1978). It is also necessary to take into account the rigidity induced by devices which stabilize forms of arrangement of relations and which format information mobilized for the action. Composed of objects and incorporated habits, they are costly to rearrange.

How do agents behave at level II? The maps drawn in comparative approaches aim at simulating debate between several action regimes (whether these take place between several people or in a single person's mind). Apart from a strong reflexive capacity, agents are thus presumed to be interdisciplinary (without knowing it): they understand the advantages of the market but also of the institution, network or interaction, and choose between these different action regimes. At level I, the decision concerns the parameter which balances the interactions in a given frame, for example as regards wages. At level II, it is the method used to fix wages that is at issue, that is, the procedures and devices used to determine them. At this level of action anticipation cannot be complete. The agent forms a general idea of the subsequent course of the action, depending on the regime, but obviously without being able to foresee all the convolutions.

Economists and managers might be tempted to reduce these systems to their informational dimension, in which case the concept of a convention could focus attention on problems of coordination. The adoption of one convention rather than another does not modify the players' respective positions, since the essential thing is to follow the same convention. 'Relational immitation' is then posed as an elementary mechanism of coordination (Gomez, 1996). Yet the situations of 'pure coordination' on which these approaches are based are exceptional. Most often, changes in conventions have effects on the respective benefits of the different actors. Any modification in the way of calculating wages, for example, is reflected in changes in the order between people. It is then essential to maintain the articulation between conventions and values. Conventions (the term 'rule' may then be preferred to mark this dimension) convey different orders of worth for people (Boltanski and Thévenot, 1991). The different ways of calculating are not neutral from the point of view of a social order. Failures which lead to adjustments in conventions are not only cognitive (anticipation which does not materialize); they also involve moral conceptions (an order criticized for its injustice). This close articulation between managerial systems and principles of justice enhances the rigidity of conventions; any change leads to a rearrangement in the way of ordering people.

Is the ideal of coordination the emergence of a single convention? The answer given by most theories to this question is affirmative. Yet it is possible to argue for pluralism, a condition for the maintenance of institutional flexibility. Organizational learning implies the stimulation of the capacity to change conventions, as an answer to observed imbalances. There is a tension between the constraints of coordination peculiar to levels I and II. Making action routine implies a disregard for alternative conventions, which runs counter to the maintenance of a capacity for change. It may therefore be useful to favour complex arrangements of systems which maintain the plurality of action regimes and thus allow for institutional adjustments.

COMPARISON WITH MANAGEMENT RESEARCH

In the last part of this chapter, we identify common points between our approach and management studies.

J.-P. Ponssard (1994) studies the links between theoretical models developed by social scientists (especially game theory) and operational models. The typical coordination problem he analyses is a complex one of appointment. It is complex in the sense of implying difficult or even impossible calculations in order to be accurately solved. In this approach it is necessary to accept the incompleteness of theoretical models; there is no mechanical link between a theoretical model and decision making. A convention is a non-optimum operational rule which may not be followed if the actors find more interesting 'focal points'. The researcher's role is to contribute towards the construction of these conventional rules in the form of formalized models, intended to facilitate the learning of coordination (pre-game phase) and not to plan optimum solutions.

In our approach, each 'appointment' can be considered an action regime when one is at level II. The complexity then results from the plurality of ways of calculating and of information formats. Controversies between the different strategies are rather of a 'qualitative' order; it will be necessary, for example, to choose from within a range of qualities of a product or work. The conventional nature of the action results from the impossibility of choosing one of these different strategies with certainty. The role of the social science researcher is to concretize this debate by presenting several standard models of relations.

Work carried out by Argyris and Schön (1978) has been used to analyse in more detail the subject of 'double loop' organizational learning (by revising theories of action or 'cognitive maps'). In this approach all the agents, including researchers, are socially programmed according to an action model: maintain unilateral control over information, maximize gains, minimize criticism of others, be rational. Alternative models are merely 'idealizations' or 'justifications'. Behaviour induced by this model blocks the opening of alternative 'worlds' (theories), producing information which is unclear, incoherent and so on. During training, researchers present managers with games describing situations in which agents behave according to this model. The players criticize this behaviour, but in their criticism they themselves are following the same model!

The distinction in our approach between two levels of action is directly inspired by this research. But Argyris's universalistic hypothesis, in which the agents are socially programmed according to a single model, seems excessive. We have also mentioned the role of apparatus, apart from people, in the inertia of action regimes. From that point of view our organizational learning approach is more socioeconomic. There is no psychological inevitability locking individuals in an action regime. Agents are self-reflective, but they are faced with multiple costs to pay for the rearrangement of systems of relations, and the impossibility of perfectly anticipating the consequences of each regime.

Studies on the role of the coordination of management tools have many points in common with our approach. The 'organizational constructs' (Midler, 1994) mobilized by individuals – technical devices (for example, buildings) as well as management techniques (the 'invisible technology' of organizations, Berry, 1983) – ground their rationality. Thus rationality is not solely a cognitive process; it is based on apparatus and devices. Midler emphasizes organizational learning which introduces dynamics into the analysis of action in an organized situation. There is reciprocity between 'knowledge' (carried by 'organizational constructs') and action: action actualizes knowledge. Following Charue-Duboc (1995) he notes the trade-off that agents have to make between organizational change (level II) and the stability of systems and devices (level I). The 'errors' caused by the questioning of knowledge can be disagreements. Organization theory can vary according to different points of view.

We think it is useful to draw maps of the 'theories of action' between which agents must choose. There is not an infinite number of them, if we assume that they fit into general conceptions of the coordination of actions. The choice between different action regimes is not only a matter of cognitive processes; it also concerns more global political conceptions.

CONCLUSION

In this chapter we have tried to support two precepts for the organization of relations not only in firms but also in broader communities: maintaining a pluralistic environment in which relations have varied forms, and maintaining uncertainty or, in other words, the possibility of critique. These are related: critique is made possible by the plurality of action regimes. These precepts have a paradoxical nature: is it not advisable to simplify and unify the economic and social world in order to facilitate cooperation between actors by providing them with clear rules for action? Is it not also advisable to reduce the uncertainty surrounding action? Researchers who follow the dominant programme in economics surely answer these two questions in the affirmative. The perfect competition market remains the only ideal, even though it may be necessary to accept forms of 'heterodox' relations for reasons related to a lack of information. Correlatively, these economists assume that welfare is always improved when uncertainty is reduced. Thus the originality of our 'conventionalist' position stems less from a technical refinement than from the general view that maintaining pluralism and unpredictability constitutes a positive programme rather than a lesser evil.

This position can, in the first case, be justified in the name of realism. Observation clearly shows the diversity of forms of relations. It also shows how unrealistic it is to reduce them to a single form, without it being possible to observe historically a movement of unification – on the contrary. Current economies cannot be reduced to a unified world market, even though the forces in that direction have probably never been so strong. The massive place occupied by organizations, which often constitute forces rivalling those of states, is proof enough that the market is not the only mode of coordination. The cultural peculiarities of the different national or infranational spaces remain strong. Industrialists, who closely adapt their products to local contexts, are well aware of that fact. Have the substantial developments in information technology brought our economies closer to the ideal of predictable societies? Here, again, the answer is clearly no. A single example is enough to support this assertion. A young person who tries to forecast her or his career path is unquestionably in a highly uncertain position, for the persistence of mass unemployment is a strong factor of uncertainty. But firms which try to anticipate tomorrow's products are in the same situation.

The analysis tool must therefore incorporate the plurality of modes of coordination, instead of concentrating on an ideal type – a lazy way out which enables one to disregard reality. But it is also necessary to go further and to adopt a normative standpoint. Diversity of forms of relations and unpredictability are conditions for maintaining a form of democracy in economic life. In a way, this message is not all that original, for the market economy advocates entrepreneurial initiative, the fight against monopolies and the maintenance of a wide variety of choice for consumers. Its precepts have always drawn on a democratic ideal. But it is essentially a democracy of consumers and savers, intended to be realized by the maintenance of the diversity of goods and the lowering of prices. We aim to extend this democratic ideal to producers and, in particular, employees. Moreover, we think that it is necessary to maintain the diversity not only of goods but also, and more profoundly, of forms of relations between people. This is the condition of critique and controversy, as L. Boltanski (1990) so rightly argues. A unified and certain environment has a single, stable order for people and goods. The perfect market leads to a static state, although actors are theoretically endowed with a high level of autonomy. Behaviour becomes completely rigid and predictable. Divergences from the model are due to a lack of rationality and not the manifestation of critical behaviour initiating debate. By contrast, plurality of coordination models opens a space for critique.

In our view, the conditions for good coordination are therefore a diversified economic environment from the point of view of mediums for coordination, and economic actors who are able to mobilize several levels of communication and who are vigilant and open to criticism of the action regime they follow. We do not, for all that, neglect the economies generated by everything that makes it possible to regularize action and to make it routine, for example, institutional and technical devices, and incorporated routines which constitute basic mechanisms and without which no coordination would be possible. They have a role which is both cognitive and political, consolidating rules on what has to be done.

NOTES

1. This article was published in French in *Gérer et comprendre* (June 1999). The translation from French to English was performed by L. Libbrecht.
2. Institut national de la statistique et des études économiques, the French national institute of statistics and economic surveys.

REFERENCES

Akerlof, G.A. (1970), 'The market for "lemons": qualitative uncertainty and the market mechanism', *Quarterly Journal of Economics*, 84 (3), 488–500.

Akrich, M., M. Callon and B. Latour (1988), 'A quoi tient le succès des innovations', *Gérer et comprendre*, 12.

Aoki, M., B. Gustafsson and O. Williamson (eds) (1990), *The Firm as a Nexus of Treaties*, London: Sage Publications.

Argyris, C. and D.A. Schön (1978), *Organizational Learning: A Theory of Action Perspective*, Reading, MA: Addison-Wesley.

Berry, M. (1983), *Une technologie invisible? L'impact des instruments de gestion sur l'évolution des systèmes humains*, Paris: École Polytechnique.
Bessy, C. and F. Chateauraynaud (1995), *Experts et faussaires*, Paris: Métailié.
Boisard, P. and M.T. Letablier (1987), 'Le camembert: normand ou normé. Deux modèles de production dans l'industrie fromagère', *Entreprises et produits*, Paris: Cahiers du Centre d'Études de l'Emploi, Presses universitaires de France.
Boltanski, L. (1990), *L'amour et la justice comme compétences*, Paris: Métailié.
Boltanski, L. and L. Thévenot (1991), *De la justification. Les économies de la grandeur*, Paris: Gallimard.
Boyer, R. and A. Orléan (1994), 'Persistance et changement des conventions. Deux modèles simples et quelques illustrations', in A. Orléan (ed.), *Analyse économique des conventions*, Paris: Presses universitaires de France.
Boyer, R. and Y. Saillard. (eds) (1995), *Théorie de la régulation, l'état des savoirs*, Paris: La Découverte.
Callon, M. (1986), 'Éléments pour une sociologie de la traduction', *L'année sociologique*, 36, 169–208.
Charue-Duboc, F. (ed.) (1995), *Des savoirs en action*, Paris: L'Harmattan.
Chiappori, P.A. and K. Orfali (1997), 'Préférences et interactions: une mise en perspective', *Revue française de sociologie*, XXXVIII, 465–95.
Corcuff, P. (1996), 'Ordre institutionnel, fluidité situationnelle et compassion', *Recherches et prévisions*, 45.
Dodier, N. (1995), *Les hommes et les machines*, Paris: Métailié.
Eymard-Duvernay, F. (1989), 'Conventions de qualité et formes de coordination', *L'économie des conventions, Revue économique*, March, 329–59.
Eymard-Duvernay, F. and E. Marchal (1994), 'Les règles en action: entre une organisation et ses usagers', *Revue française de sociologie*, XXXV, 5–36.
Eymard-Duvernay, F. and E. Marchal (1997), *Façons de recruter. Le jugement des compétences sur le marché du travail*, Paris: Métailié.
Favereau, O. (1989), 'Marchés internes, marchés externes', *L'économie des conventions, Revue économique*, March, 273–328.
Favereau, O. (1994), 'Règles, organisation et apprentissage collectif: un paradigme non standard pour trois théories hétérodoxes', in A. Orléan (ed.), *Analyse économique des conventions*, Paris: Presses universitaires de France.
Favereau, O. (1997), 'Rationalité', in Y. Simon and P. Joffre (eds), *Encyclopédie de gestion*, 2nd edn, Paris: Economica.
Favereau, O. and L. Thévenot (1996), 'Réflexions sur une notion d'équilibre utilisable dans une économie de marchés et d'organisations', in G. Ballot (ed.), *Les marchés internes du travail: de la microéconomie à la macroéconomie*, Paris: Presses universitaires de France, pp. 273–314.
Friedland, R. and A.F. Robertson. (eds) (1990), *Beyond the Market Place. Rethinking Economy and Society*, New York: Aldine de Gruyter.
Gomez, P.-Y. (1996), *Le gouvernement de l'entreprise*, Paris: InterEdition.
Granovetter, M. (1985), 'Economic action and social structure: the problem of embeddedness', *American Journal of Sociology*, 91 (3), 481–511.
Hirschman, A.O. (1986), *Vers une économie politique élargie*, Paris: Éditions de Minuit.
Hutchins, E. (1995), *Cognition in the Wild*, Cambridge, MA: MIT Press.
Kreps, D.M (1990), 'Corporate culture and economic theory', in James E. Alt and Kenneth A. Shepsle (eds), *Perspectives on Positive Political Economy*, Cambridge: Cambridge University Press.

Larquier (de), G. (1997), 'Approche macro-économique du marché du travail et qualité des appariements', in C. Bessy and F. Eymard-Duvernay (eds), *Les intermédiaires du marché du travail*, Paris: Presses universitaires de France.

Livet, P. (1994), *La communanté virtuelle Action et Communication*, Paris: L'Éclat.

Marsden, D. (1989), *Marchés du travail. Limites sociales des nouvelles théories*, Paris: Economica.

Midler, C. (1994), 'Évolution des règles de gestion et processus d'apprentissage: une perspective cognitive', in A. Orléan (ed.), *Analyse économique des conventions*, Paris: Presses universitaires de France.

Orléan, A. (1991), 'Logique Walrasienne et incertitude qualitative: des travaux d'Akerlof et Stiglitz aux conventions de qualité', *Économies et sociétés*, Série Economica, PE no. 14, January, 137–60.

Piore, M. and C. Sabel (1984), *Les chemins de la prospérité. De la production de masse à la spécialisation souple*, Paris: Hachette.

Piore, M., R. Lester, F. Kofman and K. Malek (1997), 'L'organisation du développement des produits', in B. Reynaud (ed.), *Les limites de la rationalité*, vol. 2, Paris: La Découverte, pp. 265–98.

Ponssard, J.-P. (1994), 'Formalisation des connaissances, apprentissage organisationnel et rationalité interactive', in A. Orléan (ed.), *Analyse économique des conventions* , Paris: Presses universitaires de France.

Reynaud, B. (1992), *Le salaire, la règle et le marché*, Paris: Christian Bourgois.

Salais, R. and M. Storper (1993), *Les mondes de production. Enquête sur l'identité économique de la France*, Paris: Édition de l'EHESS.

Simon, H. (1976), 'A behavioral model of rational choice. From substantive to procedural rationality', in S.J. Latsis (ed.), *Methods and Appraisal in Economics*, Cambridge: Cambridge University Press, pp. 129–48.

Simon, H.A. (1960), *The New Science of Management Decision*, New York: Harper & Row.

Simon, H.A. (1983), *Reason in Human Affairs*, Oxford: Basil Blackwell.

Stiglitz, J.E. (1987), 'The causes and consequences of the dependence of quality on price', *Journal of Economic Literature*, 25, 1–48.

Thévenot, L.(1997), 'Le savoir au travail: attribution et distribution des compétences selon les régimes pragmatiques', in B. Reynaud (ed.), *Les limites de la rationalité*, vol. 2, Paris: La Découverte, pp. 299–322.

3. Institutional embeddedness of economic exchange: convergence between new institutional economics and the economics of conventions

Christian Bessy

Certain developments in new institutional economics (NIE) over the past few years have created areas of overlap with the French school of thinking called 'Economie des Conventions' (economics of conventions, EC) on the question of the institutional embeddedness of economic exchange and its type of organization. Since the work of Williamson (if not of Coase), the comparison between different coordination mechanisms or organizational forms, depending on the characteristics of the institutional environment and, more analytically, the hypothesis of 'bounded' rationality, have constituted research perspectives common to both approaches. In his work on institutional change, North's interest in the part played by 'informal' institutions (conventions, behavioural norms and so on) caused him to move further away from neoclassical economics (North, 1990). More recently, the emphasis on the articulation between cognitive processes and institutions (Knight and North, 1997) has brought him even closer to the research programme of the economics of conventions.

These new perspectives initiated by NIE can be considered as slight divergences which are unlikely to fundamentally undermine the initial embeddedness of the neoclassical tradition, other than as 'ad hoc' additions (Guerrien, 1990), so that many divergences remain with the economics of conventions. The aim of this chapter is not, however, to list the similarities and divergences of the two approaches – which both show a degree of heterogeneity when we move away from the broad lines of the founders[1] – but to identify the main similarities, taken from the most recent work of North, for NIE, and certain representatives of EC.[2] These similarities will be based on the two main difficulties facing any economic analysis of institutions and to give a coherent analytical content to the concept of an institution and to define a mode of empirical understanding of the concept and validate the analysis.

The first difficulty derives from the concern, shared by NIE and EC, to take into account different institutional mechanisms. The second is present in particular in the analysis of the articulation between cognitive processes and institutions. This new analytical approach helps to define new avenues for empirically investigating the part played by institutions similar to those at work in sociology or the cognitive sciences. This leads researchers to redefine their methods of observation and to propose new modes of validation of their analyses.

In the first part we consider the plurality of institutions, with a particular focus on the problems of analytical coherence facing both approaches. In the second part we analyse more precisely the interdependence between cognitive processes and institutions. Both parts highlight problems of empirical investigation and validation of analyses.

PLURALITY OF INSTITUTIONAL MECHANISMS

The idea of an institution is far from being a unified concept in economics and its use usually indicates a move towards other disciplines such as sociology or law. It was this type of convergence that spawned the tradition of institutional economics of which Veblen was a founder and to which NIE and EC now belong. Several meeting points between these two approaches can be identified.

1. With regard to problems of cooperation or coordination, both highlight the impact of institutions on economic behaviour. This contradicts standard theory in which coordination between agents is the result of individual calculation, with practically no reference to the social context.
2. In general, the concept of an institution is considered to be a model of interaction between agents. Because of its normative power, this model is a source of regularity in their behaviour and expectations, but also a factor of inertia.
3. This concept of an institution is based on behavioural hypotheses which challenge the assumption of substantial rationality defended by neoclassical theory and support a Simon-type procedural rationality, even if, in certain models, use of game theory results in reference to the first type of hypothesis. The idea of a convention as developed by Lewis (1969) as a solution to the problem of coordination is a good illustration.
4. Finally, the two approaches agree to take into account the plurality of institutional mechanisms.

The latter point prompts us to characterize these different institutional mechanisms. This characterization poses a number of problems that both approaches solve in more or less similar ways. Among these problems we shall successively consider questions of the nature of institutional rules, based on whether or not they are self-emergent and self-enforcing, on their dynamic dimension and on their distinction in relation to the concept of organization.

Self-emergence and Self-enforcement of Rules

EC does not explicitly propose a theory of institutions. In general, it studies coordination rules which defy the binary opposition between rules designed to balance inter-individual interests and rules considered to be pure constraints. One of the basic hypotheses of this programme is to consider that interactions between agents, even when they are simply trading goods, are impossible without a common framework, a constituent 'convention' that is naturally imposed on the agents. This particular type of behavioural model consists of rules which are not necessarily accompanied by legal sanctions, and of which the origins and formulation may remain vague. In fact, far from being limited to conventional rules, it may be extended to a whole body of rules, including legal rules, owing to the conventional component inherent in their application and interpretation.[3] Thus there are no rules or institutions without an underlying convention.

This extension of the concept of a convention goes beyond the characterization given by Lewis (1969), according to whom the distinctive feature of a convention is that, among a set of possible choices, only one is really implemented. This uniqueness of the convention is consistent with the idea that a convention makes it possible to formally solve problems of indeterminacy of interactions when several solutions exist to achieve equilibrium. Its self-enforcing nature derives from the fact that it is in everyone's interests to comply when everyone else is complying (equilibrium in non-cooperative games). Conventions are chosen relatively arbitrarily, based on the 'common knowledge' hypothesis. From a less formalistic viewpoint, EC highlights the unrealistic aspect of this hypothesis. As a result, it opens the way to different foundations of conventions by mobilizing, in particular, Keynesian analysis or other commonsense philosophies (Dupuy, 1989). The scope of conventions is widened, to include problems of coordination in which the players not only have different interests (unlike the case in pure games of coordination) but also have the possibility of communicating, if not of opening a critical debate to select the most suitable convention (Thévenot, 1989). The latter perspective tends to reduce the arbitrary nature of the process. It also has the result[4] of reducing the self-emergent and self-enforcement characteristics most often associated with the idea of a convention. These two characteristics are opposed to the regulating dimension of explicit rules of interaction imposed by a normative, legislative or legal authority.

The typology of institutions proposed by North (1990) establishes a clear distinction *a priori* between different institutional mechanisms. It opposes codes of conduct, conventions (in Lewis's sense) and behavioural norms, which characteristically emerge during interaction between agents, on the one hand, and rules and constitutions which are the product of the state authority that guarantees compliance, on the other. In this perspective North (1990) qualifies the former as informal institutional constraints and the latter as formal constraints. The formal character of an institution is primarily related to the normative power conferred on it by the state. North (ibid., p.40) also distinguishes three categories of informal constraint:

- extensions and amendments to formal rules;
- behavioural norms which are socially sanctioned and may be in use despite the existence of formal rules prohibiting behaviour governed by the norm. North gives the example of the duel as a mode of resolving disputes between gentlemen;
- internally enforced codes of conduct.

North uses the traditional idea of a convention to explain the emergence and persistence of these informal constraints. This makes it possible to identify obvious links with EC. In particular, two types of similarity can be identified. The first category of informal constraints, 'extensions and modifications to formal rules', can be compared to the conventions underlying legal rules in EC. Contrary to a mechanistic approach of the rule of law, both approaches emphasize interaction between the two types of rule. Thus legal rules may consolidate recurrent practices[5] and, inversely, usage or norms may accompany or amend legal apparatus, at least in the form of implicit rules of interpretation. Similarly, codified knowledge is always based on tacit knowledge, attesting to processes of learning and mediation related to particular usage, situations or aims.

Secondly, for North, certain informal constraints are not self-enforcing in the absence of mechanisms related to reputation. Anonymity among economic agents makes their relations more complex. Thus quality standards defined in a business sector are considered to be cooperative behavioural norms, that is, informal constraints which are not 'self-enforcing' and are therefore enforced by the authorities that produce standards (ibid., p.41).[6] An analogy can be drawn here with the concept of 'quality convention' developed by Eymard-Duvernay (1989). This type of convention which regulates inter-firm competition is the subject of an explicit debate between firms. It is based on the intervention of a third party, which limits its self-enforcing nature. We note, moreover, that with the concept of a quality convention, emphasis can be put on the fact that any convention constitutes a summary of information in which the relevant characteristics of actors' choices can be represented – in this case the attributes of goods. It is this characteristic of a summary that generates significant cognitive economies.

The general problem encountered by both approaches is therefore that of the entanglement of rules of a different nature.[7] This challenges the opposition between self-emergent and self-enforcing rules, on the one hand, and rules with a regulatory purpose, enforced by the courts or other third parties, on the other.

The Dynamics of Institutional Constraints

Another series of problems confronting the economic analysis of institutions relates to their dynamics. This dimension of institutions raises questions on their field of validity and their stability or persistence.

As far as the field of validity is concerned, the question is to know whether institutional mechanisms can be ordered according to a decreasing degree of normativity, from the most general rules to those rooted in collectives such as organizations, groups or communities. This hierarchy is present *a priori* in North's typology, where constitutional and legal rules are claimed to have more normative power and therefore a more constraining aspect. North thus justifies the historical development of economic exchange on a large scale, based on the anonymity of transactions. He shows, however, that legal rules can be supplanted by local rules peculiar to certain social groups.

More generally, legal rules are interpreted locally and, as we have seen, this is one of the points of convergence between North's approach and EC. When this reasoning is taken to the extreme, it becomes difficult to grade the different levels of institutional normativity. Furthermore, the extension of an interpretive convention peculiar to a group or domain can lead to the redefinition of the general norm.

These dynamic procedures of extension of local conventions prompt us also to question the stability or inertia of the different categories of institution. For North (1990), informal institutional constraints are characterized by more inertia than formal rules, and therefore generate 'path dependency' phenomena. In particular, they do not change immediately in reaction to changes in formal rules. In any case, the interdependencies between different institutional mechanisms are the cause of their stability. This type of argument is totally acceptable to EC, even though EC does not propose a framework of analysis specifically for institutional change. It mentions only the conditions under which certain conventions are called into question (Salais, 1989).

To explain the evolution of formal rules, North (1990) emphasizes the fact that certain economic or political actors can exert pressure on normative authorities, leading to institutional solutions of varying degrees of efficiency from an economic point of view.[8] This type of argument, added to that of the inertia of informal constraints, helps to relativize the criticism often levelled at NIE, of having a purely functionalist view of institutions, since they are only the most effective solutions for increasing the potential benefits of exchange. High transaction costs may be a powerful factor explaining the birth and evolution of institutions, but it is not the only one and North provides many illustrations of this in his 1990 book. In particular, the second part shows the relations of interdependence that he weaves between cognitive processes and institutions.

Institution and Organization

While a large part of North's reasoning (North, 1990) tends to explain institutions in terms of their capacity to increase exchange or improve allocative efficiency, he focuses on institutional mechanisms that promote adaptive efficiency, that is, efficiency which allows an institution to solve problems ad hoc by developing new know-how through trial and error. Thus certain institutions are said to be more favourable to collective learning and innovation than others.

This type of reasoning can be compared to that of Favereau (1986) when he distinguishes between conventions that function as stimulants to the market and those that promote organizational learning favourable to the creation of new resources. One difference remains, however, in so far as, with Favereau, the latter type of convention runs counter to market mechanisms, like the concept of an internal labour market as developed by Doeringer and Piore (1971, 1985).

This perspective has the effect of blurring the distinction between institution and organization. Favereau (1989) therefore develops an institutionalist typology of markets according to the nature of rules (constituent of or limiting the market, intentional or not, and so on). This enables him to formalize different market–organization articulations, with each of the terms having different meanings depending on the nature of the articulation (organized market, market of organizations and anti-market organizations).

North's approach, by contrast, owing to the importance it attributes to economic exchange (versus the economy of production) and to associated transaction costs, tends to take into account only 'organized markets' or 'markets of organizations', as Favereau put it, by considering institutions as the 'rules of the game' between organizations.

The difficulty of distinguishing between the concepts of institutions and organizations also derives from the fact that the main function of some organizations is to facilitate economic exchange between independent actors, either by acting as an intermediary or arbitrator, or by defining quality standards or rights.[9] These organizations produce rules, norms or instructions, guarantee compliance with them, and are themselves subject to other rules. Thus characterized in terms of their normative power and the market structure, they can be considered as institutions ('institutional organization'). In this perspective, the concept of institution encompasses both the rule and the authority that produced it and enforces it. It is in this sense that an institution can denote an actor among others and not only the rules of the game between actors. We have in mind here the state or public authorities, but also all legal authorities and other organizations that exercise normative, if not coercive, power.

Empirical Perspectives

The characterization of different institutional mechanisms poses numerous problems because of the difficulty of isolating them individually or distinguishing them from other analytical concepts. We can, nevertheless, draw up a list of characteristics common to both approaches – with the exception of the differences mentioned. Thus, an institutional mechanism may be characterized (a) by its degree of self-emergence, as opposed to a normative authority's wish to regulate, (b) by its self-enforcing nature, as opposed to reliance on a coercive authority, and (c) its field of validity degree or stability or persistence.

We could add the tacit dimension of the institution, but this dimension is, in a sense, covered by the first two characteristics. This list provides us with parameters that are useful for empirically identifying and characterizing institutional mechanisms, even if it is probably difficult to establish such parameters with a wide degree of generality; that is to say, without taking into account the aims of the research and its mode of empirical validation. On the other hand, it is necessary to take into account their entanglement and interdependence.

These parameters can then be used to describe the conditions in which the set institutional environment can be considered, so that contractual variants or organizational forms based on actors' calculations can be analysed. That is the approach adopted by Williamson (1985). In a set institutional environment, the 'governance structure' opted for by the actors to manage their relationships will depend on the attributes of the transactions (specificity of assets, uncertainty, frequency). Although this approach is tinged with a degree of functionalism, in the sense that the chosen governance structure is supposed to be the most efficient from an economic point of view, it can be used as a basis for a comparative approach to different forms of coordination by using the comparative static method. In the EC context, the identification of a multiplicity of forms of coordination within the same activity usually tends to have a descriptive purpose, without giving explanatory factors on the use of any particular form of coordination (Bessy, 1997b).

By contrast, changes in the spatial or temporal scale of the analysis modify the data of the institutional environment. Intersectoral studies have to take into account the diversity of institutional environments, which poses the problem of finding relevant empirical indicators (Bessy and Brousseau, 1997b).

Macrohistorical analysis over a long period will be in a far better position to gain insight into institutions if it is able to identify regularities and discontinuity by means of economic aggregates: growth rate, price levels and so on. North's cliometric research (North and Thomas, 1973) on growth in the west is a good illustration of this, but it considers a single model of economic functioning and is unable clearly to identify the nature of the institutional mechanisms involved.[10] Such an approach is difficult to implement when trying to take into account different coordination models, in the way that EC does.

COGNITIVE PROCESS AND INSTITUTION

Another empirical position consists of focusing on elementary transactions and the single framework in which they are set. The aim is to concentrate the analysis on the identification of institutional mechanisms and their entanglement, based on observation of the situations in which the players act or interact. This modifies the terms of the analysis, compared to a macrohistorical approach to institutional change or a mesoeconomic approach based on highly stylized facts. It leads to a more microanalytical approach to the dynamics of institutions, which makes these dynamics more difficult to identify and which relies on the development of observation methods that initially resemble ethnographic inquiry or observations by cognitive science researchers.

Before addressing these empirical questions, we shall revert to the relations of interdependence between cognitive processes and institutions, based on an approach in terms of 'distributed cognition' which diverges from an individualistic conception of cognition and rationality. We see that this type of perspective, which currently seems to be shared by North and EC, tends to give wider scope to the concept of an institution.

Distributed Cognition

Starting with distributed cognition, North clearly shows the limits of the economic approach in which rationality is defined independently of social context (Knight and North, 1997). Cognition is evaluated solely in terms of individual ability to assimilate and process information correctly. Cognitive work, the elaboration of representations, takes place only at an individual level. This approach does not facilitate a clear understanding of the relationship between individual representations and collective representations stemming from history and current experience.

It therefore seems important to explore other approaches which adopt a more complex point of view on cognition, rationality and social context, and in which a significant proportion of the cognitive work is carried out by the institutional framework and not only in individuals' 'minds'.[11] Decisions are then the product of representations which are incorporated in institutions and in other cultural symbols.

Work by Hutchins (1995) – to which both North (Knight and North, 1997) and EC (Favereau, 1998) refer[12] – provides an excellent model of the approach in terms of distributed cognition. Hutchins' project is to re-embody cognitive processes, as opposed to the mentalistic approach that predominates in cognitive science, including that in Simon's work (Bessy, 1997a). The accent is placed on the way in which knowledge is distributed, not only among economic agents, but also between economic agents and their sociomaterial environment. The way in which an activity is performed is modelled on the trajectory of transformation of representations of knowledge through the different media, since knowledge is not only in agents' 'minds'. With time, solutions proposed to frequent problems help to enhance the agents' competencies and to define the organization and division of labour. They are also embodied in these representational media and, in particular, in material devices (tools, instruments, equipment, spatial arrangement and so on) and 'cognitive artefacts' (such as plans, languages) on which agents' daily activities are based. This has both theoretical and empirical consequences.

From a theoretical point of view, the sociomaterial context influences cognition in two different ways: through the content of institutional rules and cultural symbols, and through the way in which these rules and symbols structure and organize cognitive processes themselves.[13] From the latter point of view, the modes of interaction among agents and between agents and their material environment are anchored in representational media that are partly exogenous. These frames of interaction may be considered as institutional forms which are not in people's minds only, whether in the form of tacit knowledge[14] or of explicit rules of action. Because of their stability, they are mediums for learning, while simultaneously crystallizing previous learning.

By taking into account these collective cognitive devices, to use Favereau's (1989) expression, the concept of an institution is broadened extensively to include any coordination medium outside the agents. In particular, technical devices can thus be considered as institutions. It is probably necessary to limit use of the concept of an institution to the most stable coordination mediums, with wide areas of validity and strong normative or enrolment powers over other actors (Callon, 1993). The latter parameter raises the question of who imposes the reference to a particular collective cognitive device (or who benefits most from it), and therefore also the question of its emergence. In the case of network technologies, the economics of standards shows that, when there are two competing technological standards, small events can favour one of the two, irrespective of its quality, because of economies of adoption. This process can be modelled, based on the concept of a convention, to account for the random nature of election of one technology from a set of possibilities. Once the technology has become a standard, it constrains the agents but also coordinates them in their productive activities. This type of coordination must not be confused with the coordination of expected technological choices. They are two different institutional mechanisms; the first emphasizes the cognitive aspects of coordination and the second its strategic aspects.

Finally, these collective cognitive devices interact, in turn, on the most 'formal' rules. By proposing frameworks for understanding and interpreting such rules they help to define their use and scope, and even to alter them. This perspective is particularly important for analysing normative authorities which produce legal rules and enforce them. Thus the normative power of a legal rule largely depends on the organization of the courts and the cognitive devices on which their daily functioning is based.

From an empirical point of view, these different mediums outside people, as well as the modalities of interaction they mediate, can be observed in agents' daily practices. Their observation allows the study of cognitive properties (cognitive effort, quality of representations, capacity of adaptation and learning and so on) of the sociomaterial systems in which the agents (here, organizations) interact, rather than analysing only the cognitive properties of individual agents; like experimental approaches to rationality. Thus differences in the performance of two groups, practising the same activity, can be imputed to the mode of organization of cognitive processes rather than to agents' individual competencies alone.

This perspective can be a fertile avenue for research, for grasping the frameworks of interaction between agents, from both an intraorganizational and interorganizational point of view, and for examining the weight of the different institutions. We can thus identify different coordination models by considering their analytical coherence. We can, in particular, also distinguish between those interactions which are based on stabilized institutional forms, and those which create new institutions during a collective learning process (Bessy and Eymard-Duvernay, 1997). This analytical work, aimed at achieving coherence and generalization, may appear to be very disappointing 'proof' compared to a positive demonstration or real experimentation. It nevertheless has heuristic value and can guide the setting up of observation apparatus based on the identification of regularities. This requires some repetition of observations, in order to be able to translate the regularities observed into action rules which are not necessarily clarified by the actors when researchers limit themselves to an interview. Similarly, only observation continued over a long period can provide access to resources which for the actors are obvious, such as the use of networks of interpersonal relations. These resources do not spontaneously become available, owing to the constraint of objectification that our presence alone imposes on our interlocutors in most cases.[15]

This phase of more detailed observation facilitates the identification of 'intermediate' indicators of coordination models that can then be implemented in the form of a questionnaire for statistical purposes. That was partly our approach with regard to technology licence agreements (Bessy and Brousseau, 1998), where we included questions that facilitate an understanding, in particular, of the distribution of knowledge throughout the different resources transferred in that context (texts, plans, experimental or commercial data, delegation of personnel, training and so on). We thus showed that the nature of the information transmitted is correlated with the contractual form of the agreement. This type of questionnaire and even the examination of written contracts does not help to reveal all the resources and all the constraints at play in the negotiation of agreements and, particularly, in the implicit clauses. It would be necessary to observe the negotiations which govern all the contracts in our database.

CONCLUSION

Observation constraints peculiar to a research programme common to both approaches, as defined here with reference to ties between cognition and institutions, are therefore very costly, especially as validation constraints based on statistical proof increase. We shall essentially retain the idea of the possibility of establishing parameters of the different institutional mechanisms, making it possible to characterize empirically the frameworks of interaction of economic agents and to adopt comparative approaches. Once the parameters have been established, possibly in a less costly manner based on existing surveys, most of the observation will focus on the leeway of agents within a given institutional frame, and the strategies they develop to manage their relations and investments.

Apart from the empirical difficulties inherent in the understanding of institutional mechanisms, theoretical questions remain. In this chapter we have highlighted only certain possible similarities between the work of North and that of EC, based entirely on our own experience and understanding of the two research programmes. Most of our comparison focused on the identification of different institutional mechanisms and on their entanglement. Little was said on the factors of evolution of institutions, or on the factors explaining them, in the sense of knowing why a particular institution develops in one place and not another. It is in this dynamic perspective that the divergences between the two currents of thinking are greatest. North's approach gives most weight to explanation in terms of transaction costs or power strategies of certain social groups, but by considering a single space of calculation, which brings it closer to standard economic calculation. EC, by considering a plurality of spaces of calculation and by emphasizing problems of interpretation of relevant rules of calculation, has difficulty integrating the divergent strategies and interests of the economic actors and their consequences for institutional evolution.[16]

NOTES

1. For NIE, for example, the work of Williamson (1993) remains more attached to neoclassical theory than that of North (1990, 1997).
2. We refer essentially to the articles published in the special issue of *Revue économique* (1989) on the economics of conventions. We nevertheless also highlight the work of Favereau and of Eymard-Duvernay, and particularly their more recent studies. See their contribution in this volume.
3. For Favereau (1989), in relation to the hypothesis of bounded rationality, there is no system of rules of behaviour which can propose an exhaustive and objective list of its cases of correct application. The question of the interpretation of legal rules is addressed particularly well by Favereau who, following Reynaud (1986), considers rules as models. See also Bessy and Brousseau on patent rights (1997a).
4. Another consequence is that EC is based on multiple meanings of the concept of a convention, which can harm its clarity.
5. Young (1996) illustrates this in his own 'Economics of conventions' by means of traffic rules. In many countries laws simply endorsed established custom. But the central authority may also counter custom. Thus, during the French revolution, it was decreed that traffic would travel on the right to symbolize changes in the social order, since the left was identified with aristocratic practices (jousting). Note that Young always refers to conventions, even when they have been ratified by law, to emphasize the fact that an alternative does exist, and thus the arbitrary dimension of any convention even if its choice can be linked to a political intention.
6. North compares this type of informal constraint to the emergence of 'early law merchants' publicized codes of merchant conduct' which he explains in terms of a game theory model (Milgrom *et al.*, 1990).
7. For example, Aoki's solution to the problem (1999) is a radical way emphasizing the self-emergent (self-organized) and self-enforcing nature of institutions. In this perspective, 'public authorities' are not considered to be neutral third parties responsible for enforcing rationally conceived legal rules. The public authority behavioural model can be defined as the endogenous result of its strategic interaction with private actors. In general, institutions are seen as spontaneous responses by individuals to their limited capacities for cognition and action. It proposes a formalization of their emergence and stability, based on game theories borrowed from both the standard approach and evolutionary game theory.

8. Some authors, such as Guerrien (1990) see in it only a liberal critique of state intervention. However, North's argument cannot be considered on an ideological level only.
9. We give numerous examples of these organizations or 'private institutions' in our research on the collective management of intellectual property (Bessy and Brousseau, 1997b).
10. This work can be compared to that of the theory of regulation (Boyer, 1986) which evaluates the 'accuracy' of the Fordist model in terms of macroeconomic indicators such as productivity gains, growth and employment trends, and so on.
11. Knight and North are thus prompted to criticize experimental approaches which highlight the 'internal' activities of individuals disconnected from the social context, such as experiments performed by Kahneman and Tversky (1984). These researchers evaluate the rationality of individual decisions with reference to a conception of rationality that is theoretically constructed. Differences in comparison with the model are then attributed to cognitive weaknesses in the individual actors.
12. Work by the Centre for the Sociology of Innovation and, in particular, that of Callon (1993) can also be cited here.
13. Calculation and especially accounting rules are a good example.
14. It is in this sense that this type of analysis differs from the evolutionary approach of Nelson and Winter (1982). The hypothesis is that evolutionary routines are based on cognitive devices which guarantee their stability. It is still necessary, however, to explain what differentiates the concept of an institution common to both approaches considered from that of routine peculiar to evolutionary theory. In both cases we have two models of interaction between the agents, which are sources of regularity in behaviour. One way of distinguishing the two models would be by contrasting 'rules', which would imply a clarification and effort to demonstrate their effects, and 'norms' which are supposed to be separate from actors' interpretive activity and imposed on them without much reflexive activity on their part. Now, EC and North's approach tend to mix these two concepts based on that of a convention, even if they try to take into account different conventional mechanisms. It seems that one of the sources of confusion is the use of game theory which causes agents to act as though behavioural norms were the result of a process of optimization of individual interests.
15. With the method of structural analysis oriented towards the rigorous recording of relations between actors within a system, it is possible to account for its relational structure and the nature of resources circulating in it. On this point, see Lazega (1998).
16. We note, however, that recent work by Favereau (1998) shows how the choice of a mode of representation or of a framework for interpreting information is not neutral and can benefit certain actors at the origin of the choice.

REFERENCES

Aoki, M. (1999), 'Towards a comparative institutional analysis', Cambridge, MA: MIT Press.

Bessy, C. (1997a), 'L'hypothèse de connaissance tacite dans la théorie évolutionniste de la firme', Working paper, CEE/ATOM.

Bessy, C. (1997b), 'Les marchés du travail des photographes', in C. Bessy and F. Eymard-Duvernay (eds), *Les intermédiaires du marché du travail*, Cahiers du Centre d'Etudes de l'Emploi, 36, Paris: PUF.

Bessy, C. and E. Brousseau (1997a), 'Brevet, protection et diffusion des connaissances: une relecture néo-institutionnelle des propriétés de la règle de droit', *Revue d'économie industrielle*, numéro spécial 'Economie industrielle de la science', premier semestre.

Bessy C. and E. Brousseau (1997b), 'The governance of intellectual property rights: patents and copyrights in France and in the US', Inaugural Conference of the Society for New Institutional Economics, Washington University.

Bessy, C. and E. Brousseau (1998), 'Licensing of technology: various contracts for diverse transactions', *International Review of Law and Economics*, 18, 451–9.

Bessy C. and F. Eymard-Duvernay (eds) (1997), *Les intermédiaires du marché du travail*, Cahiers du CEE, 36, Paris: PUF.

Boyer, R. (1986), *La théorie de la régulation: une analyse critique*, coll. Algama, Paris: La Découverte.

Callon, M. (1993), 'Is science a public good?', Fifth Mullins Lecture, Virginia Polytechnics Institute, March.

Doeringer, P.B. and M.J. Piore (1971), *Internal Labor Markets and Manpower Analysis*, 2nd edn, with a new introduction, New York: Sharpe, 1985.

Dupuy, J.-P. (1989), 'Convention and Common Knowledge', *Revue économique*, 40 (2), March, 361–400.

Eymard-Duvernay, F. (1989), 'Conventions de qualité et formes de coordination', *Revue économique*, 40 (2), March, 329–60.

Favereau, O. (1986), 'La formalisation du rôle des conventions dans l'allocation des ressources', in R. Salais and L. Thévenot (eds), *Le travail. Marchés, règles, conventions*, Paris: INSEE/Economica.

Favereau, O. (1989), 'Marchés internes, marchés externes', *Revue économique*, 40 (2), March, 273–328.

Favereau, Olivier (1998), 'Décisions, situations, institutions', in A. Vinokur (ed.), *Décisions économiques*, Paris: Economica.

Guerrien, B. (1990), 'Quelques réflexions sur institutions, organisations et histoire', *Economie appliquée*, XLIII (3), 89–110.

Hutchins, E. (1995), *Cognition in the Wild*, Cambridge, MA: MIT Press.

Kahneman, D. and A. Tversky (1984), 'Choices, values and frames', *American Psychologist*, 39 (4), 341–50.

Knight, J. and D. North (1997), 'Explaining economic change: the interplay between cognition and institutions', *Legal Theory*, 3, 211–26.

Lazega, E. (1998), *Réseaux sociaux et structures relationnelles*, Paris: PUF.

Lewis, D. (1969), *Convention, a Philosophical Study*, Cambridge, MA: Harvard University Press.

Milgrom, P.R., D.C. North and B.R. Weingast (1990), 'The role of institutions in the revival of trade: the law marchant, private judge and the champagne fairs', *Economics and Politics*, 2 (1), 1–23.

Nelson, R. and S. Winter (1982), *An Evolutionary Theory of Economic Change*, Cambridge, MA: Harvard University Press.

North, D. (1990), *Institutions, Institutional Change and Economic Performance*, Cambridge: Cambridge University Press.

North, D. and R. Thomas (1973), *The Rise of the Western World: a New Economic History*, Cambridge: Cambridge University Press.

Reynaud, B. (1986), 'Le modèle hiérarchique: une méthode d'analyse des relations salariales', thèse d'Etat, Université de Paris X – Nanterre.

Salais, R. (1989), 'L'analyse économique des conventions du travail', *Revue économique*, 40 (2), March, 198–240.

Thévenot, L. (1989), 'Équilibre et rationalité dans un univers complexe', *Revue économique*, 2, March, 147–97.

Williamson, O.E. (1985), *The Economic Institutions of Capitalism: Firms, Markets, Relational Contracting*, New York: Macmillan, The Free Press.

Young P. (1996), 'The economics of conventions', *Journal of Economic Perspectives*, 10 (2), 105–22.

4. Transaction cost economics and governance structures: applications, developments and perspectives

Didier Chabaud and Stéphane Saussier

INTRODUCTION

It is now widely recognized that transaction cost economics is an 'empirical success story' (Williamson, 1996). Hundreds of empirical tests exist and often corroborate propositions of this theoretical framework (Klein and Shelanski, 1995; Crocker and Masten, 1996; Masten and Saussier, 2000), especially concerning the make or buy decision (Coeurderoy and Quélin, 1997). Even if progress is still to be made (Williamson, 1993; Masten, 1995; Masten and Saussier, 2000), it is not well known that recent developments allow the theory to give good explanations of complementary phenomena such as inter-firm contractual relationships or internal organization.

In this chapter we would like to illustrate what the weaknesses and recent improvements are of the theory, focusing most especially on the analysis of inter-firm agreements and intra-firm organization. After a brief presentation of transaction cost economics' basics, we come back to the main developments concerning inter-firm relationships. We show that empirical tests provide a strong support for the theory's propositions. Furthermore, we emphasize the needed improvements that still have to be done and we give insights and several examples of recent studies. Lastly, we analyse what the explanatory power of the theory is concerning internal organization. Results are more mitigated because the theory is only beginning to investigate this question in depth. A brief conclusion closes the chapter.

A BRIEF PRESENTATION

Here we do not provide an exhaustive presentation of what transaction cost economics is (see Williamson, 1996, on this point). We only want to briefly present what new institutional economics is, what institutions are and how they are articulated with governance structures.

Transaction Cost Economics and New Institutional Economics

Transaction cost economics (TCE hereafter) exist within the new institutional economics framework (NIE hereafter). NIE took shape in two complementary parts. One deals with background conditions, that is to say the 'rules of the game'. The second deals with the mechanisms of governance and is what transaction cost economics has been concerned with (see Figure 4.1).

The crucial distinctions between governance structures and institutions are that the institutional environment is given as a set of fundamental political, social and legal ground rules (North 1990). Governance structures are

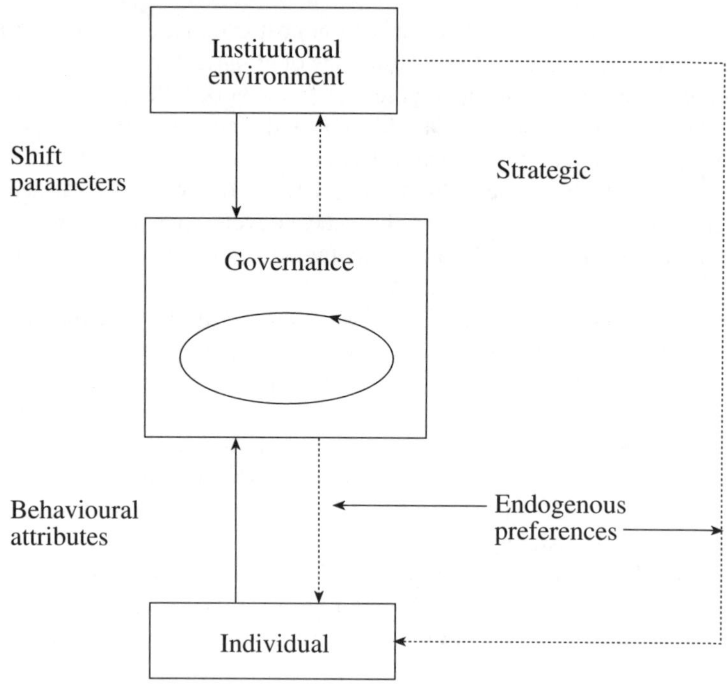

Note: Main effects are shown by the solid arrows, and the feedback effects are the broken arrows.

Source: Williamson (1996, p. 326).

Figure 4.1 Institutions and governance structures

arrangements between economic units that govern the way they cooperate and/or compete.

Of course, governance structure mechanisms and institutions are not independent. Nevertheless, there is no unified framework to analyse *these* two complementary parts, even if the 'governance line' proposed to join these two by treating the institutional environment as a set of parameters that may influence the comparative costs of governance (Williamson, 1991). Improvements are in progress concerning this issue, but we will not talk about it (see Bessy, 2000, also Chapter 9 of the present volume).

Transaction Cost Economics and Governance Structures

Transaction cost economics[1] is mainly concerned with governance structures. This theoretical framework relies on behavioural assumptions that gave rise to propositions concerning contractual arrangements.

Behavioural assumptions

The transaction cost theory (TCT hereafter) wants to analyse 'man as he is'. Behavioural assumptions that are retained insist on the fact that economic actors have a bounded rationality but have a far-sighted behaviour and *may behave* opportunistically.[2] Those behavioural assumptions are at the source of transaction costs, but only really matter when two conditions are verified (see Table 4.1).

The fact that economic actors have a bounded rationality is not a problem as long as the uncertainty characterizing the world they live in is not present. As long as their limits are not reached, bounded rationality is not a problem for economic agents to coordinate their activities. With high levels of uncertainty, the main consequence is that agents can only sign incomplete contracts.

Signing incomplete contracts is not usually a problem, even if you may face opportunistic behaviours, as long as you can use market sanctions in the event of opportunistic behaviour. That is the case as long as contracting parties are not dependent. But when they are in a 'small number' relationship

Table 4.1 Sketch of the argument

Behavioural assumptions	Transaction characteristics	Consequences of contracting process
Bounded Rationality	Uncertainty	Incomplete contracting
Opportunism	Specific assests	Credible commitments
Far-sighted behaviour		Economizing behaviour

(Williamson, 1975), the problem is more crucial as they cannot shift from one partner to another. That is typically the case when one or both of the parties develop specific investments in order to realize a transaction. Specific investments, that can be defined as a specialized investment that cannot be redeployed to alternative uses or by alternative users except at a loss of value, generate a bilateral dependency. Such dependency generates contractual hazards in the face of incomplete contracting and opportunism. The main consequence is that contracts cannot rely on promises but must be supported by credible commitments.

Propositions

Propositions of the transaction cost economics framework rely on the characteristics of the transactions (mainly specific investments and uncertainty) and are at the source of transaction costs. Many different kinds of governance structures may be chosen. This is a question for which transaction cost economics' point of view has evolved through time: 'Whereas I was earlier of the view that transactions of the middle kind[3] were very difficult to organize and hence unstable, I am now persuaded that transactions in the middle range are much more common' (Williamson, 1985, p. 89).

This perception gave rise to the analysis of a new kind of governance structure, hybrids, where economic agents are not independent (as on markets) but are still partly autonomous (contrary to what the case is in hierarchies). Hybrids are analysed as being adequately able to respond to transactions 'of the middle kind'. Their stability is assured by contractual safeguards that may be implemented by contracting parties to make their relationships rely on credible commitments (Williamson, 1996; Ménard, 2000). Transaction cost economics maintains, as Williamson (1996, p.101) describes it, that transactions, 'which differ in their attributes, are aligned with governance structures, which differ in their cost and competence so as to economize (mainly) on transaction costs' (see Figure 4.2). Each governance structure is characterized (1) by a contract law that is more or less secure (for parties investing in specific investments) and more or less flexible (to deal with uncertainty) and (2) by a differentiated capacity to generate incentives (Williamson, 1991).

The differential of incentive intensity that characterizes governance structures is essential as it allows us to understand why every transaction is not integrated. If hierarchies are characterized by a forbearance contract that permits great adaptations in the face of uncertainty and makes contracting parties feel secure (the main advantages of integration), they do not permit as high a level of internal incentive, as in hybrids or markets. A selective intervention is not possible. Hybrids and markets cannot replicate flexibility and secure feelings of hierarchies. On the other hand, hierarchies cannot replicate incentive levels of hybrids and markets. Here is the trade-off[4] that is supposed to be made by

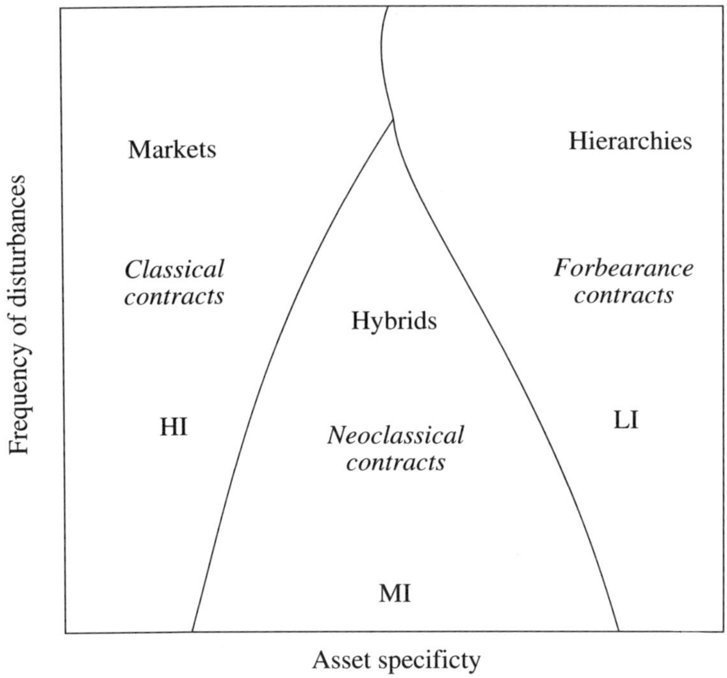

Note: HI = high incentives, MI = middle incentives, LI = low incentives

Figure 4.2 The choice of governance structures

economic agents in order for them *to economize on transaction costs and production costs.*

INTER-FIRM RELATIONSHIPS: ILLUSTRATIONS

Because transaction cost economics has generated a large number of refutable propositions, it invites empirical testing. Tremendous progress has been made, but several issues still need to be improved upon (see Masten, 1995; Masten and Saussier, 2000, concerning this issue).

What Propositions?

Transaction cost economics view contracts as devices for structuring ex post adjustments and for constraining wasteful (rent-dissipating) efforts that influence the distribution of gains from trade. It especially includes ex post bargaining and 'hold-up' activities in transactions supported by relationship-specific investments and ex ante sorting and search in contexts where additional information serves merely to redistribute rather than expand the available surplus.

To achieve this, contracting parties can choose between a secure contract that specifies how the quasi-rent generated by their relationships will be shared ex post and a flexible contract that allows them to benefit from future non-anticipated opportunities. Secure contracts give good incentives ex ante to invest in specific assets, at the risk of being trapped in a bad contract ex post, once uncertain events emerge. Flexible contracts permit dealing with uncertainty but at the cost of possible opportunistic behaviours that do not produce high incentives to invest in specific assets. The kinds of contracts that will economize on transaction costs depend on the characteristics of the transaction. Very uncertain transactions need flexible contracts. Transactions that necessitate high levels of specific assets need secure contracts. Uncertain transactions that need a high level of specific assets are good candidates for integration (see Figure 4.2).

What Tests and Needed Improvements?

Past Improvements

Coase's paper (Coase, 1937), that points out the need to incorporate transaction costs in the analysis, has often been viewed as giving tautological propositions concerning the driving forces behind what should explain the choice of a particular organizational arrangement (Coase, 1993; Masten *et al.*, 1991). The great improvement that came from the analysis of Williamson is that sources of transaction costs are now identified.

The choice of a particular organizational arrangement to govern a transaction can be represented as:

$$\text{Organizational arrangement } G^*: \quad \begin{cases} G^* = G1 \text{ if } CG1 < CG2 \\ \text{with } CG1 = f(\textit{uncertainty, asset specificity}) \\[1em] G^* = G2 \text{ if } CG2 \leq CG1 \\ \text{with } CG2 = f(\textit{uncertainty, asset specificity}) \end{cases}$$

where G^* is the chosen organizational form; $G1$ and $G2$ are the two alternative organizational forms; $CG1$ and $CG2$ are transaction costs associated with organizational forms $G1$ and $G2$.

On the condition of being able to find adequate data to measure asset specificity and uncertainty levels at stake in transactions, transaction cost economics propositions are thus refutable.

Data have been collected and numerous tests have been done (Klein and Shelanski, 1995; Crocker and Masten, 1996; Coeurderoy and Quélin, 1997; Masten and Saussier, 2000 for a survey). Data have been collected, mainly through case studies or through questionnaires, where econometric testing was the issue. Such a way of collecting data is questionable with regard to measurement errors. For example, concerning the Masten *et al.*, (1991) study on shipbuilding procurements, a low correlation has been found between respondents of questionnaires and responses of a naval architect with experience on the subject (Masten, 1995, pp. 48–9). Respondents often have difficulties understanding questions, more especially what specific assets are as compared to specialized assets.

Few empirical studies are based on the contracts themselves, which are usually confidential. Exceptions often concern regulatory filings (Mulherin, 1986; Joskow, 1987, 1988; Masten and Crocker, 1985), but not always (Saussier, 1999, 2000a).

Observed regularities in econometric studies

Empirical studies allowed for a dramatic advance in our understanding of contractual relationship structures. Several aspects of the contracts have been under scrutiny.

One of the first aspects of contract design to be studied was the issue of *contract length* (Joskow, 1985, 1987; Crocker and Masten, 1988; Saussier, 1999). The trade-off considered is the one between the marginal cost of writing longer agreements and the marginal benefits of mitigating opportunism (avoiding renegotiation) by extending the agreement for an additional period (see Masten, 1986; Crocker and Masten, 1988, for a formal analysis). The problem is then with the way characteristics of the transaction governed by the contract affect this trade-off. What is usually retained is that (1) the more the asset specificity level is needed to realize the transaction, the longer the contract should be (because asset specificity, by increasing the quasi-rent, increases the likelihood of ex post opportunism) and (2) the more uncertain the transaction, the shorter the contract should be (because uncertainty increases contracting costs, especially ex post maladaptation costs).

Those propositions have been corroborated by several studies, in several kinds of contracts. For example, Joskow studied coal contracts signed between US electrical plants and coal mines (Joskow, 1987). His econometrical tests, concerning 277 contracts confirmed the role of asset specificity in the contract length decision. Nevertheless, he was not able to appreciate the influence of uncertainty on this issue. Crocker and Masten confirmed those results taking into account the role of uncertainty on contractual duration decisions on another set of contracts (Crocker and Masten, 1988). Their study is concerned with natural gas contracts signed between well owners and natural pipelines.

A more recent study concerning contracts signed between EDF[5] coal transporters and coal carriers confirmed the results obtained from US data, using European data (Saussier, 1999).[6]

Another aspect of contract design studied was the issue of *contractual completeness*. The trade-off considered is between the marginal cost of writing more incomplete agreements and the marginal benefits of mitigating opportunism (avoiding renegotiation) by extending the completeness level of the agreement.[7]

Several empirical studies have shown that characteristics of the transaction that may affect the cost of a complete contract (complexity and uncertainty of the transaction) have a negative influence on the completeness level of contractual agreements. On the other hand, characteristics of the transaction that may affect the gain of a complete contract (probability of opportunistic behaviour, asset specificity levels) have a positive influence on the contract completeness level chosen by the contracting parties (see Crocker and Masten, 1991; Crocker and Reynolds, 1993; Saussier, 2000a).

These regularities show that the transaction cost economics framework does well to explain contractual choices observed in the real world. Nevertheless, if tremendous progress has been made to make the transaction cost concept operational, needed improvements are still on the agenda.

Needed improvements

Structural tests First of all, empirical tests concerning the transaction cost theory are often based on reduced-form analysis: 'To be sure, there is much to be done, hence there is no basis for complacency . . . most (empirical studies) are regressions in which asset specificity (and sometimes uncertainty and frequency) appear as independent variables' (Williamson, 1993, p. 27).

This point requires urgent attention with regard to the development of empirical tests of the theory: 'The specificity of assets and the level of investment in those assets that determine the size of appropriable quasi-rents are themselves decision variables. The location of facilities, the adoption of specialized designs or equipment, and the scale of investments should all, by rights, be treated as endogenous variables' (Masten, 1995, p. 60).

In fact, in most of the econometrical studies, reduced-forms are tested, whereas the complete model proposed by Williamson, compared to the heuristic one (compare Williamson, 1985, chapter 4, with Riordan and Williamson, 1985), is not really tested. As Williamson noted, concerning his heuristic presentation: 'It assumes a sequential process whereby technology is selected first and choice among feasible organizational modes is made thereafter. In fact, however, technology and organizational modes ought to be treated symmetrically; they are decision variables whose values are determined simultaneously' (Williamson, 1985, p. 83).

Data that would allow simultaneous estimation of the choices of technology and organizational modes would be very useful, in order to disentangle some effects that cannot be included in reduced-form analysis: namely the direct effect of specific investments on organizational choices instead of the effect of proxies, and the possible sequentiality that is not postulated by transaction cost economics but that may exist between the choices of technology and organizational form. Such tests are only beginning. The only one we are aware of, at the moment, is made by Saussier (1999). The study concerns coal transport and unloading contracts signed by EDF (the French owned power utility) between 1977 and 1997. Looking at contract duration, and using precise data (direct measures) with regard to asset specificity and uncertainty levels at stake in each transaction concerned by each contract, an econometrical test is proposed using instrumental variables to endogenize asset specificity at stake in transactions, estimating an equations system instead of a single reduced-form equation. The study shows that contract duration is positively influenced by asset specificity at stake in transactions (the need for a secure contract takes the form of a longer-term contract) and negatively influenced by the level of uncertainty (the need for a flexible contract takes the form of a shorter-term contract). Those results hold even when asset specificity levels are endogenized, providing an even more convincing test of the transaction cost economics propositions.

Such needed improvements in the way the theory's propositions are tested are thus possible, at the cost of collecting very precise data.

Direct tests concerning the underlying structure of transaction costs Estimation of reduced-form hypotheses greatly eases data requirements, but at the cost of misconstruing the source of transaction cost differentials too. It would be interesting to be able to estimate the underlying structure of transaction costs postulated by transaction cost economics, that permit empirical tests, but that is never tested. Such tests are possible.

We know of only one study that estimated the underlying structure of transaction costs in order to check if transaction costs vary with the characteristics of the transactions (Masten *et al.*, 1991). This study concerns the make or buy decision in the organization of transactions in the shipbuilding procurement. Results were interesting. If the reduced-form results supported all of the transaction cost predictions, the structural estimations supported only some of the underlying hypotheses (see Masten, 1995, on this issue). Furthermore, this study allows for the estimation of the cost of a bad decision (Table 4.2), showing the importance of transaction cost expenses, especially in the case of a bad decision.

Lastly, it is very interesting to note that such a result was obtainable only because the authors supposed that the underlying structures of transaction

Table 4.2 Estimated organization costs

	Make items (n=43)	Buy items (n=31)	Total (n=74)
Estimated costs	$1 863 620	$1 717 710	$3 581 330
Costs if all components made internally	$1 863 620	$2 945 930	$4 809 260
Costs if all components subcontracted	$5 435 200	$1 717 710	$7 155 060

Source: Masten et al., (1991).

costs in the firm were not exactly the same as those in the market. This issue highlights the fact that it would be interesting to go further in the analysis of intra-firm relationships to see if transaction cost sources on the markets stay the same in the firm. The study of internal relationships should give insights on this issue. But as we will see, transaction cost economics did not make as many improvements as inter-firms' contractual relationships did, regarding this issue.

INTERNAL RELATIONSHIPS: ILLUSTRATIONS

If the analysis of hybrid forms has been developed in recent years, the study of internal properties of organization remains suggestive but broad: only a few studies provide theoretical or empirical insights regarding organizations. More precisely, after some initial studies such as Williamson *et al.* (1975), Williamson (1980), Williamson and Ouchi (1981), the topic of internal organization seems to have been neglected, as Klein and Shelanski (1995) show in their survey of empirical works in TCT.

Only recently, this 'benign neglect' has been challenged, leading to a few studies that try to enhance the explanatory power of TCT (Williamson and Bercovitz, 1994; Chabaud, 1998, 2000; Ménard, 1996, 1997; Nickerson, 1999).

Transaction Cost Theory and Organizations: First Insights and Critics

From the beginning, the analysis of internal structures belonged in the research agenda of transaction cost economics. In his 1975 book, Williamson states that there should be provided 'a study in the economics of internal organization'. He maintains his objective by saying that TCT can provide a basis for the 'incipient science of organization' (Williamson, 1990) and develops some suggestive insights (Williamson, 1998). Nevertheless, only a few empirical and theoretical studies have been made that provide an analysis of the internal structures of the firm. The analysis of the firm appears to lead to a general characterization.

Symptomatically, Williamson characterizes the firm as hierarchy since his 1975 book. In his analysis of work organization, Williamson (1985) emphasizes the superiority of hierarchy over all other kinds of work organization (inside contracting, peer group and so on). This analysis has led some scholars to argue that transaction cost economics is unable to cope with 'employee involvement' (Pfeffer, 1994) and 'horizontal coordination' (Aoki, 1988). Also the hypothesis of opportunism has been challenged, and leads Ghoshal and Moran (1996) to depict transaction cost theory as 'bad for practice'. However, these analyses seem to draw more on Williamson (1985) than on earlier or more recent works of Williamson (1980, 1991).

First, Williamson (1980) develops a more subtle view than that of the affirmation that hierarchy is the best work organization principle: 'the Peer Group comes off rather well in the composite efficiency rating of (work organization) modes. The Peer Group, however, experiences severe limitations as firm size is scaled up' (Williamson, 1980, p. 33). Thus the peer group – that is, the incarnation of a democratic form of work organization – can be efficient on a small scale. Moreover, the valuation made by Williamson asserts that hierarchy and peer group are quasi-equal in their efficiency properties. So it seems peremptory to condemn the transaction cost theory on this aspect.

Second, Williamson (1991) constitutes a sharp evolution in the analysis of organization. The explanation of fiat in force in hierarchy is developed: 'One explanation is that fiat has its origins in the employment contract (Coase, 1937; Barnard, 1938; Simon, 1951; Masten, 1988). Although there is a good deal to be said for that explanation, I propose a separate and complementary explanation: The implicit contract law of internal organization is that of forbearance' (Williamson, 1996, p. 98). Forbearance is used to signify that organizations create a private judicial order that defines its functioning principle. Notice that this topic is an old one as 'internal organization supplants markets partly because it assumes and effectively discharges certain quasijudicial functions' (Williamson, 1975, p. 30). So a distinction between the analysis of the characterization of the firm (forbearance) and of its mode of command (hierarchy versus/together with the use of decentralized decision making) has to be made.

Critics of the transaction cost theory's analysis of the firm point out effectively that, when we look at the inside of the firm, the focus on organization as its proper 'court of ultimate appeal' (Williamson, 1996, p. 378) is limited in its explanatory and descriptive power. The analysis of the functioning mode of the firm has to be made precisely in the transaction cost theory corpus.

Some works exist that emphasize the role of human asset specificity in order to understand the functioning principle of the firm. Suzuki (1991) applies this approach in historical analysis to explain the emergence of the Japanese way of organization. The development of human asset specificity inside the firm necessitated a long-term relation with manpower, and explains the kind of management in force in Japan. Also, in a suggestive study, Ménard (1995, 1997) provides some refutable insights into the connection between organization forms and the attributes of internal transactions, and more specifically on human asset specificity. Ménard points out that creation of human asset specificity has two facets: 'From the point of view of organization: a negative side, related to the possibility opened by specificity of human assets to post-contractual opportunistic behaviour (Klein, Crawford and Alchian, 1978); and a positive side, which is the capacity it opens, through cooperation and/or adequate monitoring, of generating performance superior to what can be specified in contracts' (Ménard, 1997, pp. 32–3).

So a first examination of the interest of using the transaction cost theory as a tool to analyse internal organization leads to deepening the nature of human asset specificity,[8] to looking for its operationalization and to inquiry on the nature of the mode of coordination in force inside the firm, in order to answer both the limitations of Williamson's works and the general critics of TCT. Several studies made progress on the two parts of the jigsaw puzzle.

Human Asset Specificity: Content and Operationalization

According to Williamson (1975), 'almost every job involves some specific skills', as human asset specificity arises in learning by doing (Williamson, 1991, p. 281). Human asset specificity is endogenous (as pointed out above, 'Needed improvements') and comes from the principles of work organization. Nevertheless, we can consider that we lack a precise definition of the concept of human asset specificity in order to operationalize it, as the characterization of the concept remains loose. Clarifying the dimensions of human asset specificity becomes necessary, to understand what kinds of (specific) skills are linked to various kinds of work organizations.

On this topic, Koike (1988) can be useful, as his analysis of the skills of Japanese workers combines theoretical insights and empirical observations. Koike emphasizes the importance of intellectual skills and of mutual aid in the Japanese plants, making it possible to distinguish between: (1) operational skills, (2) intellectual skills and (3) relational skills:

> Operational skill refers to the control of the technical content of the job. In the automotive industry for example, where there is mass production, these skills refer essentially to tasks that are repetitive and monotonous, with little knowledge content. Nevertheless, the individual can develop a specific know-how for these tasks, for improving his performance when accomplishing it.[9]
>
> Intellectual skill refers to the ability to deal skilfully with 'unusual operations',

i.e. changes and problems that arise on the shopfloor. Intellectual skill necessitates the worker to be able to cope with these unusual operations, i.e. to detect, diagnose and rectify/manage them. On this topic, it seems necessary to refer to the different kinds of indirect tasks controlled by the worker (maintenance, quality control, problem solving, etc.) to evaluate his intellectual skill.

Relational skill refers to the ability of individuals to mobilize collectively in order to deal with problems or changes. When facing a problem, either the job is strictly delineated and the worker has to react individually to solve it or there is a loose demarcation of jobs and the worker can benefit from the help of his co-workers.

Relational skill is the ability of a worker to cooperate with other workers, and to give help or mutual aid. These skills can be evaluated by the existence or absence of the overlap in jobs (ambiguity in the job definition). Also, the valuation by the firm of the mutual aid of workers reflects the importance of relational skills in the work organization.

Each form of work organization will require different kinds of skills. The principles of organizing work, dividing it into jobs, organizing coordination, and problem solving make it necessary for workers to more or less possess each of these three dimensions of specific skills. This distinction makes it possible to distinguish different kinds of work organization depending on the kinds of skills needed, and their depth. The first part of the jigsaw puzzle is completed, but it needs to be matched with the analysis of modes of command to provide a complete picture and to be able to make empirical studies.

From Human Asset Specificity to Mode of Command

What pattern of decision making is used in the different forms of work organization? We have seen that it is generally asserted that transaction cost theory is unable to cope with this topic, owing to its overemphasis on hierarchical relationships as a way of coordinating agents' actions. In fact, the distinction between the nature of the firm (and the fact that organization is its 'own court of ultimate appeal': Williamson, 1991) and the coordination modalities inside the firm is suitable. Ménard (1994, 1995) suggests distinguishing between two patterns of decision making, that can be connected with the characteristics of the work organization in force in the firm. A brief presentation of this distinction and of its possible operationalization has to be made in order to evaluate the interest of TCT.

Two modalities of command

Ménard (1994, 1995) distinguishes two patterns of decision making inside the firm: authority and hierarchy.[10] If A is the set of possible actions within an organization, and I and J are two classes of agents, for $j \in J$ and $i \in I$, it can be said that j has authority over i, if i allows j to choose an action a, $a \in A$. It is important to note that this definition emphasizes that 'authority involves intention and requires some form of explicit acceptance' (Ménard, 1995, p. 155). Decision making is delegated to agent *j* within a precisely defined area of acceptance. Also authority can be taken away from agent *j*. When authority is practised within a team, we can think of peers remaining in a symmetrical (statutory) position.

Conversely, it can be said that *i* is subordinate to *j* if *i* refers to the goals defined by *j* rather than to his own goals when it comes to the choice of *a*, and if the decisions of *j* prevail over those of *i* when there are ambiguities or conflicts about choices to be made (Ménard, 1995, p. 156). So a hierarchical relationship is based on a non-negotiable asymmetry between individuals: the subordinate *i* has to accept orders from *j*, his superior. The firm is conceived as a pyramidal structure in which only ranks are important.

Note that this distinction between authority and hierarchy enables us to distinguish two different kinds of structure of decision making in which there is, to a certain degree, centralization of decision making. If hierarchy prevails, the superior possesses an extensive power of decision making over his subordinates, who only have to obey orders. The superior is at the centre of all communication channels, which limits the costs of communication (Williamson, 1975). In contrast, if authority prevails, we can observe that for every kind of decision a different leader prevails: for quality troubles it will be agent j_1, for absenteeism management it will be j_2, and so on. In fact, it is conceivable that inside a workgroup every member will have authority over one class of action. In this sense, with hierarchy only one member possesses decision power, whereas with authority everyone may decide.

So authority enables allocation of decision power according to agents' abilities, whereas in hierarchy the origin of decision power remains statutory.

What about work organization? We can conceive that firms will design a work organization that will use essentially either hierarchy or authority, according to the comparative efficiency of these patterns of decision making. In this sense, we have to distinguish between the organization as its own court of ultimate appeal (which is to say that organization is hierarchical by nature) and the organization as the locus of coordination of decision making (which is to say that the modalities of command are authority and/or hierarchy).

What is alignment of modalities of decision making and of work organization?

Some observations As a consequence, we have to study the comparative efficiency of hierarchy and authority in order to understand the modalities of command on the shopfloor. For this, we have to qualify the influence of asset specificity on the efficiency of the patterns of decision making.

Chabaud (1998, 2000) proposed relating human asset specificity to the pattern of decision making, and confronting these propositions with data, focusing on assembly shops of 43 plants of the automotive industry.[11] This attempt first necessitated operationalizing the distinction between authority and hierarchy.

Human asset specificity and modalities of decision making Human asset specificity allows workers to develop a local knowledge. They are able to occupy more job stations, to treat unusual operations alone or to help co-workers. A complete use of their skills is needed to give them more autonomy in the decision-making process. In this sense, we can consider that high human asset specificity requires more authority than hierarchy, as workers have to use their skills efficiently. Conversely, low human asset specificity, which implies more routine tasks and the lack of local treatment of unusual operations, leads to use of the hierarchical relationship in the process of decision making, as workers do not possess (officially) the skills to deal locally with problems.

Operationalization of the authority–hierarchy delineation Chabaud provided an operationalization of the authority–hierarchy delineation, distinguishing between the global responsibility of the team, the origin and the role of the team leader, and the prerogatives of workers (see Table 4.3). In every case, the criterion consisted of measuring either the asymmetric statutory origin of decision making (hierarchy) or the weight of individual skills and consent in the allocation of the decision power.

A confrontation with data This empirical study allows contrasting the frequency of these dimensions in the different kinds of work organization

Table 4.3 Criteria of authority and hierarchy

Criterion	Authority	Hierarchy
Team responsibility	Obtain results	Obey orders
Origin of leaders' prerogatives	Delegated by members	Conferred by status
Nomination of leader	By peers	By hierarchy
Function of leader	Animation	Locally omnipotent
Role of workers	Deciding, in function of peers' decisions	Obey orders
Origin of decision	Skill	Status

Table 4.4 Authority and hierarchy in forms of work organization

Work organization	Plants with low human asset specificity (n = 8)		Plants with high human asset specificity (n = 35)	
Criterion	A	H	A	H
Team responsibility		100	100	
Origin of leaders' prerogatives		100		100
Nomination of leader		100	86	14
Function of leader		100	86	14
Role of workers		100	100	
Origin of decision		100	100	

Note: A indicates a component of authority as criterion, whereas H indicates a hierarchical component; data in percentage of plants surveyed.

observed in plants. Even if the observations remain general and incomplete (from about 43 assembly plants), the facts are clear and coherent with hypotheses (see Table 4.4).

When work organization is based more on human asset specificity, it entails the predominance of authority over hierarchy in the work group. It is observed that the mode of command differs sharply among plants. The only exception lies in the fact that prerogatives of the leader are hierarchically defined: designers of the work process choose to delegate decision making to teams, organizing them along authority or hierarchy. But, as studied work groups are on the production process, this is not so astonishing: they take place inside a whole organization that delimits their prerogatives.

Besides this point, the alignment between mode of command and level of human asset specificity is confirmed by data, except for a few cases. The five plants that differ according to the 'nomination' and the 'function of leader' criterion appear to be the last arrivals in the trial to change work organization. It seems that leaders retain hierarchical power (while being officially the agents of change and animation).

So we can conclude that a TCT viewpoint does not prevent us from thinking of decentralization as an efficient way of organizing work. Also it allows us to anticipate the kind of decision-making process in force in the plant. But, in order to do so, we have to endogenize asset specificity variables and search for accurate micro data, that is, data of the internal structure of the firm (see Nickerson, 1999, on this point). This need implies the use of case studies and empirical methods complementary to the traditional one used in economic science, and enables TCT to contribute to organization science.

CONCLUSION

In this chapter, we have reflected on recent advances of the transaction cost theory. First, we showed that inter-firm relationships have been carefully analysed by the theory. According to our point of view, convincing advances and results have been made, permitting real improvements in the understanding of contractual practices observed in the real world, even though we have stressed several topics concerning empirical studies still to be dealt with.

Second, we showed that, if Williamson considers the theory to be adequate in analysing internal structures of firms, it did not provide the same kind of empirical evidences until now. Nevertheless, we showed that recent studies allowed us to provide first answers to the critics, and to develop an analytical framework that should enable us to make improvements in the understanding of internal structures.

Nevertheless, as we mentioned at the beginning of the chapter, the analysis has been conducted in an institution-free framework. If this methodological choice provides fruitful results, and permits exhibition of empirical and theoretical developments, a number of researches will try to make the connection between institutional environment and governance structures, and should give us an even deeper understanding of the mechanisms of governance.

NOTES

1. More precisely the 'governance line' as it has been developed by Williamson (Williamson, 1975, 1985, 1996): in what follows, we will speak alternatively of 'transaction cost economics' and 'transaction cost theory', referring to these works.
2. This point is not always well understood. Transaction cost economics is often criticized on the grounds that economic actors do not always behave opportunistically (Ghoshal and Moran, 1996, versus Williamson, 1996).
3. That is to say, between markets and hierarchies (Williamson, 1975).
4. We must note that the incomplete contract theory that emerged recently (Grossman and Hart, 1986; Hart, 1995), with the initial objective being to formalize transaction cost economics reasoning, is giving an alternative explanation of vertical integration that is not based on this trade-off (see Favereau and Picard, 1996; Fares and Saussier, 1998; Saussier, 2000b and Masten, 1999, on this particular point).
5. The French state-owned power utility.
6. It is useful to confirm results obtained with US data using European data because results may be driven by institutional characteristics that are always fixed if we do not consider data from several countries. One of the main topics on the agenda of the theory is certainly to analyse, for the same kind of transactions, how they are organized in several institutional frameworks (that is to say how institutions influence contractual relationships at the governance level).
7. There is no agreement regarding the way to appreciate the completeness level of a contract. In Crocker and Masten (1991) and Crocker and Reynolds (1993), the question concerns the completeness level of price provisions. The way to proceed is to consider that 'the most complete contract is one where the price is set initially and invariant to future economic conditions' (Crocker, 1996, p.97). On the other hand, in Saussier (2000a), the question

concerns the completeness level of entire contracts. The way to proceed is to give a new definition of completeness, a feasible completeness compared to the definition of the contract theory. Incompleteness may then appear as 'a solution' more than a problem (Favereau, 1996).

8. This does not mean that other sources of specificity are unimportant. Notably, 'temporal specificity' (Masten *et al.*, 1991; Nickerson, 1999); 'specificity of building and equipment design' can be useful to understand the constraints of work organization (Clipson *et al.*, 1995; Hounshell, 1984), but human asset specificity appears to have a good discriminating power in the analysis of work organization (see Chabaud, 1998, for detailed analysis on the automotive industry).
9. Even with standardized work, it can be observed that workers develop a particular way of doing it (De Terssac, 1992).
10. The origin of this distinction is in Barnard (1938).
11. These data drive from: (1) an international survey of assembly plants, sponsored by MIT's International Motor Vehicle Program (MacDuffie and Pil, 1997), (2) Extensive case studies realized by the 'Groupe d'Etudes et de Recherches Permanent sur l'Industrie et les Salariés de l'Automobile' (GERPISA, permanent group for the study of the automobile industry and its employees), and (3) extensive case studies performed by the author on two European car makers, Renault and Volvo.

BIBLIOGRAPHY

Adler, P.S. (1993), 'The Learning Bureaucracy: New United Motor Manufacturing, Inc.', in L.L. Cummings and B.M. Staw (eds), *Research in Organizational Behavior,* vol. 15, Greenwich, Connecticut: JAI Press, pp. 111–94.

Aoki, M. (1988), *Information, Incentives and Bargaining in Japanese Economy,* Cambridge: Cambridge University Press.

Barnard, C. (1938), *The Function of the Executive*, Cambridge, MA: Harvard University Press.

Bessy, C. (2000), 'L'ancrage institutionnel des échanges économiques: convergences entre la nouvelle économie institutionnelle et l'économie des conventions', mimeo, ATOM.

Chabaud, D. (1998), 'Equipes et coûts de transaction. Une analyse néo-institutionnelle de l'organisation du travail dans l'industrie automobile', thesis, Université de Paris I.

Chabaud, D. (2000), 'Asset specificity, work organization and mode of command: first insights from the automotive industry', in C. Ménard. (ed.), *Institutions, Contracts and Organizations. Perspectives from New Institutional Economics*, Cheltenham, UK and Northampton, MA, USA: Edward Elgar, pp. 349–64.

Clipson, C., J. Steen, A. Törnqvist and P. Ullmark (1995), 'Building for new production concepts', in A. Sandberg (ed.), *Enriching Production. Perspectives on Volvo's Uddevalla Plant as an Alternative to Lean Production,* Aldershot: Avebury, pp. 137–56.

Coase, R.H. (1937), The nature of the firm, Economica, New Series, 4, 386–405.

Coase, R.H. (1993), 'The nature of the firm: influence', in O.E Williamson and S.G. Winter, (eds) *The Nature of the Firm*, Oxford University Press, pp. 61–74.

Coeurderoy, R. and B. Quélin (1997), 'L'économie des coûts de transaction. Un bilan des études empiriques sur l'intégration verticale', *Revue d'économie politique*, 107, 145–81.

Crocker, K.J. (1996), 'Regulatory issues with vertically disintegrated public utilities: a transaction cost analysis', in John Groenewegen (ed.), *Transaction Cost Economics and Beyond*, Amsterdam: Kluwer Academic Press, pp. 85–105.

Crocker, K.J. and S.E. Masten (1988), 'Mitigating contractual hazard: unilateral options and contract length', *Rand Journal of Economics*, 19, 327–43.

Crocker, K.J. and S.E. Masten (1991), 'Pretia ex Machina? Prices and process in long term contracts', *Journal of Law and Economics*, 34, 64–9.

Crocker, K.J. and S.E. Masten (1996), 'Regulation and administered contracts revisited: lessons from transaction-cost economics for public utility regulation', *Journal of Regulatory Economics*, 9, 5–39.

Crocker, K.J. and K.J. Reynolds (1993), 'The efficiency of incomplete contracts: an empirical analysis of air force engine procurement', *Rand Journal of Economics*, 24, 126–46.

De Terssac (1992), *L'autonomie dans le travail*, Paris: Presses universitaires de France.

Fares, M. and S. Saussier (1998), 'Théorie des coûts de transaction et contrats incomplets : où en sommes-nous?', working paper ATOM-Université de Paris I.

Favereau, O. (1996), 'L'incomplétude n'est pas le problème, c'est la solution', in *Limites de la rationalité et constitution du collectif*, Actes du colloque de Cerisy, vol. 2, Paris: La Découverte, pp. 219–35.

Favereau, O. and P. Picard (1996), 'L'approche économique des contrats: unité ou diversité', *Sociologie du travail*, 4, 441–64.

Foss, N.J. (1996), 'Knowledge-based approaches to the theory of the firm: some critical comments', *Organization Science*, 7 (5), 470–76.

Ghoshal, S. and P. Moran (1996), 'Bad for practice: a critique of the transaction cost theory', *The Academy of Management Review*, 21, 13–47.

Grossman, S.J. and O.D Hart (1986), 'The costs and benefits of ownership: a theory of vertical integration', *Journal of Political Economy*, 94, 691–719.

Hart, O.D. (1995), *Firms, Contracts and Financial Structure*, Clarendon Lectures in Economics, Oxford: Oxford University Press.

Hounshell, D.A. (1984), *From the American System to Mass Production, 1800–1932. The Development of Manufacturing Technology in the United States*, Baltimore: John Hopkins University Press.

Joskow, P.L. (1985), 'Vertical integration in long term contracts: the case of coal-burning electric generating plants', *Journal of Law, Economics and Organization*, 33, 33–80.

Joskow, P.L. (1987), 'Contract, duration and relationship-specific investment: empirical evidence from coal markets', *American Economic Review*, 77, 168–85.

Joskow, P.L. (1988), 'Price adjustment in long term contracts: the case of coal', *Journal of Law and Economics*, 31, 47–83.

Klein, P. and H. Shelanski (1995), 'Empirical research in transaction cost economics: a survey and assessment', *Journal of Law, Economic and Organization*, 11, 335–62.

Klein, B., V.P. Crawford and A. Alchian (1978), 'Vertical integration, appropriable quasi-rents and the competitive contracting process', *Journal of Law and Economics*, 21, 297–326.

Koike, K. (1988), *Understanding Industrial Relations in Modern Japan*, London: Macmillan.

MacDuffie, J.P. and F.K. Pil (1997), 'Japanese and Local Influences: Human Resource Practices and Policies of Japanese Transplants in North America', 5th international meeting of GERPISA, June, Paris, 253–69.

Masten, S.E. (1986), 'Institutional choice and the organization of production: the make or buy decision', *Journal of Institutional and Theoretical Economics*, 142, 493–509.

Masten, S.E. (1988), 'A legal basis for the firm', *Journal of Law, Economics and Organization*, 4, 181–98.
Masten, S.E. (1993), 'Transaction costs, mistakes, and performance: assessing the importance of governance', *Managerial and Decision Economics,* 14, 119–29.
Masten, S.E. (1995), 'Empirical research in transaction-cost economics: challenges, progress, directions', in John Groenewegen (ed.), *Transaction Cost Economics and Beyond*, Amsterdam: Kluwer Academic Press.
Masten, S.E. (2000), 'Contractual choices', in B. Boukaert and G. De Geest (eds), *Encyclopedia of Law & Economics*, Cheltenham, UK and Northampton, MA, USA: Edward Elgar Publishing and the University of Ghent.
Masten, S.E. and K.J. Crocker (1985), 'Efficient adaptation in long term contracts: take-or-pay provisions for natural gas', *American Economic Review*, 75, 1083–93.
Masten, S.E. and S. Saussier (2000), 'Econometrics of contracts: an assessment of developments in the empirical literature of contracting', *Revue d'Économie Industrielle*, June.
Masten, S.E., J.W. Meehan and E.A. Snyder (1991), 'Costs of organization', *Journal of Law, Economics and Organization,* 7, 1–27.
Ménard, C. (1994), 'Organizations as coordinating devices', *Metroeconomica,* 45 (3), 224–47.
Ménard, C. (1995), 'Inside the black box: the variety of hierarchical forms', in J. Groenowegen (ed.), *Transaction Cost Economics and Beyond,* Amsterdam: Kluwer Academic Press, pp. 149–71.
Ménard, C. (1997), Internal characteristics of formal organizations, in C. Ménard (ed.), *Transaction Cost Economics: Recent Developments*, Cheltenham, UK and Lyme, US: Edward Elgar.
Ménard, C. (2000), 'The enforcement of contractual arrangements', C. Ménard (ed.), *Institutions, Contracts and Organizations. Perspectives from New Institutional Economics*, Cheltenham, UK and Northampton, MA, USA: pp. 234–54.
Mulherin, J.H. (1986), 'Complexity in long term contracts: an analysis of natural gas contract provisions', *Journal of Law, Economics and Organization,* 2, 105–17.
Nickerson, J.A. (1999), 'Teams and the organization of work in the garment industry – refining, extending and applying the governance framework', working paper, Washington University, St Louis, MO.
North, D.C. (1990), *Institutions, Institutional Change and Economic Performance*, Cambridge: Cambridge University Press.
Pfeffer, J. (1994), *Competitive Advantage Through People. Unleashing the Power of the Work Force,* Boston: Harvard Business School Press.
Riordan, M.H. and O.E. Williamson (1985), 'Asset specificity and economic organization', *International Journal of Industrial Organization*, 3, 365–78.
Saussier, S. (1999), 'Transaction cost economics and contract duration: an empirical analysis of EDF coal contracts', *Louvain Economic Review,* 65 (1), 3–21.
Saussier, S. (2000a), 'Transaction cost economics and contractual completeness', *Journal of Economic Behavior and Organization,* 62 (2), 189–206.
Saussier, S. (2000b), 'When incomplete contract theory meets transaction cost theory: a test', in C. Ménard (ed.), *Institutions, Contracts and Organizations. Perspectives from New Institutional Economics*, Cheltenham, UK and Northampton, MA, USA: pp. 376–99.
Simon, H. (1951), 'A formal theory of the employment relationship', *Econometrica*, 19, 293–305.

Suzuki, Yoshitaka (1991), *Japanese Management Structures, 1920–80*, London: Macmillan.
Williamson, O.E. (1975), *Markets and Hierarchies: Analysis and Antitrust Implications – A Study in the Economics of Internal Organization*, New York: Free Press.
Williamson, O.E. (1980), 'The organization of work. A comparative institutional assessment', *Journal of Economic Behavior and Organization,* 1, 5–38.
Williamson, O.E. (1985), *The Economic Institutions of Capitalism*, New York: Free Press.
Williamson, O.E. (1990), 'Chester Barnard and the incipient science of organization', in O. E. Williamson (ed.), *Organization Theory: From Chester Barnard to the Present and Beyond*, New York: Oxford University Press, pp. 172–206.
Williamson, O.E. (1991), 'Comparative economic organization: the analysis of discrete structure alternatives', *Administrative Science Quarterly*, 36, 269–96.
Williamson, O.E. (1993), 'The economic analysis of institutions and organisations in general and with respect to country studies', Working paper no. 133, OECD.
Williamson, O.E. (1996), *The Mechanisms of Governance*, Oxford: Oxford University Press.
Williamson, O.E. (1998), 'Human Actors and Economic Organization', 2nd Annual Conference of The International Society for New Institutional Economics, Paris, September.
Williamson, O.E. and J. Bercovitz (1994), 'The Modern Corporation as an Efficiency Instrument: The Comparative Contracting Perspective', mimeo, University of California, Berkeley.
Williamson, O.E. and W.G Ouch (1981), 'The markets and hierarchies program of research: origins, implications, prospects', in A.H. Van de Ven and W.F. Joyce (eds), *Perspectives on Organization Design and Behavior*, New York: John Wiley & Sons, pp. 347–71.
Williamson, O.E., M.L. Wachler and J.E. Harris (1975), 'Understanding the employment relationship: the analysis of idiosyncratic exchange', *Bell Journal of Economics,* 6 (1), 250–78.

5. Organizational ecology

David N. Barron

INTRODUCTION

Reviews of organizational ecology usually start by making reference to Hannan and Freeman's (1977) now famous article.[1] Along with work published around the same time by authors such as Aldrich (1979) and McKelvey (1982), this article was the foundation for the large body of research that has developed over the past 20 years or so. The central question posed by Hannan and Freeman (1977) was 'Why are there so many kinds of organizations?' Although little, if any, empirical research has sought to answer this question directly, ecologists are always concerned with explaining how 'social, economic, and political conditions affect the relative abundance and diversity of organizations and attempt to account for their changing composition over time' (Baum, 1996, p.77). To this end, most empirical research in this tradition has concentrated on explaining the rates at which new organizations are founded and/or the rate at which existing organizations disband, a sub-branch of organizational ecology that is sometimes called *organizational demography* (Carroll and Hannan, 2000). The other main sub-branch of the field has been concerned with changes in individual organizations. This sub-branch has developed out of the work of another American sociologist, Miller McPherson (1983). Recently, a few scholars have been attempting to combine some of the features of these two sub-branches of ecological research.

The encapsulation of the concerns of ecological researchers quoted above summarizes some of the key characteristics of ecological research. First, it is concerned with the effect of the *environment* on organizations. In this sense, it is an example of what Scott (1992) calls an open systems theory. Second, it seeks to explain characteristics of *collections* of organizations: populations and communities.[2] Third, it is explicitly concerned with the dynamics of these collections of organizations. In this chapter I will discuss each of the two main categories of ecological research in turn. I will then discuss a number of studies that have attempted to combine some of the insights of ecological theory with those of structural analyses of markets.

ORGANIZATIONAL DEMOGRAPHY

This is the largest category of ecological research. It is concerned with understanding entry into and exit from populations of organizations. A few studies have also looked at rates of growth of organizations. These processes are clearly of fundamental importance if one is interested in understanding organizational diversity. A striking regularity has emerged in the course of 20 years of ecological research (and also in recent work in evolutionary economics). The regularity is in the trajectory followed by the number of organizations in a population. The numbers start small, and grow slowly at first but at an accelerating rate. Growth in numbers slows again, reaching a peak and then declining. In some cases, the decline has been reversed in recent years. However, the decline in numbers is not a result of the organizations becoming less successful in any simple sense, because if one also collects data on some measure of the scale of the organizations' activities, this typically continues to increase long after the decline in the number of organizations. Figure 5.1 shows a typical example: labour unions in the United States. One of the important things

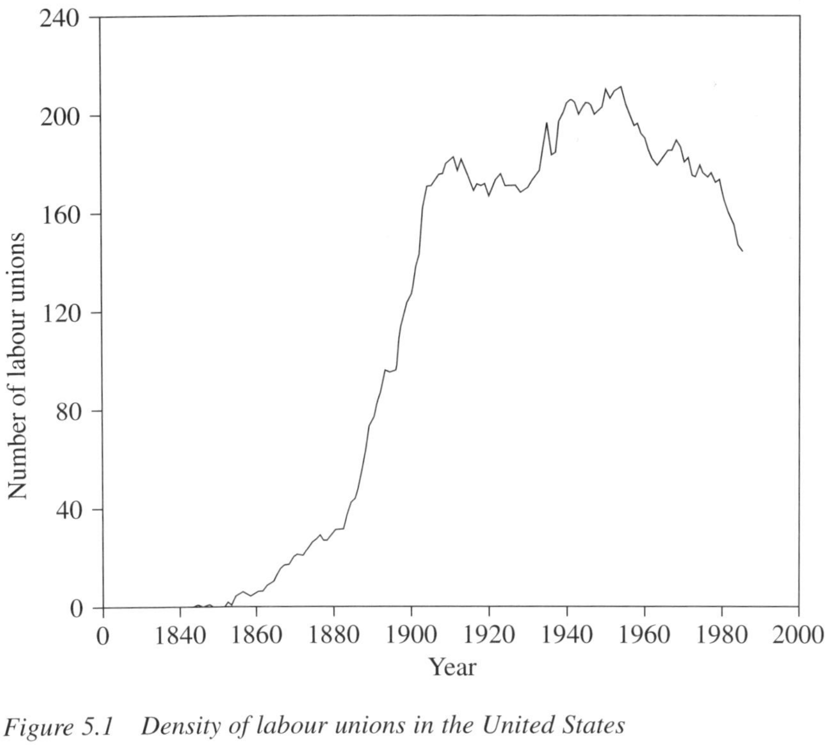

Figure 5.1 Density of labour unions in the United States

to note is that a very diverse set of organizations have been found to follow this path, including manufacturing, service and non-profit organizations as well as labour unions. This implies that a very general mechanism could be operating – more general, for example, than is provided by the industry life cycle model recently developed by some evolutionary economists (Gort and Klepper 1982; Klepper, 1996, 1997).

One model has been used to explain founding, failure and growth rates: the density-dependence model. I will discuss this first, followed by other models that use characteristics of the population as an explanatory variable. Failure and growth models can also take into account characteristics of individual organizations; I shall discuss these next. Finally, I will discuss models that rely on other characteristics of the environment for their explanatory power.

DENSITY-DEPENDENCE

The density-dependence model has become so important that it is sometimes mistakenly thought that density-dependence is population ecology. However, the model was first reported in Hannan (1986), and the first empirical study that used it was published in Hannan and Freeman (1987). Density is defined simply as the number of organizations in a population. The density-dependence model uses functions of density to explain founding, failure and growth rates. Density has this effect via its relationship to two important variables: legitimacy and competition.

Legitimacy

One of the important and distinctive features of organizational ecology research has been the extent to which it has become linked to institutional theory. It is important to re-emphasize that the institutional theory of organizations is completely different from institutional economics. In particular, it is not a rational-action theory. The roots of the institutional theory of organizations are important articles by Meyer and Rowan (1977) and DiMaggio and Powell (1983). The essence of their work is that organizations enhance their survival chances if they are able to achieve legitimacy.

It is important to distinguish three forms of legitimacy that are often conflated in the organizational literature. Following Suchman (1995), I call these three forms *pragmatic*, *moral* and *cognitive* legitimacy, respectively (Barron, 1998b). Pragmatic legitimacy 'rests on the self-interested calculations of an organization's most immediate audiences' (Suchman, 1995, p. 578). Potential members, customers or sponsors of an organization must believe that such an involvement will be in their interests. Moral legitimacy 'reflects a positive normative evaluation of the organization and its activities' (ibid., p. 579). This is perhaps the definition of legitimacy that is closest to its meaning in common usage. However, ecologists have stressed that moral acceptability is not necessary for an organizational form to be legitimate in other ways.

Most ecological research has concentrated on the third form: *cognitive legitimacy*. An organizational form that is legitimate in this sense is taken for granted as the natural way of structuring some type of collective action (Hannan and Freeman, 1989; Meyer and Rowan, 1977). This does not imply any evaluation either of pragmatic interest or of moral acceptability (Jepperson, 1991). Taken-for-grantedness can be considered an 'end point' of a process of legitimation, when enough (most) people both know about an organizational form and accept it as a natural way of achieving some end. The legitimation process is viewed as the spread of knowledge and beliefs through a certain set of actors.

I argue that, if an organizational form gains any or all of these types of legitimacy, this will affect rates of founding, failure and growth of organizations with that form. Other things being equal, gaining legitimacy means that foundings will be more numerous, risk of failure will decline and rates of organizational growth will increase. I also argue that it is possible for organizations to act so as to increase their legitimacy. Individual organizations within a population, or representatives and sponsors, can attempt to enhance their pragmatic, moral and cognitive legitimacy. At the same time, legitimacy is also affected by factors that are beyond the control of 'institutional entrepreneurs'. One of the difficulties that researchers have to deal with when wanting to test hypotheses about the effects of legitimacy on the vital rates of organizations is how to measure it. Indeed, much of the debate that has taken place about the use of legitimacy in ecological models has centred on the measurement issue, particularly with respect to the use of one particular variable: population density (Zucker, 1989).

The link between density and cognitive legitimacy is straightforward. Hannan (1989) argues that an organizational form cannot be taken for granted as the natural way to effect some kind of collective action when it is very rare. Therefore, when density is low, legitimacy will also be low. Increasing numbers of organizations, however, will raise people's awareness of the existence of the organizational form. Therefore there should be a positive association between density and the legitimacy of an organizational form. Hannan's density-dependence model also assumes that there is a ceiling on this effect: legitimation is a process or a variable rather than a state, but it cannot go on increasing for ever. The final step in the the density-dependence model, as it applies to legitimacy, is to posit an association between the degree of legitimacy of an organizational form and the rate at which new organizations are created and existing organizations leave the population. Increasing legitimacy is expected to make it easier for organizations to obtain the resources they need to thrive: skilled employees, customers, members, contracts, government approval, and so on. This is expected to raise founding rates and lower failure rates, always subject to the ceiling on the effect. There are a number of different functional forms that could be used to model this relationship. The most common is:

$$
\begin{array}{ll}
 L_{\mathrm{t}} & \lambda_t \, \alpha \, L_t; \\
L_{\mathrm{t}} = \mathrm{N}_{\mathrm{t}}^{\alpha} & 0 < \alpha < 1,
\end{array}
\qquad (5.1)
$$

where λ_t is the founding rate at time t, L_t is legitimacy, and N_t is density. Models for failure and growth rates can easily be developed by analogy.

Competition

Competition is one of the most important environmental factors that affects both organizational demography and organizational attributes. Observing competition between organizational populations directly usually proves to be difficult because competitive influences are often indirect and diffuse. Hence empirically-minded analysts look for ways to study competition indirectly. Concentrating on the relationship between density and competition as a way to do so makes sense because the intensity of competition depends both on the degree of intersection of fundamental niches and on the *numbers* of competitors involved. Even when two populations in the same system have intersecting fundamental niches,[3] they presumably do not compete intensely if their numbers are very small (relative to the abundance of resources). Mathematical models of ecological competition represent abundance as a scalar 'carrying capacity' of the environment for a population. This term refers to the numbers that can be sustained in a particular environment in isolation from other populations. A useful way to formalize the concept of competition builds on the idea that the presence of a competitor in the system lowers the carrying capacity for the focal population.

To this point we have considered *inter*-population competition. The density-dependence model also applies to *intra*-population competition – processes of competition within populations of organizations. This focus greatly simplifies the problem of identifying competition because one can safely assume that members of the same population have (very nearly) the same fundamental niche. It follows that members of a population compete in the sense that the life chances of any one organization depends on the number of other organizations in the system.

According to the theory, adding an organization to the population has only a slight effect on the frequency and strength of competitive interactions when density is low relative to abundance of resources. But when density is high, adding an organization strongly increases competition. In other words, the qualitative implication is that *density* (N) *increases competition (C) at an increasing rate*:

$$\frac{dC}{dN} > 0 \text{ and } \frac{dC^2}{d^2N} > 0. \tag{5.2}$$

The literature on density dependence and competition has assumed an exponential relation between competition and the square of density:

$$C(t) = c_t \exp(bN_t^2), \quad b > 0, \tag{5.3}$$

where c_t represents the effects of factors other than density that affect levels of competition. Choice of an exponential relationship rather than a simple linear relationship between competition and the square of density reflects the definition of a rate as non-negative. As far can be determined from empirical research, this choice of specification does a reasonably good job of representing density dependence in the vital rates.

One possible motivation for the specification in equation (5.3) comes from considering the net of possible ties among actors in a population. Suppose that the level of (indirect) competitive pressure is proportional to the number of pairs that can be formed:

$$\left(\frac{N}{2}\right) = \frac{N^2}{2} - \frac{N}{2}.$$

As population size grows large, the squared term dominates, so that the number of pairs is approximately $N^2/2$. Thus the specification in (5.3) can be considered an approximation to a model in which the strength of intra-population competition is proportional to the number of possible pairwise interactions (with the accuracy of the approximation improving as density increases, meaning that N^2 dominates N). This interpretation deserves attention because it can serve as a point of departure for integrating ecological and network conceptions of interaction and competition.

The model I have presented applies to founding rates, but the underlying theory is just as applicable to rates of organizational failure and growth. Increasing legitimacy is expected to reduce failure rates and cause growth rates to rise. Higher density should raise the risk of failure and lower growth rates. It is straightforward to derive the analogous functional forms for the relationship between density and failure and growth rates.

ELABORATIONS OF DENSITY DEPENDENCE

Other Forms of Legitimacy

We have already seen that density can be thought of as affecting only one form of legitimacy. If this is expected to increase founding and growth rates and reduce failure rates, it is logical to expect that other forms of legitimacy will have the same effect. There have been a number of studies now that have measured legitimacy in other ways. For example, Baum and Oliver (1992) argue that legitimacy is increased by relationships between an organization and community organizations and government agencies. Barron (1998b) found evidence that moral legitimacy was affected by social movement-like activity and mass media attention, while pragmatic and cognitive legitimacy were spread via the social networks of organizational members.

Other Forms of Competition

Size-localized competition

Density-dependent competition has an important characteristic: each additional member of the population increases the total amount of competition experienced by all other members of the population by the same amount. Several authors have questioned the validity of this. For example, the size-localized competition model suggested by Hannan and Freeman (1977) and developed by Hannan *et al.* (1990), Baum and Mezias (1992), and Ranger-Moore *et al.* (1995) suggests instead that organizations compete most strongly with those that are closest to themselves in size. This argument is related to the resource partitioning model, one interpretation of which is that large, dominant organizations compete more strongly amongst themselves than they do with small, peripheral competitors. The model rests on the assumption that organizations of different sizes will often depend on different resources. According to Carroll, when populations become highly concentrated, this implies that there are a small number of dominant organizations competing among themselves for market share. This may lead them to neglect relatively peripheral resources in their niche. For example, major construction companies are not generally thought to compete for business with local building firms. Carroll argues that high concentration actually increases the founding rate and reduces the failure rate of small, specialized organizations. So density decline associated with increasing concentration can be reversed. The best evidence for this phenomenon so far comes from studies of wineries and breweries (Carroll, 1985; Carroll and Swaminathan, 1992).

An important implication of the size-localized competition model is that size distributions should evolve so as to become bimodal. This is because medium-sized organizations will suffer competition from both small, specialist organizations and from large, generalist organizations. Thus medium-sized organizations will have a higher failure rate than small and large organizations in the same population.

Density delay

Carroll and Hannan (1989) proposed a model in which an organization's risk of failure was affected not only by (time-varying) contemporaneous density but also by the (time-invariant) density at the time an organization was founded. The motivation behind the development of this model was the realization that the density-dependence model could not explain why density often declines from its peak. They reasoned that organizations founded when density was high would face a more challenging environment than those founded when density was low. High density is associated with high competition, and so organizations starting out under such conditions would find it harder to attract the resources needed to operate. They would tend to be forced far from the centre of the population's niche, causing lasting problems for such organizations, significantly and permanently reducing their life chances.

The density delay model can clearly only be applied to analyses of an organization-level process such as failure and growth. It cannot be used as an explanatory variable in models of population-level processes such as founding. This is the fundamental reason why density delay on its own cannot in fact explain a permanent decline in population density. It is easy to see that density delay could result in density declining from a peak, as organizations founded at peak density will have a high rate of failure. In fact, the average failure probability of the organizations in a population will rise as density rises, other things being equal. The consequent rise in the failure rate will reduce density. However, this reduction in density in turn reduces the intensity of competition in the population, allowing the founding rate to rise. Furthermore, these newly founded organizations are created when density is relatively low, reducing their risk of failure. Consequently, density will rise again. This pattern will then be repeated indefinitely. Computer simulations reported by Hannan and Carroll (1992) reveal just such a cyclical pattern. So density delay on its own cannot explain density decline.

Mass dependence

Barnett and Amburgy (1990) suggested that large organizations generate stronger competitive forces than small organizations. Larger organizations, they reason, can benefit from economies of scale and scope, greater market power and easier access to resources. They test this idea using the aggregate size of the population as an independent variable in analyses of founding and failure rates of telephone companies. Their model implies that, as mass increases, founding rates should fall while failure rates should rise.

Support for the mass dependence hypothesis has been relatively weak. Barnett and Amburgy (1990) obtained estimated effects of mass in the opposite direction from those they predicted. Hannan and Carroll (1992) report no statistically significant effects of mass in the several populations they studied. Baum and Mezias (1992) and Baum (1995) found mass-dependent competitive effects in analyses of failures of Manhattan hotels. However, they did not find the expected pattern of *density*-dependent competition. Barnett (1997, p. 135) argues that the weak evidence for mass dependence results from a 'failure to think about organizational size in an evolutionary way'. His interpretation is that large organizations may be less likely to fail, as much evidence shows (see, for example, Barron *et al.*, (1994)), but this does not necessarily mean that they are stronger competitors. If they are not, then increasing mass does not necessarily increase the intensity of competition experienced by the members of the population. Barnett's (1997) argument is that the 'fitness' of large organizations is the average of the fitness of their subunits. Since subunits with low fitness will be protected by their membership of a large organization, rather than being forced out of business as they would be if they were stand-alone organizations, the average fitness of large organizations is likely to be lower (after selection has taken its toll) than that of small organizations. Consequently, *smaller* organizations will provide the stiffest competition.

There are a number of problems with this model, however. First, not all populations contain the sort of highly differentiated organizations that are implied by the model. Second, Barnett implies that the model works for large organizations that are multi-product or vertically differentiated, performing functions in-house 'which might otherwise be outsourced by small organizations'. However, this begs a number of questions. For example, Barnett implies that small organizations can achieve some maximum level of fitness, which large organizations can only hope to match (never exceed) in the unlikely event that all their subunits are individually also optimally fit.[4] For it to be true that a large, differentiated firm can never exceed the fitness of a smaller, specialized competitor there must be no economies of scale or scope (or, at least, these must become insignificant at a level below that of the size of the largest unitary firm). This may be true in some industries, but how widespread is this likely to be?

Can mass-dependent founding and failure rates explain density decline? The evidence is inconclusive. It is clearly impossible to draw any conclusions from those studies that analyse only failure rates. If mass-dependent competition does not also depress founding rates, then, as density declines, the founding rate will increase as a result of the reduction in density-dependent competition, leading to the sort of cycles that we have previously seen result from density delay. Unfortunately, none of the authors who have studied both vital rates found evidence of mass-dependent competition, so it is not possible to analyse specific results. Nevertheless, we can make some general points about the impact of mass dependence on the evolution of density if increasing mass does indeed generate higher competition.

Consider what would happen in a population that did experience both density-dependent and mass-dependent competition. If the mass of a population continues to rise as density reaches its peak, then it must follow that the organizations are getting larger. If large organizations do generate stronger competition, then the overall strength of the competitive forces experienced by population members (the sum of density-dependent and mass-dependent competition) will increase. We would therefore expect that the failure rate will rise and the founding rate will fall. This would result in a decline in density. However, such a decline would produce a reduction in density-dependent competition, reducing the failure rate and allowing the founding rate to increase. This seems to imply that the population density would again cycle around an equilibrium level rather than experience a sustained decline. However, if mass continued to increase, this might produce an increase in mass-dependent competition that outweighs the decline in density-dependent competition. The actual implications for density would, therefore, depend on the relative strength of density–dependent and mass-dependent competition *and on the evolution of population mass*. Conceivably, then, mass-dependent competition could explain why density declines while mass continues to increase. However, empirical studies have failed to find combinations of density and mass dependency that are consistent with such an explanation.

Niche overlap

Studies such as those by Baum and Mezias (1992) into Manhattan hotels and by Baum and Singh into children's day nurseries (Baum and Singh, 1994a, 1994b, 1996) have investigated how organizational founding and failure rates respond to competition, with competition being a function of how closely substitutable organizations are for each other from the point of view of customers. In a sense, this is a more sophisticated version of size-localized competition, since size is used as a proxy for the segment of the market a firm serves, while niche overlap models attempt to measure this directly. The essence of these models is that the 'contribution' of an organization to the strength of competition experienced by a firm is weighted by the extent to which their niches overlap. In the most recent of their series of articles, Baum and Singh (1996) also studied how organizational niches change in response to competition. Interestingly, they were able to measure an organization's *fundamental* niche, in that their measures were the age groups to which each nursery was licensed to offer places. They were able to show that organizations' niches do respond by contracting or expanding in response to competition. However, they did not distinguish between these two possible outcomes: they did not develop ideas about when organizations' niches are likely to become narrower (more specialized) and when they are likely to become wider (more generalized). This a theme to which we will return when we discuss ecological models of organizational change.

Environmental Variation

The final category of research into organizational demography that I would like to discuss is that which investigates the role of environmental variation. For example, Freeman and Hannan (1983) focus on two aspects of environmental variation: variability and grain. Variability refers to the variance of environmental fluctuations about their mean over time. Fine-grained variation implies that this variance consists of many, small, rapid changes. Coarse-grained variation, on the other hand, consists of long but large variations. Making the assumption that environmental variations are large relative to the organizations' ability to adapt to them, Hannan and Freeman (1989) made predictions about the relative ability of generalist and specialist organizations to survive different types of environmental variability. These are summarized in Table 5.1.

The intuition behind these predictions is as follows. Specialists are always favoured when grain is fine, because they can survive the short periods over which the environment is not favourable to them. The variability of the environment is, therefore, not a significant factor. When the grain is coarse, however, generalists are favoured when variability is high because it is necessary to have a reasonable degree of fit to whatever environmental conditions are likely to be encountered, as these conditions are likely to persist for a relatively long time. Specialists are still favoured when variability is low,

Table 5.1 Niche width theory predictions of relative fitness of specialists and generalists

	High variability	Low variability
Coarse grain	Generalist	Specialist
Fine grain	Specialist	Specialist

Source: Adapted from Hannan and Freeman (1989, p. 311).

however. Hannan and Freeman (1989) tested these ideas in an empirical study of the failure rates of restaurants, in which they were supported.

POPULATION DYNAMICS

I began the section on organizational demography by pointing to empirical regularities in the trajectories followed by density and mass in many organizational populations. It is important to point out that the density-dependence model cannot explain this pattern. On its own, the density dependence model predicts that density will follow an S-shaped trajectory. That is, it can account for the rise of a population to a peak, but not its subsequent decline. The density delay model was introduced partly in response to this weakness, but, because it cannot affect founding rates, it cannot fully explain the phenomenon. We have seen that mass dependence is also a weak explanation. Recent efforts to explain this phenomenon that seem to hold out the most promise have been proposed by Hannan (1997) and Barron (1999).

Hannan's (1997) model implies that density becomes 'decoupled' from legitimacy and competition as a population matures. Legitimacy is relatively stable, and not easily eroded even if the population density declines. Competition also becomes decoupled as organizations become more fixed into networks of alliances, develop specialization, and so on. In other words, the population becomes more 'structured' as it gets more mature.

The latter hypothesis is particularly interesting. In fact, we know very little about the dynamics of this kind of structure, and this is a subject ripe for research. Hannan's (1997) model works in the sense that declining density no longer reduces competition, and so does not allow founding rates to rise. However, it is not clear why the elimination of an organization does not reduce competition, notwithstanding the structuredness of the population. More direct evidence in needed.

Barron's (1999) model is unique in addressing organizational founding, failure *and growth*. It is thus uniquely placed to explain both decline in density and increase in mass. He found evidence that increasing competitive intensity does not have the same impact on all organizations in a population. Rather, organizations that have some sort of survival advantage – in this case scale – gradually come to predominate in the population. Although any source of advantage would operate in the same way, scale is particularly important. This is partly because the liability of smallness is so common, but also because, once the process has started, it may become self-accelerating. Surviving organizations may be able to take over the resources previously utilized by failed organizations, growing still more, and so increasing their survival advantage.

ORGANIZATIONAL CHANGE

Niche Overlap

Two possible ways by which competition can affect the niches of organizations are shown in Figures 5.2 and 5.3. In 5.2(a), the niches have a large overlap; these populations are attempting to obtain very similar resources. This implies that competition will be very strong between these populations. A possible result of this competition is that the niches of the two populations move apart. This might be because the organizations that exist in the shaded overlap region are more likely to fail because of the greater difficulty they have in obtaining resources. The result is that the mean of the niches moves apart, reducing the amount of overlap, as shown in Figure 5.2(b).

A model that relies on this type of process has been developed by McPherson and his colleagues to explain the dynamics of voluntary associations (McPherson, 1983; McPherson and Ranger-Moore, 1991). In developing his theory, McPherson made the important assumption that the concept of the niche could be applied to individual organizations as well as to populations. This seems reasonable as an organization has a set of resource requirements, and it will fail if these requirements are not met. Furthermore, the image of niche overlap describing the intensity of competition also has an intuitive appeal.

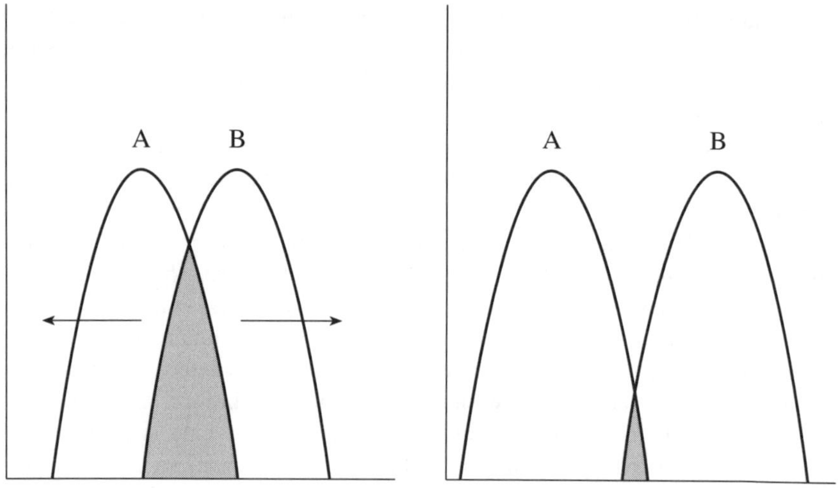

(a) Intense competition (b) Weak competition

Figure 5.2 Competition affecting niche position

In his work on the dynamics of voluntary associations, McPherson argued that organizations would tend to lose members more rapidly in areas of overlap, and would also find it harder to attract new recruits from these regions. New members would be more likely to come from the side of the niche where there was no competition, and the organization would also be more likely to hang on to its existing members in these regions. If the *x* axis in Figure 5.2 represents, say, the ages of organizational members, McPherson would expect that the proportion of middle-aged members of both organizations would fall, while the proportion of young members of organization A should increase, as should the proportion of old members of organization B.

McPherson's model is more complex than this, however, in that he also takes into account how the exploitation of resources in different regions of social space deviates from the *carrying capacity* of the environment. For McPherson, the carrying capacity is constant over time; it represents the average potential resource available to organizations. Actual resource use may deviate from this carrying capacity in the short term, and this creates a *landscape* of hills, representing regions of social space that are over-exploited, and valleys, where resources are relatively abundant. Other things being equal, McPherson expects organizations to move 'down hill'. Differentiation will result if the landscape contains more than one valley. It is worth noting that this model also explains why there are limits to differentiation (the number of valleys) and why it is difficult for organizations to change from one form to another (they would have to get over a hill to reach a different valley).

Figure 5.3 shows another possible outcome of competition. Instead of the niches shifting away from each other, but staying the same width, in this case the means of the niches remain the same, but they become narrower. The result is, however, the same: the overlap between the two niches is greatly reduced. In this case, organizations respond to competition by becoming more specialized. They consume a narrow range of resources, but probably make more efficient use of them. This is essentially the division of labour model. Not only is competition reduced by specialization, but the person who concentrates on a single occupation probably does it better than a jack-of-all-trades.

These figures also illustrate another important concept: the distinction between a *realized niche* and a *fundamental niche*. The latter is the niche that an organization would occupy in the absence of any competition from other organizations. Fundamental niches are shown in Figures 5.2(a) and 5.3(a). As we have seen, though, competition can affect the niche of an organization. The niches that we actually observe, therefore, are usually realized niches, as shown in Figures 5.2(b) and 5.3(b).

An implication of the effects of competition on niches is that an apparent lack of overlap between two organizations' niches may in fact be the outcome

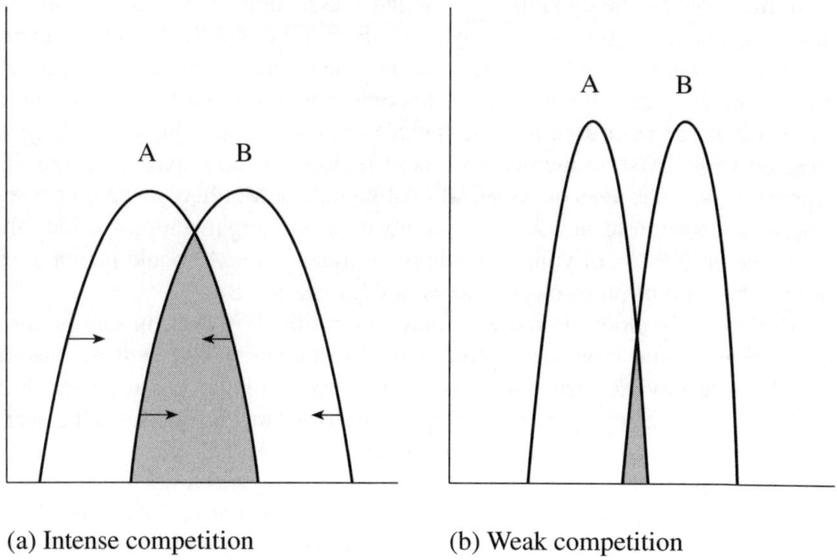

Figure 5.3 Competition affecting niche width

of intense competition at an earlier time. This is one of the reasons why competition is notoriously difficult to observe. The solution to this problem is to observe organizations over time. By this means it is possible to see how organizations respond to changes in the level of competition.

Apart from McPherson's work, there have been several other studies that have used similar concepts. A recent study by Barron (1998a) found good evidence that newspapers and magazines respond to increasingly intense competition by differentiating themselves from their competitors. That is, there is good evidence that niche positions shift in response to fluctuations in the level of competition (Figure 5.2). Less clear-cut was the impact of changes in the carrying capacity on the degree of specialization. It is possible that this is due to opposing effects of resource abundance. On the one hand, an increase in the carrying capacity might reduce the impact of niche overlap, so tending to reduce the pressure to become more specialized. On the other hand, it might make specialist organizations more viable. These two opposing effects might tend to cancel each other out. In addition, there is an important interplay between specialization and size. Relatively specialist organizations tend to be smaller than more generalist competitors, but we know that large organizations have a much lower risk of failure than do small organizations, an advantage that tends to increase as competition becomes more intense (Barron, 1999; Barron *et al.*, 1994). So, while increasing competition might, other things being equal, tend to increase specialization, the better survival rate of larger generalists might outweigh this effect.

Inertia

Ecological theory has often been criticized as being deterministic. This criticism stems in part from a misunderstanding of the statistical models that are used. More important, though, is the status of the 'structural inertia' theory proposed by Hannan and Freeman (1984). They argued that, contrary to conventional wisdom, managers often find it very difficult to achieve change, and certainly find it difficult to change their core operations quickly and accurately enough to be said to be adapting to changes in their environment. More radically, they argue that organizations need to develop a degree of inertia, because it is only by increasing reliability of performance that they can survive. So organizations are caught in a bind, short-term survival requiring that they develop in such a way that their long-term survival may well be jeopardized. To some critics, this leaves managers helpless to affect the performance of their firms. Ecologists, however, generally argue that individual efforts at adaptive change are possible, but ecological theory does suggest that change in the *core structure* of a firm will be very difficult to achieve. Even when such fundamental change is realized, it is unlikely that it will turn out to be adaptive, given the difficulty of predicting the future demands of the environment and the full consequences (including the unintended ones) of change. So ecologists generally view their approach as providing a useful corrective to standard, overoptimistic accounts of management.

ECOLOGY AND STRUCTURAL ANALYSIS

In this section, we will explore four areas where ecological and structural theories have been drawn together: (1) the use of network concepts and data to define and identify population niches (and hence organizational forms) (Burt 1992; Burt and Talmud, 1993); (2) the diffusion of organizational forms via social networks (Barron, 1998b); (3) the role played by networks in organizational dynamics (McPherson and Ranger-Moore, 1991); (4) technology networks and organizational niches (Podolny *et al.*, 1996).

Networks and Niches

An important point of contact between network theory and organizational ecology is the concepts of the *niche* and *organizational form*. DiMaggio (1986) was the first to point out that the social network theory concept of structural equivalence could be used to define sets of organizations occupying what ecologists would call a niche. This idea was developed by Burt and Talmud (1993) and Burt (1992, pp. 208–27).

The bio-ecological roots of the concept of the niche most commonly used by organizational ecologists can be found in the pioneering work of Hutchinson (1957). He conceived of populations existing in an environment consisting of an N-dimensional space, with each dimension being some environmental condition relevant to the survival and reproduction of the members of the population. Each point in this space then defines a unique set of environmental conditions, though of course only a small subset of them may actually occur. The *fundamental niche* of a population can then be defined as a 'hypervolume formed by the set of points [the set of environmental conditions] for which the population's growth rate (fitness) is non-negative'.

The extension of the concept to organizations is straightforward. Like plants and animals, organizations require resources from their environments to survive. Classical organizational theorists such as Max Weber explain the rise of large classes of organization, such as rational-legal bureaucracy, in terms of environmental conditions like the availability of literate employees, implicitly recognizing the relationship between resources in the environment and the development of organizational forms. However, most organizational research does not operate at such a general level of analysis. More typically, researchers are interested in specific types of organization, such as labour unions, banks or car manufacturers. How can we define the niches of organizational forms like these? The ecological approach is summarized by Hannan and Freeman (1989, p. 96):

> Specifying the niche of an organizational form requires intensive analysis of its natural history. Learning about the social, economic, and political conditions required to sustain a form of organization requires study of the details of the organizational form and the functioning of organizations that embody it. In fact the concept of the fundamental niche of a form provides a felicitous device for incorporating institutional knowledge about kinds of organizations into systematic theory about population dynamics and evolution. It fits well with the actual practice of social scientists and others who provide detailed accounts of the functioning of various kinds of organizations.

It is worth repeating that such an approach would not identify the *fundamental* niche of an organizational form (see note 3). The fundamental niche is a theoretical concept; it is the region of resource space that a population would occupy in the absence of any competition for resources from other populations. In practice, all populations do compete for resources, and so they occupy a smaller region of resource space than that in which they could, theoretically, survive. This smaller region is the *realized niche*: the actually occurring set of environmental conditions in which an organizational form survives in the face of competition from other organizational forms.

The problem with this approach to identifying a population's niche is that it relies on a procedure that appears to be essentially ad hoc. Each population's niche is identified on the basis of whatever seems appropriate for that organizational form. In the case of car manufacturers, for example, members of the population are identified primarily on the basis of what products they manufacture. There are, however, grey areas where the boundaries are unclear. Some sorts of light trucks could be considered cars, but how heavy does a truck have to be to no longer count as a car? Should makers of small numbers of hand-built vehicles be counted as part of the same population as mass producers?

Network theorists have proposed a method of identifying a niche that seems to get round at least some of these problems. The basis of the network approach is the claim that all the organizations that occupy a niche are *structurally equivalent*. Structural equivalence is an important network concept; two positions in a network are structurally equivalent to the extent that they have an identical pattern of ties to the same set of alters. For example, a husband and wife will be structurally equivalent if they have exactly the same set of friends.

Figure 5.4 shows a producer with ties to the first, fourth and last resource

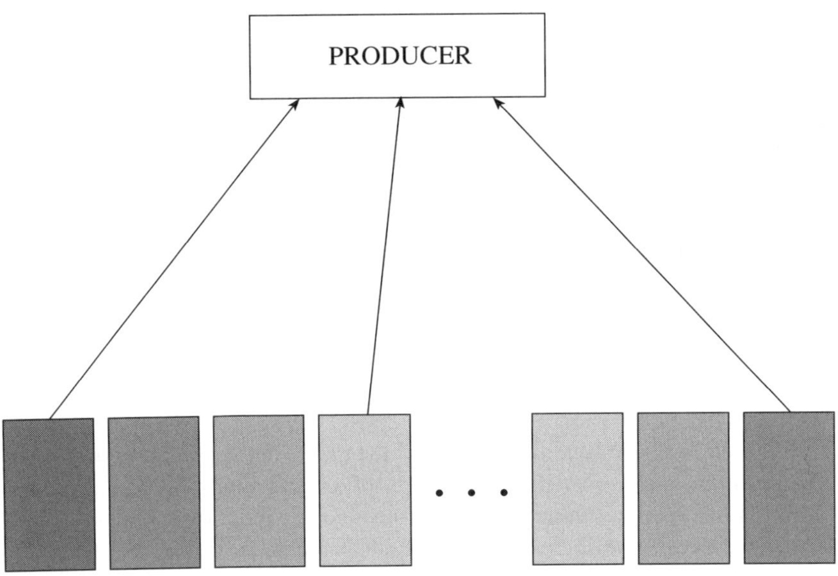

Source: Burt (1992, p. 209)

Figure 5.4 A producer in a differentiated resource environment

segments. That is, the producer requires the first, fourth and last type of resources in order to be able to produce its goods or services. It would be possible to draw a similar set of ties to one or more downstream markets. Organizations are structurally equivalent if they have the same pattern of ties to upstream and downstream markets. All such organizations occupy the same niche.

The attractions of this definition are clear. In principle, one can identify sets of structurally equivalent organizations without the need to make any a *priori* assumptions. This would enable researchers to classify organizational forms, since there is a one-to-one relationship between an organizational form and a niche. This would address a frequent criticism of ecological research, that it does not pay sufficient attention to the problem of classification and identification of boundaries around organizational forms.

However, in my view this promise is largely illusory. It is not always possible to distinguish clear boundaries using conventional measures of structural equivalence. In practice, organizations almost never have identical patterns of ties, and these patterns are not in any case stable over time. In reality, one is looking for sets of organizations that are 'more alike' than others, but there is still a great deal of room for ambiguity about where boundaries around organizational forms should be drawn.

Burt (1992, p.211) addresses concern about stability by claiming that 'market boundaries are defined in terms of transactions between classes of structurally equivalent establishments, not between firms'. This seems to beg several questions. In particular, how are the resource segments shown in Figure 5.4 defined? Why is it easier to identify structurally equivalent 'establishments' than firms, and why should we expect the pattern of ties between such establishments to be more stable than those between firms? Burt's empirical work involves resource flows between 'markets' defined by the US government's Standard Industrial Classification, and therefore depends on a pre-defined classification that is certainly no less ad hoc than those used in ecological research. Therefore, although the insight into the relationship between an ecological niche and structural equivalence in networks of resource flows is interesting theoretically, it has yet to prove useful in empirical research.

Some studies have used the concept of the niche, but applied it to individual organizations, rather than to populations of organizations or organizational forms. Miller McPherson and his colleagues locate voluntary associations in a 'space' defined by attributes of the individual members of the organizations, such as age, sex and education (McPherson and Ranger-Moore, 1991). However, he made no attempt to identify organizational forms or population niches using this approach. Similarly, studies by Baum and Haverman (1997) into Manhattan hotels and Baum and Singh (1994a; 1994b; 1996) into children's day centres have used similarity in the attributes of organizations (how close they are to each other geographically, and how much they overlap in the age range of children for whom they are licensed to provide care, respectively) to model the intensity of interorganizational competition. However, in both these cases, the organizational forms (hotels and day centres, respectively) and the geographical extent of the population (Manhattan and Toronto, respectively) were defined *a priori*.

In addition to his discussion of niches, Burt (1992) also uses network concepts to develop an argument about the *structural autonomy* of organizations in a population and their survival chances. Structural autonomy is defined by Burt (p. 45) as the extent to which an agent is best positioned for the 'information and control benefits that a network can provide'. This occurs when an agent is not easily replaced by other agents as a provider of some key resource, and when the agent occupies a position bridging many otherwise unconnected networks. Burt refers to these gaps in networks as *structural holes*. He hypothesizes that rates of failure should be higher in populations where organizations have relatively low levels of structural autonomy, whereas failure rates should be lower when structural autonomy is relatively high.

To understand the reasoning, it is helpful to refer to Figures 5.5, which is taken from Burt (1992). Figure 5.5(a) shows what in the ecological literature is a standard representation of the density-dependence model that was discussed above.[5] In the shaded area of the figure, legitimacy effects dominate competitive effects. That is, for all densities below N^{**} the failure rate is lower than it was when the population first came into existence, even though the *marginal* effect of increasing density will have been to increase the failure rate for densities above N^{*}. In Figure 5.5(b), however, competition never dominates in this absolute sense, though it is still the case that when density is greater than N^{*}, increasing density causes the failure rate to rise from its minimum.[6]

It is important to emphasize that both parts of the figure produce a non-monotonic relationship between density and the rate of failure, as predicted by the density-dependence model. However, it is clear that, in Figure 5(b), legitimacy (represented by the dotted curve) is a much more potent factor in the dynamics of the population than competition. Hannan and Carroll (1992) find that populations vary considerably in the relative strength of legitimation and competition in a discussion of organizational founding rates. They compare populations of banks, brewers, labour unions, life insurance companies and newspapers in Argentina, Ireland and the San Francisco Bay Area. Of these, only for banks and life insurance companies did competition come to dominate legitimation as shown in Figure 5.5(a). The other populations resembled Figure 5.5(b), with the most extreme cases being the newspaper populations in Ireland and the San Francisco Bay Area.

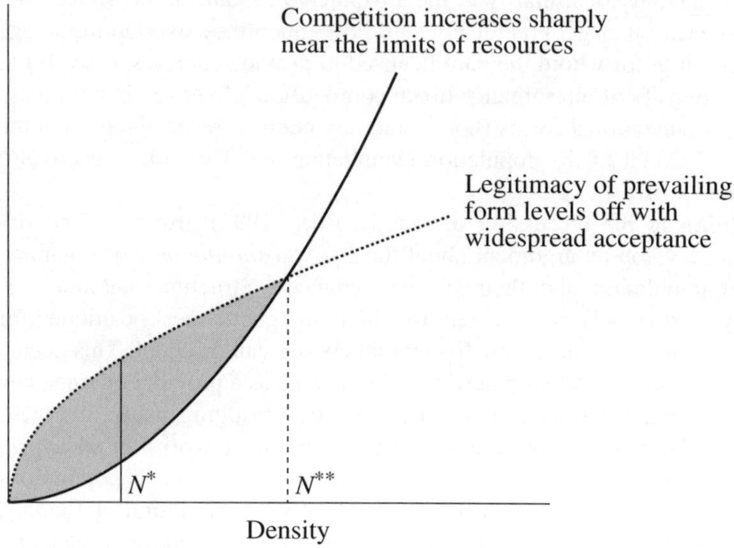

(a) Low autonomy

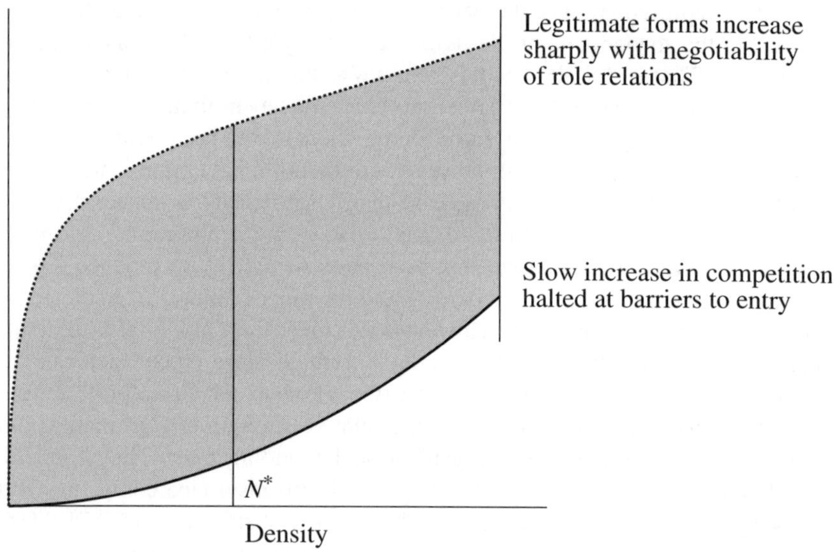

Source: Burt (1992, p. 217).

Figure 5.5 Competition and legitimacy

While Hannan and Carroll (1992) describe these interesting differences in the pattern of density-dependent population dynamics, they do not attempt to explain in any systematic way why these differences occur. Burt (1992), however, does provide an explanation, rooted in his concept of *structural autonomy*. Burt argues that the relationships shown in figure 5.5(a) are characteristic of populations with low structural autonomy. In these populations, competition becomes intense because there are few structural holes, and the products of the population's members are readily substitutable. On the other hand, Figure 5.5(b) shows a population with high structural autonomy. Competition rises much more slowly than in the low autonomy population, while legitimacy increases more sharply.

Burt argues that competition increases slowly for two reasons. First, 'structural holes among suppliers and customers allow entrepreneurial firms to set a higher market price for their commodity, which allows more establishments to survive in the market. Second, competition in high-autonomy markets is managed more through the social organization of players'. Consequently, the population can support larger numbers of members. In addition, autonomous member organizations have the ability to impose barriers to entry, preventing competition from increasing above some level. Similarly, legitimacy increases rapidly because players connected to a high-autonomy role 'are more in a position of putting up with the preferences of the autonomous people performing the role. Where acquiescence is acceptance, the social acceptance of whatever performances appear in a high-autonomy role increases quickly'.

Burt goes on to argue that a firm is more likely to find somewhere to survive in the larger shaded area in Figure 5.5(b). That is, the carrying capacity of the niche is higher when structural autonomy is higher. This should be reflected in lower failure rates. Burt is able to provide some 'illustrative evidence' in support of his hypothesis.

In summary, there is in principle a connection between the ecological concept of the niche and the network concept of structural equivalence. However, this has not so far proved useful in empirical applications. Burt's concept of structural autonomy, however, provides a potentially powerful explanation of observed differences in the relationship between population density and organizational vital rates across populations.

Networks and Organizational Forms

As discussed above in the section on 'Elaborations of density dependence', the concept of *legitimacy* plays a key role in the density-dependence theory of population dynamics. Legitimacy has several different dimensions or forms. Suchman (1995) defined three forms: pragmatic, moral and cognitive. As already mentioned, pragmatic legitimacy 'rests on the self-interested calculations of an organization's most immediate audiences' (Suchman 1995, p. 578). Moral legitimacy 'reflects a positive normative evaluation of the organization and its activities' (ibid., p. 579). Cognitive legitimacy implies that an organizational form is taken for granted as the natural way of structuring some type of collective action (Hannan and Freeman 1989; Meyer and Rowan 1977). Taken-for-grantedness can be considered an end point of a process of legitimation, when enough (most) people know about an organizational form and accept it as a natural way of achieving some end.

The legitimation process is, then, the spread of knowledge and beliefs through a certain set of actors. Viewed in this way, it seems natural to think of legitimacy as involving some sort of diffusion process. As Barron (1998b, p. 216) put it,

> Once the first organization of a particular type has been founded, its members, clients, customers, and staff become potential sources for the further diffusion of information about that organizational form. Presumably, such people are convinced of the usefulness of the organization of which they are a part. In the case of credit unions, for example, they are likely to have a more favourable attitude than the general public towards consumer borrowing in general, and credit unions in particular. Therefore, it is reasonable to suppose that they might act as sources for the propagation of such attitudes, thereby boosting pragmatic, moral and cognitive legitimacy.

In an excellent review of the literature on diffusion in organizations, Strang and Soule (1998) enumerate some of the mechanisms by which ideas, practices and so on might diffuse. There are a variety of ways in which new organizational forms can spread; in many cases, no doubt, several processes operate simultaneously. External sources such as mass media are sometimes important, as Barron (1998b) found in his study of the institutionalization of credit unions in New York. High levels of media attention have also been associated with the spread of managerial innovations such as matrix management (Burns and Wholey, 1993) and with 'management fads' more generally (Abrahmson, 1996). 'Institutional entrepreneurs', one or more individuals with a stake in the success of an innovation, can also be important (DiMaggio, 1988).

Alternative accounts stress network diffusion of innovations from prior to potential adopters. Barron (1998b) finds evidence that such a process increases the rate at which new credit unions are founded in New York. Firms tend to copy each other, a process DiMaggio and Powell (1983) call 'mimetic isomorphism'. Such diffusion is most likely to occur between firms in the same industry and when firms are strong competitors. For example, Osterman (1994) shows that management styles influenced by Japanese practice were adopted most readily by firms exposed to external competition. Other authors have suggested that prestige and geographic proximity are important determinants of the diffusion process.

Strang and Soule (1998, p. 276) also point out that the cultural basis of diffusion is important: 'An analysis of the cultural (in some usage, institutional) bases of diffusion speaks more directly to what spreads, replacing a theory of connections with a theory of connecting.' However, as we have seen, networks can also be seen as playing a key role in the diffusion of culture (or legitimacy). Notwithstanding the important role that networks undoubtedly play in the diffusion of new organizational forms, there have been very few empirical studies that have attempted to analyse such processes in combination with ecological models of population dynamics. Even Barron's (1998b) study, which takes the role of network diffusion seriously, uses indirect measures of network effects. No doubt the lack of such studies reflects the extreme difficulty of collecting network data over the long time spans required to test ecological models.

Networks and Organizational Dynamics

Miller McPherson and colleagues (McPherson and Ranger-Moore, 1991; McPherson *et al.*, 1992; Popielarz and McPherson, 1995) have explored how social networks affect the dynamics of voluntary associations. As we have already seen, they envisage these organizations as existing in a multidimensional 'space', the dimensions of which are defined by characteristics of the individual members of the organizations, such as age, education and sex.

Figure 5.6 shows how individuals and organizations can be located in such a space, only two dimensions of which are shown on the figure for clarity of presentation. The individuals, shown as points in the figure, are a random sample of residents of Lincoln, Nebraska. A sample of organizations in the same city are shown as boxes, the width of which represents the dispersion of members along the two dimensions shown. Clearly, organizations tend to specialize; the dispersion of their membership characteristics is much smaller than that of the residents of the city.

McPherson *et al.* (1992) argue that this occurs as a result of the *homophyly principle*. This principle simply states that network ties are more likely to be found between actors who are adjacent to each other in social space than those who are far apart. Of course, the extent to which this is true depends on the network relation we are considering. Friendship ties are more homophilous than kinship ties along age and sex dimensions, for example. However, McPherson *et al.* (ibid., p.154) argue:

> Distance in sociodemographic space stands as a proxy for social distance in great generality; people at extremes of distance do not share the same social world. They

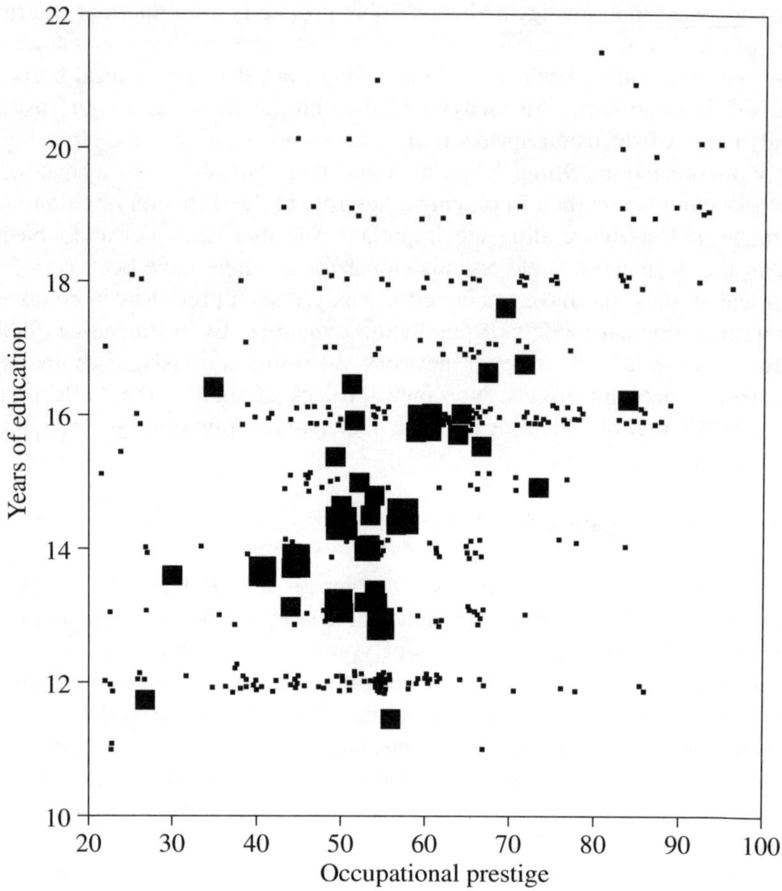

Note: Points = individuals, squares = groups.

Source: McPherson *et al.* (1992, p. 155).

Figure 5.6 Groups and individuals in two dimensions

> interact with different others; they are exposed to different views and interests; they have different lifestyles and tastes, and so forth.

This in turn accounts for the diversity in organizations shown in Figure 5.6. Since voluntary associations tend to recruit new members via the social networks of existing members, their memberships reflect wider social boundaries. One can use the homophyly principle to do more than explain the fact that there are many different kinds of voluntary association, however. It can also be used to explain the movement of these organizations through social space.

First, assume that membership recruitment is more likely if a non-member has a network tie to an existing member:

> direct communication between a group member and a nonmember increases the probability that the nonmember will be drawn into the group, or conversely, that the member will be drawn out of the group by connection to the nonmember. The more connections a nonmember has to members, the greater the probability that the nonmember will join the group.

The authors find considerable evidence in support of this hypothesis. Second, assume that network ties tend to be homophilous. This means that organizations will generally recruit new members from areas of social space close to their current location. They are therefore unlikely to move quickly across large social distances. Third, assume that people have a finite amount of leisure time, and that therefore to some extent voluntary associations are in competition for members (McPherson *et al.*, 1989). Fourth, assume that the average number of memberships held by people in different regions of social space fluctuates over time, and that, when this number is low, organizations operating in this region of space will find it easier to recruit new members than when it is high. McPherson and Ranger-Moore (1991) called these fluctuations in the number of memberships changes in the degree to which organizations were 'exploiting' the pool of potential members. In Figure 5.7, we see a hypothetical 'exploitation curve', calculated by subtracting the current level of exploitation from a long-run average. McPherson and Ranger-Moore (1991) assume that recruitment opportunities will be greater when this curve is low, and that members will tend to be lost where the curve is near a peak.

We can now make predictions about the way organizations at different points on this exploitation curve (that is, in different regions of social space) will move and whether they will grow or decline in size. Organization D is in a region of low exploitation, and so is likely to grow as it recruits new members. Since the curve is symmetrical around its position, it is equally likely to attract new members on both sides of its current position, so it is likely that the diversity of its members will increase somewhat. Group A will find it easier to recruit new members with more years of education, while it is likely to lose members to its left on the curve. Therefore organization A's membership will tend to become more highly educated. Group C will also recruit new members, but as it is at a peak in the curve it can recruit in both directions. Group B is trapped in a region of high exploitation. It is trapped because the homophyly principle predicts that it is unlikely to be able to recruit members in the low exploitation region occupied by group D because its

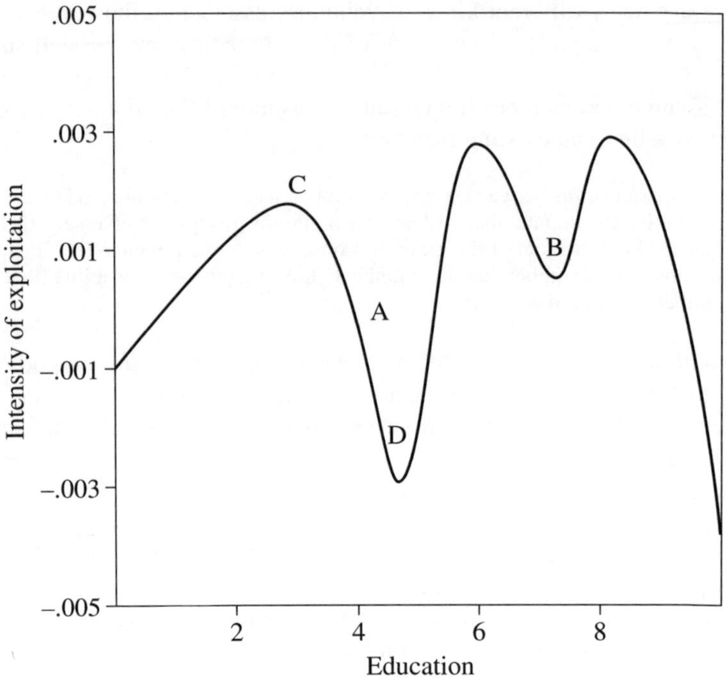

Figure 5.7

current members will have few ties to people there, while it is difficult for it to recruit new members in adjacent regions because they are already highly exploited. This organization is therefore likely to shrink in size. McPherson and Ranger-Moore (1991) provide some evidence in support of their model, though their data are not ideal as they consist of information about organizational *types* rather than individual organizations. However, they do find evidence that these aggregate niches move through social space in the way that their theory predicts.

Technology Networks, Status and Niches

A number of articles by Podolny and colleagues outline a theory linking technology networks, organizational status, niche overlap and organizational life chances (Podolny, 1993; Podolny and Stuart, 1995; Podolny *et al.*, 1996). The connections between these concepts are made most explicit in Podolny *et al.* (1996). Organizations are conceived of as being actors in a technological network. That is, patented inventions by any given organization can be linked to antecedent inventions made by the same or other organizations. Data on patents make this possible, because patent applications must list the inventions on which the new innovation is based. Figure 5.8 shows a hypothetical technology network (see Podolny *et al.*, 1996, p.664). There are 12 inventions, each one shown by a box. Inventions eight and nine are patented by organization A, while inventions seven and 10 are patented by organization B. The ties between boxes show that the later invention depended on the technology of the earlier invention in some way. Podolny *et al.* (ibid.) use this pattern of ties to define organizational niches: 'an organization's niche is its position in technology space, as defined by the pattern of technological ties involving its inventions'.

Calculating niche positions requires that one specify the dimensionality of this technology space. Podolny *et al.* (1996) use two dimensions. The first dimension involves the *pattern* of ties among the inventions of organizations. Where the patterns are similar, it implies that the organizations concerned are using very similar technologies, and that therefore they are close competitors.

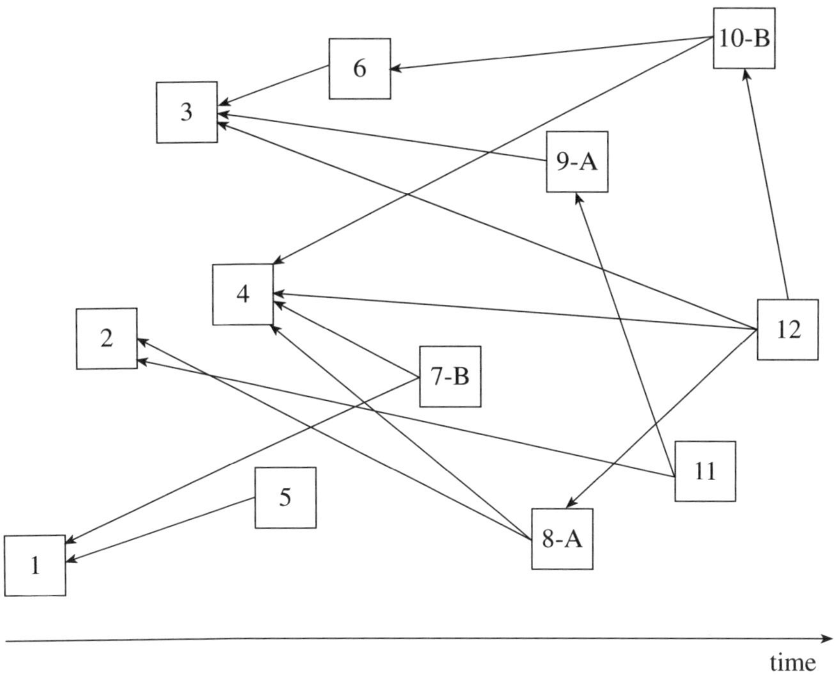

Source: Podolny *et al.* (1996, p. 664).

Figure 5.8 Hypothetical technology network

In other words, mirroring Burt's ideas, niche overlap is measured in terms of structural equivalence, though in this case the network is of links between inventions rather than flows of resources. The central idea, however, remains the same: structural equivalence implies substitutability and therefore high levels of niche overlap. Niche overlap in turn implies high levels of competition. Podolny *et al.* hypothesize that the sum of an organization's niche overlaps, which they term *crowding*, should be related to its life chances: increasing total niche overlap increases competition and thus reduces its life chances.

The second dimension reflects the *direct* ties between the inventions of a set of organizations. Such ties could also imply niche overlap. However, Podolny *et al.* (1996) argue that they imply 'a certain *deference* by one organization to the contribution of the other . . . By building in an observable way on another organization's innovation, an organization confers a certain legitimacy or status on the innovative activity of the pioneer'. If the first dimension is closely related to the network concept of structural equivalence, the second dimension is allied to the concept of network centrality. Podolny *et al.* argue that the centrality accorded by this conferral of status should increase an organization's life chances where it operates in an uncrowded niche. However, they expect this positive effect to decline as an organization's niche becomes more crowded.

Podolny *et al.*'s (1996) empirical research on growth rates of firms in the US semiconductor industry supports their hypotheses. That is, organizations in crowded niches grow more slowly than organizations in less crowded niches. In less crowded niches, growth is highest among high-status organizations, but the effect of status declines as crowding becomes more intense. They note that the finding that niche crowding affects life chances links with McPherson *et al.*'s (1992) study of voluntary associations, discussed above. 'Niche overlap defined as similarity in patterns of ties has implications not only for voluntary organizations but also for market-based organizations.' Similarly, the finding that status increases organizational growth rates parallels the results of Podolny's (1994) comparison of investment-grade and non-investment-grade debt markets. In this study, status affected perceptions of quality more strongly in the non-investment-grade market, reflecting the greater uncertainty of this market. Podolny *et al.* (1996, p. 684) argue that their findings in the semiconductor industry are similar, because 'less crowded niches are likely to have the greatest uncertainty about competing technological possibilities'.

CONCLUSION

Organizational ecology is a very active field of empirical research. Within the sociology of organizations, it asks unique questions and has developed unique theories. The very large number of empirical studies that have been done (I have barely scratched the surface in this review) have entailed much detailed data collection. The theories are, however, couched in very general terms. Although particular studies usually require detailed knowledge of an industry, the dynamics of that specific set of organizations is not usually the primary concern. This is both a strength and a weakness. General theories are clearly appropriate for explaining very common regularities. On the other hand, not all populations are the same, and little attempt has been made to address these differences in a systematic way. In other words, comparative ecological research could be better developed. Nevertheless, in my view ecological theories of organizations have provided many important insights, and I expect this to be a field of growing importance in years to come.

NOTES

1. Scholars interested in organizational ecology are fortunate in that a large number of excellent review articles have been published (for example, Aldrich and Wiedenmayer, 1993; Baum, 1996; Carroll, 1984; Singh and Lumsden, 1990; Wholey and Brittain, 1986). As a result, I make no attempt at completeness in this chapter. My intention is to highlight what I consider to be the most important areas of current research activity.
2. Because ecological research is not concerned exclusively with properties of populations, I prefer to call the field organizational ecology rather than population ecology.
3. The fundamental niche of an organizational form consists of the social, economic and political conditions required to sustain the functioning of organizations that embody the form. If two populations rely on completely different kinds of resources and depend on different kinds of social and political institutions, then their fundamental niches do not intersect. Otherwise, they do intersect, and it makes sense to measure their similarity in terms of the degree of intersection. Viewed ecologically, the potential for two populations to compete is proportional to the intersection of their fundamental niches. When populations with intersecting fundamental niches inhabit the same system, potential competition is converted into actual competition. Under such conditions, the expansion of one population changes the conditions of existence of the others. In the case of competition, the presence of the competitor reduces the set (range) of environments in which another population can sustain itself. The realized niche is the subset of the fundamental niche in which growth rates are positive in the presence of competitors. Except in the highly unusual case in which a population exists in isolation from all competitors, what can be observed in any concrete setting is realized niches.
4. The best-managed evolutionary process in a large organization would end up with all fit units and so would just match the level of fitness that occurs consistently among small organizations under environmental selection, which is the limiting case' (Barnett 1997, p. 137).
5. For example, a similar figure can be found in Hannan and Carroll (1992, p. 95).
6. Hannan and Carroll (1992, pp. 94–7) discuss this issue in more detail. The point N^* is the density after which the gap between the two curves starts to shrink.

REFERENCES

Abrahmson, E. (1996), 'Management Fashion', *Academy of Management Review*, 21, 254–85.

Aldrich, Howard E. (1979), *Organizations and Environments*, Englewood Cliffs, NJ: Prentice-Hall.

Aldrich, Howard E. and Gabriele Wiedenmayer (1993), 'From Traits to Rates: An Ecological Perspective on Organizational Foundings', in *Advances in Entrepreneurship, Firm Emergence, and Growth*, vol. 1, Greenwich, CT: JAI Press, pp. 145–95.

Barnett, William p. (1997), 'The dynamics of competitive intensity', *Administrative Science Quarterly*, 42, 128–60.

Barnett, William P. and Terry L. Amburgy (1990), 'Do Larger Organizations Generate Stronger Competition?', in Jitendra V. Singh (ed.), *Organizational Evolution: New Directions*, Newbury Park, CA: Sage, pp. 78–102.

Barron, David N. (1998a), 'Competition and Organizational Niches', paper presented at the American Sociological Association Annual Meetings, San Francisco.

Barron, David N. (1998b), 'Pathways to legitimacy among consumer loan providers in New York City, 1914–34', *Organization Studies*, 19 (2), 207–33.

Barron, David N. (1999), 'The structuring of organizational populations', *American Sociological Review*, 64, 421–45.

Barron, David N., Elizabeth West and Michael T. Hannan (1994), 'A time to grow and a time to die: growth and mortality of credit unions in New York City, 1914–1990', *American Journal of Sociology*, 100, 381–421.

Baum, Joel A.C. (1995), 'The changing basis of competition in organizational populations: the Manhattan Hotel Industry, 1898–1990', *Social Forces*, 74, 177–205.

Baum, Joel A.C. (1996), 'Organizational Ecology', in Stewart R. Clegg, Cynthia Hardy and Walter R. Nord (eds), *Handbook of Organization Studies*, London and Thousand Oaks, CA: Sage, pp. 77–114.

Baum, Joel A.C. and Heather A. Haverman (1997), 'Love thy neighbour? Differentiation and agglomeration in the Manhattan Hotel Industry, 1898–1990', *Administrative Science Quarterly*, 42, 304–38.

Baum, Joel A.C. and Stephen J. Mezias (1992), 'Localized competition and organizational failure in the Manhattan Hotel Industry, 1898–1990', *Administrative Science Quarterly*, 37, 580–604.

Baum, Joel A.C. and Christine Oliver (1992), 'Institutional embeddedness and the dynamics of organizational populations', *American Sociological Review*, 57, 540–59.

Baum, Joel A.C. and Jitendra V. Singh (1994a), 'Organizational niches and the dynamics of organizational mortality', *American Journal of Sociology*, 100, 346–80.

Baum, Joel A.C. and Jitendra V. Singh. (1994b), 'Organizational niches and the dynamics of organizational founding', *Organization Science*, 5, 483–501.

Baum, Joel A.C. and Jitendra V. Singh (1996), 'Dynamics of organizational responses to competition', *Social Forces*, 74, 1261–97.

Burns, L.R. and D.R. Wholey (1993), 'Adoption and abandonment of matrix management programs: effects of organizational characteristics and interorganizational networks', *Academy of Management Journal*, 36, 106–38.

Burt, Ronald S. (1992), *Structural Holes: The Social Structure of Competition*, Cambridge, MA: Harvard University Press.

Burt, Ronald S. and I. Talmud (1993), 'Market niche', *Social Networks*, 15 (2), 133–49.

Carroll, Glenn R. (1984), 'Organizational Ecology', in *Annual Review of Sociology*, vol. 10, Palo Alto, CA: Annual Reviews, pp. 71–93.

Carroll, Glenn R. (1985), 'Concentration and specialization: dynamics of niche width in populations of organizations', *American Journal of Sociology*, 90, 1262–83.

Carroll, Glenn R. and Michael T. Hannan (1989), 'Density delay in the evolution of organizational populations: a model and five empirical tests', *Administrative Science Quarterly*, 34, 411–30.

Carroll, Glenn R. and Michael T. Hannan (2000), *The Demography of Corporations and Industries*, Princeton, NJ: Princeton University Press.

Carroll, Glenn R. and Anand Swaminathan (1992), 'The organizational ecology of strategic groups in the American brewing industry from 1975 to 1990', *Industrial and Corporate Change*, 1, 65–97.

DiMaggio, Paul (1986), 'Structural Analysis of Organizational Fields: A Blockmodel Approach', in B. Staw and L. Cummings (eds), *Research in Organizational Behavior*, Greenwich, CT: JAI Press, pp. 335–70.

DiMaggio, Paul J. (1988), 'Interest and Agency in Institutional Theory', in Lynn G. Zucker (ed.), *Institutional Patterns and Organizations: Culture and Environment*, Cambridge, MA: Ballinger, pp. 3–21.

DiMaggio, Paul J. and Walter W. Powell (1983), 'The iron cage revisited: institutional isomorphism and collective rationality in organizational fields', *American Sociological Review*, 48, 147–60.

Freeman, John H. and Michael T. Hannan (1983), 'Niche width and the dynamics of organizational populations', *American Journal of Sociology*, 88, 1116–45.

Gort, Michael and Steven Klepper (1982), 'Time paths in the diffusion of product innovations', *The Economic Journal*, 92, 630–53.

Hannan, Michael T. (1986), 'Competitive and Institutional Processes in Organizational Ecology', Technical Report 86–13, Cornell University, Department of Sociology.

Hannan, Michael T. (1989), 'Competitive and Institutional Processes in Organizational Ecology', in Joseph Berger, Morris Zeldich, Jr. and Bo Andersen (eds), *Sociological Theories in Progress: New Foundations*, Newbury Park, CA: Sage, pp. 388–402.

Hannan, Michael T. (1997), 'Inertia, density and the structure of organizational populations: entries in European automobile industries, 1886–1981', *Organization Studies*, 18, 193–228.

Hannan, Michael T. and Glenn R. Carroll (1992), *Dynamics of Organizational Populations*, Oxford and New York: Oxford University Press.

Hannan, Michael T. and John Freeman (1977), 'The population ecology of organizations', *American Journal of Sociology*, 56, 929–64.

Hannan, Michael T. and John Freeman (1984), 'Structural inertia and organizational change', *American Sociological Review*, 49, 149–64.

Hannan, Michael T. and John Freeman (1987), 'The ecology of organizational foundings: American Labor Unions, 1836–1985', *American Journal of Sociology*, 92, 910–43.

Hannan, Michael T. and John Freeman (1989), *Organizational Ecology*, Cambridge, MA: Harvard University Press.

Hannan, Michael T., James Ranger-Moore and Jane Banaszak-Holl (1990), 'Competition and the Evolution of Organizational Size Distributions', in Jitendra V. Singh (ed.), *Organizational Evolution: New Directions*, Newbury, CA: Sage, pp. 246–68.

Hutchinson, Evelyn G. (1957), 'Concluding remarks', *Cold Spring Harbor Symposium on Quantitative Biology*, 22, 415–27.

Jepperson, R.L. (1991), 'Institutions, Institutional Effects and Institutionalism', in Walter W. Powell and Paul J. DiMaggio (eds), *The New Institutionalism in Organizational Analysis*, Chicago: University of Chicago Press, pp. 143–63.

Klepper, Steven (1996), 'Entry, exit, growth, and innovation over the product life cycle', *American Economic Review*, 86, 562–83.

Klepper, Steven (1997), 'Industry life cycles', *Industrial and Corporate Change*, 6 (1), 145–81.

McKelvey, Bill (1982), *Organizational Systematics*, Berkeley, CA: University of California Press.

McPherson, J. Miller (1983), 'An ecology of affiliation', *American Sociological Review*, 48, 519–35.

McPherson, J. Miller and James R. Ranger-Moore (1991), 'Evolution on a dancing landscape: organizations and networks in dynamic Blau Space', *Social Forces*, 70, 19–42.

McPherson, J. Miller, Pamela A. Popielarz and Sonja Drobnic (1992), 'Social networks and organizational dynamics', *American Sociological Review*, 57 (2), 153–70.

McPherson, J. Miller, Elizabeth West and David N. Barron (1989), 'The Market for Members: Competition, Facilitation and Inhibition of Voluntary Affiliation', paper presented at the American Sociological Association Annual Meeting.

Meyer, John W. and Brian Rowan (1977), 'Institutionalized organizations: formal structure as myth and ceremony', *American Journal of Sociology*, 83, 340–63.

Osterman, P. (1994), 'How common is workplace transformation and who adopts it?', *Industrial and Labor Relations Review*, 47, 173–88.

Podolny, Joel M. (1993), 'A status-based model of market competition', *American Journal of Sociology*, 98, 829–72.

Podolny, Joel M. (1994), 'Market uncertainty and the social character of economic exchange', *Administrative Science Quarterly*, 39, 458–83.

Podolny, Joel M. and Toby E. Stuart (1995), 'A role-based ecology of technological change', *American Journal of Sociology*, 100, 1224–60.

Podolny, Joel M., Toby E. Stuart and Michael T. Hannan (1996), 'Networks, knowledge, and niches: competition in the worldwide semiconductor industry, 1984–1991', *American Journal of Sociology*, 102 (3), 659–89.

Popielarz, Pamela A. and J. Miller McPherson (1995), 'On the edge or in between: niche position, niche overlap and the duration of voluntary association memberships', *American Journal of Sociology*, 101, 698–720.

Ranger-Moore, James, Robert S. Breckenridge and Daniel L. Jones (1995), 'Patterns of growth and size-localized competition in the New York State Life Insurance Industry, 1860–1985', *Social Forces*, 73 (3), 1027–49.

Scott, W. Richard (1992), *Organizations: Rational, Natural and Open Systems*, Englewood Cliffs, NJ: Prentice-Hall.

Singh, Jitendra V. and Charles J. Lumsden (1990), 'Theory and research in organizational ecology', *Annual Review of Sociology*, 16, 161–95.

Strang, David and Sarah A. Soule (1998), 'Diffusion in organizations and social movements: from hybrid corn to poison pills', *Annual Review of Sociology*, 24, 265–90.

Suchman, Mark C. (1995), 'Managing legitimacy: strategies and institutional approaches', *Academy of Management Review*, 20, 571–610.

Wholey, Douglas R. and Jack W. Brittain (1986), 'Organizational ecology: findings and implications', *Academy of Management Review*, 11, 513–33.

Zucker, Lynne G. (1989), 'Combining institutional theory and population ecology: no legitimacy, no history', *American Sociological Review*, 54, 542–5.

6. Interdependent entrepreneurs and the social discipline of their cooperation: a research programme for structural economic sociology in a society of organizations

Emmanuel Lazega, Lise Mounier[1]

INTRODUCTION: BUREAUCRACY AND COLLEGIALITY AT THE INTERORGANIZATIONAL LEVEL

Economists have long focused on markets as exchange mechanisms, and many economic sociologists have also used the same approach. This focus emphasized the importance of price and that of the social embeddedness of economic transactions among actors, whether individuals or organizations. Focusing on the production side of economic activity, however, underlines the fact that society is a society of organizations (Presthus, 1962; White, 1981b; Stokman *et al.*, 1985; Coleman, 1990; Perrow, 1991), with specific social mechanisms underlying collective action. From the latter's perspective, saying that society is an organizational society is also equivalent to saying that its intrinsically multi-level dimension should frame – much more than it currently does – sociologists' perspective on human, including economic, activity. In our view, this additional focus reframes analyses of both market exchange and social exchange (Blau, 1964) of resources as they are connected in production. This approach advocates new combinations of theories of individual action and theories of collective action. Within such a perspective, priority is given here to the study of social exchange and cooperation among *interdependent entrepreneurs*, at the intraorganizational and interorganizational levels. In short, this study is about the social discipline that helps interdependent entrepreneurs in their collective action. Entrepreneurs are not conceived as individuals acting on their own, but as individuals, and organizations, interacting with, and investing in, other entrepreneurs as peers or quasi-peers in order to make collective action possible.

The sociology of organizations has been able to design an ideal-typical distinction between two forms of collective action at least at the intraorganizational level. The two forms are bureaucracy and collegiality (Weber, 1978; Crozier, 1963; Lazega, 2001a). The first imposes an order in routine production; this order is built on formal hierarchy and rule circumvention by weaker parties in the collective. The second organizes non-routine work based on formal equality between interdependent entrepreneurs and identifiable social mechanisms of cooperation that can only be understood on the basis of structural analyses of multiplex social exchanges among economic actors.

For the last decades, structural analyses of social processes taking place within and between organizations have contributed, more or less intentionally, to such a development in economic sociology. In this chapter, we sketch some of the main aspects and limitations of this early development. We then review new directions for research based on these expanded ambitions for current economic sociology. In particular, we ask whether it is possible to extend to the interorganizational level theory and models developed at the intraorganizational level to account for collective action among interdependent entrepreneurs (especially when production is not routinized and products are not standardized). A multi-level approach does not presuppose, for example, that the relationship between a boss and his worker is the same as a relationship between a large company and its subcontractor. Nor does it consider the distinction between market and hierarchy as a useful one for economic sociology.[2] It is argued here that, although there is no scale invariance in the social sciences, the ideal–typical distinction between bureaucratic and collegial forms of collective action can be useful to understand coordination at the interorganizational level.

For example, at the interorganizational level, bureaucratic order is comparable to state planning ('external' regulation of the economic world, redistribution of resources providing forms of 'universal' solidarity and, sometimes, of generation of change).[3] In recent history, the social systems in which this order was reified have not been able to muster the capacity to grow and innovate to an extent comparable to that of less bureaucratic systems. In the latter, exceptional growth is often exclusively attributed to the dynamics of the 'market economy'. In our view, it can also be attributed to the logic of politicized social exchange and to the derived generic social mechanisms that make it possible for an oligarchy of interdependent entrepreneurs to cooperate and get involved in collective action by acting at the interorganizational level. This level refers to the specific social phenomena that transform micro individual and relational behaviour into social mechanisms that structure the collective at the macro level. Generic social mechanisms – for example, that of generalized exchange (that is, bounded solidarity), control and regulation – were identified using a structural approach at the intraorganizational level, and concatenated under the label of the 'corporate social capital' (Lazega and Pattison, 2001). They combine entrepreneurial investments in relationships and the subsequent quest for social niches and status competition, two phenomena that come out of members' rationality in social exchange. These phenomena make the meso level a tangible and measurable reality. Our chapter asks how and to what extent such meso-specific mechanisms, that is mechanisms relying on the creation of social niches and more or less consistent forms of status, operate at the interorganizational level.

Differences between the intraorganizational and the interorganizational levels abound. At the macro level, for example, more brutal and often more impersonal forms of status – impersonal concentrations of resources that stress raw power more than symbolic authority – are sought and used. The social niches that can be found at the interorganizational level combine resources that are different from that of social niches at the intraorganizational level. But similarities across levels are also striking. For example, the idea of an intraorganizational social niche is similar to that of a group of corporate actors depending on similar resources and providing each other with such resources at a lower price than would be expected with other exchange partners (Granovetter, 1994). Thus it makes sense to try to extend to the interorganizational level reasoning that was developed on interdependent entrepreneurs at the intraorganizational one, with adjustments concerning kinds of resources, niches and statuses that make sense at that higher level.

The existence of a meso level of analysis between the micro and the macro levels is a precondition of this theory connecting individual and collective economic behaviour. The current neostructural renewal of economic sociology rests on the development of multi-level methods of data analysis (particularly network analysis[4]) and on theories of action that do not accept a narrow conception of individual rationality. Any sociological theory of economic behaviour must rely on a realistic conception of the actors who produce and exchange. Early structural sociology used conceptions of actors that ranged between the automaton and the narrow cost–benefit maximizer. Here we build on an approach that seems more adequate for our purpose, one that brings in politicized social exchange to account for the social mechanisms characterizing cooperation in the organizational society more generally. In effect, our approach assumes that social mechanisms are triggered by relational choices made by actors. Such choices select exchange partners and this selection is understood as a niche-specific *relational investment.* Investments and their underlying commitment (to exchange partners) contribute in turn to the emergence of meso-level relational structures (regularities in the exchanges of resources), but also trigger the generic social mechanisms mentioned above. Without such mechanisms, we argue, collective action among interdependent entrepreneurs would not be possible at the micro and macro levels. Relational investments and generic social mechanisms build up a *social discipline* that characterizes both individual and collective behaviour.

In effect, relational investments and commitments are made under specific conditions characterizing social exchange. They sometimes appear to be dyadic in nature (that is, to be 'gifts'), but they actually presuppose the existence of collectives in which dyads are embedded. Commitments have a multilevel dimension. They are made to actors (exchange partners) in social niches, using identity criteria. They happen when actors can define their situation using appropriateness judgments and identity criteria in the selection of exchange partners, from whom they expect, directly or indirectly, successfully or unsuccessfully, reciprocal investments and commitments (Lazega, 1992a). From the inside of the quasi-group, such commitments are perceived as homophily; from the outside as density and embeddedness.

Contextualizing their economic activities in this way helps actors seek social niches and compete for status (with attached authority arguments and control of various kinds of resources). In effect, in our view, that would surely be consistent with that of many organizational sociologists (Crozier and Friedberg, 1977), these investments in exchange partners are part of actors' micropolitical behaviour. Actors tend to *politicize their exchanges*. They try as much as they can to shape and *reshape their opportunity structure* by influencing events at the meso level. This broadly conceived theory of rationality in social exchange includes an actor's capacity to contextualize his or her action. It brings in power and resource dependencies, but also social and cultural disciplines subsumed under regulatory activities (Reynaud, 1989; Favereau, 1989, 1999; Lazega, 1999a). In that respect, this neostructural approach combines rational choice ideas with more institutionalist, symbolic interactionist and strategic perspectives that will be outlined below – but also with formal and systematic modelling.

This chapter thus outlines the contribution and limitations of this broadly conceived structural approach to the study of organizations and markets. The specificity of structural studies is in their use of network analysis as a method for tracking and understanding flows and exchanges of resources, their control and rule enforcement, and finally the negotiation of rules commanding such flows and terms of exchanges. We mainly argue that the collegial model (developed to analyse social mechanisms of non-routine cooperation between interdependent intrapreneurs at the intraorganizational level) can offer insights into, and hypotheses for, the study of interorganizational cooperation between interdependent entrepreneurs. Based on such an approach to economic activity, the strong difference between markets and organizations tends to be replaced by the dialectic interplay between mechanisms characterizing bureaucratic and collegial coordinations in each of the two contexts (intraorganizational and interorganizational). The boundary between the two forms of coordination, however, is a permanently shifting one. In effect, the forms taken by actors' social exchanges and politicized contextualization of their actions – and therefore their efforts to reshape their opportunity structure – depend heavily on the extent to which their tasks in collective action can be routinized, which is an unstable constraint. In our conclusion, we raise this issue of a possible typology of equilibrium points stabilizing the mix of collegiality and bureaucracy that can be found in any real-life organization and perhaps between them as well.

EARLY STRUCTURAL APPROACHES TO ORGANIZATIONS AND MARKETS

Network analysis in itself is a method, and its early users did not rely on many complex behavioural assumptions. They often used a conception of action that very generally looks at structural constraints imposed on the behaviour and opportunities of members of a social setting (White, 1970) and of reactions to such constraints (recorded as cutting and switching ties) that are eventually supposed to lead to a change in the structure. In early structural explanations in sociology, individuals were portrayed as being subject to these particular sets of constraints and opportunities defined by their social context, such as specific and pre-existing social networks through which many resources can circulate (White *et al.*, 1976). Although this micro–macro relationship has not been examined systematically, the approach has been productive for the study of organizations and for economic sociology. Of particular importance to understanding such constraints, social relations are part of the contextual conditions influencing behaviour, including economic calculations. Early structural approaches to organizations and markets use this method without, or with minimal, theory of action: narrow rational choice and resource dependence theory (Salancik and Pfeffer, 1977), the latter being primarily interested in the relationship between exchange, dependence and power.[5]

These constraints were theorized by the concepts of status and role without much reflection on the use of authority that status provides or on the enactment of such roles. In our view, this means that structural approaches should beware of explanations of actors' behaviour and achievements simply by stating that they were 'at the right place, at the right time'. This is where a theory of politicized management of resource interdependencies and status competition is needed.

Early Intraorganizational Network Studies

For the last 30 years, organizations have been among the social settings most studied by network analysts: mines and shop-floors (Kapferer, 1969, 1972), monasteries (Sampson, 1969; Breiger *et al.*, 1975; Reitz, 1988), banks (Eccles and Crane, 1988), advertising agencies (Ibarra, 1992), hospitals (Stevenson,

1990), corporate law firms (Lazega, 1992b) and many others (Baker, 1984, 1992; Blau and Alba, 1982; Brass, 1984; Burt and Ronchi, 1990; Knoke and Wood, 1981; Krackhardt, 1990; Lemieux, 1979, 1982; Shrader *et al.*, 1989; Thurman, 1980). Although some issues are dominant in this body of work (organizational integration; relationship between centrality, autonomy and power; influence of relationships on decision making; invisible inequalities), intraorganizational studies using network analysis deal with a wide variety of topics. For example, they describe the ways in which work, advice or friendship ties cut across internal formal boundaries such as departmental or status boundaries (Baker, 1992; Brass, 1984; Lazega, 1992b). They show how a system filters information that reaches its members (Rogers and Agarwala-Rogers, 1976) and influences the flows and exchanges of various resources (Stevenson, 1990).

For example, a study by Burt (1992), following Harrison White and Mark Granovetter, stresses the importance, in a social structure, of absences of relationships between actors. A 'structural hole' is defined as an absence of ties between redundant others (that is contacts who give access to the same social resources). Burt uses the concept to develop a measurement of structural autonomy. An actor is autonomous when his or her contacts are not connected to each other – for many possible reasons – and cannot put together a strong constraint on his or her behaviour. A simple example is that of two competing suppliers that a firm can play off against each other. With the idea of structural holes, Burt generalizes his theory of autonomy, adding that it provides benefits in information and control that every entrepreneur needs to seize opportunities. Absences of ties among others are exploitable by a *tertius gaudens* (in the Simmelian sense of a third party taking advantage of a blocked situation between two persons). With these premises, Burt develops a theory of this entrepreneur. An actor whose network is rich in structural holes will benefit from this structural feature when he can play them against each other or become an intermediary. On the basis of this advantage, a productive 'social capital', he or she will be in a better position to win in selection processes such as promotions. Actors paralysed in positions where they have to manage many heterogeneous relations simultaneously and where they have few opportunities to become unavoidable intermediaries, are destined for quick burnout. Burt thus pushes his structural theory of autonomy and social capital towards a theory of inequality and selectivity of social systems. His work leads to a focus on actors' manipulation of relations (network surgery including cutting and adding ties from and to one's network) and cooptation as a defence mechanism (if you can't beat them, join them) where a strategic player tries to avoid competition or diminish his or her dependence upon a constraining party. These manœuvres can also be indirect (Gargiulo, 1993; Lazega and Vari, 1992; Lazega and Lebeaux, 1995; Lazega, 1995; Lazega and Krackhardt,

2000). In Burt's early approaches, members' behaviour and management of ties are assumed to be driven exclusively by cost–benefit calculations.

Early Interorganizational Networks Studies

Many resources also flow among organizations, for example capital, personnel, information, goods (Aldrich and Marsden, 1988; Galaskiewicz and Marsden, 1978). In addition, as shown by studies such as that of Bauer and Cohen (1981) or Stokman *et al.* (1985), interorganizational relationships are also characterized by a great number of 'non-economic' exchanges. Again the dominant literature on this field is that of resource dependence theory. These approaches differentiate themselves from atomistic approaches by defining the environment as a set of other organizations. For example, organizational systems can be centralized and hierarchical, as with a group with a dominant holding company at the top, or they can be fragmented in a large number of small organizations, disorganized as in the beginning of an industry or in a highly competitive system (Mintz and Schwartz, 1985); or they can display a limited number of coalitions as in the system of financial and marital alliances between houses in 15th century Florence (Padgett and Ansell, 1993).

Davis and Powell (1992) identify three different directions taken by research on interorganizational networks. The first two remain merely descriptive. The third develops a complete approach which has been particularly influential in current economic sociology.

The first direction is concerned with formation and maintenance of these networks. It uses mainly interlock ties (that is, ties between two companies created by the fact that one person sits on both boards). The reason for this interest in these ties goes back to problems raised at the beginning of the 20th century by cartels, collusion and antitrust action taken to be consistent with an ideology of open competition in capitalist economies (Mizruchi, 1982, 1992; Schwartz and Mizruchi, 1988). The second direction is represented by studies of the way position in the network of organizations, or organizational 'field ' (DiMaggio, 1986), influences corporate actions, for example philanthropic giving (Galaskiewicz, 1979, 1989), top managers' political ideology (Useem, 1984), choice of a defence strategy against hostile takeover bids (Davis, 1991), and many others. In the same direction, Laumann and Knoke (1987) studied empirically the influence of interorganizational networks on lobbying and policy making in two ministries (health and energy) in the United States.

Finally, the third direction is concerned with evaluating profitability and chances of survival of companies given their position in the informal structure of their sector (Burt, 1983, 1992; Burt and Talmud, 1993). Market stability (Burt, 1988) and firm survival in a competitive arena are also among the main dependent variables.[6] For example, Barley *et al.*, (1992) try to explain strategic behaviour of companies in the new biotech industry, behaviour such as alliances and management of uncertainties arising from interdependencies with competitors. They show that one cannot explain these firms' behaviour without knowing their position in the structure created by all the organizations of the same sector. Analysing relationships between 900 organizations, as well as 700 contracts among them, they show that the firms may be clustered in blocks in which members tend to have the same alliance strategies and same level of participation in various segments of the market. Another example in the financial sector is Baker's (1984, 1990) empirical study of the informal structure of the Chicago options exchange. He has shown that price volatility of some products is higher at the periphery of the structure than at its centre, thus depending on the status of brokers.

This approach has generated fundamental ideas with regard to cooperation and competition in collective action. Pioneering work by Harrison White (1981a, 1981b, 1988, 2001) renews economic sociology by emphasizing the importance of the social structure of markets and the way in which social relations (as opposed to prices) regulate economic behaviour of competitors on specific markets, or the way in which the social structure influences pricing itself and other behaviour on competitive markets (Burt, 1992; Burt and Talmud, 1993; Leifer and White, 1988). White built an early sociological model of the market economy (recently extended, White, 2001) based on the existence of niches and blocks of producers watching each other's revenues, commitments to volume and choices of quality of products. As in Schumpeter's theory, producers do not focus first on demand, but on other producers. By definition, exchanges are never bilateral, always multilateral (and thus politicized). Instead of converging towards a single optimal price, they attempt to find a niche (defined as a combination of volume and the quality/price ratio) that allows them to create an ever-precarious market situation. Markets are thus organized from the perspective of niche-seeking producers and tend to segment into temporarily protected but fragile non-competitive economic niches.

It is interesting to notice here that several authors have used the concepts of niche to account for economic phenomena. In his seminal paper (1981b) and book (2001), White looks for conditions under which a market comes into existence and sustains itself. He considers a niche to be a market footing for a single firm and a single product, created mainly by consumers' quality judgment about (and ranking of) the product offered by this firm. This niche is thus socially constructed by producers watching each other, and by a 'typical consumer's' decision; notice that this construction is not a form of collective action because there is no joint and coordinated involvement of producers and consumers in the process. Obviously, this does not necessarily overlap with the definition of a social niche provided below as a set of exchange partners allowing easier access to multiple resources and developing common identifications and commitments. In the new version of his model, White (2001) 'turns the downstream model inside out' and models the behaviour of producers concerned with their upstream connections. But although, paradoxically, Harrison White is one of the pioneers of structural approaches to markets, his own model assumes the existence of an underlying social structure (connecting producers) without actually looking at the social and political mechanisms that maintain a market (including professional associations, political parties, country clubs and non-profit organizations). Managers are concerned with the size of their production runs, not with joining or creating groups of organizations to concentrate their power or deal with their interdependencies. In White's view, a niche is not a segment of a market in which actors agree to a partial suspension of strategic behaviour and competition, in exchange for more control of each other's behaviour, be it informal. It is mainly a monopolistic position of the firm to be secured and derived from a characteristic of the product and to be obtained from the typical consumer's quality orderings. Thanks to network analytical partition methods, one finds here familiar segmentation processes such as that characterizing labour markets (Granovetter, 1985, 1992; Swedberg, 1990, 1992).[7]

Other work in this third direction (Berkowitz *et al.*, 1979; Berkowitz, 1988; Berkowitz and Fitzgerald, 1995; as well as Mokken and Stokman, 1978), uses capital ownership ties combined with control interlock ties to define entities called *enterprises*. A company in a context of multinational groups operating at the global level is not a unit of analysis that must attract interest first in order to define a market. Berkowitz defines *market areas* as clusters of companies producing, distributing and consuming various goods in an upstream–downstream flow. This new overlay offers a picture of competitive markets at various levels of complexity. These models are more realistic than definitions of markets in purely technological terms in that they bring out institutional structures that protect market areas. Network analysis helps identify classical forms of market relationships (such as monopolies, duopolies, oligopolies or monopsonies) as well as unnamed but simple and constraining socioeconomic structures.

This work often goes beyond simple monographs of informal structures of organizations or of interorganizational systems to test embeddedness hypotheses on the articulation of structure, access to resources and behaviour. They build sociological theories reinterpreting economic activity through a detailed and ethnographic knowledge of the business world and its relationships with the institutional, local and national, context. Such theories are not yet complete and able to explain collective action coordinated by mechanisms other than competition. However, their capacity to explain many economic phenomena reformats the debate between sociology and economy in the grand tradition of

Weber and Polanyi, who conceive of markets as social institutions facilitating exchanges, that is, more than a pricing mechanism. It also suggests that it is useless to imagine interorganizational structures of cooperation that do not rely on multiple social resources and formal organizations, for example interorganizational 'structures' that would be made exclusively of contracts. By isolating the network of contracts from a formalized and organized social exchange, one kills its specificity.

Most of this early work was often based exclusively on narrow resource dependence theories taking into account social embeddedness. As shown by Lindenberg (1996), few behavioural assumptions, other than the prevalence of short term cost–benefit theories mitigated by social ties, were used to explain members' behaviour. It is, however, insufficient to explain how actors generate structures that encourage cooperation (as opposed to competition), or how to account for high levels of social exclusion provoked by contemporary market economies (Perrow, 1992). Therefore the next generation of structural sociologists has been trying to enrich the definition of the actor that is used to account for economic action. Specifically, since actors get involved in, and manage, exchanges of multiple resources, this calls for a theory of social exchange and barter.

RATIONALITY, SOCIAL EXCHANGE AND STRUCTURE: THE IMPORTANCE OF THE MESO LEVEL

Beyond utilitarian and embeddedness studies, a broader structural approach adds behavioural assumptions and multiplexity to a sociological theory of economic action. It assumes a form of actors' rationality that is compatible with social exchange, not only with market exchange. Social exchange includes calculations, but also symbolic activity[8] such as *appropriateness judgments*, commitments and relational investments (based on boundary management and identity claims) and value judgments (negotiation of precarious values and norms) that allow individuals to *contextualize* and *politicize* these calculations and exchanges, at least by selecting reference groups, priorities in allegiances and authorities (Lazega, 1992a, 1997; Favereau, 1998, 1999). In our view, it is useful to assume that actors invest in relationships in order to act at the meso level, not only to move within given opportunity structures but to try to *reshape their opportunity structure*, that is, to try to structure the context of their interactions and exchanges. They can do so, for example, in the process of selecting exchange partners. These selections are neither random, nor entirely free, nor entirely determined. As seen in the previous section, they are themselves subject to previous structural and normative constraints. But they nevertheless reflect the idea that actors invest in relationships at least in order to make some direct or indirect reciprocity possible. Actors often assume that they will benefit from this reciprocity in social niches, that is, if others share the same identities and rules of exclusivity. Rationality from a broadly conceived structural approach is inseparable from the processes characterizing social exchange.

One example that illustrates this approach to rationality is the importance of barter. In economics, barter is a slow, expensive and highly restrictive way to do business. The barter economy is inefficient compared to the cash economy. Barter transactions are opaque and approximate. At the macro level, barter undermines good government because it makes tax collection difficult, tax evasion easier (for example, the tax man has to work harder, with much less precise information to understand a company's business). A country cannot prosper unless barter is replaced by conventional money. For economists, people barter, for example, when inflation is too high or because they make goods that are unsalable at any price, and barter then becomes a way for them to restore price flexibility. There is barter entrenchment. It also becomes easier for people in power to manage barter to their advantage. However, in social life, barter is much more widespread than is usually acknowledged. It is used much more often than cash for many types of multiplex exchanges. And it has its own rules. It is indeed much more restrictive and it falls under a logic of membership, a symbolic logic; it is much more demanding in terms of solidarity with 'one's own people'. Basically, it identifies criteria that drive the barter economy, that is, a principle that is the exact opposite of the perfect market mechanism, in which people tend to be anonymous and unrelated. The barter economy is much more visibly politicized than the cash economy. It requires identifications, appropriateness judgements and interpretations. And it is much more pervasive in the economy than conventional economists acknowledge. In effect, pricing many goods or resources is next to impossible for actors involved in transactions connected to production and collective action. This is especially the case for knowledge.

In addition, investments in relationships are not independent of status comparisons. In effect, actors need to define terms of social exchange, and status is an enviable position from which to negotiate such terms. The dynamics of status auctions in brainstorming is a good illustration: it is a multiplex process relying on several forms of status (Lazega and Pattison, 2001). There is, however, a permanent risk of opportunism attached to such relational investments. They therefore presuppose a definition of – and possibly a resort to – authorities. A social niche cannot operate on its own, without such external authorities. The latter are central in the processes of the definition of the situation, but also for the meso-level social mechanisms such as generalized exchange or regulatory deliberation.

We thus use the concept of rationality in a wide sense. Rational action means that one has a goal (or a series of competing or successive goals) and a series of scarce means to reach these goals efficiently. For example, niche seeking is not an exclusive goal in itself but a strategy to reach a series of higher order goals. Niche seeking is sometimes based on a series of intuitive relation-specific investments guided by homophily. Therefore it belongs to a form of rationality that is not exclusively concerned with cost–benefit calculation. The fact that it is not always experienced as rational in a narrow sense does not mean that it is not rational in a broader sense. The criterion of what is rational is not necessarily what is experienced as such on the spot. Therefore attributing such a form of rationality to interdependent entrepreneurs cannot be considered to be a form of 'scholastic fallacy' denounced by Bourdieu with regard to narrow rational choice theories. On the contrary, this form of rationality can be shown to be highly correlated to position in the structure (Lazega and van Duijn, 1997).

In the next section, we provide an overview of the contribution of strategic analysis and symbolic interactionism as underlying sets of assumptions concerning actor's behaviour when involved in social exchange. We then look at their implications for economic activity at the individual level. Finally, we raise the issue of extending such a view of actors' behaviour at the interorganizational level.

Resource Interdependencies and Investments in Relationships

Actors depending on each other for resources are rational when they look for social niches, that is, contexts where their investments in relationships (with such selected partners) have a better chance of ensuring reciprocity both at the dyadic level and via generalized exchange (indirect reciprocity), and make social exchange, or barter, possible. They are trying to shape as much as possible their opportunity structure. This of course depends on their acceptance by others in the niche, so decisions to invest are not decisions that they can make exclusively on their own. These investments are the basis of generic social mechanisms that are multiplex and multi-level: multi-level because niches create a micro–meso and meso–macro articulation; and sometimes multiplex because some of these investments are exchanges of various kinds of resources needed for collective action (for example, both arm's-length and 'embedded' ties, as described by Lazega and Pattison, 1999, or Uzzi, 1999). Once investments in relationships have been made and once niches provide such positive returns, it can even make sense to risk (apparently sacrifice) some of these relationships themselves for the common good (see the case of lateral control regimes below) and for legitimacy needed to change the rules or maintain the status quo.

In other words, relation-specific investments are triggers for social mechanisms of cooperation. Before developing this proposition, it is useful to acknowledge two bodies of work that are particularly useful to this structural theory of social exchange focusing on investments in relationships and attempts to reshape opportunity structures. The first is an approach of power in terms of resource interdependencies, the second is an approach to commitment and identity. As we define it, social exchange requires both politicization of these exchanges, or barters, and coorientation with exchange partners.

Trying to Reshape Opportunity Structures: the Contribution of Strategic Analysis

An organizational approach to social life means, among other requirements, that individuals must be seen as interdependent members who need to get access to production-related resources (Crozier and Friedberg, 1977). At the level of organizations as units, resource dependencies are even more obvious. Because they rely on theories of power and resource dependencies, structural analyses are close to theories of collective action such as the French school of organizational analysis. Following the sociotechnical tradition of the 1950s, these interdependencies can be functional, that is related to a formal division of work, or structural, that is related to more informal circulation of all sorts of resources through social relationships. In that respect, structural analysis is compatible with what Crozier (1963; Crozier and Friedberg, 1977) calls 'strategic' analysis. Indeed, the former presupposes the latter.[9] This is particularly the case because structural analysis offers sophisticated measurements of resource interdependencies, status and power that are basic concepts of both approaches. Both rely on inductive reasoning avoiding reification of the notion of structure.

In effect, to the notion of formal structure, strategic analyses (Crozier, 1963; Crozier and Friedberg, 1977; Sainsaulieu, 1987) add the notion of a concrete action system. This system is partly defined by the relationships that are established among interdependent members in the organization or between organizations. Part of the task of strategic analyses involves bringing out patterns of informal relationships on which unexpected forms of order depend. In the structural perspective too, actors contribute to the raising of structures that end up constraining them. Formal and informal structures are now defined in the same terms, those of resource dependencies. Notions such as power and autonomy are measured in various types of centrality and constraint scores that take into account the relational and systemic dimensions of these phenomena. Structural advantage and disadvantage are made more visible.

Beyond these general similarities, structural and strategic analyses also meet in the study of two fundamental dimensions of power games: first, actors' capacity to manage relationships, invest in them and disinvest; second, in the ways in which they politicize their exchanges. Sainsaulieu (1977, 1987) has long insisted on the type of trained capacities that members develop in order to 'become actors' – whether cognitive capacities (identifying key players and relationships among them) or manipulative capacities (creating coalitions, letting relations dissolve or cutting ties). Such an approach is very close to that of Krackhardt (1987, 1990, 1992; Krackhardt and Hanson, 1993) and his exploration of the relationship between power and perception of relations; or to that of Kapferer (1969, 1972), Burt (1992) and other network analysts interested in direct or indirect cooptation and influence (Brass, 1984; Gargiulo, 1993; Lazega and Vari, 1992; Lazega and Lebeaux, 1995; Lazega, 2000b; Lazega and Krackhardt, 2000). As a moment (analytically speaking) of politicized exchanges, the logic of regulatory work and deliberations has also been closely tracked by Reynaud (1989).

Trying to Reshape Opportunity Structures: the Contribution of Symbolic Interactionism

The contribution of symbolic interactionist theory to our assumptions concerning social and economic behaviour is less straightforward. The easiest way to theorize this connection is to use the notion of commitment underlying selection of exchange partners. Commitment to others, but also to shared identifications and allegiances, is an old symbolic interactionist topic. From this perspective, social order is constructed through meaningful, self–other interaction (Blumer, 1969) under the 'surveillance' of reference groups, an audience which is not necessarily empirically present, but nevertheless exercising social control, and thus constraining behaviour by judging of its appropriateness and legitimacy. Such concepts are necessary because actors have many conflicting memberships, and therefore interests. Defining one's interest is not as easy as narrow rational choice theorists would suggest. In this context, the question of the structure is raised in terms of institutional constraints influencing negotiations of identities that, in turn, weigh on appropriateness judgments (McCall and Simmons, 1966; Lazega, 1992a). Since most interactions take place in situations that are never completely structured, nor necessarily clearly defined in actors' minds, actors may not necessarily know which of their identities will be involved, as a priority, in the current interaction, and which behaviour is more appropriate given the commitment to such identity. A phase of mutual identification, of identity negotiation and hierarchization, is necessary for interactions to take place. For example, joint identification with the image and attributes of a profession is all the more common in the business world that people have to 'sell themselves' in order to hold their own. The link between the structure of the social setting and the interactive processes which take place within them is theorized through analyses of this negotiation.

Social exchange necessary for production cannot be theorized without the notions of commitment, identity and appropriateness judgment. In collective action, formal and informal identities are combined. A context can be modelled as a set of formal identities bestowed upon some members, with their attached power and authority. The informal set of identities is not necessarily recognized institutionally and thus rarely associated with authority. Actors' method of contextualization of behaviour is thus close to a symbolic interactionist conception of rationality. Certainly, networks are not providing actors with 'pure' and 'essential' identities but with a sense of the appropriateness in using formal attributes here and now when orienting or coorienting behaviour. Identity is not a benefit that actors extract from belonging to a network. It is a structural green light both for construction of ties (access to resources) and for coorientation of actions within a specific context (formal and informal structure). This approach goes beyond embeddedness studies that do not often explain how actors use and develop social ties for their exchanges and cooperation.

Another angle from which to grasp the conceptual proximity between structural and symbolic interactionist theories comes from analysing 'crystallized' ways in which economic actors participate in social exchange. This crystallization can be understood through the notion of role as used in both perspectives. As seen above, the conceptual link between structure and behaviour in network analysis is often provided by the notion of role, which can be understood as the function performed from a position (for example, a subset of approximately structurally equivalent members), or as a specified combination of relations compounding two or more different networks. Such operationalizations of the concept of role, like any model, simplifies the description of constraints on behaviour, especially because they are exclusively relational. For critics (Brint, 1992; DiMaggio, 1991, 1992), the role of cultural (in the sense of normative) orientations may be as important in the explanation of actors' behaviour, especially when structural constraints are multiple and sometimes contradictory. For most general theories of action, such as that of Nadel (1957), a role results from normative expectations and from relations with associates carrying these expectations and sanctioning deviance. This is true even if it may be difficult to find a relational basis for all rights and duties, for instance by identifying authority figures that represent them or speak on their behalf. Therefore roles are useful as a synthesis of individual and social levels, but also of normative and relational dimensions.

Accepting that economic actors try to reshape their opportunity structure by entering social exchanges as role performance does not mean subscribing to a rigid conception of roles. Blumer (1969) sees roles as sets of informal rules created and recreated through interactions, especially through negotiations between individuals and their associates. Actors and their interactions construct the roles and rules that govern their behaviour. Individuals participate in defining their own roles, which have many variations, and they usually undergo change (Stryker, 1980; Stryker and Statham, 1985). In that sense, two largely descriptive steps are involved in the analysis of roles. One is the description of the extent to which the informal definition of the role (role making) is closely related to the formal definition (role taking). The second is the description of the extent to which this redefinition is itself subject to relational constraints. These negotiations recreate and reshape roles, often with dogmatic emphasis on (always temporary forms of) conformity and consensus among stakeholders. Individuals' role-related behaviour is determined by expectations of their associates, and such expectations are themselves culturally coded. In order to link the institution and the individual, this approach defines roles as sets of norms that are widely endorsed by actors in their interactions, even if associates may change. At a very general level of abstraction, this symbolic interactionist approach to social exchange is also compatible with a conventionalist theory of economic activity. Indeed, rules subsume relational and cultural devices that are needed to make economic decisions, both calculating and interpretive.

In sum, individuals trying to reshape their opportunity structure can be represented as strategic but interdependent entrepreneurs who seek contexts in which they can find and exchange these resources at low cost. Once in such contexts, they seek various forms of concentration of these resources so as to be in a position to define the terms of such exchanges. This means that two notions are important to a structural approach of collective action: *social niches* and *multidimensionality of status*. Both are indispensable for members' durable commitment to a labour contract. They are basic components, not only of production, but also of a series of relatively general mechanisms that together characterize coordination of collective action from a structural perspective. A structural approach is more than just a refinement of strategic analysis and symbolic interaction. Access to production-related resources by interdependent members, as well as participation in power plays, are particularly visible in niche seeking and status competition. The latter activities are both consequences of actors' attempts to reshape their opportunity structures and the building blocks of the social mechanisms that help them achieve cooperation even with their competitors.

Interdependent Entrepreneurs Seeking Bounded Solidarity in Social Niches

Interdependent members of organizations must have access to various production-related resources (for example clients, co-workers' goodwill, advice). The social niche of an actor can also be broadly defined as a subset of members of the organization with whom the actor has succeeded in creating especially *durable* exchange relations, whether directly or indirectly, as a consequence of his or her previous (and mutual, although not necessarily symmetric) investments. It is a pool of partners with whom exchanges are characterized by a certain density, which implies that sociologists can detect a niche through a strong relational cohesion, if not a generalized exchange system (Lazega and Pattison, 1999).[10] Actors contextualizing their behaviour also detect the existence of niches, but they often use the criterion of a certain social homogeneity to do so: they use similarities (for example in terms of office membership, or speciality, or hierarchical status) between exchange partners to identify the boundaries of the niche in which they assume that dense exchanges do or will take place (Lazega and van Duijn, 1997).[11] Ideally, such niches operate as pumps mixing and spreading various types of resources to members.

Members operate within micro structures such as niches, that are themselves part of a *system of niches* in the wider organization. Indeed, niches only make sense in a system of niches. It is rational for members to be niche-seeking because it is rational for them to look for multifunctional contexts that provide them with resources needed to produce, and with relative protection from rivalry and competition for these resources.[12] The multifunctional character of niches means that several resources can be exchanged by members. Indeed, such niches are also built for that very purpose, that is, to allow multiplex barters of resources without 'general equivalent'. Niche building is strategic, but, once built, niches have the advantage of allowing *partial suspension of purely calculating behaviour* (Ekeh, 1976). They help members, as economic actors, identify partners with similar long-term interests and combine, through identity criteria, these long-term interests and management of multiple resources. Niches and identities come together because they introduce long-term stability in members' choices and definitions of interests.[13] This stability is based on the intuition that common characteristics make long term common interests more likely, and therefore the existence of indirect reciprocity that is necessary to collective action. As seen above, there is no barter without identities and a very important symbolic dimension. Therefore they can be characterized by a form of *bounded solidarity*. This bounded solidarity is connected to a form of contextualization of action (Lazega, 1997) and limited rationality, in the sense that members do not always use the same criteria to evaluate the fairness of their multiplex barters. It can be measured in several ways: for example, by the stability of members' choices of exchange partners; or by boundary management (Lazega, 1992a) allowing for the existence of generalized exchange cycles, that is, of indirect reciprocity, among such partners; or by the presence of informal rules imposing multiplexity or marginalizing, then excluding, members who grab all the credit for successful actions.

To get access to such resources, members do not rely entirely on formal organization and rules. They are selective in their relational choices, and this selectivity, together with institutional constraints, produces patterns which are interesting for understanding exchanges in the firm. Members manage their interdependence in their own ways, that are both economic and political (Crozier and Friedberg, 1977). As seen above, to get access to such resources, they enter exchanges that are multilateral and multiplex.[14] The contextual rationality that is at work in such exchanges plays with attributes and ties.[15] It intervenes in the process of resource allocation by using formal attributes in 'politicized' ways or by introducing other particularistic attributes and preoccupations (for example gender, or school attended). The latter are more informal and ad hoc; they are not necessarily officially recognized by the organization as characteristics that should be used to promote cooperation and allocate resources. The main concept to understand this stability in social niches is that of *identification*. As mentioned above, identity is usually a relatively stable and multidimensional set of attributes that members use to make judgments of appropriateness, define themselves and get recognition as sources of their actions (for credit and accountability) on a continuing basis. In practice, an actor is always 'loyal' to some allegiance (represented by an attribute) while 'betraying' another (represented by another attribute). Identity is what introduces time in action by defining long-term individual and collective interests. Identities enter the exchange as bearings or markers or criteria for selection of exchange partners. Members use identity criteria to choose exchange partners who will presumably share values leading to some sort of solidarity. The idea here is that identity is introduced in transfers and exchanges of resources to avoid measuring the value of the heterogeneous resources in multiplex exchanges. The use of identities in multiplex exchanges creates a form of bounded solidarity.

In sum, a social niche offers its members resources, a sense of identity and of common long-term interests, a context for the enforcement of their own rules, and the stimulation that is needed to produce in common. Its generalized exchange system sustains cohesive and durable work relationships in contexts often dominated by flexibility and short-term calculations. It constitutes a bounded solidarity bloc. But recall that it can also become a difficult and very constraining environment, especially when members lose control of the status competition process.

Interdependent Entrepreneurs Competing for Multiple Forms of Status

Together with seeking or building niches as appropriate and protected contexts for part of their exchanges, members try to reshape their opportunity structure by attempting to manage the exchanges that take place in them. In this context of bounded solidarity, one way of influencing exchanges with colleagues is to accumulate resources needed for production, thus reaching a form of status. The role of status in the mechanisms supporting organizations is complex. In general sociological theory, status refers to a member's relative position in the group, both in the formal hierarchy and in the networks of exchanges in the group. In organizations, status comes from contributions to the firm, from credentials, from a history of achievements and establishment of competence. It means that the individual is considered worthy of being granted an extensive mandate, regarding both personal responsibility and corporate responsibility to regulate community, professional or internal firm affairs (Bosk, 1979). This mandate is derived from – and made measurable by – concentration of production-related resources, or by the privileges that are granted to members who control such resources. These privileges may include financial compensation, decision-making priorities, more respectful treatment by peers, symbolic and moral licensing, as well as escaping pressure for accountability, tests of commitment, and blame for many errors. In addition to being less vulnerable to criticism from colleagues, and being insulated from cross-pressures, members with status have functional prerogatives including more freedom to select interesting matters and cases on which to work, thus authoritatively deciding how such cases will be handled and dividing the work among others.

It is not surprising, therefore, that members of a group compete for status,[16] even if the latter comes with responsibilities, for example that of exercising a form of leadership, of being responsible for the long-term future of the organization. Other members expect from them solutions to their collective action problems and these convergent and constraining expectations play an important role in the structuration of cooperation. Elites are challenged to solve problems by alternating constraint and persuasion, to combine diverging interests of fractions hanging on to their rents within often confused and unstable coalitions. They are supposed to help maintain solidarity within the organization at large. But this leadership cannot be exercised without a concentration of social resources. This is where a relational and structural definition of power becomes important to understand status (Crozier and Friedberg, 1977). In effect, it is often the concentration of social resources that allows members to reach a form of status. And once in a leadership position, members need these resources to perform, to use others' dependencies and define terms of exchanges.

From a structural perspective, the concept of status is a composite of titles (official function) and accumulation of different types of social resources. This composite character is translated by the existence of multiple forms of status that can be used by actors to stabilize their definition of interests and priorities, as well as to politicize their exchanges. Sociological classics have long stressed the importance and many dimensions of social status and social approval. Max Weber used to distinguish dimensions that were economic (based on revenue), social (honour, prestige, not only from birth, but from human capital – education) and political. For him, collective action is possible only because status has heterogeneous sources. As stressed by Parsons, then by Bourricaud, the functions of leadership are always exercised by several persons. The role of the leader is 'diffuse', not specialized. This multidimensionality of status is derived from the concentration of different resources, from an endogenous heterogeneity (and not only an exogenous one, as in Weber) of sources. For example, the official member, the most competent, the most popular, the most committed, all have some sort of status, and participate in coordination of collective action.

The question may be raised of the relationships between these different forms of status, if not their coexistence. Given that it is multidimensional, each of its forms may or may not go hand-in-hand with another form, often capitalized by someone else. For the individual, heterogeneity of sources of status may correspond to various levels of status consistency. In fact, it is the possibility of playing, at the individual level, with this status inconsistency that gives oligarchic systems the capacity to maintain themselves in equilibrium and to define a hierarchy of values (for more on this, see the end of this chapter). In collegial systems, for example, multidimensionality of status comes usually with processes that help the organization maintain a *balance of powers* between oligarchs. Heterogeneity of sources of status often means that an oligarchy reaches a form of equilibrium or stability based on the interdependency of oligarchs.

Investments in Relationships and Social Mechanisms

The fact that actors are niche-seeking entrepreneurs, status competitors and judges of the appropriateness of their own (as well as others') social exchanges is important to understanding sociologically economic activity. Reaching and enforcing economic decisions are processes that depend heavily on the existence of social niches, of multi-dimensionality of status and of normative coorientation. The contribution of a broadly conceived structural approach to a theory of economic activity needs to take them into account. This is done by acknowledging that, when investing in relationships and trying to reshape their opportunity structure, actors trigger social mechanisms that can be vicious or virtuous.

In other words, relation-specific investments are triggers for social mechanisms. This raises a chicken-and-egg issue. We do assume that actors always act in situations that are already structured, but we do not assume that these structures entirely determine behaviour. For example Uzzi's (1999) work shows that organizational change may sometimes come from importing into the organization (banks) types of ties (social relationships with clients) that are built outside the organization. Signals providing a *structural green light* for specific kinds of imports, however, remain to be examined more closely. Do actors invest in ties before generalized exchange exists? How do they take a risk in a situation of uncertainty? In our view, actors may try to import exogenous structures but there is a limit to this process because the number of (compatible) identity criteria that each of us can credibly use is limited by preexisting constraints.

In the next section, based on a case study, we illustrate this point by specifying several *social mechanisms* (Stinchcombe, 1991; Hedström and Swedberg, 1998) that drive collective action in economic partnerships. Specifying such mechanisms goes beyond simple statements of embeddedness seeking to prove the economic efficiency of the existence of social ties, or 'relational capital'. These mechanisms spell out processes that are key to collective action, mainly exchanges of resources, control of commitment and oligarchic negotiation of precarious values. A good definition of such mechanisms exemplifies the usefulness of added behavioural assumptions in a structural approach to economic activities. It also provides new understanding of the relationship between the micro and macro levels of collective action, not just a criticism of the limitations of orthodox economic sciences in their approach to economic activity. In the following sections we sketch a definition of these mechanisms.

SOCIAL MECHANISMS FOR COOPERATION AT THE INTRAORGANIZATIONAL LEVEL

Framing the structural contribution to the study of markets and organizations through the notion of social mechanism goes beyond narrow structuralism.[17] Examples of social mechanisms in organizations include solidarity (generalized exchange), management of status competition, control and rule enforcement, and 'constitutional' processes (that is, redefinition of the rules of the game). An old sociological tradition focuses on social mechanisms supporting and enhancing economic performance, beginning with Durkheim in 1893 and now strongly established (Burt, 1992; Macaulay, 1963; Bourdieu, 1980; Coleman, 1990; see Flap *et al.*, 1998, and Gabbay, 1997, for a review). Here maximizing performance not only means improving technology, product and organizational innovation, managerial coordination or financial management. It also means maintaining the specific local constellations of relationships that are the basis of social mechanisms and that help organizations to solve problems of coordination.[18]

This conception of a structural approach of collective action in terms of social mechanism helps in this analysis of exchange, control and social change. It is compatible with a theory of action such as that outlined above. In this section, we illustrate this approach at the intraorganizational level by using a structural study of a professional partnership. This study offers a description of the three generic social mechanisms that are needed to sustain the collegial form of collective action (a multiplex generalized exchange system, a lateral control regime, and the process of negotiation of precarious values). Looking at such mechanisms helps in understanding how an organization provides structural solutions to problems of collective action. These mechanisms and their efficiency have been examined in a medium-sized northeastern US corporate law partnership (Lazega, 2001a). Some characteristics of this firm made it easier to study these mechanisms: in particular, partners have locked themselves in a very cooperative situation and constraining structure: they have adopted a compensation system that helps (or forces) them to take a long-term view with regard to cooperation and solidarity; they can expel one of their own only if there is near unanimity against him or her. They also belong to a profession that is usually favoured with monopoly returns, thus loosening the relationship between efficiency, performance and scarcity of resources.

The firm can indeed be seen as an exchange system for various forms of resources, and members as (broadly conceived rational) status competitors managing and accumulating these resources needed to work and survive in this environment. The production process is based on the use of social ties in a *generalized, multiplex and multilevel exchange system.*[19] This system can be shown to rest on rules of partner selection and to be effective at cultivating and mitigating status competition among members. The analysis of the ways in which these resources are bartered leads to the identification of informal entities such as niches that are shaped by members' use of the formal structure of the firm. The effects of relevant differences in members' selective choices of exchange partners such as hierarchical status (partner/associate), speciality (litigation/corporate), office membership, gender and law school (Ivy League/non-Ivy League) were examined to confirm the emergence of these social niches. The existence of these entities can then be used to provide insights into the way collegial organizations find structural solutions to additional key problems: first, motivating tenured partners; second, quality control; third, opportunism in the form of free-riding; and fourth, firm integration.

The firm can also be seen as a control system (against behaviour considered to be opportunistic, such as shirking) in which issues of cost of control and rule enforcement are as central, if not more so, as in any form of collective action. A structural perspective also helps focusing on the relationship between status and control of enforcement of decisions made by the partnership. This issue is of particular importance in formally egalitarian bodies in which practitioners are all nominal equals and interdependent. Free-rider problems quickly arise in such settings because even a member who did not contribute effectively to the firm's revenues imposes a cost on the organization as a whole by reaping the benefits of membership (Olson, 1965). As a consequence, monitoring and policing, especially early graduated sanctions, are considered to be particularly important for ensuring that members' individual commitment to contribute remains credible. A second-order free-rider problem arises as well: the problem of who will bear the costs of monitoring and enforcement of previous agreements among the formally equal members (Heckathorn, 1989; Oliver, 1980; Yamagishi, 1986). In such contexts, hierarchical control being relatively weak, there is reluctance, at an early stage, to use formal procedures against colleagues to overcome free-riding and maintain solidarity. Direct command or use of administrative hierarchy are not considered appropriate means for exercising control because professionals have many ways of neutralizing formal authority (Gouldner, 1954; Freidson, 1975, 1986; Bosk, 1979.) In fact, early monitoring and sanctioning in collegial organizations also rely on specific forms of interdependencies in the exchanges of resources to protect overall prosperity against individual opportunism or parochial interests. Knowledge of such relational constraints helps to understand how members try to keep early monitoring costs low, and themselves motivated to carry on monitoring and sanctioning each other. These constraints take the form of a *lateral control regime* (Lazega, 2000b) that is also part of firm social capital in Coleman's sense because it helps peers find an early solution to this second-order free-rider problem in formally egalitarian interdependent groups. In this regime, status, particularly that of members called 'protectors of the common good', is shown to be central. Thanks to this social mechanism, individuals find it advantageous, credible and safe to pursue contingent commitment to rule compliance and mutual control.

Beyond economic performance (Lazega, 1999b), the exchange system can also be shown to be useful in maintaining firm integration, that is, in dealing with many centrifugal forces threatening the organization (for example, disputes about sharing profits, secession of rainmakers – partners controlling access to important clients – and their more or less permanent team to another firm, status competition in the work process, disputes between subgroups representing different offices or specialities). The study shows that members of a collegial organization have an interest in maintaining a stable oligarchy, a subset of members with various forms of status. Oligarchs are often under pressure not to fight. They are all the more appreciated in that they do not raise controversies, keep a low profile and present their agreements as renegotiable. Multi-dimensionality of status comes usually with processes that help the collegial organization maintain a *balance of powers* between oligarchs. This is the case at this law firm, where economic and administrative powers are separate, informally but in a strong structural way. This allows two forms of solidarity and integration to coexist, one based on a 'welfare system' of bureaucratic distribution of work, the other on an informal and 'clientelistic' distribution. Each form of solidarity (welfare and clientelistic) is made possible by members with different forms of status in the organizations ('minders', who are more responsible for the long-term time frame in the organization, and 'finders' who bring in and control access to new clients) that are kept dependent upon each other. In many ways a collegial organization replaces an autocrat with a set of oligarchs who prevent each other from accumulating enough resources to be independent. Collegiality (thus called polycracy) presupposes the interdependency of oligarchs. Cohesion in the oligarchy is reached by a balance of powers and integration *à la* Montesquieu (Lazega, 1992b, 2000a; Kuty, 1998). Maintaining heterogeneity and interdependence of forms of status is often the condition under which rivalry among oligarchs leads to equilibrium.

Finally, this structural approach also helps us to understand the 'constitutional' process of such collective actors by looking at their *members' negotiation of precarious values* underlying policy options and derived rules of social exchange. As seen above, in the section on symbolic interactionism and roles, members of an organization do not have rigid overarching 'common values' (Crozier and Friedberg, 1977) and derived rules. For example, in decisions on recruitment through cooptation, peers often reach a conflict between loyalty (typically clientelistic criterion) and excellence (ideally bureaucratic criterion). Managerial, professional and entrepreneurial ideologies can conflict in the redefinition of organizational rules and policies. Actors, if they want to win, sometimes have to redefine their priorities in terms of values (Friedberg, 1993). In a collegial organization, for example, partners feel free to develop their own conception of professionalism. They calculate their interests, but they also 'negotiate' their values (Kuty, 1998). They must accept debates concerning professionalism even when members with superior economic power (for example controlling access to large and lucrative clients) try to impose their own hierarchy of values, their own rules of the game, their terms for multiplex exchanges. In particular, given that no member can have the last word once and for all in such discussions, a *modus vivendi* is usually established among them. A structural approach can help understand, in part, this *modus vivendi*.

A structural approach looks at the social mechanism helping members control this constitutional process in the firm, that is, the renegotiation of the rules of the game. A precarious value (Selznick, 1957) is one that is essential to the viability of the collectivity but in which most members may have no direct stake. Examples of precarious values include, in collegial organizations, hierarchical authority and professional ethical principles. Subunits fight for the particular values entrusted to them and may continually redefine them to assert their priority over potentially competing values. Client satisfaction, internal coordination, innovation and quality of professional knowledge, societal needs and employee interests would not be defended or promoted if not represented by powerful subunits or members to whom the values in question are paramount, and the organization as a whole would be the poorer (Simpson, 1971).

This social mechanism helps collegial organizations solve the problem of endless deliberation about norms and values, and thus about firm management policies regarding issues such as compensation, peer review, work intake and assignment, marketing, and many others.[20] It can be shown to make use of the multi-dimensionality of status ahead of the deliberations themselves. It consists in authorizing specific forms of status inconsistency so as to prevent certain legitimate values from being later defended forcefully by the appropriate oligarchs. In effect, regulatory decisions are also made from within the organizational exchange system. The social mechanism of definition of rules is based on a selection of bi- or multi-status oligarchs who play a leadership role by defining priorities.[21] Their selection brings into the deliberation only oligarchs who have several forms of status and represent several precarious values, thus able to give priority to one of these forms without disqualifying the others. The negotiation of precarious values, or the emergence of a priority value, requires a cohesive core of multi-status oligarchs clearly identified with such values and in a position to defend their rank with their peers, if not to prescribe them to each other. In short, the debate about precarious values uses in a constraining way the heterogeneity of sources of status observed by the classics. Structure mediates between interests and values because oligarchs can promote some norms and conventions while playing down the importance of others (Lazega, 2000e).

This is also part of the politicization of exchanges as defined above and as part of cumulating power in the sense of capacity to set premises and to define terms of exchanges. Structural approaches remain limited as long as they are not associated with the study of forms of politicization of exchanges allowing for the circulation of resources, that is, the choice of exchange rules among members. This work, however, goes beyond the capacity of narrow structuralism to use qualitative methods. Rules surely have an endogenously dynamic dimension. They develop within a relational structure and they themselves have an effect on the evolution of these structures, especially through their influence on the selection of exchange partners (see Kellerhals *et al.*, 1988 for an example). In this field, much remains to be done with economists of conventions, both in the normative and in the interpretative dimensions of the concept.

SOCIAL MECHANISMS OF COOPERATION AT THE INTERORGANIZATIONAL LEVEL IN STUDIES OF MARKETS

At the beginning of this chapter, we argued that the social mechanisms characterizing collective action at the intraorganizational level, as well as their modelling, may also characterize collective action and coordination at the interorganizational level. Beyond early structural approaches that were often limited to statements of embeddedness, the same broadly conceived structural approach can be used to look at organizations as actors trying to structure their environment and shape their opportunity structure, and at the derived mechanisms of cooperation.

Specifically, we argue that the collegial form of organization (and its network analysis) offers models for examining the social organization of a market economy, an economy that is not bureaucratized by state planning, especially for the coordination of activities among interdependent entrepreneurs. This does not mean that the state does not intervene in such an economy, but that its interventions are now looked at as competing with those of all the other stakeholders of the economy, including small and medium-sized financial or business groups, large multinationals, independent or supranational watchdogs and regulatory bodies, and many other organizational entities. In this organizational society, the state still wields strong powers – not least a power of legitimate violence – but so do some of the other entities that play an entrepreneurial role or control the circulation and allocation of enormous amounts of resources. In addition, there are many levels of cooperation between the two ideal-type models of collective action, as well as within each type. Levels of involvement in cooperation go from temporary but multiplex contracts (such as that characterizing services industries) to strong alliances and eventually mergers.

Organizations, whether public administrations or private businesses, do not conduct their affairs as isolated units. Their resource dependencies (Salancik and Pfeffer, 1977) force them to form cooperation ties with other organizations, and these relationships are expressed by more or less clear legal and social boundaries.[22] Recall that Levine and White (1961) already framed interorganizational relationships in terms of exchanges of resources and resource dependencies (Aldrich and Marsden, 1988). Resources exchanged through multiplex ties at that level can be learning goods, services that may or may not come attached to financial credit, and so on. This view underlies Harrison White's seminal work (1981b; 2001) in which transfers and exchanges of production-related resources are the defining features of production markets. It is the basis of the sociological approach to markets as social institutions facilitating exchanges without being reduced to price definition mechanisms (for a summary, see Swedberg, 1994).

Is this extension to cooperation at the interorganizational level (of a reality previously examined at the micro level) acceptable? To what extent are higher-order entities such as organizations 'rational' in a broad sense? Individuals, when they represent organizations and make decisions on behalf of them, make a special effort to be efficient cost–benefit maximizers. But do their organizations select 'identities' and get involved in 'social' exchanges in order to shape their opportunity structure? Does it make sense, at that level, to get involved in identity politics, to join meso-level niches for better and easier access to resources?[23] Does cooperation at the interorganizational level rely on any form of social discipline that can be differentiated from a purely utilitarian attitude? The same question applies to competition for status, that is, for better control of the terms of exchange and prices of resources, or for rule enforcement and regulatory clout. A positive answer could make it worthwhile to identify multiplex social mechanisms for collective action because it would provide a new vision of productive systems in regions, sectors or other levels. It would lead structural approaches towards a more general theory of collective action at the meso and macro levels. There is certainly no scale invariance with regard to rationality and social phenomena, but it is nevertheless possible to assume that, just like individuals, organizations follow similarly politicized principles when making decisions concerning transactions with partners such as other organizations (Raub and Weesie, 2000). This, however, is a true challenge for a broadly conceived structural economic sociology. Elements of answers to the above questions – the first building blocks of this structural research programme in economic sociology – are available already.

All exchanges between organizations are not necessarily 'purely' market exchanges. For many years, research has been conducted on the ways in which individuals working in or running such social settings, even if they often tend to behave as 'rationally' as possible (by definition of the organization of work), also use them for purposes that are not immediately and directly connected to purely focused production activities. In many such situations, cost–benefit calculations, with regard to many activities, although mechanically performed, have a fictitious dimension. For firm A, putting a precise price tag on a specific R&D operation involving cooperation between its own scientists and that of firm B is formally possible, but it is a bet that very often does not reflect any clearly defined costs or market value for the outcome of this operation. For the same companies, putting up a million Euros to support a political campaign is also an expense measurable in monetary terms, but the amount of this form of investment cannot be reduced to a price as usually defined on a market (again, a rational value that can be associated with a specified outcome). Many such expenses and investments cannot be traced back to clear cost–benefit calculations. The price of trying to structure one's environment to get 'Pareto protection' is not easily defined. To look at them, in part, as forms of relational investments or social exchange is useful in the sense that such practices, which are important for economic activity, have a logic that differs from the price mechanism. Our point is that this logic can easily be compared to that of social exchange, and lead to the niche building and status competition examined above.

Although the conditions under which such exchanges can be defined as barter are not entirely spelled out yet, it is helpful to assume that they can be and that organizational politics include learning the mechanics of social exchange: this perspective brings together various contributions by structural sociologists in that domain.

Social Niches and Status Competition at the Interorganizational Level

Actual structural network studies of multiplex ties in interorganizational 'fields' (DiMaggio, 1986) are rare because such data are sensitive and strategic. Visible elite family ties, for example, no longer constitute a strong basis for social discipline in the business world, as they did in 19th-century forms of capitalism (Berle and Means, 1932; Chandler, 1977). Therefore, in order to look at contributions, at the interorganizational level, to the broadly conceived structural approach outlined here, it is useful to focus directly on pioneering work echoing more or less directly our reasoning about niches and about status. Concerning niches,[24] DiMaggio (1986) exhorted organizational analysts to reason in terms of observed patterns of exchange relations. As mentioned above, a few exceptional studies in the 1980s – pioneering in their analyses of transfers and exchanges of resources – were conducted with this preoccupation in mind (for a presentation of their place in the history of market analyses, see Swedberg, 1994). For example, it is possible to read Berkowitz's work (1982, 1988; Berkowitz and Fitzwilliam, 1995) as a first approach to niche building. As seen above, this author combines control (interlock ties) and ownership (capitalistic) ties among companies to provide early network modelling of market structures. He defines new entities called 'enterprises', then 'market-areas' as a new kind of clustering of production activities in which these enterprises operate and get new business footings. Although he does not provide much understanding of how these 'enterprises' operate, these new contours also offer an original overlay of competitive markets at various levels of complexity, one that is separable from more standard technology-based approaches.

Studies of business groups (including conglomerates such as Japanese *keiretsus* and Korean *chaebols*) could also be used as proxies for systematic detection of social niches. Selection of exchange partners may be studied through choices of suppliers, subcontractors or distributors that are in themselves investments in relationships. Granovetter's (1994) programmatic text on business groups also exemplifies this structural approach to interorganizational ties. He considers business groups to be interorganizational entities in which exchanges of resources are dense and multiplex, but who also raise 'private', non-tariff barriers to economic dealings with the 'outside' of the cartel, thus restraining trade. There are forms of particularistic solidarity, ways of giving premiums to loyalty, that are more or less visible. Sharing costs of exploring new markets, lower financial costs of raising capital, sharing personnel and so on are indicators of such forms of solidarity even among competitors. Granovetter (1994) offers a research programme on business groups, which he defines as formal and informal federations of companies that constitute a more or less coherent social structure.[25] He emphasizes the fact that in many countries the choice between a business group federation and consolidation is affected not only by economic contingencies, but also by political and symbolic factors. Ties between organizations include commercial transactions, but also mutual ownership, solidarity ties based on religion, political allegiances, ethnicity and family or regional ties. Granovetter includes moral constraints as a component of the social discipline underlying economic transactions in such business groups.[26] Such formal and informal ties allow them to become more than the sum of their parts. Coordination depends on this embeddedness of economic decisions in social ties. Systematic data about these phenomena are obviously missing.

In effect, in business groups, for example, connected partners both force and help their managers to deal with and share common risks. It is at the level of groups that real risks are taken in business strategy, but only when member organizations are mobilized and committed to carrying out such policies. These ties can be analysed as multiplex networks of easier access to capital, information and personnel (thus creating internal group-level labour markets), but also strategic advice with or without transactions or common responsibilities. These resources give a concrete meaning to the term 'group', even when multiplexity is reduced compared to what it can be at the intraorganizational level. This presupposes the capacity to detect meso-level forms of bounded solidarity that represent forms of short-term rationality embedding themselves in longer-term rationality on which they depend. Studying groups is not easy: these resources must be sharable and appropriable ones, both at the national and the international levels (Boccara, 1999a, 1999b). Unpredictability and uncertainties are invisibly delegated or passed on to subcontractors or to certain categories of employees; those at the lower end of the dumping chain (whose labour contracts become increasingly 'flexible') incur the maximum of risks and costs.[27]

An empirical phenomenon that provides an opportunity to look at niches based on ties with exchange partners is the phenomenon of strategic alliances. This topic has received considerable attention in the organizations and business strategy literatures (for example, Gulati, 1995; Uzzi, 1997). Firms establish alliances because they expect benefits from access to resources provided by such ties. Organization scholars have been particularly impressed by the learning advantages of these alliances which provide firms with fresh know-how and skills (Kogut and Zander, 1996; Powell *et al.*, 1996). However, the existence of 'knowledge niches' has not been examined as an object in a social and relational space, only as a phenomenon characterizing a 'technological space' (see below).[28]

From the perspective outlined here, it is worth arguing that three approaches to the existence of social niches remain underdeveloped. The first is concerned with the role of state administrations (and associated *corps d'Etat* in countries such as France) in the creation of social ties among executives. The second is the role of the non-profit sector (Anheier and Seibel, 1990), including business schools, in the creation of such ties, a role that has not been fully exposed. The third is that of illegally (trust) cooperative ties in which information and commitments are exchanged (Baker and Faulkner, 1993, Baker *et al.*, 1998). Looking at such niche-building contexts that bring together businesses for various purposes should be a productive area of research.

The second concept that could be used to account for social mechanisms at the interorganizational level is that of multidimensional status competition. The concept of status has been only partly exploited in a broadly conceived structural approach to markets. It is still not very clear how status exists at the interorganizational level, at least from a perspective combining social and market exchange. Studying market uncertainty, Podolny (1993, 1994; Podolny and Stuart, 1995) uses this traditional concept to account for the selection of business partners. Firms use evaluations of status to signal quality and select exchange partners. Partners with status inspire confidence, attract risk-averse customers and are able to define favourable terms of exchange with lesser status partners. This use of the concept, however useful at early stages of structural analyses of markets, remains vague because the various dimensions of status are not clearly defined and compared; power generated by the concentration of various kinds of *social* resources is neglected. But this work nevertheless shows how difficult it is today to look into interdependencies between entrepreneurs, even at the descriptive stage, and how useful it would be to identify such forms of status more clearly. This difficulty is even greater at the explanatory level required to account for the social mechanisms of cooperation. Data for studying these social mechanisms at the interorganizational level are scarce. Recall that structure is defined as regularities in multiple resource interdependencies among entrepreneurs with a business footing; interdependencies are always multiplex (defined for several resources) and multilateral.

Finally, the relationships between niche seeking and status competition at the interorganizational level deserve special attention. Just as endless brainstorming fuelled by status competition among peers is dealt with (kept under control) by oligarchs, the latter can also replace dysfunctional markets with more viable ones, although more brutally at that level (Lazega, 2000e). For example, it is sometimes indispensable for large companies to agree to impose a common technological standard without which markets would unravel. However, at the interorganizational level, the effects of social niches and those of status and power may not be combined and balanced as efficiently as they can be at the intraorganizational level, because corporate actors are run by individuals who are trained to make particular efforts to be as cost–benefit maximizing as they can. Corporate leaders still look for social niches, using identities, or membership in ethnic groups (Saxenian, 1994), but this does not necessarily predispose them to lenient behaviour when survival is at stake. The fact that oligarchs' power may be more brutal (than it is at the intraorganizational level) does not identify their interventions with those of a formal hierarchy such as a state administration's. At the interorganizational level, distinctions between status (Weberian *Herrschaft*) and raw power (*Macht*) may matter less because power here is less often confronted with or challenged by various forms of status. Distinctions such as that used by Podolny et al. (1996) (legitimacy produced by endorsement) are not always necessary when power and several forms of authority are concentrated in the same hands. In this situation, there may not be much social exchange: calculating strategies anticipate the decisions and movements of asymmetrically distributed resources generated by threatening repositionings of oligarchs (big firms). On the other hand, commonsense accounts of governance of business often have it that, at the interorganizational level, the notions of private resources and relation-specific investments seem to be less relevant than at the intraorganizational level. But this statement is highly questionable. High-level managers need multiple resources to interact with the interorganizational environment and they usually do not rely exclusively on resources provided by the formal organization itself (indeed, they are often hired for their own personal network). In sum, the relationship between niche seeking and status competition at the inter-organizational level remains to be researched more sociologically.

Collegial Social Mechanisms at the Interorganizational Level

The general idea that studies of relational structures should go beyond the description of embeddedness and account for social mechanisms that are grounded in exchanges of resources among firms can actually be found in Granovetter's (1985) own work and in a more recent preoccupation with the 'governance benefits' of embeddedness.[29] Current 'embeddedness studies' sometimes provide glimpses of such mechanisms. Given the constraints on data collection, such studies remain mostly at the dyadic level and are unable to reach (as intraorganizational studies sometimes do) the structural level.

At the dyadic level such studies are different from most economic research on the question of inter-firm arrangements promoting governance benefits for firms in their interorganizational transactions. This economic research focuses on how formal 'governance' arrangements, such as contracts, hostage taking or hierarchy, enable exchange partners to capture gains through trade (Williamson, 1996; Dyer and Singh, 1998; Raub and Weesie, 1996; Batenburg *et al.*, 1997). By contrast, recall that other theories argued that governance benefits are achieved through the embedding of commercial transactions in social attachments and networks (Granovetter, 1985, 1994). The latter studies are conducted with thorough investigation of the formal economic structure of the market (number of firms, concentration, market shares, quality niches, intermediaries and so on). They offer the equivalent of the above-mentioned glimpses because they show that social embeddedness offers a useful account of how social life matters, at the dyadic level, for economic benefits in markets. Using measurements of social embeddedness in a financial market, Uzzi (1999) shows that firms get easier access to loans and lower interest rates from mid-market banks when entrepreneurs maintain social ties to a privileged bank officer and arm's-length ties to other bankers. He argues that embedding commercial transactions in social attachments and networks facilitates dyadic exchanges by initiating 'self-organizing governance arrangements' that operate through expectations of trust and reciprocity and access to private knowledge. At the level of the bank–firm tie, increased embeddedness enhances governance benefits. Firms' networks composed of a complementary mix of embedded and arm's-length ties are said to produce optimal governance by reducing the need for costly formal governance of loan contracts.

Another example of research that comes close to identifying social mechanisms based on niche seeking and status competition is that of Podolny and Stuart (1999). Building on their previous work (1995) on patents citations, they show that position in what they call a 'technological space' can drive alliances and their performances in specific industries.[30] This technological space is thus assumed to have its own dynamics,[31] which, together with firms' considerations of relative 'status', would drive the evolution of the industry. This evolution is thus linked to considerations of power (that are considered social-structural in that they are different in nature from technology). Although it assumes the existence of an exchange system (of which alliances would be an indicator) between firms, this research does not examine it as a multiplex and structural phenomenon. Rather, it switches to a different (more ecological) conception of 'niche' to account for survival of firms in the industry. Podolny *et al.*, (1996) develop a conception of an organization-specific niche (defined by 'crowding' and 'status' – itself built from citations of an organization's patent portfolio, not through analysis of dense and multiplex exchanges of resources) in a technological network to show that it can enhance the firm's growth and survival chances.[32] This approach loses even White's insight about the importance of structural equivalence (with respect to the pattern of ties to upstream and downstream organizations) for niche building, not to mention the importance of any form of density in the exchanges between firms.[33] Nevertheless, there is much to learn from these studies in terms of looking at outcomes such as survival, growth rates and innovation as effects of niche building and status competition, as described above.

The importance of niche seeking and status competition for control and enforcement of regulation has largely escaped analysis up to now. Status competition may make sense at the interorganizational level even in increasingly oligarchic (monopolistic or duopolistic) forms of competition. Niches, often identifiable through either corruption or violation of antitrust laws, make sense at that level when rents cannot be extracted from a monopolistic position. The balance between status competition and niche seeking should be in itself the very stuff of competition policies that are attempts to regulate production and exchanges on markets.

More even than at the intraorganizational level, relation-specific investments between organizations raise the problem of sunk costs (when one party behaves opportunistically) and therefore social mechanisms, in addition to legal ones, are also needed here to deal with first- and second-order free-riding. For example, the issue of commercial justice can be framed in terms of formal external regulation (Hawkins, 1984; Reiss, 1984; Shapiro, 1984; Vaughan, 1983, 1996) or self-regulation (Lazega, 1994b, 2001a; Lazega and Mounier, forthcoming), but also in terms of more informal conflict resolution mechanisms (Macaulay, 1963) or private arbitration practices created by corporate law firms (Dezalay and Garth, 1999). The contribution of social ties (and derived niches and forms of status) to social control mechanisms in the business world remain, to our knowledge, poorly studied. Governance mechanisms in Williamson's (1996; also Raub and Weesie, 1993) sense only scratch the surface of all the processes that help interdependent entrepreneurs monitor and sanction each other before (or through) resorting to well-defined but costly court procedures (Cheit and Gersen, 2000; Dunworth and Rogers, 1996; Macaulay, 1963; Rooks *et al.*, 2000) and how society attempts to exercise control over their activities.[34]

Finally, since niche building and status competition are inseparable from a politicization of economic activity, attention has also focused on political management of economic activity, but in a way that does not yet provide new general insights on political economy. Neoclassical economics with its ideology of pure competition has often permeated studies of markets. White's and Burt's approaches helped question such views by connecting reasoning in terms of network analysis with ideas on monopolistic competition. But they do not focus on how economic actors such as interdependent firms spend time and resources structuring their environment so as to escape competitive markets. As well described by Pareto and Schumpeter, entrepreneurs as political 'courtesans' try to dump market competition on others, and to look for niches in which rents and discounts are available. If organizations follow this logic as well, it makes sense to assume that they all vie both for collusion (Baker and Faulkner, 1998) with specific suppliers, subcontractors and consumers, and for forms of status that would both attract clients and give them power to negotiate terms of trade with partners outside the niche. Markets are often rigged and constructed in interorganizational contexts in which power is usually in the hands of a very politicized establishment. In this establishment, actors recognize each other or identify with one another (using identity criteria) and act politically to keep their shared power, instead of (or at the same time) competing, for example, on the basis of innovation.

However, unsurprisingly, data are also missing to test the effect of such behaviour and check for the existence of the self-regulatory social mechanisms underlying transactions among firms. The influence of niche seeking and status competition on regulatory work is also a domain that is underresearched. Institutional economics and sociology have often looked at contexts in which economic activities and competition take place as legally and culturally defined (Hirsch, 1997). Markets cannot emerge without appropriate legal property rights, and also many derived rules such as bankruptcy laws, that are defined and negotiated in a political sphere (Carruthers and Halliday, 1998). Fligstein and Mara-Drita's (1996) work on the construction of the European common market fleshes out this idea of politically constructed competition, with an important role played especially by the state. Fligstein distinguishes stages of market development, calling attention to endogenously formed institutions as sources of order, echoing White's approaches to niches and adding focus on firms 'conceptions of control'. But truly structural studies of the regulatory process (using measurements of multiple forms of status and power in complex oligarchies negotiating the rules of the game) are almost non-existent.

The effect of resource dependencies on the capacities of some actors to redefine the rules, the terms of exchange and priority values, has barely been examined, with the exception of studies of lobbying such as that of Laumann and Knoke (1987) and Pappi and König (1995). Criticism for such a lack of interest for data collection has long been around (Fligstein, 1990; forthcoming). Studies of intraorganizational relational structures have been used to look at the reasons for which some businesses try to redefine the rules of their competition (Lazega, 1994b) as they apply to their sector, for example rules about conflicts of interests in professional services. Professional firms use organizational devices to reassure the market about the ethics of their economic behaviour. Another example of regulatory effort is provided by struggles to impose a standard upstream of production (not so much for market share in mature markets). Such standards can even be called for by first- and second-rank subcontractors who prefer universal standards even if they impose a cascade of new adjustments and constraints. But very few structural studies have been able to show how organizations participate in shaping their normative and regulatory environment. Concerning the study of that generic mechanism, which is the most visibly politicized of all such mechanisms, almost all remains to be done. The dynamics that it calls for are only barely perceived.

We know that companies pay large campaign contributions to ruling political parties (Useem, 1984; Carruthers, 1996). Lobbying studies mentioned above, while examining the influence of interorganizational networks on policy making (Laumann and Knoke, 1987; Pappi and Koenig, 1995; Stokman *et al.*, 2000), and on attempts to use and impose their industry customs and rules on others (Swedberg, 1993), show how economic policy is partly shaped by lobbying practices of large companies and industries. This is, however, where a more complex behavioural assumption about corporate actors (such as that used above when outlining a theory of politicized appropriateness judgment) is needed to make progress. A broadly conceived structural approach must focus on such regulatory activities much more than it has up to date. In our view, this is precisely where conventions and structures combine (Lazega, 1999a, 2001a). In particular, various dimensions of economic status need to be differentiated in order to look at various forms of influence in the regulatory process.

In sum, pioneering structural studies of interorganizational ties suggest the feasibility of more systematic examination of social mechanisms and their role in the economy, but, owing to lack of access to data, very little has been achieved in that respect. Studies in progress nevertheless illustrate the search for various forms of balance between collegiality and bureaucracy in different kinds of collective actors (Comet, 2001; Stofer, 2001; Varanda, 2001; Wattebled, 2001) producing both standardized and unstandardized goods, particularly by looking at the social mechanisms that their potential or actual rival members in their efforts to cooperate.

CONCLUSION: A PERMANENTLY SHIFTING BOUNDARY BETWEEN BUREAUCRACY AND COLLEGIALITY AT THE INTERORGANIZATIONAL LEVEL

In this chapter, we have sought to evaluate the extent to which it is possible to reason at the interorganizational level in the same terms as at the intraorganizational level. Do interdependent corporate actors get involved in multiplex social exchange and politicize their behaviour through niche seeking and status competition? If so, could this lead to collegial social mechanisms such as those identified at the intraorganizational level? In that case, it would have many consequences in reasoning about policy, given the existence of macrosociological constraints that need to be taken seriously.

Switching from the intraorganizational level to the interorganizational level with the same theory is not an obvious research programme. Nevertheless, the ingredients of an 'extended' structural contribution to the study of markets and organizations, one that goes beyond the contribution of pioneering structural studies, was presented above. From this perspective, economic sociology does not need to start with the distinction between markets and hierarchies. It is based on a different conception of the economy, one in which it is too limiting to explain the emergence of collective actors such as organizations or groups of organizations as a result of a 'make or buy' decision based on the evaluation of transaction costs and what they would otherwise be on a supposedly unstructured market. Rather, it is much closer to a strategic analysis of economic activity, and to political economy.

It is based on a conception of rationality that is broader than traditional rational choice. It includes economic calculus but integrates also symbolic reasoning allowing bounded solidarity and politicized exchanges of multiple resources, delegation of control and deliberation on precarious values. It allows for actors' attempts at shaping their opportunity structure at the (analytically speaking) meso level, whether inside or between organizations. In many ways, we would like to argue that it is a broadly conceived structural approach that can bridge the gap between economic and sociological approaches to coordination of collective action.

The specificity of broadly conceived structural studies is in their use of network analysis as a method for tracking and understanding flows and exchanges of resources, their control, and negotiation of rules commanding such flows and terms of exchanges. We argued that the models developed to analyse social mechanisms allowing for cooperation between interdependent entrepreneurs at the intraorganizational level, the collegial model, can offer insights into, and hypotheses for, the study of interorganizational cooperation between interdependent entrepreneurs. Based on such an approach to economic activity, the strong difference between markets and organizations tends to be replaced by the dialectic interplay between mechanisms characterizing bureaucracy and collegiality in each of the two contexts (micro and macro). These mechanisms are triggered by selective investments in relationships within social niches and for status competition. They represent a meso-level social and cultural discipline that underlie both intraorganizational and interorganizational coordination.

Every organization and/or interorganizational system, however, is different with respect to the temporary balance between bureaucracy (that shapes collective action for standardized, more repetitive, production) and collegiality (that shapes collective action for unstandardized, more innovative, production) that it can achieve. One of today's most intriguing issues in theoretical economic sociology is perhaps to figure out a typology of equilibrium points between the two models. Because real-life organizations are different and because they change, and because economic institutions weigh on the redefinition of such equilibrium points, the boundary between the two is permanently being redefined, and these kinds of balance are moving targets. A theory of these equilibrium points can therefore only be developed by using longitudinal approaches and analyses of the dynamics of organizational and interorganizational structures.

Current research insists on multiplexity, on constraints coming from multiple relationships between exchange partners, whose recurrent interactions compose relational structures maintained by sanctions and helping in enforcing formal contracts. These contributions use multiplex databases very little. A quick review of the literature on this issue shows that economic sociology develops very slowly in that respect. This rhythm is due to difficulties related to systematic data collection, particularly on economic transactions (buying and selling) between sets of organizations (such as groups, or local or regional industries, or 'market areas' in Berkowitz's sense, or more standard sectors). Measuring commercial ties systematically is difficult; combining such measurements with systematic information on social ties among actors is even more difficult. Accounting and social data are strategic to companies (especially with respect to competition and regulatory authorities). Therefore social niches and status competition – and derived mechanisms – are not easily detectable empirically. Most of the work therefore remains to be done in that respect. In particular, more research is needed on actors' investments in social exchange and on the social mechanisms of cooperation (among individuals or among organizations) that such investments trigger. In addition, generic mechanisms are connected to each other: the last two (control and regulation) are attempts to protect the first: bounded solidarity between interdependent entrepreneurs.

This broadly conceived structural approach, and especially the challenge of using multiplexity in intraorganizational and interorganizational studies, has the potential to renew economic sociology. Although many 'embeddedness' studies assert the importance of social ties and 'gifts' for individual economic performance, the embeddedness framework has often justified lack of efforts from researchers to look for complete networks and structural solutions provided for basic problems of social discipline in collective action such as solidarity, control and regulation. Only complete network data of specific intraorganizational and interorganizational systems, of economic institutions and elites, at several points in time, can provide systematic ways of linking micro and macro levels of analysis by describing relation-specific investments and social mechanisms derived from them. Unless such methodological efforts are made, multi-level structural studies of organizational change and evolution of markets will remain even scarcer. A thorough understanding of the organizational society and its social mechanisms will not be developed. Organizations and markets will not be held accountable for some of their externalities and social costs. Much more remains to be done in order to fulfil this goal.

NOTES

1. A first draft of this paper was presented at the 1998 Cnrs Summer school on 'Markets and Organizations', at the Maison Suger in Paris. It was revised for presentation at the Seminar of Economic Sociology at the Maison des Sciences de l'Homme, Nantes, November 2000, then at the Seminar of Economic Sociology at the University of Paris IX-Dauphine, January 2001, and finally at the Journées du Clersé on 'The Social Organization of the Economy', University of Lille 1, June 2001. We would like to thank the organizers of these events as well as Sébastien Delarre, Alexis Ferrand, and André Torre for their comments on a previous version.
2. We do recognize (Lazega, 1996) the heuristical value and usefulness of this distinction for economists opposed to the neoclassical dogma, from Williamson (1975) to Favereau (1989).
3. Order imposed by a tightly connected oligarchic banking system can sometimes have the same effect on society, especially when the state delegates some of its power of legitimate use of violence (Lazega and Mounier, forthcoming).
4. For general network analysis, see Wasserman and Faust (1994). For the specific network models that test for the existence of social mechanisms of generalized exchange, lateral control and self-regulation in a collegial organization, see the references to our more technical papers in the bibliography.
5. Several papers provide overviews of this early work (see, for example, Swedberg, 1994; Lazega, 1994a) and demonstrate how useful network analysis combined with even this minimal theory of action can be to economic sociology and its many substantive topics.
6. Burt (1988) observes stability at the ultimate macro level of aggregation using Leontief input–output tables of national accounts (where the organization is lost as a unit of analysis). In his view, for example, politicized multiplexity of ties (or resource dependencies) between organizations does not play any role in the mechanisms that account for stability in markets. This stability is conceived of as entirely 'structural' without any behavioural assumption at that level of aggregation.
7. For a detailed presentation of White's market models, see White (1981b, 2001), but also Eymard-Duvernay and Favereau (1990), Biencourt *et al.*, (1994a, 1994b, and Chapter 8 in this book). For an analysis of the effects of introducing uncertainty about quality of goods in the analysis of economic activity, see also Karpik (1989).
8. This symbolic activity may be partly construed as a form of interpretation, as conventionalists understand this term.
9. On the relationships between network analysis and strategic analysis, see Lemieux (1982) and Lazega (1994a).
10. A generalized exchange system refers to the existence of cycles of postponed and indirect reciprocity. In the case of organizations, cycles are often short, involving only three or four persons; nevertheless, they indicate the existence of a form of bounded solidarity and social discipline.
11. A social niche is not necessarily a group because it does not always have the legitimacy that would be granted to an independent entity by an outside authority. The organization can recognize the importance of niches for efficient circulation of resources, but it does not favour the emergence of detachable subunits. Just as a social niche can be either a shelter or

hell for an individual member, it can be an advantage or a threat for the organization that encompasses it (Lazega, 2000a).

12. This conception of the relationship between rationality and protectionism is entirely compatible with Pareto's approach to entrepreneurial activity, except that it does not consider it to be a 'residual' form of activity.
13. On the relationship between identity, appropriateness judgments, definition of interests and contextualized behaviour, see Lazega (1992a; 1997).
14. For additional insights into cooperation as routine transfers or exchanges of various kinds of resources, see Bearman (1997), Breiger and Ennis (1997), Cook (1987, 1990), Ekeh (1976), Flap *et al.*, (1998), Galaskiewicz and Marsden (1978), Gouldner (1960), Granovetter (1994), Han and Breiger (1999), Lazega and Pattison (1999), Lin (1995, 2001), Levi-Strauss (1949), Raub and Weesie (1990), Saxenian (1994).
15. As shown by Festinger (1954), the comparisons that matter for people are the comparisons with others most like themselves. Combination of criteria (office similarities, speciality similarities, hierarchical status similarities and so on) push members to compare themselves first to same niche people.
16. It is not our purpose to assume that status competition is omnipresent in society. In many arenas, especially when production is routinized, actors do not try to accumulate resources and forms of status, thus accepting bureaucratic formal hierarchy. But at the interorganizational level, among interdependent entrepreneurs, such a competition, although limited by niche seeking, is in itself an instrument for the definition of terms of exchange, and therefore unavoidable.
17. The use of the notion of social mechanism is meant to convey a criticism of the use of the word 'governance', which overemphasizes the capacity of management to control collective action.
18. One feature characterizing this network approach to social mechanisms compared to many early ones is that it takes into account multiplexity in a much more systematic way. This accent on several types of resources leads to a more precise understanding of power and interdependencies among economic actors participating in collective action, and needed to describe social mechanisms. As an example, take the difference between the human relations tradition and the structural approach to relationships at work (Lazega, 2001a).
19. The combined use of structural analysis and rational choice approach leads to abstract concepts such as multiplex relationships. The word 'multiplex' qualifies a rich relationship between two persons. It refers to the fact that the two persons have a relationship in which they can transfer and exchange multiple types of resources (Wasserman and Faust, 1994). For example, two partners have a multiplex relationship because they are co-workers on many cases, because they also seek each other for advice in difficult professional situations, and finally because they also have social activities outside work. From a structural perspective, this means that specific local and multiplex substructures of social ties must crystallize for members to be able to cooperate on a continuing basis in the context of wider collective actors such as organizations.
20. One obvious way of controlling the deliberation about rules is to marginalize or exclude some members from the reference group itself, that is from the collective that is perceived to be the best arena for interpretation and enforcement of these rules. As previously noted, racism and other forms of discrimination are never far away from all the mechanisms that are based on barter and particularism.
21. Constitutional change is not the only form of change that multi-status oligarchs can promote. They are also in a structurally advantageous position to promote new products because they can afford both to invest in an innovation and to lose from abandoning the production of 'old' products.
22. In many ways, the structural approach has attracted representatives of economics of organizations, often based on transaction costs economics (Williamson, 1975, 1981). However, the distance between the two approaches remains considerable. For example, in this presentation, we do not use the word 'network' in the sense of a separate kind of entity that represents a specific form of coordination of collective action between market and hierarchy, a third 'hybrid' form. Many authors have questioned the usefulness of a transaction costs approach. Eccles (1985) has shown that in some large organizations transactions (based on

transfer pricing) may be more difficult and costly than outside the organizations. For a critique of this approach, see Lindenberg (1996) and Lazega (1996).

23. In particular, one might object that, at the intraorganizational level, one finds a form of homogeneity between members and a focus on one common objective, two features that cannot characterize society at large. However, in our view, as in that of strategic analysis, there is not necessarily a greater heterogeneity of actors and of goals at the interorganizational level than at the intraorganizational level. Another objection to that approach is that relationships between organizations are less a product of a choice of exchange partners than at the intraorganizational level. In our view, however, the choices of partners and level of investment are not necessarily available to agents within organizations more than between organizations. Prototypical of such choices is the selection of subcontractors (Lazega and Mounier, 1999). Equally questionable is the idea that a relation specific investment and the notion of a private resource make less sense at the interorganizational level than at the intraorganizational level. As often stressed by embeddedness studies, managers need multiplex ties to run their organization and create markets (White, 2001). They cannot count exclusively on the resources formally provided by their organization. Relation-specific investment still raises the problem of sunk costs (when one party behaves opportunistically) and therefore the social mechanisms of control are also needed (Raub and Weesie, 1993; Williamson, 1996). But these investments with requests for commitment from the others in the niche do make sense at the interorganizational level too.
24. It is important to mention again that the niche concept has been the object of important debates, at least at this interorganizational level. The first protagonist of this debate is Harrison White, whose niche concept represents a specified level of quality in a quality array helping consumers compare products and quality/price ratios. This is obviously not the same meaning as a densely connected subgroup in which members have multiplex ties to one another, although it is not entirely different insofar as such dense groups are also positions of approximately structurally equivalent actors (see Borgatti and Everett, 1992, for a dedramatization of the distinction between cohesion and structural equivalence). Extending White's approach, Burt and Talmud (1993) also use the niche concept. They do reason in terms of ties representing transfers and exchanges of various types of resources, but they are mainly interested in looking for elementary substructures (especially ones that represent the existence of 'structural holes' and derived opportunities) that make sense regardless of the type of tie. This represents a simplification of the structural approach, particularly with regard to multiplexity, one that earlier contributions did not accept. This approach remains untested and is different from approaches assuming density of resource flows within the niche. It is not necessarily different if niches are also dense, since internal density in positions can increase the level of approximated structural equivalence between actors. But stressing such ties would introduce arguments about cooperation, not about competition between members of the niche. Actually, in these studies, interorganizational ties are rarely measured as such, often derived from similarity along common characteristics (using similar technology, developing interdependent innovations).
25. Formally, business groups are not simply strategic alliances or consolidated conglomerates. They are sets of organizations connected for economic, social and political goals. Stable cartels could be considered business groups. Granovetter uses the example of Korean *chaebols* and Japanese *keiretsus*, in which many kinds of resources, including symbolic, circulate, and where individual companies keep a separate legal identity. These groups include sets of companies that are neither integrated in a single holding nor completely independent. They are collective actors that do not exist legally as one single entity and that are not identified in the official census (Strachan, 1976). Careful attention to groups in other countries yields similar observations. Such a network may be costly in terms of price, but it might also be efficient in the long term with regard to innovation, investments, personnel management and social costs. In addition, sanctions may include marginalization, but also illegal ones (sometimes carried out by mafias).
26. Granovetter thinks that such groups have characteristics of moral communities in the Durkheimian sense. Moral constraints may have integrative force for members who know what behaviour they are entitled to expect from each other, especially with regard to behav-

iour perceived to be opportunistic. However, the effects of moral forces are difficult to measure and to disentangle from those of economic calculations.

27. This will lead increasingly to research on the capacity of the state to regulate by redefining firms' social responsibilities and obligations in this new context, particularly those of organizations and groups of organizations that build internal labour markets.
28. A related issue is that we do not think that sociological research should distinguish, at the interorganizational level, between social niches and ecological niches. Sociologists such as Podolny *et al.*, (1996) think that, in the second type of niche, companies depending on the same resources and endorsement mechanisms making coordination possible are enough to justify this distinction. In our view, the notion of a social niche encompasses this type of ecological niche and recognizes that more aggressive power relationships should often characterize interorganizational ties. Power relationships should not be distinguished in nature from simple 'endorsements'. Power that seems to be raw power is never very far from legitimization; indeed, what makes its use very often so scandalous is the fact that it is actually and silently legitimized by authorities (such as the state). Organizational ecology does not address issues of raw power in the ecological niche. Our approach using the idea of a social niche is an extended view of such entities, one that is able to include both endorsements and more brutal expressions of power. Organizational ecology and its emphasis on codependency on similar resources is not to be neglected. But without the power of a hierarchy between organizations, standardization of products, for example, is impossible and markets destroy themselves. Just as brainstorming at the intraorganizational level (example used above) would not stop, owing to status competition, without the intervention of hierarchical status, markets would not reach any standards. Hierarchy manages what is dysfunctional with the collegial social niche at the micro and meso levels. This transposition also works with regard to the use of identities (ethnic groups, 'classe patronale') underlying a social niche. Instead of asking what triggers the choice of an ecological over a social niche, we think that a social niche should account for market structuration, including firms' codependency on similar resources usually attributed to ecological niches. The social niche does not require only contacts and relationships; sometimes it also requires power, thanks to one's control of resources. Berkowitz's work (see above) can be seen as an example of the overlap of the two approaches. Actions influenced by the fact that one is a director of a company are not necessarily different from those deriving from the fact that one belongs to the same ethnic group. In our view, it is simpler to assume that there is only one kind of society in the market, even if two organizational forms (bureaucracy and collegiality) account for coordination among its actors.
29. White's (2001) approach to production markets actually reasons in terms of mechanisms, but it assumes their existence more than it actually models them, even from the perspective of individual entrepreneurs, not to mention the coordination of interdependent ones.
30. Stuart (1998) tries to show that strategic alliances have a positive effect on organizations' performance (growth and capacity to innovate) when the partners are themselves large and innovative.
31. Podolny and Stuart (1999) assume a technologically closed 'space', in which inventions at time *t2* are always derived from inventions from that same field at time *t1*. Inventions in that industry, however, may come from firms in different industries (plastics, chemistry, biology) or from labs in the public sector (universities). Thus their account of industry evolution is limited to specific 'endogenous' processes and (probably) routine developments in the semiconductor industry.
32. This certainly improves on Hannan and Freeman's (1989) approach to competition in terms of numbers of producers in an industry. They claim that their definition of a niche is 'fundamental', as opposed to 'realized' (or based on market exchange relations which, they assert, have a 'transitory' character, that is, defined at one point in time and therefore not constraining on the actions of an organization). What makes this 'fundamental' character, however, is unclear: it may be the stability of the niche over time, or its lack of dependence on agency. More generally, it is possible to envisage that markets, when not regulated externally by the state, are structured in two different ways (that is, by two different types of niches): in an extended ecological way (organizational ecology plus power relationships in the construction of markets) and in a social way. But the extent to which it is useful to assume that there are two kinds of society

in the market remains to be tested. The two often overlap to such an extent that the distinction may be useless. But, in special cases, they may not. For example, in private R&D ventures, social niches may matter much more than extended ecological ones. A social niche requires heavy reliance on contacts, relationships and associated social mechanisms. The extended ecological niche simply requires a way to notifying the other parties of one's power over them via unchallengeable control of vital resources. The second is easier to enforce. However, structures being multi-level, social niches might need a level of structuration that is superior in order to gain the level of influence that has the same effect as power in the extended ecological niche.

33. Such an approach was extended by the recent look at activities of endorsement (Podolny *et al.*, 1996) and at coordination based on more aggressive power relationships, which was neglected in population ecology and recent attempts to combine it with structural sociology.
34. For example, control at the interorganizational level is being examined in our study of the balance between external (state-controlled) regulation and self-regulation of the business world commercial courts in France (Lazega and Mounier, forthcoming). In these courts, 'consular' (that is, not professional) and voluntary judges are appointed by the business community through the Chamber of Commerce. These judges come from various sectors of the economy (with an overrepresentation of the banking and financial services), sectors that are particularly well positioned to exercise control at the interorganizational level when state agencies withdraw from part of their enforcement tasks. While performing such tasks, competitors do rely on this social discipline in order to cooperate, thus combining 'bureaucratic' and 'collegial' models of collective action.

REFERENCES

Aldrich, Howard E. and Peter M. Marsden (1988), 'Environments and Organizations', in Neil J.Smelser (ed.), *Handbook of Sociology*, Beverly Hills: Sage.

Anheier, Helmut and Wolfgang Seibel (1990), *The Third Sector, Comparative Studies of Non-Profit Organization*, Berlin: De Gruyter.

Baker, Wayne E. (1984), 'The social structure of a national securities market', *American Journal of Sociology*, 89, 775–811.

Baker, Wayne E. (1990), 'Market networks and corporate behavior', *American Journal of Sociology*, 96, 589–625.

Baker, Wayne E. (1992), 'The network organization in theory and practice', in Nitin Nohria and Robert G. Eccles (eds), *Groups, Leadership and Men*, Pittsburgh: Carnegie Press.

Baker, Wayne E. and Robert R. Faulkner (1993), 'The social organization of conspiracy: illegal networks in the heavy electrical equipment industry', *American Sociological Review*, 58, 837–60.

Baker, Wayne E., Robert R. Faulkner and Gene A. Fisher (1998), 'Hazards of the market: the continuity and dissolution of interorganizational market relationships', *American Sociological Review*, 63, 147–77.

Barley, S.R., J. Freeman and R.C. Hybels (1992), 'Strategic Alliances in Commercial Biotechnology', in N. Nohria and R. Eccles (eds), *Networks and Organizations*, Cambridge: Harvard Business School Press.

Baron, James N. and Michael T.Hannan (1994), 'The impact of economics on contemporary sociology', *Journal of Economic Literature*, 32, 1111–46.

Batenburg, Ronald, Werner Raub and Chris Snijders (1997), 'Contacts and contracts: temporal embeddedness and the contractual behavior of firms', Utrecht, Iscore Papers, no. 107.

Bauer, Michel and Elie Cohen (1981), *Qui gouverne les groupes industriels?*, Paris: Seuil.

Bearman, Peter (1997), 'Generalized exchange', *American Journal of Sociology*, 102, 1383–1415.

Berkowitz, Stephen D. (1982), *An Introduction to Structural Analysis*, Toronto: Butterworth.

Berkowitz, Stephen D. (1988), 'Markets and market-areas', in B. Wellman and S.D. Berkowitz (eds.), *Social Structures, A Network Approach*, Cambridge: Cambridge University Press.

Berkowitz, Stephen D. and William Fitzgerald (1995), 'Corporate control and enterprise structure in the Canadian economy, 1972–1987', *Social Networks*, 17, 11–127.

Berkowitz, S.D., P.J. Carrington, Y, Kotowitz and L. Waverman (1979), 'Enterprise Groups', *Social Networks*, 1, 391–413.

Berle, Adolf A. and G.C. Means (1932), *The Modern Corporation and Private Property*, revised edn (1969), New York: Harcourt, Brace & World.

Biencourt, Olivier, François Eymard-Duvernay and Olivier Favereau (1994a), 'Concurrence par la qualité et viabilité d'un marché: le cas du transport routier de marchandises', rapport au Commissariat Général du Plan, Laboratoire FORUM, Université Paris X et Centre d'Etude de l'Emploi, Novembre.

Biencourt, Olivier, François Eymard-Duvernay and Olivier Favereau (1994b), 'L'économie doit définir le marché à partir de l'entreprise, plutôt que l'inverse', Communication présentée au colloque de la Society for the Advancement of Socio-Economics, Paris, July.

Blau, J.R. and R.P. Alba (1982), 'Empowering Nets of Participation', *Administrative Science Quarterly*, 27, 363–79.

Blau, Peter M. (1964), *Exchange and Power in Social Life*, New York: John Wiley.

Blumer, H. (1969), *Symbolic Interactionism*, Englewood Cliffs, NJ: Prentice-Hall.

Boccara, Frédéric (1999a), 'Facts and myths in employment and SME growth: The role of enterprise groups (1984–1992)', Insee Working papers of the Direction des statistiques d'entreprise.

Boccara, Frédéric (1999b), 'Globalization, business groups and growth factors in France', Insee Working papers of the Direction des statistiques d'entreprise.

Boorman, Scott A. and Ronald L. Breiger (1976), 'Social Structure from Multiple Networks, I. Blockmodels of Roles and Positions', *American Journal of Scoiology*, 81, 730–80.

Boorman, Scott and Paul Levitt (1980), *The Genetics ofAltruism*, New York: Academic Press.

Borgatti, Stephen and G. Martin Everett (1992), 'Notions of position in social networks analysis', *Sociological Methodology*, 22, 1–35.

Bosk, Charles (1979), *Forgive and Remember*, Chicago: University of Chicago Press.

Bourdieu, Pierre (1980), 'Le Capital social: Notes provisoires', *Actes de la recherche en sciences sociales*, 3: 2–3.

Bourdieu, Pierre (1990) [1984], *The Logic of Practice*, Stanford: Stanford University Press.

Bowles, Samuel (1995), 'Compte rendu sur le *Handbook of Economic Sociology*', *Contemporary Sociology*, 24, 304–7.

Bowles, Samuel and Herbert Gintis (1998), 'How communities govern: the structural basis of prosocial norms', in Avner Ben Ner and Louis Putterman (eds), *Economics, Values and Organization*, Cambridge: Cambridge University Press.

Brass, Daniel J. (1984), 'Being in the right place: a structural analysis of individual influence in an organization', *Administrative Science Quarterly*, 29, 518–39.
Breiger, Ronald L. (1974), 'The duality of persons and groups', *Social Forces*, 53, 181–90.
Breiger, Ronald L. and J. Ennis (1997), 'Generalized exchange in social networks: statistics and structure', *L'Année Sociologique*, 47, 73–88.
Breiger, Ronald L., S. Boorman and P. Arabie (1975), 'An algorithm for clustering relational data with applications to social network analysis and comparison with multidimensional scaling', *Journal of Mathematical Psychology*, 12, 328–83.
Brint, Stephen (1992), 'Hidden meanings: cultural content and context in Harrison White's structural sociology', *Sociology Theory*, 10, 194–208.
Burt, Ronald S. (1983), *Corporate Profits and Cooptation*, New York: Academic Press.
Burt, Ronald S. (1988), 'The stability of American markets', *American Journal of Sociology*, 94, 356–95.
Burt, Ronald S. (1992), *Structural Holes, The Social Structure of Competition*, Cambridge, MA: Harvard University Press.
Burt, Ronald S. (1993) 'Market integration', in S. Lindenberg and H. Schreuder (eds), *Interdisciplinary Perspectives on Organization Studies*, Oxford: Pergamon Press.
Burt, Ronald S. and D. Ronchi (1990), 'Contested Control in a Large Manufacturing Plant', in *Social Networks Through Time*, J. Weesie and H. Flap (eds), Utrecht: ISOR.
Burt, Ronald S. and I. Talmud (1993), 'Market niche', *Social Networks*, 8, 97–117
Capecchi, Vittorio (1987), 'Formation professionnelle et petite entreprise: le développement industriel à spécialisation flexible en Emilie-Romagne', *Formation-Emploi*, no. 19, July–September, La Documentation française.
Carruthers, Bruce (1996), *City of Capital: Politics and Markets in the English Financial Revolution*, Princeton: Princeton University Press.
Carruthers, Bruce G. and Terence C. Halliday (1998), *Rescuing Business: the Making of Corporate Bankruptcy Law in England and the United States*, Oxford: Clarendon Press.
Chandler, Alfred D. (1962), *Strategy and Structure: Chapters in the History of Industrial enterprise*, Cambridge, MA: MIT Press.
Chandler, Alfred D. (1977), *The Visible Hand. The Managerial Revolution in American Business*, Cambridge, MA: Harvard University Press.
Chandler, Alfred D. (1990), *Scale and Scope: The Dynamics of Industrial Capitalism*, Cambridge, MA: Harvard University Press.
Chazel, François (1983), 'Pouvoir, structure et domination', *Revue Française de Sociologie*, 24, 369–93.
Cheit, Ross E. and Jacob E. Gersen (2000), 'When businesses sue each other: an empirical study of state court litigation', *Law & Social Inquiry*, 25, 789–816.
Coase, Ronald H. ([1937] 1988), *The Firm, the Market and the Law*, Chicago: University of Chicago Press
Coleman, James S. (1990), *Foundations of Social Theory*, Cambridge, MA: Harvard University Press.
Comet, Catherine (2001), 'Les coopératives de petites entreprises du bâtiment', PhD thesis in preparation, University of Lille I.
Cook, Karen (ed.) (1987), *Sociological Exchange Theory*, London:Sage.
Cook, Karen S. (1990), 'Linking Actors and Structures: An Exchange Network Perspective', in C. Calhoun, M.W. Meyer and W.R. Scott (eds), *Structures of Power and Constraint*, Cambridge: Cambridge University Press.
Crozier, Michel (1963), *Le phénomène bureaucratique*, Paris:Seuil.

Crozier, Michel and E. Friedberg (1977), *L'acteur et le système*, Paris: Seuil.
Davis, G.F. (1991), 'Agents without principle? The spread of the poison pill through the intercorporate network', *Administrative Science Quarterly*, 36, 583–613.
Davis, Gerald F. and Powell, Walter W. (1992), 'Organization-Environment Relations', in M.D. Dunnette and L.M. Hough (eds), *Handbook of industrial and organizational psychology*, second edition, volume III, Palo Alto: Consulting Psychology Press.
Degenne, Alain and Michel Forsé (1994), *Les réseaux sociaux*, Paris: Colin.
Dezalay, Yves and Garth, Bryant (1996). *Dealing in virtue: International commercial arbitration and the construction of a transnational legal order*, Chicago: Univeristy of Chicago Press.
DiMaggio, Paul (1986), 'Structural analysis of organizational fields', in B. Staw and L.L. Cummings (eds), *Research in Organizational Behavior*, Greenwich, CT: JAI Press, vol. 8, pp. 335–70.
DiMaggio, Paul (1991), 'The micro/macro dilemma in organizational research: implications of role-systems theory', in J. Huber (ed.), *Macro–Micro Relationships*, Newbury Park, CA: Sage.
DiMaggio, Paul (1992), 'Nadel's paradox revisited: relational and cultural aspects of organizational culture', in Nitin Nohria and Robert G. Eccles (eds), *Groups, Leadership and Men*, Pittsburgh: Carnegie Press.
Dunworth, Terence and Joel Rogers (1996), 'Corporations in court, big business litigation in U.S. Federal Courts, 1971–1991', *Law & Social Inquiry*, 21, 497–592.
Dyer, J.H. and H. Singh (1998), 'The relational view, cooperative strategy and sources of interorganizational competitive advantage', *Academy of Management Review*, 23, 660–79.
Eccles, Robert (1985), *The Transfer Pricing Problem*, Lexington, MA: Lexington Books.
Eccles, Robert G. and Dwight B. Crane (1988), *Doing Deals: Investment Banks at Work*, Boston: Harvard Business School Press.
Ekeh, Peter (1976), *Social Exchange Theory: The Two Traditions*, Cambridge, MA: Harvard University Press.
Encaoua, David and Alexis Jacquemin (1982), 'Organizational efficiency and monopoly power. The case of French industrial groups', *European Economic Review*, 19, 25–51.
Eymard-Duvernay, François and Olivier Favereau (1990), 'Marchés internes, modèles d'entreprises et conventions de qualité, matériaux pour une formalisation non standard du marché des biens', Communication aux 7èmes journées de Micro-Economie Appliquée, Université du Québec à Montréal, May.
Farkas, George, Kevin Lang and Paula England (1994), 'Economic sociology and social economics: where are we now?', in George Farkas and Paula England (eds), *Industries, Firms and Jobs, Sociological and Economic Approaches*, New York: De Gruyter.
Favereau, Olivier (1989), 'Marchés internes, marchés externes', *Revue économique*, 40(2), 273–328.
Favereau, Olivier (1998), 'Décisions, situations, institutions', in A.Vinokur (ed.), *Décisions économiques*, Paris: Economica.
Favereau, Olivier (1999), 'L'Economie des conventions et le constructivisme en économie', in G.R.A.S.C.E. (ed.), *Entre systémique et complexité, chemin faisant. Mélanges en l'honneur de J.L. Lemoigne*, Paris: Presses Universitaires de France.
Ferrand, Alexis (1997), 'La structure des systèmes de relations', *L'Année Sociologique*, 47, 37–54.
Festinger, Leon (1954), 'A theory of social comparison processes', *Human Relations*, 7, 117–40.

Flap, Hendrik D., Bert Bulder and B. Völker (1998), 'Intra-organizational networks and performance: a review', *Computational and Mathematical Organization Theory*, 4, 1–39.

Fligstein, Neil (1990), *The Transformation of Corporate Control*, Cambridge, MA: Harvard University Press.

Fligstein, Neil (forthcoming), *Ruling Markets: An Economic Sociology of Capitalist Societies*, Princeton: Princeton University Press

Fligstein, Neil and Iona Mara-Drita (1996), 'How to make a market', *American Journal of Sociology*, 102, 1–33

Freidson, Eliott (1975), *Doctoring Together: A Study of Professional Social Control*, New York: Elsevier.

Freidson, Eliott (1986), *Professional Powers*, Chicago: University of Chicago Press.

Friedberg, Erhard (1993), *Le pouvoir et la règle*, Paris: Seuil.

Gabbay, Shaul M. (1997), *Social Capital in the Creation of Financial Capital: The Case of Network Marketing*, Champaign, IL: Stipes Publishing.

Galaskiewicz, J. (1979), 'The structure of community interorganizational networks', *Social Forces*, 57, 1346–64.

Galaskiewicz, J. (1989), 'Interorganizational networks mobilizing action at the metropolitan level', in Perucci R. and H. R. Potter (eds), *Networks of Power*, New York: Aldine de Gayter.

Galaskiewicz, J. and P.V. Marsden (1978), 'Interorganizational Resource Networks: Formal Patterns of Overlap', *Social Science Research*, 7, 89–107.

Gargiulo, Martin (1993), 'Two-step leverage: managing constraint in organizational politics', *Administrative Science Quarterly*, 38, 1–19.

Ghoshal, S. and J. Nahapiet (1998), 'Social capital, intellectual capital and the organizational advantage', *Academy of Management Review*, 23, 242–66.

Gouldner, Alvin W. (1954), *Patterns of Industrial Bureaucracy*, New York: Free Press.

Gouldner, Alvin W. (1960), 'The norm of reciprocity', *American Sociological Review*, 25, 161–78.

Granovetter, Mark (1985), 'Economic action and social structure: the problem of embeddedness', *American Sociological Review*, 91, 481–510.

Granovetter, Mark (1992), 'Problems of explanation in economic sociology', in N. Nohria and R. Eccles (eds), *Networks and Organizations*, Cambridge, MA: Harvard, Business School Press.

Granovetter, M. (1994), 'Business Groups', in Neil Smelser and Richard Swedberg (eds), *Handbook of Economic Sociology*, Princeton, NJ: Russell Sage Foundation.

Gulati, Ranjay (1995), 'Social structure and alliance formation patterns: A longitudinal analysis', Administrative Science Quarterly, 40, 619–50.

Han, Shin-Kap and Ronald L. Breiger (1999), 'Dimensions of Corporate Social Capital: Toward Models and Measures', in Roger Leenders and Shaul Gabbay (eds), *Corporate Social Capital and Liability*, Boston: Kluwer.

Hannan, Michael T. and John Freeman (1989), *Organizational Ecology*, Cambridge, MA: Harvard University Press.

Harrison, Bennett (1994), *Lean and Mean: The Changing Landscape of Corporate Power in the Age of Flexibility*, New York: Basic Books.

Hawkins, Keith O. (1984), *Environment and Enforcement*, Oxford: Oxford University Press.

Heckathorn, Douglas (1989), 'Collective action and the second-order free-rider problem', *Rationality and Society*, 1, 78–100.

Hedström, Peter and R. Swedberg (1998), *Social Mechanisms*, Cambridge: Cambridge University Press.
Hirsch, Paul M. (1997), 'Sociology with social structure. Neoinstitutional theory meets brave new world', *American Journal of Sociology*, 102, 1702–23.
Hirsch, Paul M., Stuart Michaels and Ray Friedman (1987), 'Dirty hands versus clean models. Is sociology in danger of being seduced by economics?', *Theory and Society*, 16, 317–36.
Ibarra, H. (1992), 'Homophily and Differential Returns: Sex Differences in Network Structure and Access in an Advertising Firm', *Administrative Science Quarterly*, 37, 422–47.
Kalleberg, Arne L. (1995), 'Sociology and economics, crossing the boundaries', *Social Forces*, 73, 1207–18.
Kapferer, B.C. (1969), 'Norms and the manipulation of relationships in a work context', in J.C. Mitchell (ed.), *Social Networks in Urban Situations*, Manchester: Manchester University Press, pp. 181–245.
Kapferer, B.C. (1972), *Strategy and Transaction in an African Factory*, Manchester: Manchester University Press.
Karpik, Lucien (1989), 'L'économie de la qualité', *Revue Française de Sociologie*, 30, 187–210.
Kellerhals, Jean, Marianne Modak and Massimo Sardi, with the collaboration of Noëlle Languin and Renaud Lieberherr (1995), 'Justice, sens de la responsabilité et relations sociales', *L'Année Sociologique*, 45, 317–49.
Knoke, David (1987), *Political Networks*, Cambridge: Cambridge University Press.
Knoke, D. and J. Wood (1981), *Organized for Action: Commitment in Voluntary Associations*, New Brunswick, NJ: Rutgers University Press.
Kogut, Bruce and Udo B. Zander (1996), 'What firms do: Coordination, identity and learning', *Organization Studies*, 7, 502–18.
Krackhardt, David (1987), 'Cognitive Social Structures', *Social Networks*, 9, 109–34.
Krackhardt, David (1990), 'Assessing the political landscape: structure, cognition and power in organizations', *Administrative Science Quarterly*, 35, 342–69.
Krackhardt, David (1992), 'The Strength of Strong Ties: The Importance of Philos in Organizations', in Nohria, N. and R. Eccles (ed.) (1992), *Networks and Organizations*, Cambridge, Harvard Business School Press.
Krackhardt, David and J.R. Hanson (1993), 'Informal networks: the company behind the chart', *Harvard Business Review*, July–August, 104–11.
Kuty, Olgierd (1998), *La négociation des valeurs : introduction à la sociologie*, Brussels: De Boeck & Larcier.
Laumann, Edward O. and Peter V. Marsden (1982), 'Microstructural analysis in interorganizational systems', *Social Networks*, 4, 329–48.
Laumann, Edward O. and David Knoke (1987), *The Organizational State*, Madison: University of Wisconsin Press.
Laville, Jean-Louis (1994), 'Economie et société, pour un retour à une problématique fondatrice de la sociologie', *Sociologie du Travail*, 36, 239–49.
Lazega, Emmanuel (1990), 'Internal Politics and the Interactive Elaboration of Information in Workgroups: An Exploratory Study', *Human Relations*, 43, 87–101.
Lazega, Emmanuel (1992a), *The Micropolitics of Knowledge: Communication and Indirect Control in Workgroups*, New York: Aldine–de Gruyter.
Lazega, Emmanuel (1992b), 'Analyse de réseaux d'une organisation collégiale: les avocats d'affaires', *Revue Française de Sociologie*, 33, 559–89.

Lazega, Emmanuel (1993), 'Bureaucratie et collégialité dans les firmes américaines d'avocats d'affaires', *Droit et Société*, 23/24, 15–40.

Lazega, Emmanuel (1994a), 'Analyse de réseaux et sociologie des organisations', *Revue Française de Sociologie*, 35, 293–320.

Lazega, Emmanuel (1994b), 'Les conflits d'intérêts dans les cabinets américains d'avocats d'affaires: concurrence et auto-régulation', *Sociologie du Travail*, 35, 315–36.

Lazega, Emmanuel (1995), 'Concurrence, coopération et flux de conseil dans un cabinet américain d'avocats d'affaires: Les échanges d'idées entre collègues', *Revue Suisse de Sociologie*, 1, 61–84.

Lazega, Emmanuel (1996), 'Arrangements contractuels et structures relationnelles', *Revue Française de Sociologie*, 37, 439–56.

Lazega, Emmanuel (1997), 'Network analysis and qualitative research. A method of contextualization', in Gale Miller and Robert Dingwall (eds), *Context and Method in Qualitative Research*, London: Sage.

Lazega, Emmanuel (1999a), 'Le phénomène collégial: une théorie structurale de l'action collective entre pairs', *Revue Française de Sociologie,* 4 (40) 639–70.

Lazega, Emmanuel (1999b), 'Generalized exchange and economic performance', in Roger Leenders and Shaul Gabbay (eds), *Corporate Social Capital and Liabilities*, Boston: Kluwer.

Lazega, Emmanuel (2000a), 'Teaming Up and Out? Cooperation and solidarity in a collegial organization', *European Sociological Review*, 16, 245–66.

Lazega, Emmanuel (2000b), 'Enforcing rules among peers: A lateral control regime', *Organisation Studies*, 21, 193–214.

Lazega, Emmanuel (2000c), 'Les entrepreneurs interdépendants et les mécanismes sociaux de leur coopération', Communication à la Journée d'étude *Le réseau, acteur et objet de régulation,* Maison des Sciences de l'Homme, Nantes, 17 November.

Lazega, Emmanuel (2000d), 'Le troc comme mécanisme social: une approche structurale', Présentation à la journée d'étude *De la sociologie économique à la sociologie de l'action économique*, Ecole Normale Supérieure-Cachan, 10 November.

Lazega, Emmanuel (2000e), 'Structure and Culture in the Constitutional Process: Multistatus Oligarchs and the Negotiation of Precarious Values', paper presented at the American Sociological Association Annual Meeting, Social Networks section, Washington DC, August.

Lazega, Emmanuel (2000f), 'Networks, distributed knowledge and economic performance', conference on 'The Economics and Socio-Economics of Services, International Perspectives', Lille-Roubaix, 22–3 June.

Lazega, Emmanuel (2001a), *The Collegial Phenomenon. The Social Mechanisms of Cooperation among Peers in a Corporate Law Partnership*, Oxford: Oxford University Press.

Lazega, Emmanuel (2001b), 'Who Guards the Guardians? A Lateral Control Mechanism as a Form of Corporate Social Capital', in Roger Leenders and Shaul Gabbay (eds), *Research in the Sociology of Organizations*, vol. 8, 263–91.

Lazega, Emmanuel and Marijtje van Duijn (1997), 'Position in formal structure, personal characteristics and choices of advisors in a law firm. A logistic regression model for dyadic network data', *Social Networks*, 19, 375–97.

Lazega, Emmanuel and David Krackhardt (2000), 'Spreading and shifting costs of lateral control in a law partnership: A structural analysis at the individual level', *Quality and Quantity,* 34, 153–75.

Lazega, Emmanuel and Marie-Odile Lebeaux (1995), 'Capital social et contrainte latérale', *Revue Française de Sociologie*, 36, 759–77.

Lazega Emmanuel and Lise Mounier (1999), 'Analyse secondaire de l'enquête. *Liaisons industrielles* d'un point de vue sociologique: une expérience inaboutie', Rapport au service des Statistiques industrielles du Ministère de l'Industrie, Paris, Lasmas.

Lazega, Emmanuel and Lise Mounier (forthcoming), 'Interlocking judges: commercial courts and the governance of markets in France', *Research in the Sociology of Organizations*.

Lazega, Emmanuel and Philippa Pattison (1999), 'Multiplexity, generalized exchange and cooperation in organizations', *Social Networks*, 21, 67–90.Leifer, Eric M. and Harrison C. White (1988), 'A structural approach to markets', in Mark S. Mizruchi and Michael Schwartz (eds), *Intercorporate relations: the structural analysis of business*, New York: Cambridge University Press.

Lazega, Emmanuel and Philippa Pattison (2001), 'Social mechanisms as a form of corporate social capital: status auctions among peers', in Nan Lin, Karen Cook and Ronald Burt (eds), *Social Capital: Theory and Research*, New York: Aldine–de Gruyter.

Lazega, Emmanuel and Stéphane Vari, (1992), 'Acteurs, cibles et leviers. Analyse factorielle des relations de contrôle indirect dans une firme américaine d'avocats d'affaires', *Bulletin de Méthodologie Sociologique*, 37, 41–51.

Leifer, Eric M. and Harrison C. White (1988), 'A structural approach to markets', in Mark S. Mizruchi and Michael Schwartz (eds), *Intercorporate relations: the structural analysis of business*, New York: Cambridge University Press.

Lemieux, V. (1979), *Les cheminements de l'influence*, Québec: Presses de l'Université Laval.

Lemieux, V. (1982), *Réseaux et appareil*, Québec: Edisem, Paris: Maloine.

Levi-Strauss, C. (1949), *Les formes élémentaires de la parenté*, Paris:Plon.

Levine, Sol and Paul E. White (1961), 'Exchange as a conceptual framework for the study of interorganizational relationships', *Administrative Science Quarterly*, 5, 583–601.

Lin, Nan (1982), 'Social resources and instrumental action', in Peter V. Marsden and Nan Lin (eds), *Social Structure and Network Analysis*, London: Sage.

Lin, Nan (2001), *Social Capital*, Cambridge: Cambridge University Press.

Lindenberg, Siegwart (1991), 'Homo socio-oeconomicus: the emergence of a general model of man in the social sciences', *Journal of Institutional and Theoretical Economics*, 146, 727–48.

Lindenberg, Siegwart (1992), 'An extended theory of institutions and contractual discipline', *Journal of Institutional and Theoretical Economics*, 148, 125–54.

Lindenberg, Siegwart (1996), 'Multiple-tie networks, structural advantage, and path-dependency: another look at hybrid forms of governance', *Journal of Institutional and Theoretical Economics*, 152, 188–96.

Macaulay, Stewart (1963), 'Non-contractual relations in business, a preliminary study', *American Sociological Review*, 28 , 55–67.

McCall, G.J. and J.L. Simmons (1966), *Identities and interactions*, New York: Collier–Macmillan.

Mintz, Beth and Michael Schwartz (1985), *The Power Structure of American Business*, Chicago: University of Chicago Press.

Mizruchi, Mark (1982), *The American Corporate Network: 1904–1974*, Beverly Hills: Sage.

Mizruchi, Mark (1989), 'Similarity of political behavior among large American corporations', *American Journal of Sociology*, 95, 401–24.

Mizruchi, Mark (1992), *The Structure of Corporate Political Action: Interfirm Relations and their Consequences*, Cambridge, MA: Harvard University Press.

Mokken, R. and F. Stokman (1978), 'Corporate governmental networks in the Netherlands', *Social Networks*, 1, 333–58.
Morin, François and Claude Dupuy (1993), *Le cœur financier européen*, Paris: Economica.
Nadel, Sigfried F. (1957), *The Theory of Social Structure*, London: Cohen & West.
Nee, Victor (1998), 'Norms and networks in economic and organizational performance', *American Economic Review*, 88, 85–9.
Nohria, Nitin and Robert Eccles (eds) (1992), *Networks and Organizations*, Cambridge, MA: Harvard Business School Press.
North, Douglass (1993), 'Institutions and Credible Commitments', *Journal of Institutional and Theoretical Economics*, 149,11–23.
Oliver, Pamela (1980), 'Rewards and punishments as selective incentives for collective action: theoretical investigations', *American Journal of Sociology*, 85, 356–75.
Olson, Mancur (1965), *The Logic of Collective Action*, Cambridge, MA: Harvard University Press.
Padgett, John F. and C. K. Ansell (1989), 'Robust action and the rise of the Medici, 1400–1434', American Journal of Sociology, 98, 1259–1319.
Padgett, John F. (2000), 'Organizational genesis, identity and control: the transformation of banking in Renaissance Florence', in A. Casella and J. Rauch (eds), *Markets and Networks*, New York: Russell Sage.
Pappi, F.U. and T. König (1995), 'Les Organisations centrales dans les réseaux du domaine politique: Une comparaison Allemagne-Etats-Unis dans le champ de la politique du travail', *Revue française de sociologie*, 36, 725–42.
Perrow, C. (1992), 'Small-firm networks', in N. Nohria and R. Eccles (eds), *Networks and Organizations*, Cambridge, MA: Harvard Business School Press.
Perrow, Charles (1991), 'A society of organizations', *Theory and Society*, 20, 725–62.
Perucci, R. and H. R. Potter (eds.) (1989), *Networks of Power*, New York: Aldine-de Gruyter.
Piore, Michael and Charles Sabel (1984), *The Second Industrial Divide*, New York: Basic Books.
Pizarro, Narciso (1999), 'Appartenances, places et réseaux de places: la reproduction des processus sociaux et la génération d'un espace homogène pour la définition des structures sociales', *Sociologie et Sociétés*, 31, 143–61.
Podolny, Joel M. (1993), 'A status-based model of market competition', *American Journal of Sociology*, 98, 829–72.
Podolny, Joel M. (1994), 'Market uncertainty and the social character of economic exchange', *Administrative Science Quarterly*, 39, 458–83.
Podolny, Joel M. and Toby E. Stuart (1995), 'A role-based ecology of technological change', *American Journal of Sociology*, 100, 124–1260.
Podolny, Joel M., Toby E. Stuart and Michael T. Hannan (1996), 'Networks, knowledge, and niches, competition in the worldwide semiconductor industry, 1984–1991', *American Journal of Sociology*, 102, 659–89.
Podolny, Joel and Stuart, Toby (1999), 'Positional causes and correlates of strategic alliances in the semiconductor industry', *Research in the Sociology of Organizations*, 16, 161–82.
Powell, Walter W. (1990), 'Neither market nor hierarchy: network forms of organization', in L.L. Cummings and B. Shaw (eds), *Research in Organizational Behavior*, vol. 12, Greenwich, CT: JAI Press.
Powell, W.W., K.W. Koput and L. Smith-Doerr (1996), 'Interorganizational collabora-

tion and the locus of innovation: networks of learning in biotechnology', *Administrative Science Quarterly*, 41, 116–45.
Presthus, R. (1962), *The Organizational Society*, New York: Knopf.
Raub, Werner and Jeroen Weesie (1990), 'Reputation and efficiency in social interactions: an example of network effects', *American Journal of Sociology*, 96, 626–54.
Raub, Werner and Jeroen Weesie (1993), 'Symbiotic arrangements, a sociological perspective', *Journal of Institutional and Theoretical Economics*, 149, 716–24.
Raub, Werner and Jeroen Weesie (1996), 'The management of matches: decentralized mechanisms for cooperative relations with applications to organizations and households', Utrecht, Iscore Papers, no. 62.
Raub, Werner and Jeroen Weesie (eds) (2000), *The Management of Durable Relations. Theoretical and Empirical Models for Households and Organizations*, Amsterdam: Thela Publishers.
Reiss, Albert J. Jr. (1984), 'Selecting strategies of social control over organizational life', in Keith O. Hawkins and James M. Thomas (eds), *Enforcing Regulation*, Boston: Kluwer-Nijhof.
Reitz, K.P. (1988), 'Social Groups in a Monastery', *Social Networks*, 10 (4), 343–57.
Reynaud, Jean-Daniel (1988), 'Les régulations dans les organisations: régulation de contrôle et régulation autonome', *Revue Française de Sociologie*, 29, 5–18.
Reynaud, Jean-Daniel (1989), *Les règles du jeu*, Paris: Armand Colin.
Rogers, E.M. and R. Agarwala-Rogers (1976), *Communication in Organizations*, New York: Free Press.
Rooks, Gerrit, Werner Raub, Robert Selten and Frits Tazelaar (2000), 'How inter-firm cooperation depends on social embeddedness. A vignette study', *Acta Sociologica*, 43, 123–37.
Sabel, Charles (1989), 'Flexible specialization and the re-emergence of regional economics', in P. Hirst and J. Zeitlin (eds), *Reversing Industrial Decline?*, London: Berg.
Sabel, Charles (1993), 'Constitutional ordering in historical context', in Fritz W. Scharpf (ed.), *Games in Hierarchies and Networks*, Frankfurt am Main: Campus Verlag.
Sainsaulieu, Renaud (1977), *L'Identité au travail*, Paris, Presses de la Foundation Nationale des Sciences Politiques.
Sainsaulieu, Renaud (1987), *Sociologie de l'organisation et de l'entreprise*, Paris: Presses de la Fondation Nationale des Sciences Politiques.
Salancik, G.R. and J. Pfeffer (1977), 'Who gets power – and how they hold onto it: a strategic contingency model of power', *Organizational Dynamics*, 5, 3–21.
Sampson, S. (1969), 'Crisis in a Cloister', PhD dissertation, Cornell University.
Saxenian, Anna Lee (1994), *Regional Advantage. Culture and Competition in Rt. 128 and Silicon Valley*, Cambridge, MA: Harvard University Press.
Schwartz, M. and M. Mizruchi (eds) (1988), *The Structural Analysis of Business*, Cambridge: Cambridge University Press.
Scott, W.R. (1975), 'Organizational structure', in A. Inkeles, J. Coleman and N.Smelser (eds), *Annual Review of Sociology*, Palo Alto, CA: Annual Reviews Inc.
Selznick, Philip (1957), *Leadership in Administration*, Evanston, IL: Row, Peterson & Co.
Shapiro, Susan P. (1984), *Wayward Capitalists. Target of the Securities and Exchange Commission*, New Haven: Yale University Press.
Shrader, C.B., J.R. Lincoln and A.N. Hoffman (1989), 'The network structures of organizations: effects of task contingencies and distributional form', *Human Relations*, 42, 43–66.

Simpson, Richard L. (1971), 'Imperative Control, Associationalism, and the Moral Order', in Turk, Herman and Richard L. Simpson (eds.), *Institutions and Social Exchange*, New York: Bobbs-Merrill.
Smelser, Neil and Richard Swedberg (eds) (1994), *Handbook of Economic Sociology,* Princeton, NJ: Princeton University Press, and New York: Russell Sage Foundation.
Stevenson, William B. (1990), 'Formal structure and networks of interaction within organizations', *Social Science Research*, 19, 113–31.
Stinchcombe, A.L. (1989), 'An outsider's view of network analyses of power', in Perucci, R. and H. R. Potter (eds), *Networks of Power*, New York: Aldine-de Gauyter.
Stinchcombe, Arthur L (1991), 'The conditions of fruitfulness in theorizing about mechanisms in the social sciences', *Philosophy of the Social Sciences*, 21, 367–88.
Stofer, Rafaël (2001), 'Réseaux de relations sociales et professionnelles au sein de l'élite des chercheurs sur le cancer en France', Phd thesis, University of Lille I.
Stokman, F.N., M.A.L.M. van Assen, J. van der Knoop and R.C.H. van Oosten (2000), 'Strategic Decision Making', *Advances in Group Processes* (17), 131–53.
Stokman, Frans N., Rolf Ziegler and John Scott (eds) (1985), *Networks of Corporate Power*, Cambridge: Polity Press.
Strachan, Harry (1976), *Family and Other Business Groups in Economic Development*, New York: Praeger.
Stryker, Sheldon (1980), *Symbolic interactionism: a social structural version*, London: Benjamin/Cummings.
Stryker, Sheldon and Statham, A. (1985), 'Symbolic Interaction and Role Theory', in Gardner Lindzey and Elliot Aronson (eds), *Handbook of Social Psychology*, 3rd ed;. vol. 1, New York: Random House.
Stuart, Toby E. (1998), 'Network positions and propensities to collaborate: an investigation of strategic alliance formation in a high-technology industry', *Administrative Science Quarterly*, 43, 668–98.
Stuart, Toby E. and Joel M.Podolny (1999), 'Positional causes and correlates of strategic alliances in the semiconductor industry', in *Research in the Sociology of Organizations*, 16, 161–82.
Swedberg, Richard (ed.) (1990), *Economics and Sociology*, Princeton, NJ: Princeton University Press.
Swedberg, Richard (ed.) (1992), *Explorations in Economic Sociology*, New York: Sage.
Swedberg, Richard (1993), 'Economics and custom', *Journal of Institutional and Theoretical Economics*, 149, 204–9.
Swedberg, Richard (1994), 'Markets as social structures', in Neil Smelser and Richard Swedberg (eds), *Handbook of Economic Sociology,* Princeton, NJ: Princeton University Press, and New York, Russell Sage Foundation.
Talmud, Ilan and Gustavo S. Mesch (1997), 'Market Embeddedness and Corporate Instability: the Ecology of Inter-Industrial Networks', *Social Science Research*, 1–23.
Thurman, B. (1980), 'In the office: networks and coalitions', *Social Networks*, 2, 47–63.
Useem, Michael (1984), *The Inner Circle: Large Corporations and the Rise of Business Political Activity in the US and UK*, Oxford: Oxford University Press.
Uzzi, Brian (1996), 'The sources and consequences of embeddedness for the economic performance of organizations: The network effect', *American Sociological Review*, 61, 674–98.
Uzzi, Brian (1997), 'Social structure and competition in interfirm networks. The paradox of embeddedness', *Administrative Science Quarterly*, 42, 35–67.

Uzzi, Brian (1999), 'Embeddedness in the making of financial capital: how social relations and network benefit firms seeking capital', *American Sociological Review*, 64, 481–505.

Uzzi, Brian and James J. Gillespie (1999), 'Interfirm ties and the organization of firm's capital structure in the middle financial market', in David Knoke and Steven Andrews (eds), *Research in the Sociology of Organizations*, Greenwich, CT: JAI Press.

Varanda, Marta (2001), 'Réseaux et mobilisation de PME commerciales dans le cadre d'un réaménagement urbain', PhD thesis in preparation, University of Lille I.

Vaughan, Diane (1983), *Controlling Unlawful Organizational Behavior*, Chicago: University of Chicago Press.

Vaughan, Diane (1999), 'The dark side of organizations: mistake, misconduct and disaster', *Annual Review of Sociology*, 25, 271–305.

Wasserman, Stanley and Katherine Faust (1994), *Social Network Analysis: Theory and Applications*, Cambridge: Cambridge University Press.

Wattebled, Olivier (2001), 'Bureaucratie et collégialité dans le Diocèse de Versailles', PhD Thesis in preparation, University of Lille I.

Weber, Max (1978), *Economy and Society*, Berkeley: University of California Press.

Wellman, Barry and Stephen D. Berkowitz (eds) (1988), *Social Structures: A Network Approach*, Cambridge: Cambridge University Press.

White, H.C. (1970), *Chains of Opportunity: System Models of Mobility in Organizations*, Cambridge, MA: Harvard University Press.

White, Harrison C., Scott C. Boorman and Ronald L. Breiger (1976), 'Social Structure from Multiple Networks I. Blockmodels of Roles and Positions', *American Journal of Sociology*, 81, 730–80.

White, Harrison C. (1981a), 'Production markets as induced role structures', in S.L. Leinhardt (ed.), *Sociological Methodology*, San Francisco: Jossey-Bass, pp. 1–57.

White, Harrison (1981b), 'Where do markets come from?', *American Journal of Sociology*, 87, 517–47.

White, Harrison (1988), 'Varieties of markets', in B. Wellman and S.D. Berkowitz (eds), *Social Structures: A Network Approach*, Cambridge: Cambridge University Press.

White, Harrison (2000), 'Markets and firms: Notes on the future of economic sociology', paper presented at the Second Annual Conference on Economic Sociology, University of Pennsylvania.

White, Harrison, with the collaboration of Matthew S. Bothner (2001), *Markets from Networks*, Princeton, NJ: Princeton University Press.

Williamson, Oliver (1975), *Markets and Hierarchies: Analysis of Antitrust Implications*, New York: Free Press.

Williamson, Oliver (1981), 'The economics of organization: the transaction cost approach', *American Journal of Sociology*, 87, 548–611.

Williamson, Oliver (1985), *The Economic Institutions of Capitalism*, New York: Free Press.

Williamson, Oliver E. (1996), *The Mechanisms of Governance*, New York: Oxford University Press.

Yamagishi, Toshio (1986), 'The Provision of a Sanctioning System as a Public Good', *Journal of Personality and Social Psychology*, 51, 110–16.

7. Employer/employee relationship regulation and the lessons of school/work transition in France

Alain Degenne

INTRODUCTION

We look at salaried employment and usually start by thinking in terms of the 'labour market', but this puts the cart before the horse, even if what we are researching does indeed square with what the term 'labour market' usually covers. We shall attempt to show that we need detailed analysis of the employer/employee relationship, its forms of regulation, varieties, etiology and the relative importance of these factors before we can understand that relationship, and that, if research does result in what we conventionally call 'labour market segmentation', the labour market should turn up as a by-product of our research (Jacob and Vérin, 1995). With this in mind, we shall outline theoretical elements that draw unusually little inspiration from standard economic analysis and, more particularly, we shall attach only relative value to the issue of salary levels (Perrot, 1998). The LASMAS-IDL longitudinal studies institute started such investigations over five years ago to extract maximum understanding from a longitudinal view of life sequences about actual practices among employers and employees alike.

Others have also stressed the longitudinal approach, including the CÉREQ job qualification research centre which has collected data and produced results that have fostered five annual seminars to date, including the last in Strasbourg in 1998. The seminars initially focused on both trajectory typologies and on methods, especially demographic methods that we call 'lifespan models'. The LASMAS team has worked mostly on trajectory typologies (Degenne *et al.*, 1996).

We started with no real theoretical foundations. We simply felt this would prove the best way to discover actor strategies. This approach taught us two types of lesson. First, we found it was feasible to regroup a sampling of fledgling job histories into a manageable number of categories that make sense and comfort certain hypotheses and acquired knowledge. Second, it taught us a number of new questions that need detailed research. The first descriptors we used to construct trajectories were all too crude, especially type of employment contract (Fénelon *et al.*, 1997). The studies from that period should be understood in light of five years of debate and follow-on studies triggered by CEREQ surveys on school/work transition. Jean Vincens is pondering over a definition of school/work transition as a state of being, i.e. as the end product of a process. In another way, this concern underlies the article on 'decisive' jobs by Catherine Rougerie and Jocelyn Courtois (1997).

In the beginning, we essentially quantified school/work transition in terms of either first job or time to first permanent job contract. But as we tracked school leavers over their first 50 months after school system exit, we accumulated data that undermined these two criteria (Degenne *et al.*, 1996). For example, a permanent job contract in the hotel industry actually guarantees zero job security while fixed-term contracts or agency 'temping' sometimes provides near-continual employment.

Studies of various French government incentives to hire youth show that they can indeed lead to a stable permanent employment on condition that jobseekers enter such jobs right after school, but sooner reveal serious personal handicaps to school/work transition in jobseekers hired through these incentives three or more years after school system exit. Available surveys on school/work transition helped enormously at the outset because they provided a homogeneous window into the world of wage-earners, but, for further headway, we needed to analyse job histories by sequences with new methodological tools.

A number of qualitative studies contributed extensively to the critique of our initial work on longitudinal studies of job histories, including papers by Chantal Nicole-Drancourt (1991, 1994, 1995) as well as a survey of 40 long-term minimum welfare beneficiaries in the town of Caen by students we advised (Bidart *et al.*, 1996) and a survey of 35 first interviews of jobseekers by Annabel Couzinet-Laroche for the ANPE national employment bureau (Degenne *et al.*, 1998).

We came to realize the importance of understanding job sequences and how they evolve in the employer/employee relationship. This relationship has an interpersonal component that complements the economic factors in play whose substance, form and duration deserve detailed attention (Galtier, 1996). The rough outline of a theory that follows offers a few ideas that should help formulate more selective questions.

THEORY AND PRACTICE OF HIRING AND PERSONNEL MANAGEMENT

To evaluate all the job trajectory data, it is imperative to consider, in all its complexity, the dynamics that combine to subdivide the labour market into widely divergent segments. We are now convinced that we need to look beyond the frequent and fortunate cases of highly educated first-time jobseekers who quickly find and keep secure jobs and to pay attention to everyone who is somehow tinkering with the very concept of employment in some way. While jobseekers surely just want a job, all employers really want is output. Yet this does not destroy the employer/employee relationship. Quite the contrary. The more market pressures bear down on employers, the greater their need for a pool of skilled/experienced resources on standby. The people in this pool must be immediately operational but only for limited periods. Here the concept of employment gives way to an employer/employee relationship, whereby employer and employee reach an understanding that the latter (generally in the weaker position) will be on constant standby. Thus employers and jobseekers each build up respective lists of labour suppliers and demanders. The upshot is relatively secure relations year in year out. Well established companies cope by calling in labour from temping agencies while others resort to a broad arsenal of hiring arrangements both on and off the books (Lochet, 1997).

Table 7.1 plots the type of employment status, or contract, against type of employer/employee relationship. Alongside standard forms of employment, it points up employer/employee relationships based on mutual understanding over time. Here conventional economists will be quick to note the paradox of services whose quality rises as their cost declines (Eymard-Duvernay, 1997; Favereau *et al.*, 1994; White, 1981, 2002).

Qualitative interviews show that long-term employer/employee relationships do exist under cover of temping, fixed-term contracts and off-the-books employment. This forces us to take into account the human dimension of the employer/employee relationship when trying to understand how the labour market actually functions, especially in segments where employees enjoy few real rights or guarantees.

Employers help structure the labour market by the way they hire and

Table 7.1 Typology of regulation

	Hiring strategies	
	Permanent employment contract	Fixed-term temping contracts or day labour
Secure employer/employee relationship	Secure conventional employment	Human resource pool
Depersonalized employer/employee relationship	'Bureaucratic' – type hiring civil service tenure	External labour market

manage personnel. While a lion's share of employees have permanent employment contracts, fixed-term contracts are on the rise, especially in early job history. Moreover, temping is on the rise to cut personnel administration costs. Lochet (1997) notes:

> Change of job contracts is quite common . . . in two out of five cases, permanent employment contracts are a form of temporary, if not precarious, employment status . . . Quitting to another company or going on unemployment does not preclude rehire by an ex-employer. Seasonal work is a textbook example of employment that is an integral part of job histories. But we are also seeing employers who cope with workload surges by calling back in the same people, now more vulnerably positioned on the labour market.

In this model, it is the job histories that count. We are a long way from the 'secondary labour market' we once designed, with an open market of unskilled labourers hired in function of fluctuating corporate needs and no attempt to retain those it regarded as interchangeable parts. In fact, employer/employee relations develop a history that restrains employee mobility in a good number of ways because of labour force structure. Both sides are trying to reduce the uncertainty factor in partner behaviour to cap hiring and downtime costs. This removes us from the open market model and drops us far closer to traditional personnel management practices of the sort that prevailed, for example, in French shipyards or the construction industry before World War II.

Temporary jobs sometimes lead to secure positions over time because company-specific experience becomes a relative asset and key permanent employees eventually need to be replaced by *trustworthy* successors, so that some selection process must be at work. Checking this hypothesis makes it essential to investigate employer/employee histories and to reconstitute the actual, mutually understood terms governing employment, which contract paper ill defines.

We need a resolutely longitudinal approach to map out individual job histories and, above all, if we are to grasp how jobseekers go about finding work, position themselves on the labour market and establish relationships with potential employers. Every job has a history: a history of employer/employee interaction in an output-oriented context. Thus we need a record of these histories to reach beyond mere analyses of hiring clauses or of the relevance of schooling to vacancies whose limitations are already well known (Tanguy, 1986).

Qualitative study data (see Couzinet in Degenne *et al.*, 1998) suggest that companies with fluctuating demand for their output and cashflow limitations make a policy of keeping staff on low-commitment contracts. Although such practices are not the general case because they seriously complicate the regulation of employer/employee relations when compared to relations with permanent employees, they highlight the mechanisms of labour market segmentation, which make them important to consider when trying to pin down the dynamics of a typology for labour market practices.

Most quantitative studies restrict the field to formal employment and it is important to reread them inside the broader context of all forms of employment, on/off the books, because qualitative studies show that off-book employment is a significant component of many job histories (Tilly and Tilly, 1994).

JOB HISTORY SEQUENCING

We need sequence breakdowns of job histories. A sequence is a period of variable duration that depends on the meaning it takes on in a given study. The sequences we have observed show that employees do not restrict themselves to legal employment and readily drift into off-the-books practices (as do employers) and into unemployment (which includes household production and other activities), especially those who tend to land low-security formal employment.

As shown in Figure 7.1, we can graph a sequence with a point in a triangle and define it as the proportion of time spent in each status. Applying our typological methods, the CEREQ yields the following four types of employment sequences:

1. stable single-company employment,
2. precarious single-company employment that firms up into a steady job (for example, temping),
3. a sustained blend of precarious legal and off-the-books jobs,
4. infrequent precarious jobs (more joblessness than employment).

We now need to look at low-security employment. This leads us to a definition of a 'job'. We see it as any identifiable period of continuous (not always continual) employer/ employee interaction. This leads to focusing on the form and regulation of this relationship. Initial terms of employment will evolve. The terms that bind both parties at the time of hiring continue operating for the duration of the contract period. But we can conceivably imagine that their relative importance will vary over time.

Employment has obvious profit-spinning value but this does not mean that either party thinks solely in terms of optimizing profits. Many studies flatly disprove this view and so do we. The main consequence of this rejection is that it calls for a hypothesis about how each party operates to reduce uncertainty about the other party's behaviour. Employers want guarantees about the people

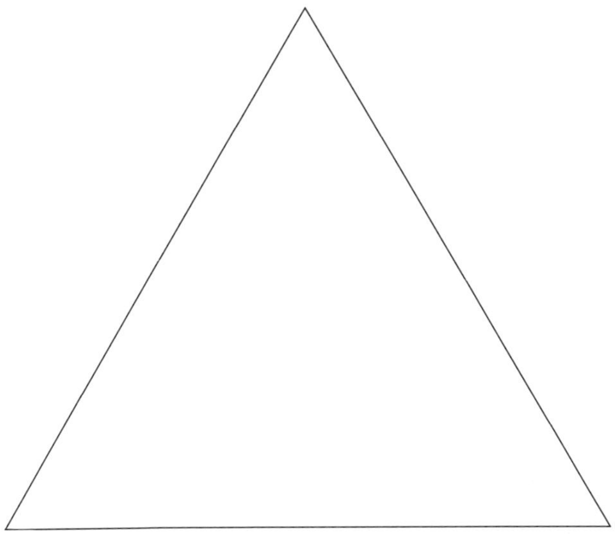

Figure 7.1 Kinds of employment

they hire and their behaviour; job applicants want as much about the company and terms of employment. Over time, familiarity with one another will affect behaviours.

By stating the problem this way, it becomes plain that it could prove helpful to go beyond Granovetter's strength of weak ties (1973, 1974) and other theories that hugely enthused us too. Valuable though it is, the weak tie theory is too general and unwieldy with field data (Marry, 1983). Actually, we are seeking to confirm the relevance of social network analysis by refining it through the investigation of the employer/employee interaction and its regulation.

TRUST AND INTERACTION REGULATION

The first two things to bear in mind here are the descriptors for trust and the objective criteria (for example, state of the economy, current demand for a given product/service, terms of employment, employee's input to output or any minimum going wage).

The notion of trust still escapes any straightforward operational definition. Fukuyama (1995) raises it to a national ethnic value and works it into large-scale models, much as Weber does with the Protestant work ethic and spirit of free enterprise. He sees trust as an ethnic trait that inhibits free-rider behaviour and incites collective action (Olson, 1966). This is like the notion of societal systems developed by Maurice *et al.*, (1982). By globalizing ethnic values, these four approaches carry the seeds of abandoning any attempt to pin down trust analytically as it develops and operates out in the field. We see trust as a *cognitive* pluridimensional concept. It describes what guarantees each party has about the behaviour of the other. So our concern is to find relevant indicators first and to postpone the issue of country-to-country variations.

Returning to the resource pool notion, one of our assumptions here is that employers have every interest in rehiring personnel with job-specific in-house experience (Lochet, 1997). Companies also have an interest in preserving off-hours ties to *trustworthy* employees. This is not new. It was once even commonplace and a return to the job security that hallmarked three golden decades in France may be on the next horizon.

But another way of viewing the issue is to ask who shoulders the consequences of any fall in the utility value of keeping on a permanent employee. First, the company, because it needs trustworthy people and because severance pay may be steep (internal market). Then the employee, because she or he will have to find alternative income. Lastly, the government, because of ex-employee entitlements to unemployment benefits it enacted to subsidize resource pools. So now we realize the need to bring government and other intermediaries into the equation.

Because *trust* is our issue, we need the means to study its foundations and how it operates. The trust rating grid presented in Table 7.2 applies conveniently to the employer/employee relationship.

The columns are based on the three categories proper to network analysis (Degenne and Forse, 1999; White, 1992). We can look at employee assets and identify complementarity including skills, brute force, health and personal appearance. We then look at what employer and employee have in common as

Table 7.2 Facets of trust

		Criteria		
		Individual traits	Intermediaries	Job/in-house experience
Standpoint	Absolute assets	1	4	7
	Adequacy	2	5	8
	Adaptability	3	6	9

persons, which is where common friends and other mediators come into play. We round out by examining track records to collar job experience and output quality.

The first way of appreciating these criteria is per se, irrespective of the actual vacancy. Another way is to test the employee's adequacy for the job. Each job has requirements (such as 20/20 vision for USAF pilots). A third way is to bet on adaptability and evolution (for example, young PhDs make good candidates for training investments). And small business also bets on adaptability because it can only afford limited staff to meet a wide variety of tasks.

Our result is a grid with nine categories that draws heavily on White (1992). All rate the same at the time of hiring but a hierarchy tends to develop over time. The objective value of educational level will pale before on-the-job experience. Adaptability only remains sovereign in leading-edge companies. Elsewhere, adequacy, experience and job adequacy prevail: the employee makes the grade or just does not work out. But the nine categories also apply to assess trust from both sides and this binocular feature stands among the grid's advantages. First, we consider the employer's standpoint.

1. Some personal assets have absolute value regardless of the vacancy. Race is an obvious example: it is illegal to turn down a candidate for this value, but the facts argue that the practice is endemic. There are also knee-jerk preferences for fellow alumni or the candidate with the highest diploma.
2. Objective assets are tallied against the job profile. Competitive exams are the extreme form of this logic in action since they rule out personal recommendations and life experience. Selection operates to pick the candidate that best fits the post but one missing skill or idiosyncratic personal appearance may suffice to disqualify an otherwise qualified candidate.
3. Objective assets are weighted against adaptive potential, not job profile. Hiring a fresh engineering graduate engineer amounts to a bet on adaptability. The candidate will need to stake out the new job. The post may even be tailored to the holder.
4. Personal recommendations and the candidate's reputation have absolute value. This calls into play the social identity of the referrer.
5. Personal recommendations are weighted against the job profile. Here the referrer's own knowledge about the job opening comes into play.
6. Personal recommendations are judged kinetically. A referral from a current employee implies that she or he has some control over her or his protégé. Hiring the offspring of a current employee is often a bet on mutual regulation. Mother has no interest in bringing in an offspring who will become an uncontrolable person while the latter would not want to tarnish her good standing in the company.

7. Experience rates as an absolute value. All the employer wants to know is that the candidate has previous work experience: young and cheap but punctual and obedient. This operates mostly at the moment of hiring, but job-specific experience probably becomes more important over time.
8. Experience is weighted against job adequacy or terms of employment. This applies to candidates with experience of similar positions. They know the job and are available now. They are temps that you may later want to lock in, or reliable seasonals, who are competent and keep coming back.
9. Experience is weighted against adaptive potential and initiative. Guilds are one example of corporate bodies that place high value on eclectic job experiences. Promoting a veteran employee to management level is another example of a bet on a hybrid of experience and adaptive potential.

The employee's standpoint is as follows:

1. The vacancy is a permanent, stimulating and well-paid opportunity.
2. The pay and working conditions are a take-it-or-leave-it proposition.
3. I can adjust to the job or adjust it to me, for example, this job works out because I can expect rises eventually and moonlight elsewhere anyhow.
4. I can identify with the objectively positive images of the company and position, with or without real job security.
5. I know the boss or have a referral from a current employee, but may have doubts about the image of the company, the position, job hazards, and so on.
6. I know current employees who assure me I can adjust to the position and terms of employment or can tailor the job to my needs and abilities.
7. I have doubts about my qualifications for this vacancy, the pay, challenges, co-workers, and so on.
8. I have doubts about doing this sort of work again.
9. I have doubts about whether my background is an asset in adjusting to this vacancy or whether I can tailor it.

These indicators would make useful components of a survey to identify the forms of employer/employee interaction. They also serve to map out frameworks for secondary studies of exploitable field data.

Contracts of employment pose several problems. Some of them grant ironclad job security regardless of performance, as in the civil service or major corporations. Longitudinal studies are almost pointless here. Other contracts are voidable or unenforceable. In some industries, 'permanent' contracts provide zero job security. Thus the best way to define 'employment contract' for our research is to ignore the clauses and reason in terms of histories and features of employer/employee interaction. Likewise, we need to requalify personnel management policy based on high recourse to temporaries. The categories outlined above should serve to design interviews and to pin down the spectrum of employer strategies and employee responses.

RELEVANCE TO THE MARKET

Employer/employee interaction is obviously subject to market conditions. Bénédicte Galtier's study is helpful here (1996). She bases a new typology for personnel management on 'temporal horizons'. Although she derives it from secondary study of the 1992 INSEE survey of labour costs and pay grids that ignores informal employer/employee interaction, she does connect our approach to segmentation by industry. However, the typology does not readily apply to the market niche that a given company exploits. The five types of regulation by horizon she proposes are (1) renovated medium-term, (2) traditional long-term, (3) short-term, (4) radical short-term and (5) goal-oriented variable-term.

This approach improves our understanding of strategies but we need data on less orthodox practices if we are to make further headway. But looking at the 'radical short-term horizon' category which covers companies whose margins are under strong competitive price pressure due to overdependence on a single client, we can infer that these companies need a high degree of operating flexibility and need to be able to hire and fire on very short notice. The resource pool strategy is doubtless highly relevant here. As Galtier (1996) concludes:

> The bottom line is that the diversity of temporal attitudes and how they fit into the broader picture reveal a big gap in conventional thinking that advocates extending the management horizon, through various forms of management planning for example. The finding is that each temporal attitude is a response to a specific set of opportunities and constraints that condition how that attitude operates.

'Short-term horizon' covers companies with very little manœuvring room because they operate in highly competitive markets. Employees here have just a little room for manœuvre because they have no other job opportunities. If we admit that wages are inflexible in small companies which operate in highly competitive markets (and that employees enjoy living standards that handicap job mobility while other local job opportunities are scarce), then these companies must be able to adjust to changes in market demand very quickly if they are to compete. This means having the right product to offer, of course, but it also means being able to adapt rapidly and slash output levels. The system needs highly flexible labour resources to survive. Thus, the more factors that structure the markets for a given product and the labour that produces it, the greater our chances of discovering informal links between employer and employee. Good places to look are in underindustrialized areas of the country and in highly competitive industries such as construction, food services, garments and industrial subcontracting. Job histories here show shifts between different jobs and industries, especially in the case of youth with no readily marketable skills.

Industrial sectors stand out as the first basis for establishing rough equivalence among employers, because they are likely to be under similar pressures to practise comparable hiring and personnel management practices. However, we need much finer analysis because of the deep differences between companies and the varying degrees of vassalage within each sector. Skilled workers have the least mobility, while managers and unskilled workers have more options.

We also need to look at local characteristics, especially at which types of jobs are available in the area. It is obviously easier to circulate in a major labour market such as Paris than in small towns or rural areas (Grelet and Timoteo, 1996).

CONCLUSION

Adopting a global view does not necessarily imply jettisoning analysis in terms of the labour market. However, new trends in the hiring of youth and substantial recent research interest in this population both indicate that these new hiring policies are now being applied to other categories of jobseekers.

Our statistical surveys have their limits: (1) they represent the population as a whole and fail to focus on the 20 per cent component at the bottom – we now know a good deal about school/work transition for the other 80 per cent; (2) they do not address off-the-books employment directly; (3) they are not the best way to understand (substantial!) resistance to job mobility; and (4) they approach from an inappropriate angle the options of last resort open to those between jobs.

We have started working on the following three hypotheses, based on various interview campaigns and a review of statistical surveys:

1. subsidized jobs, temping and other forms of precarious employment are not incompatible with the establishment of stable employer/employee relationships;
2. long periods of hopping from one precarious job to another may overlap with hiring policies and lead to a steady job (but we know little about wage-earner strategies in this domain);

3. youth (and others) take very different behaviour patterns depending on individual degree of personal autonomy. Some apply a wide range of means to position themselves on the labour market while others are more dependent on both employers and welfare.

All these considerations make precarious employment a complex phenomenon that cannot be boiled down to a by-product of the economic recession. There is no evidence that a sustained return to high growth will sweep away established behaviour patterns, especially when they result from a process of repositioning a company on its market(s). Thus it is important to understand this complexity in full detail. This chapter has attempted to offer some background data towards this end.

BIBLIOGRAPHY

Bessy, C. and F. Eymard-Duvernay (eds) (1997), *Les intermédiaires du marché du travail*, Paris: Presses universitaires de France.

Bidart, C., J. Dampuré, A. Degenne and B. Raoulx (1996), *Insertion, mobilités, réseaux, Étude auprès de bénéficiaires et ex-bénéficiaires du RMI dans le Calvados*, research report funded by Calvados Regional Council and Calvados Regional Directorate for Social Affairs and Public Health, Caen: MRSH.

Degenne, A., A. Couzinet and M.-O. Lebeaux (1998), *Une expérience d'exploitation du fichier historique de l'ANPE, en liaison avec une enquête qualitative*, report on a type of French employment bureau job contract, Caen: Lasmas-IdL.

Degenne, A., M.-O. Lebeaux and L. Mounier (1996), 'Typologies d'itinéraires comme instrument d'analyse du marché du travail', in A. Degenne, M. Mansuy, G. Podevin and P. Werquin (eds), *Typologie des marchés du travail, suivi et parcours*, Marseilles document no. 115, Céreq, pp. 27–42.

Degenne, A. and M. Forsé (1999), *Introducing Social Networks*, London: Sage.

Eymard-Duvernay, F. (1997), 'Les contrats de travail: une approche comparative', in C. Bessy and F. Eymard-Duvernay (eds), *Les intermédiaires du marché du travail*, Paris: Presses universitaires de France.

Eymard-Duvernay, F. and E. Marchal (1997), *Façons de recruter, le jugement des compétences sur le marché du travail*, Paris: Métailié.

Favereau, O., O. Biencourt and F. Eymard-Duvernay (1994), 'L'économie doit définir le marché à partir de l'entreprise plutôt que l'inverse', Communication multigraphiée, Forum, Nanterre, CEE.

Fénelon, J.-P., Y. Grelet and Y. Houzel (1997), 'Modéliser l'insertion', *Formation Emploi*, 60, 37–47.

Fougères, D. and F. Kramarz (1997), 'Le marché du travail en France: quelques pistes d'analyse', *Économie et Statistique*, 301–2, 51–60.

Fukuyama, F. (1995), *Trust*, New York: The Free Press.

Galtier, B. (1996), 'Gérer la main d'œuvre dans la durée: des pratiques différenciées en renouvellement', *Économie et Statistique*, 298, 45–70.

Granovetter, M.S. (1973), 'The strength of weak ties', *American Journal of Sociology*, 78, 1360–80.

Granovetter, M.S. (1974), *Getting a Job: A Study of Contacts and Careers*, Cambridge, MA: Harvard University Press.

Grelet, Y. and J. Timoteo (1996), 'Un outil pour l'analyse localisée de la relation emploi-formation: une typologie des zones d'emploi', in A. Degenne, M. Mansuy, G. Podevin and P. Werquin, *Typologie des marchés du travail, suivi et parcours*, Marseilles document no. 115, Céreq.

Jacob, A. and H. Vérin (1995), *L'inscription sociale du marché*, Paris: L'Harmattan.

Larquier de, G. (1997), 'Approche macro-économique du marché du travail et qualité des appariements', in C. Bessy and F. Eymard-Duvernay (eds), *Les intermédiaires du marché du travail*, Paris: Presses universitaires de France.

Le Goff, J.M. (1995), 'Les processus d'entrée dans la vie active: caractéristiques individuelles et marchés du travail', PhD. thesis, University of Paris I.

Lochet, J.-F. (1997), 'L'insertion structurée par les pratiques des entreprises', in Michel Vernières (ed.), *L'insertion professionnelle, analyses et débats*, Paris: Economica.

Marry, C. (1983), 'Origine sociale et réseaux d'insertion des jeunes ouvriers', *Formation–Emploi*, 4, 3–15.

Maurice, M., F. Sellier and J.-J. Silvestre (1982), *Politique d'éducation et organisation industrielle en France et en Allemagne*, Paris: Presses universitaires de France.

Nicole-Drancourt, C. (1991), *Le labyrinthe de l'insertion*, Paris: La Documentation Française.

Nicole-Drancourt, C. (1994), 'Mesurer l'insertion professionnelle', *Revue française de sociologie*, XXXV (1), 37–68.

Nicole-Drancourt, C. and L. Roulleau-Berger (1995), *L'insertion des jeunes en France*, Paris: Presses universitaires de France.

Olson, M. (1966), *The Logic of Collective Action*, Cambridge, MA: Harvard University Press.

Perrot, A. (1998), *Les nouvelles théories du marché du travail*, Paris: La Découverte.

Tanguy, L. (ed.) (1986), *L'introuvable relation formation–emploi; un état des recherches en France*, Paris: La Documentation Française.

Rougerie, C. and J. Courtois, (1997) 'Une étape du passage à l'âge adulte: l'emploi qui compte', *Population*, 6, 1297–1328.

Tilly, C. and C. Tilly (1994), 'Capitalist work and labor market', in N.J. Smelser and R. Swedberg (eds), *The Handbook of Economic Sociology*, Princeton: Princeton University Press.

Vernières, M. (ed.) (1997), *L'insertion professionnelle. Analyses et Débats*, Paris: Economica.

Vincens, J. (1997), 'L'insertion professionnelle des jeunes, à la recherche d'une définition conventionnelle', *Formation–Emploi*, 60, 21–36.

White, H.C. (1981), 'Where do markets come from?', *American Journal of Sociology*, 87 (3), 517–47.

White, H.C. (1992), *Identity and Control: A Structural Theory of Action*, Princeton: Princeton University Press.

White, H.C. (2002), *Markets from Networks*, Princeton: Princeton University Press.

8. Where do markets come from? From (quality) conventions!

Olivier Favereau, Olivier Biencourt and François Eymard-Duvernay

INTRODUCTION

In a 1981 issue of the *American Journal of Sociology*, sociologist Harrison White asked the economic question par excellence: where do markets come from? He devised a sophisticated and heterodox model to answer that question. His model allowed him to identify structural conditions (related to costs and preferences) under which stable markets could emerge (or not). 'Markets' should be understood here as a self-reproducing system of niches for competing firms, in a price/quality space, rather than the Walrasian fictitious place, where a benevolent auctioneer applies the law of supply and demand. So markets become another exemplification of modern social network analysis, developed by Harrison White and his Harvard group since the beginning of the 1960s.[1]

In 1989, the *Revue économique* published a special issue entitled 'L'économie des conventions', to which two of the present authors contributed. All the papers collected in that issue tried to think anew about either markets or business firms, in a more comprehensive approach to coordination and rationality, combining economics and sociology. The common key to revisiting the usual models of firms and markets is the notion of 'convention', as a social representation on what could be argued, if required, as a 'satisficing' level of coordination, inside the relevant collective entity.[2] Eymard-Duvernay's paper showed that the existence of stable goods markets is linked to implicit collective agreements between buyers and sellers, on what defines quality: these 'quality conventions' are translated by firms into coherent ways of management, whose pure forms are studied as 'enterprise models'.

This chapter is devoted to the thesis that the viable types of markets, analysed by Harrison White, can be reinterpreted to instantiate the 'quality conventions', analysed by François Eymard-Duvernay. If we are right, our thesis means that structuralist approaches (at least in terms of networks) and individualist approaches (at least in terms of conventions) may be deeply connected, contrary to the prevalent epistemological view in the social sciences.

We will proceed through this thesis in two stages. First, we will expose the building blocks of White's model, from the viewpoint of 'économie des conventions'. Second, the topology of markets derived from White's model will be shown to agree with Eymard-Duvernay's classification of quality conventions. In our conclusion, we briefly summarize the intermediary results and the next most important tasks of the joint research strategy on markets, organizations and networks that we are hinting at.[3]

WHITE'S MODEL OF MARKET AND THE ECONOMICS OF CONVENTION

We are more interested in the deep structure of White's model and its translation into the formal language of conventions than in the fine detail of its technical apparatus. The meaning of this reminder is twofold: (1) the interested reader will not find, in either sections of our chapter, an exhaustive mathematical account, for which we invite him to return to White's writings (1981a, 1981b, 1988, 2002), supplemented by the dissertations of Biencourt (1995, ch. 5) and Wächter (1999, ch. 4); (2) we will allow ourselves, in this section, to separate the essentials and the specifications of White's model. We do not suggest that the second section is less important than the first, but we need that separation in order to make as clear as possible the dual levels of discussion between White's network analysis and our conventionalist way of practising economics.

Firms

White's model

A producer market (Figure 8.1) is said to be viable when (1) there is a set of public observations, first on volume flow $y(k)$ sold by each firm k, second on the associated revenue flow $W(y(k))$, which could be approximated by a continuous function $W(y)$: the market schedule; (2) the firm k is supposed to rely on that approximation and act as if it had to choose one point, k, on that schedule; (3) the overall result of all similar choices (integrating consumer choices) is to reproduce the same approximation, proving to firms competing in that market that they were right to believe such a schedule actually exists: so we are back to (1).

The reader should notice that the index k, which enables firms to differentiate from each other, is absent from the market schedule: it is not a public (quantitative) piece of information like production y and proceeds W, which could be condensed into a single figure.

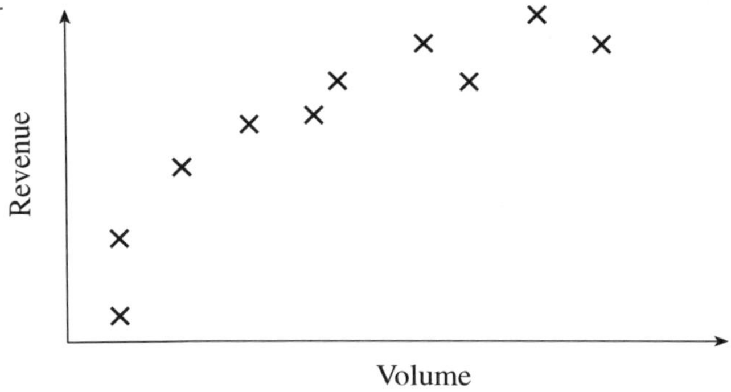

(a) A (producer) market will be a set of public observations . . .

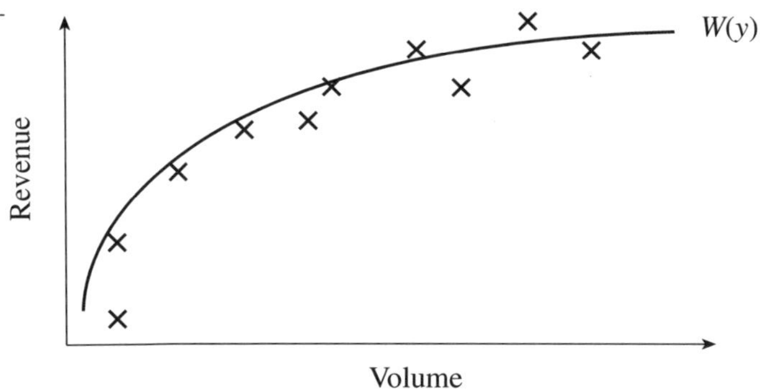

(b) . . . which can be approximated by a continuous functions . . .

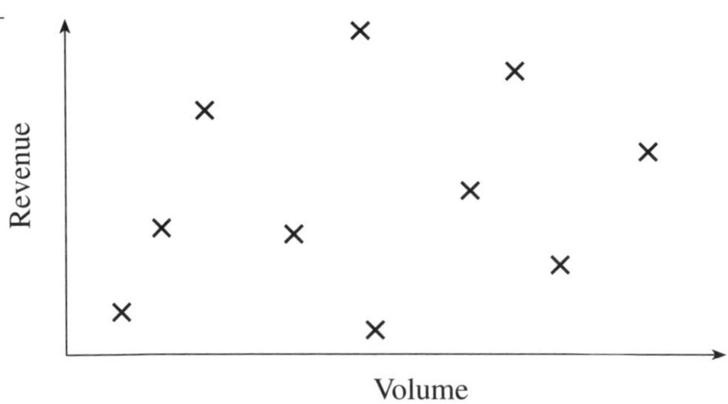

(c) . . . and this will not always be possible.

Figure 8.1 What is a (producer) market?

Each producer k tries to select $y(k)$ and, as a consequence, its price strategy $W(y(k))/y(k) = p(y(k))$, which maximizes its potential profits:

$$W(y) - C(y(k), k).$$

The cost function $C(y(k), k)$ is monotonic in its first argument: $C_1 > 0$. First order and second order conditions will be satisfied, together with a condition of non-negative profits $W - C \geq 0$. The index k could not be an endogenous variable, at this stage, since the producer uses the market schedule, from which k has been extracted. Were it not the case, the firm would choose $k = 0$ or $k = \infty$ according to the sign of the derivative C_2. Therefore the index k should be understood as something like the 'identity' of the firm, with respect to quality: it is what it is, and the choice of $y(k)$ takes place in that context. Moreover by assumption, cost functions are nested: they never intersect.[4] If costs of firm k are (say) superior to costs of firm $k + 1$ at one level of production, they will remain superior at all other levels.

So, at the end of these computations, we have a series of points $y^*(k)$ and $W(y^*(k))$, for each of the firms, like firm k, competing on the market under study.[5]

Reading in terms of conventions

We said, when commenting on our 'short' definition of 'convention' (see note 2), that it requires the economics of 'bounded rationality'[6] and interpretive social science:[7] the economic man becomes, at the same time, less rational and more intelligent than his neoclassical fellow. He is no longer able to make all the computations implied by the criterion of expected utility – which means a conversion to cognitive realism. On the other hand, he is no longer considered as the human analog of a mechanical computer. He receives an effective capacity to 'understand' (himself and others, either on an inter-individual basis or on a truly collective one) that implies he can enter into a discussion and be sensitive to arguments for and against: *homo oeconomicus* has recovered language! Let us now check to what extent White's model of firm behaviour is coherent with those postulates.

As for 'bounded rationality', there seems to be a contradiction, since firms maximize their profits. Even if recourse to maximization will make the comparison with standard microeconomics easier, we must concede we would prefer an approach with a criterion of 'satisficing', along the same lines as those followed for consumers (see the next section). Nevertheless on a closer look, 'bounded rationality' is not lost from sight. First, decisions on y^* are rather simple ones, needing very little information (the firm's variable costs and the set of proceeds/production figures for its competitors); second, optimization of y is strictly local, as far as k is fixed and y^* could easily result from adaptive adjustments;[8] third, concerning k, we must not forget $W(y)$ is, after all, only an approximation and, when we have to study business decisions about k, we will treat them as discrete choices, on a par with the 'comparative institution approach':[9] that methodology is privileged by Williamson, when he wants to justify how economic agents 'minimize' transaction costs in spite of their bounded rationality.

As for 'interpretive rationality', there has not seemed to be (up to now) much hermeneutic flesh on those structuralist bones! Once more that may be misleading, because we have a clearly important parameter, k, in search of a fuller interpretation. Moreover, what we already know is suggestive: thanks to k, the firm can identify itself as different from other firms, although they are all competing on the same market (in that limited sense, they look similar to the consumers) – and, more precisely, k is an identification key for a firm's level of costs which is neither price nor quantity. Therefore we call this first reading of k: quality factor α. It is that component of quality which lies 'in the eyes'[10] of producers. We also take notice of the striking macro absence of this strategic micro parameter.

Consumers

White's model

For consumers, the bundle of goods $y(k)$ produced by firm k is, at the same time, different from, and close to, the bundle of goods produced by firm $k' \neq k$. Otherwise firms k and k' would not be competing on the same market. So consumers' satisfaction relies, first, on a quantitative component: the number of units bought, $y(k)$; second, on a qualitative component, the identity of the product manufactured by the firm k or k': let us call it n_k or $n_{k'}$. The valuation of a flow volume of size y, from a producer indexed by k, on the part of buyers in aggregate, is designated by $S(y(n_k), n_k)$. Note that consumers are neither individualized like firms nor analysed through a representative agent: they are considered as an aggregate.

Buyers in aggregate make a 'yes or no' decision, when offered a volume/price pair by a producer. The only producers who stand out on the market are those whose offer satisfies the following constraint, whatever their location in the set of firm identities:

$$S(y(n_k)\ , n_k) = \theta \cdot W(y(n_k)).$$

The parameter θ is a sort of mark-up of satisfaction (measured in monetary terms) over the overall buying cost of a given production. Whereas each producer knows his own cost function C and the market schedule $W(y)$, the functions S are constructs of the observer, unknown to the producers, who could only register the impact of consumers' choice on their sales.

Finally, for consumers in the aggregate, we introduce the analog to the constraint of non-negative profit, for each producer (with one new parameter γ):

$$\mathbf{V} - \mathbf{W} \geq 0,$$

with $\mathbf{V} = [\mathbf{S}]^{\gamma}$, $\mathbf{S} = \Sigma_k S(y(n_k), n_k)$ and $\mathbf{W} = \Sigma_k W(y(n_k))$.

That constraint (when an equality) will be useful to calibrate the (minimum) value of θ: θ_0. Aggregate market flows for other ratios θ which allow for positive net consumer benefits are calibrated as multiples of θ_0.[11] The new parameter γ (when < 1) catches saturation effects of demand, which creates another form of interdependency, no longer internal but external, between firms: without it, the market under study would be devoid of any specificity, within the whole array of markets.

Reading in terms of conventions

'Bounded rationality' is obvious in consumer behaviour. At a micro level and notwithstanding the fact we are considering consumers in aggregate, the parameter θ can easily be interpreted as an aspiration level, in Simon's model of 'satisficing'.[12] We can go further along this line of reasoning: it shows a striking resemblance with the commonplace 'quality–price' ratio, since θ is equal to the division of S/y by W/y, that is the unit satisfaction (and so approximately the valuation restricted to quality) divided by the unit buying expenses (that is the mean price or even the unit price, if the pricing scheme is linear). Then the implementation by the aggregate consumer of a homogeneous θ throughout the various segments of the market becomes quite plausible. Each individual consumer probably has access to several of these segments, in close proximity to one another: by moving from one producer to the nearest other one, he simultaneously discovers the common value of θ and helps make it effective. Moreover, that kind of consumer behaviour implies orthodox microeconomics, as a limit. If they can be defined, marginal rates of substitution are shown to be equal, by differentiation of the θ condition.[13]

At a macro level, the θ condition exhibits an interesting property, which will prove useful, when we deal with the interpretive side of the model:

$$\theta = S(y(n_k), n_k)/W(y(n_k), n_k) = \ldots = \Sigma_k S(y(n_k), n_k)/\Sigma_k W(y(n_k)) = \mathbf{S}/\mathbf{W}.$$

So $W(y(n_k))/\mathbf{W} = S(y(n_k), n_k)/\mathbf{S}$.

Thus the model succeeds in bringing to the fore two variables which rank high in the agenda of business strategies:[14] market size ($\mathbf{W}$) and market share ($W(y(n_k), n_k)/\mathbf{W}$). That is entirely due to the introduction of the unusual (for theoreticians), though familiar (for practical people), parameter θ . . . which then disappears beneath the surface of these macro variables, somehow like k (now n), as the reader may remember, when we examined producer behaviour. We note that the market share for a single firm has a strong normative flavour, since it is built on the part of the aggregate consumer's satisfaction procured by that firm's product.

We now come to the interpretive side of the model. We have already pointed out that the key to the understanding of micro or aggregate behaviour is given by a parameter (k or n_k, θ), omnipresent in the structural forms, but absent from the reduced forms, the only ones observed at the macro level. In the next section of comments (Markets: Reading in terms of conventions), we shall have more to say about this strange property of such explanatory variables whereby they disappear: we think it is a necessary (but not conclusive) sign of a logic of interpretation coming into play inside the formal model of interacting agents.

At this stage, what is reasonably sure is that n_k, as an identification key of the product bundle offered by firm k, reveals a source of consumer satisfaction independent of quantity $y(k)$ and, taking θ into account, independent of price $W(y(k))/y(k)$. Therefore we call this second reading of k, through n_k, the quality factor ω. It is that component of quality which stays 'in the eyes' of consumers.[15]

Markets

White's model

We shall now put together the two building blocks of White's model. The existence of one viable market seems to depend on only one simple question, relative to the market schedule $W(y)$: does that approximation of a continuous function exist: that is, could firms competing on that market use that approximation to make decisions, in such a way that the approximation gets confirmed by their results?

Behind that question, lies another – the shadow question of market existence: whereas it is (intrinsically) not a problem, for producers and consumers, to agree on price (as an indisputable numeral), it is (intrinsically) a problem to agree on quality. Up to now, we have just assumed that there are no mistakes made about which firm produces which good and that this fact is valued independently by firms and by consumers: moreover, the valuation by one side of the market is not common knowledge for the other side. Obviously, we cannot stop there, in order to think about coordination, even in a world of bounded rationality.

We will now introduce a simplifying but powerful (and plausible) assumption: $n_k = k = n$. Firms lie in the same qualitative rank order[16] when judged by product label (function S) as when their cost functions C are nested.[17] We shall call n the value of the index in the common linear ordering. That simply means no asymmetry of information (and no uncertainty) at the level of the ordering itself: producers and consumers are in complete agreement with the scale of qualities, yet that does not entail the producer getting the information about valuation by consumers of n (that is, function S). That should not come as a great surprise: if firms overestimate the ranking of their product, they will quickly understand their mistake, since consumers will buy none:[18] there is no appeal left, after consumers have decided 'yes' or 'no'. Firms change their minds or go bankrupt. With that assumption, White's model catches the common sense of competition. Indeed, it goes well beyond, by assuming that the quality factors α and ω are merged into one; that is, quality in the eyes of producers unites with quality in the eyes of consumers. Behind the common sense of (order through) competition, there is a deeper phenomenon: the emergence of what we should really call a unique language on quality, jointly devised and agreed upon by consumers and producers.[19] We will soon have to make use of this family resemblance between language and quality to draw important conclusions on the individual skills inside White's model.

Then, if we go back to the question on the existence of a viable market, the link between the unknown ($W(y)$) and its shadow ($\{n\}$)[20] becomes crystal-clear: could we possibly, as observers, conceive of an ordering $\{n\}$, which could, for the actors, either producers or consumers, (re)produce the approximation of $W(y)$?

After substituting n for k and n_k, let us gather the relevant equations of the system of interactions between consumers and producers which summarize White's model of the market:[21]

$$dW(y)/dy = \delta C(y, n)/\delta y \qquad \forall n. \tag{8.1}$$

The producers' first order conditions give us n equations of type (8.1) with n endogenous variables ($y(n)$) and n predetermined variables, but we must not forget that the function $W(y)$ is really what we are in search of. We do not repeat the n second order conditions, nor the n constraints of non-negative profits.

$$S(y(n), n) = \theta \cdot W(y(n)) \qquad \forall n. \tag{8.2}$$

The consumers' demand for a homogeneous quality/price ratio across all the products available on the market gives us n equations of type (8.2) with the same n endogenous variables ($y(n)$) as in equation (8.1), the same n predetermined variables (but to be determined now), all of them conditional to θ. That crucial parameter will be calibrated through the constraint of non-negative benefit for the aggregate consumers.

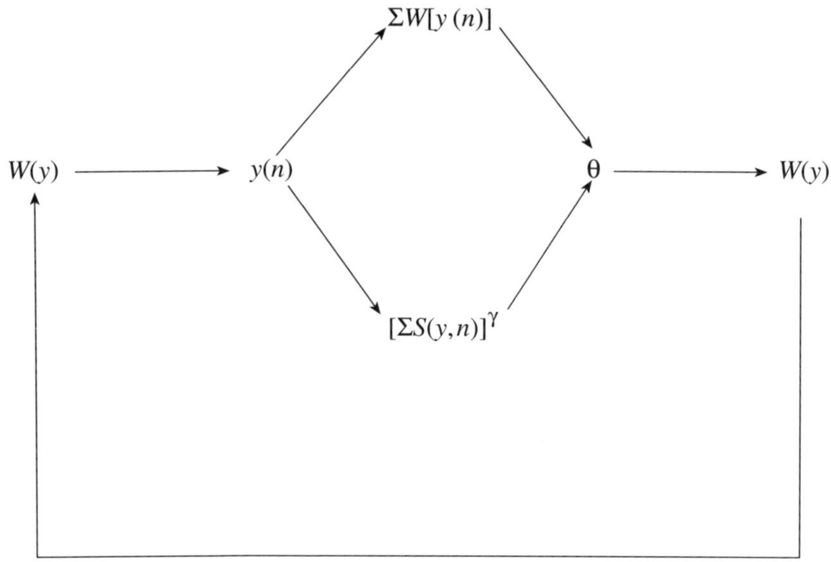

Figure 8.2 A viable market as a fixed point on quantities and with/without qualities

To conclude: we have $(2n)$ independent equations for $(2n)$ unknowns, n production variables, n quality variables (until now predetermined), all variables possibly conditional on one parameter, a quality/price ratio. Therefore our problem may have a solution (see Figure 8.2) but that is not our whole problem yet. It remains to be verified whether concrete functions $W(y)$ exist which can effectively generate such a solution.

Our initial definition of a viable market, above, at the beginning of the section on 'Firms', from the viewpoint of producers, can now be replaced by a formal definition: (1) existence of a fixed point concerning not a (price) vector as usual but a function: $W(y)$;[22] (2) computability of $(2n)$ variables $(y(n), n)$ and one parameter (θ), subject to three types of constraints (second order conditions and non-negative profits for producers; non negative benefit for aggregate consumers).

This new definition is not only more precise, it adds the viewpoint of consumers and, in so doing, it makes explicit a strange property that we have already alluded to: n does not – indeed must not[23] – appear in the function $W(y)$.

So we close our short exposition of White's model with that corrigendum: a viable market is characterized by two constitutive elements, each of which is as necessary to the other as an object and its shadow, a macrofunction $W(y)$

conditional to the macrovariable θ and a linear ordering $\{n\}$ common to producers and consumers. Whereas White insisted upon the first element, the 'market schedule', Eymard-Duvernay emphasized the second, the 'quality convention', and some years after, our intuition now is that each approach had seized only half of the truth: this chapter is devoted to the thesis that we actually need both approaches to explain markets and doing so will pave the way for a research programme in social sciences combining structures and representations or, more precisely, networks and conventions.

For the time being, let us wait until the second section of the chapter before exhibiting an explicit solution and just suppose we can find solutions verifying (1) and (2).

Reading in terms of conventions

We start from the principle that a viable producer market is fully characterized by:

$$M = \{W(y), \{n\}\}$$

when, of course, $W(y)$ and $\{n\}$ satisfy all the constraints and allow a reasonable value for θ.

We now want to prove the following proposition: M if read from $W(y)$ to $\{n\}$ gives 'markets from networks':[24] we call this reading M_N; M if read from $\{n\}$ to $W(y)$ gives markets from conventions: we call this reading M_C. The proof will be built with two kinds of arguments: first M_C displays the essential features of a convention. Second, and this part is indispensable if we are to convince the reader that we are not playing with words, the very fact that M_C has the nature of a convention should bring a deeper understanding of M_N as a mathematical model: we shall deal with the absence of n from $W(y)$ and show an important philosophical interpretation can be grafted on that seemingly mathematical constraint.

Let us begin with some technical remarks on how to solve White's model. After assuming a continuous macrofunction $W(y)$ and predetermined values of the n indices identifying firms in the area of qualities, we extract n solutions for variables $y^*[n]$ from equations (8.1). Then we insert those solutions into equations (8.2), which produce n new values of quality indices, conditional to a value of θ. Should equations (8.2) generate exactly the same $\{n\}$ as exogeneously put inside equations (8.1), while satisfying all the constraints (including an admissible level of θ), the work is done: the initial macrofunction $W(y)$ is confirmed. Leaving aside the question of finding that initial function, we can already bring to light two joint properties of M: (1) at the end of the day, $W(y)$ is just as important (not less, not more) as $\{n\}$. One is not possible without the other.[25] In this sense, M_C has the same legitimacy as M_N; (2) when we follow the line of events, we must first fix n, then solve for y. So, whereas the analytical weights of $W(y)$ and $\{n\}$ are similar, the analytical weights of y and n are not. The 'variable' n has to be considered as provisionally solved before solving the 'variable' y, as if the second is less important than the first one. That is fortunate, since n (respectively y) is interpreted as quality (respectively quantity) and it would be nonsense to speak about a number of units of a product before knowing which product we are speaking about!

It is due time to come back to the question of finding an explicit function $W(y)$ and to provide the first – technical – explanation of the strict separation between $W(y)$ and $\{n\}$ inside M_N and M_C. We quote Harrison White:

> Regard the quality index as an unspecified variable, n, that characterizes a hypothetical 'representative firm' (. . .). One cannot just integrate this apparently simple[26] differential equation [our equation (6.1)] to find the shape of $W(y)$ as a formula in known functions. Such integration would be over neighboring values of y, each of which must imply a slightly different level of n, in accord with $y[n]$.[27] That is, one needs to allow for how n must move as $y[n]$ shifts. Somehow equation [8.1] must be transformed so as to eliminate n from its statement (2002, pp. 40, 41).

So we use equation (8.2) to solve for n, which was exactly the method adopted in the previous paragraph to understand the structure of the model, and we replace n with that solution into equation (8.1).

> Thus one obtains a more complex differential equation that expresses how $W(y)$ must shift with y when one allows for n having to change in step. This issue is central: according to the model, at each separate value of n, a producer will choose a distinctive (optimal) volume. But this means that along the market profile, n will be neither a parameter, nor a constant index value (2002, p. 41).

With this technical background, we can revisit M in terms of conventions. We will proceed by steps: steps 1 and 2 gather prerequisites, steps 3 and 4 draw conclusions.

Step 1. Although (or because) it works as an approximation, the function $W(y)$ looks like the usual statement of a rule in the form of a conditional: if A, then B; that is, if the firm sells y units, then the firm earns $W(y)$ monetary units.[28] Nevertheless, it is striking that $W(y)$, as is well known of any actual rule, does not suffice to enforce any specific behaviour.[29] After all, the producer does not know where he is, or where he can move on $W(y)$: he needs some kind of connection between his present situation and other positions accessible under the rule $W(y)$, if it is to be applied by him. Since a quite plausible name for that connection is an interpretation and since $\{n\}$ provides decisive evidence about that connection, we get a first hint at our forthcoming thesis that $\{n\}$ is to be read as the interpretive base for $W(y)$.

Step 2. We find further support for our thesis from the capacities White's model confers upon the economic agents, either consumers or producers: whereas the variable y results from a computation (compatible with, if not altogether typical of, bounded rationality), the variable n results from an interpretation. That ability is a new one, in the genetic patrimony of the *homo oeconomicus*. To describe it, the shortest way is to compare the quality of a product with the meaning of a text.[30] First, a product is a set of characteristics; likewise a text is a series of sentences. So quality, like meaning, results from a global judgment, even if arguments could only be put forward piecemeal. Second, whatever the intentions of its author, a text escapes them to live on its own; similarly, the overall level (if not the basic elements) of quality intended by the producer will not have any causal influence on the consumer judgment. From that point of view, producing/consuming parallels writing/reading. Third, the meaning of a text, which becomes independent of its author's intention, becomes inversely dependent on all the other relevant texts, by the fact that it is embedded in a network of texts which Ricoeur calls a 'literature'; there is a close analogy with quality, as a multi-criteria rating (therefore fuzzy: see Blin, 1977): a product could not be qualified before being embedded into the whole series of rival objects – which may be the best definition of a 'market'. Our 'interpretive' approach to quality can be extended and strengthened by appeal to Schön's (1983) theory of management as an art (rather than a science) or Piore *et al.*'s (1994) hermeneutic theory of product design, (see Biencourt and Jolivet (2000) for a development).

Step 3. So economic agents in White's model show features of behaviour, unusual with respect to orthodox microeconomics, if not to the most commonplace observation. We shall make extensive use of them, when rephrasing $\{W(y), \{n\}\}$ in terms of conventions. In the meanwhile, we will have refined the usual definition of conventions: a subset of the set of rules, singled out by four aspects (relative vagueness, non-canonical expression, unknown origin, absence of legal enforcement). Lewis (1969) developed the very first game-theoretical model of conventions, on the uncontroversial idea that agents are quite often in interaction structures dubbed 'games of coordination' where it is crucial to select one among several equilibria, but the selected one may be arbitrary: the fact of coordination matters more than the form of coordination. Unfortunately, Lewis was not conscious that all his cases dealt with strictly observable behaviours: what is needed for coordination consists in a definite kind of physical action, rather than a definite kind of mental representation, which was introduced much earlier by Keynes (1936), to understand coordination on financial markets.[31] Our definition, stated at the very beginning of this chapter (a social representation, on what could be argued, if required, as a 'satisficing' level of coordination, inside the relevant collective entity) extends Keynes's definition, in two directions: (1) it is not restricted to financial markets; (2) it is not (only) a special type of rules but a general property of nearly any rule: since no rule is really complete, agents need something more to interpret rules (including the conventions covered by Lewis!). Let us call Keynes's definition (and ours) convention_1 and Lewis' definition[32] convention_2. Then we can establish that $W(y)$ has the nature of convention_2 and $\{n\}$ the nature of convention_1:

- The proof that $W(y)$ is some kind of convention_2 is easy: first, we have already noticed that $W(y)$ looks like a rule: if y, then W; second, this rule displays the four characteristic features of conventions according to David Lewis; third the variables implied in the function $W(y)$ are correlated with observable data.
- The proof that $\{n\}$ is some kind of convention_1 (to be called a quality convention) is hardly more challenging. First, $\{n\}$ obviously defines a collective order on quality, which is an emergent property of the interacting decisions of producers and consumers: thus it has the four properties of conventions, just like $W(y)$, although – this is our second point – it does not consist in observable data as y and W. Third, it has some normative properties and could be argued as a satisfactory framework of coordination,[33] at both the level of firms (positive – but not necessarily equal – profits) and that of consumers (homogeneous ratio quality/price[34] throughout the market). A quality convention is illustrative of a principle of justice – not overall, of course, but quite significant as far as the goods market is uniquely concerned. We must not forget, moreover, that the agreement between producers and consumers about n means that they have found a common language by which to speak to one another.

Step 4. We conclude that in M_C, $W(y)$ is the rule to be interpreted and $\{n\}$ is the interpretation of the rule, whereas in M_N, $W(y)$ is rather the set of resources from the consumers available to the firms and $\{y\}$ is the set of niches where those resources from the consumers are accessible to firms: the two sets should be intertwined to reveal the network structure of the market.

To put the whole thing in a nutshell:

$$M = \{W(y), \{n\}\} = M_C = \{\text{convention}_2, \text{convention}_1\}$$
$$= M_N = \{\text{resources, niches}\}.$$

The substitution of M_C to M_N is not simply a new coat of paint on an unchanged structure: one mathematical property of White's model now receives a deep philosophical justification. The mathematical property is the necessary exclusion of n from the macrofunction $W(y)$, although it plays a fundamental role in its determination, at a micro level; the philosophical justification is the finding that the meaning of a rule can never be part of the rule.[35]

White's model revisited by the economics of convention recovers the most provocative result of Wittgenstein's second philosophy, strongly confirmed by present-day cognitive sciences and philosophy of law: rules are never complete in their way of controlling actions,[36] and their completion cannot proceed from interpretive meta rules (which would fall into an infinite regression, be logically unsound and anyway unrealistic), but from collective interpretive schemes, like our conventions_1. This is our first explanation – the most philosophical one – for the fact that the absence of n from the function whose making it contributes to is correlated with the extension of rationality as calculus to rationality as interpretation. There will be two more explanations, forthcoming in the next section.

So our tentative conclusion for the first section of our chapter is twofold:

- quality conventions reveal the deep meaning of market schedules,
- market schedules provide the tangible marks of quality conventions.

WHITE'S TOPOLOGY OF MARKETS AND QUALITY CONVENTIONS

Our reading is not only possible, it is highly productive: the best proof of which will be given, in this second section, by the mutual support each theoretical corpus brings to the other, when no longer dealing with the general idea of a viable market/a quality convention, but with the various types of markets/the various quality conventions. This is the test of 'concreteness'.

In fact, that test will only be our second step in this section. Before reviewing these various cases, we have first to exhibit an instance of a fixed point on $W(y)$, in order to convince the reader we are not investigating an empty world. We will follow Harrison White's decision to adopt simplified specifications, rather than general functional forms: the maximum weight is put on the objective of obtaining explicit solutions.[37] This is the test of 'constructiveness'.

The last step of this second section will be devoted to the examination of remaining problems, on the way of building a truly general theory of markets and business firms, through networks and/or conventions. This is the test of 'robustness'.

Constructiveness

Specifications

For the valuation function of consumers, White chose $S(y, n) = r \cdot y^a \cdot n^b$ and, for the cost function of producers, $C(y, n) = q \cdot y^c \cdot n^d$, with parameters $q, r > 0$, and elasticities $a, b, c > 0$, but $d > 0$ or < 0: the reader is urged to take notice of this last possibility, which will turn out to be attractive. It is not *a priori* excluded, as in orthodox industrial economics, that *higher* quality could mean *lower* costs.

Parameters q and r are simple numerical scaling factors, common across all the firms. As illustrated by the constant elasticities, White adopted Cobb–Douglas functional forms for producers and consumers, the computational convenience of which is well known in economics.[38] But there may be something more than plain tractability behind these choices: each of these elasticities connects the rate of variation of an instrument (volume produced, y, or quality aimed at, n) with respect to the rate of variation of an objective (cost of production, valuation by consumers): so each elasticity is the mathematical translation of what could be depicted as a rule of adaptation, enacted either by firms or by consumers. These rules constitute a kind of reduced form of firm or consumer behaviour, along the lines of bounded rationality.

We can now insert these specifications into equations of type (8.1), by reasoning as if n denotes a representative firm:

$$dW(y)/dy = c\ .\ q\ .\ y^{c-1}.\ n^{d}$$

As we explained above, rather than integrating that differential equation, White eliminates n, by using equations of type (8.2):

$$n = [\theta\ .\ W(y)/r\ .\ y^{a}]^{1/b}$$

After substitution for n, 'so that terms of trade are common to all firms' (1981a, p. 20), we have a new differential equation:

$$dW(y)/dy = q\ .\ c\ .\ [\theta\ .\ W(y)/r]^{d/b}.\ y^{(bc - ad - b)/b}$$

'A market profile $W(y)$ has allowable shape *only* if it satisfies this differential equation' (2002, p. 42). It is an exact differential equation with separate variables, to be integrated by a standard calculus formula: we can now reap the benefit of the adopted specifications.

Solutions

The integration of the fundamental differential equation gives us one family of solutions, with K as a constant of integration.

$$W(y) = [P\ .\ y^{G} + K]^{F}$$
$$P \equiv q\ .\ (\theta/r)^{d/b}.\ (1 - d/b)/(1 - [ad/bc]) \equiv A/G.F$$
$$A \equiv c\ .\ q\ (\theta/r)^{d/b}$$
$$G \equiv (bc - ad)/b$$
$$F \equiv b/(b - d).$$

Our first comment is that this general solution admits the usual linear price function of pure competition $W(y) = P \cdot y$ as a limit case,[39] with $G.F \to a$ (and $a \to 1$), and $K = 0$.

Our second comment will be to stress the analytical importance of the arbitrary constant K, 'not fixed in terms of other parameters and rates in the system' (White, 1981b, p. 525). The presence of an essential element of arbitrariness in the general solution strongly supports our conventionalist interpretation of White's model, since a significant amount of arbitrariness is probably the most distinctive feature of conventions.[40] The connection goes very deep indeed, as we will see immediately when studying the possible values of K.

In a preliminary version of his model, White (1976, p. 9) gave this technical warning: 'The conventional procedure, specifying the constant of integration so as to satisfy boundary conditions [second order conditions and non-negative profit conditions], should be reversed. The constant of integration K should be taken as a given fact summarising the history[41] of the process which shaped some initial (. . .) schedule into an equilibrium one. Thus K is an initial condition in terms of which the boundary conditions specify ranges of y and n which can appear in the equilibrium (. . .) schedule' (note added by present authors).

Thus conditions of positive profits for each of the n firms ($W(y) - C(y; n) > 0$) could be shown[42] to become the following inequalities, for each level produced, y:

$$[(a/c) - 1]/[(b/d) - (a/c)] \,.\, [q \,.\, (\theta/r)^{d/b} .\, y^G] > (-K)$$

and second order conditions for each of the n firms ($d^2W(y)/dy^2 < d^2C/dy^2$) could similarly be shown to become the following inequalities, for each level produced, y:

$$(bc/a) \,.\, [(a/c) - 1]/[(b/d) - (a/c)] \,.\, [q \,.\, (\theta/r)^{d/b} \,.\, y^G] > (-K) \,.\, d$$

These two inequalities can be presented on a plane whose axes correspond to the ratios (b/d) and (a/c): the first one may be positive or negative, whereas the second one is only positive. By drawing a line of coordinate $a/c = 1$, parallel to the axis (b/d) and a ray from the origin of the axes $a/c = b/d$, in the positive quadrant, we delineate six regions where we can check the sign of the left side of the two inequalities (see Figure 8.3). Only one region ($a/c > 1$ for negative values of b/d) will be excluded for its inability to sustain a viable market, because no values of K could be found to conform to both conditions (let us call them respectively **pos** and **max**).

This does not mean the five remaining regions are admissible for all values

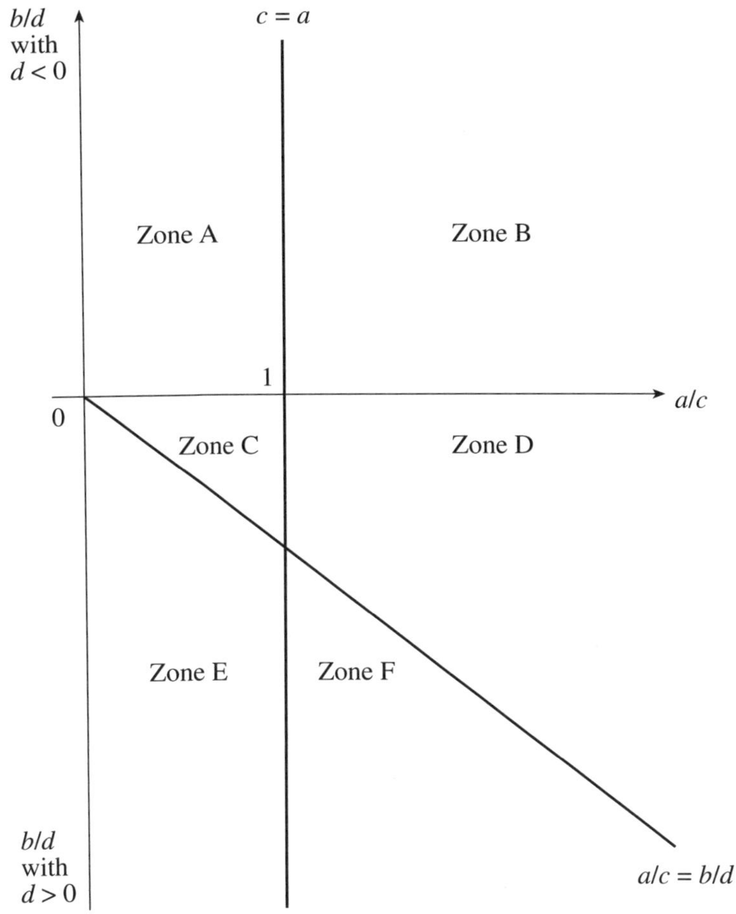

Figure 8.3 The space of possible markets

of K, with respect to the level of y (and therefore of n): (1) y must be positive in each condition; (2) the ordering of upper (or lower) bounds on y deduced from each condition, respectively $y_{\mathbf{pos}}$ and $y_{\mathbf{max}}$, is not indifferent: if we have $y_{\mathbf{max}} < y_{\mathbf{pos}}$, the market profile will be liable to 'unravel'. In that case, only a corner optimum obtains and therefore, instead of one producer (one value of n) for one volume y, several producers may be found 'choosing the same extreme value of volume, so that volume signals not a unique but a whole range of quality n. All do expect to gain positive incomes but they cannot be delivering the same payoff value over payment; so the buyers no longer accept any shipment from producers issuing that signal. But then the process repeats itself at the new lowest acceptable signal – and so on' (see White, 2002, pp. 81–3; see also White, 1981b, p. 528).

After this new test,[43] one more region is rejected as non viable (because of 'unravelling') and only one of the four remaining can be viable for any K; otherwise, one is viable for $K > 0$, one for $K \geq 0$, one for $K = 0$.[44]

This is still not the end: we have made no use of the constraint of positive benefit for consumers (see above). It would be a mistake to deduce, from the fact they are not optimizers, that consumers are passive beings through their role of accepting/rejecting whole bundles of products according to their quality/price ratios. To some extent, they can manipulate the value of θ, at least if the market under scrutiny has some specificity (because of saturation effects) with respect to other markets, that is, if $\gamma < 1$. 'Thus gamma provides a third, independent dimension for a market space: the market plane geranalized by specifying external substitutability' (White, 2002, p.140) and not only internal substitutability. That means our complete state space should be treated as a cube – or that the plane of axes (a/c) and (b/d) is drawn for one value of $1/\gamma$. Unfortunately, no analytical solution is to be expected. Nevertheless for $K = 0$, we can get some important clues. It can be proved[45] that the net benefit for consumers $\mathbf{V} - \mathbf{W}$ admits a maximum when $a/c < 1/\gamma$, and 'in the varieties of markets which have this combination, aggregate market size [$\mathbf{W}$] decreases as more firms are added',[46] whereas the net benefit is unbounded when $a/c > 1/\gamma$: $\mathbf{W}$ grows if more producers enter the market, adding more levels of n but also $\mathbf{V}$ and/or $\mathbf{S}$ more than proportionally![47] That last region – located to the right of a vertical (and dotted to reflect conditionality to $K = 0$) line on the axis (a/c) beyond the unity – should be deleted.

To conclude, after this ultimate screening, we are still left with four regions of viable markets (and three regions of non-viable markets), of which two come from the restriction of previous ones (see Figure 8.4).

Our third comment on the solutions just gathered and classified must be devoted to the fixed point methodology in White's model, revisited in our conventionalist framework.

With respect to the postulate of bounded rationality, the careful reader could point out that, after all, this heterodox model of the market formally looks like the Walrasian model, which springs too from a fixed point in Arrow–Debreu's canonical version! Have we not also as much coordination here as in mainstream economics: that is, too much? We think not, even apart from the paucity of information needed by agents in White's model. The most striking difference[48] lies in the 'constructive'[49] proof offered by White, in sharp contrast with the mainstream demonstration of the sole existence of an equilibrium (by recourse to Kakutani or Brouwer's theorem of fixed point[50]). The particular function discovered by White will allow us to make concrete connections with practical rules of action used by economic agents, even if we

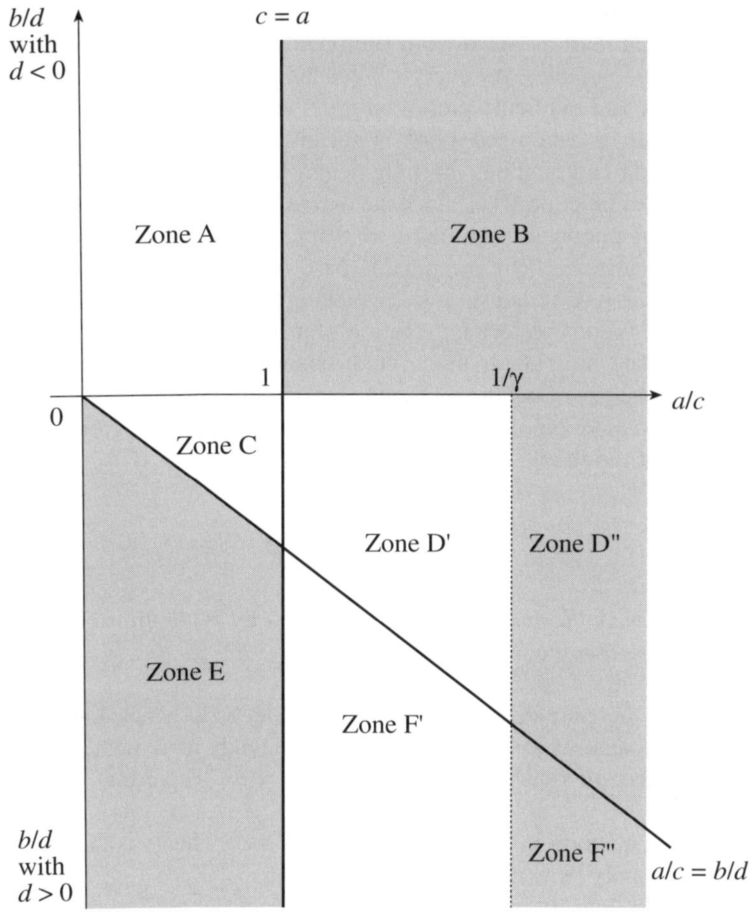

Figure 8.4 The space of viable markets

do not suggest that they use that particular function. Nothing similar could be devised in Arrow-Debreu's theory.[51]

With respect to interpretive methodology, the constructivity of White's proof gives us the opportunity to bring forth a second explanation – the most mechanical one – of the puzzle about the absence of the microvariable n from the macrofunction $W(y)$, which we want to correlate with the extension of computational rationality to interpretive rationality. We saw in the process of solving the equations that we had to eliminate n in order to find the function $W(y)$. It is time to emphasize that it was also a process that worked 'bottom-up', from micro to macro. We are accustomed to treating this process as one of aggregation, that is, of summation. Nevertheless, more realistically, aggregation comes at least as much from subtraction: only what is countable will enter the macrovariables. As every statistician knows, quality of products is only indirectly and implicitly present in gross national product data: the interpretive side of the data, once more, is not in the data because quantities (or values) are data and qualities are judgments. Therefore it is no surprise if n disappears from function $W(y)$, since the outputs of individual rationality to be collected at the aggregate level must be stripped of their interpretive component, so as to insulate their computable part. A side-effect of our view is to remind us of the risk of delusion when sticking to micro–macro models of the representative agent: 'perfect aggregation', far from being an ideal,[52] is a sign of triviality. The individuals under study show such a poor behaviour that nothing is in danger of being lost by projection onto the coarse macro level – but neither can anything novel emerge in the process of aggregation.

We now turn to the qualitative variety of equilibria.

Concreteness

Viable markets

The *first type of viable market* is called 'ordinary' by White. It is characterized by four features (see Zone C in Figure 8.4):

- $a/c < 1$: there are decreasing returns to scale. Strictly speaking, it seems as if we can only assert that C rises more quickly than S when y is growing. Since, on a viable market, we have $S = \theta \cdot W$, we may skip from S to W.[53]
- $d > 0$: if quantity is costly, so is quality. C rises when n is higher. This is the 'ordinary' way of thinking about quality.
- $a/c > b/d$: returns are decreasing with respect not only to scale but also to quality, and to a more severe degree.
- $K \geq 0$: with a negative value of the constant of integration, unravelling may occur. The role of K is to take account of 'historical idiosyncrasy' (White 1981b, p. 526).

This whole set of features obviously denotes a familiar kind of markets closest to mainstream competitive analysis: quality is hardly a disturbing factor.

Our hypothesis is that 'ordinary' markets are founded on the 'merchant' quality convention (Eymard-Duvernay, 1987, 1989). This order of quality is constituted[54] by conformity to customers' tastes. In a very precise sense, market defines quality: buyers appreciate one product essentially because it is appreciated by their reference group (which may be simply the other buyers),[55] rather than for its price. The best instance is given by teenagers' clothes but we need not restrict ourselves to fashionable products. The common thread between products dependent on 'merchant' quality convention is made of a material with two opposite properties. The first one is the irrelevance of price, as a cause, and the second one is the relevance of price, as a consequence. The explanation comes from the fact that price itself does not initially explain the success of the most appreciated products but their proximate, less appreciated, competitors could only attain the ratio θ by strongly lowering both price and quantity (because of decreasing returns to scale), so that eventually high price becomes a signal for high 'merchant' quality, whereas lower quality can be efficiently compensated by still lower prices. The 'model of firm' coherent with this quality convention is centred on variable costs (personnel expenses) in the function C: the typical firm is urged to search for flexibility. Series are short and prone to frequent changes in product lines. The lengthening of production series would be self-defeating since higher costs of higher volumes would either erase profits or increase prices at the risk of losing customers' support. As for $K > 0$, an interpretation compatible with the 'merchant' quality convention is that the price covers fixed costs (not that the whole of proceeds depends on y)[56], which suggests the absence of barriers to entry. We are close to the textbook competitive world, even if quality brings some novel traits to light.[57]

White calls the *second type of viable market* 'advanced' in its maximum extension (after elimination of the 'explosive' type). It is characterized by three features, the fourth helping to discriminate between two subtypes, 'trust' and 'crowded' (see Zones D′ and F′ in Figure 8.4):

- $d > 0$: as in the first type of viable market, a product of higher quality is more costly to produce.
- $a/c > 1$: there are increasing returns to scale. That makes a difference with the first type of viable market.
- $a/c < 1/\gamma$: The increasing returns to scale are not so great as to make the size of the market unbounded.
- $K > 0$ if $a/c > b/d$; otherwise, unravelling may occur. That area will be dubbed 'trust'. Any K is possible if $a/c < b/d$. That area will be dubbed 'crowded'.

This whole set of features pinpoints an unconventional type of market, since its viability is matched with increasing returns to scale, although this factor is considered as disruptive in mainstream industrial economics.

Our hypothesis is that 'advanced' markets are founded on the 'industrial' quality convention.[58] This order of quality is constituted by conformity to technical standards. Quality is no longer defined by one side of the market (customers in the 'merchant' convention), but by an authority external to the market: a public agency, an administration, an independent customer association, a scientific laboratory and so on. The best instances are given by medicinal products or cars. The technical norms to which they are submitted are, *de facto* or *de jure*, not produced by the producers (contrary to consumers in the 'merchant' convention).

The 'model of firm' coherent with this quality convention is centred on heavy equipment and fixed capital: the management emphasizes viability and learning by doing. The length of production series is looked for, in order to stabilize the product in consumers' minds, and to benefit from increasing returns to scale.

The condition on K is quite interesting in our conventionalist view. As in the first type of viable market and perhaps more satisfactorily, the positivity of K has a natural interpretation: it is not sufficient to get profits over variable costs, fixed costs have also to be covered by proceeds, but the condition vanishes when $a/c < b/d$. Now the equality of a/c and b/d (which should be written: $a/b = c/d$) reveals an extraordinary pattern: the satisfaction function of the consumer is structured like the cost function of the producer. Buyers and sellers are in agreement about the relative weights of quantity and quality: it is no surprise if this pattern (together with increasing returns) serves as the central axis, the spine of the 'industrial' convention. The case when $1 < a/c < b/d$ means that generally the satisfaction of the buyers (with respect to either more quantity or more quality) grows more quickly than the costs of the sellers – and specifically the gap is even larger for quality than it is for quantity: by offering higher quality, firms are most successful. Variable costs do not grow in the same proportion and furthermore the higher volumes bring still more satisfaction and, because of increasing returns, end by lowering costs! We can easily understand that the financing of fixed costs is not a strong demand (indeed not a demand at all) in such a favourable context.

This last case – illustrative of mature industries – may be nicknamed 'crowded', because buyers would be made better off if they were served by fewer firms. Indeed it can be shown that market size decreases when a new firm enters and finds a niche on the market schedule. Since buyers are neither advised, nor superseded by an omniscient auctioneer, they can say yes/no to one producer at a time, but 'they cannot change to another set of producers as a whole. (. . .) So the best here is second best' (White, 1981a, pp. 33–4).

White calls the *third type of viable market* 'paradox'; it is characterized by three features (see Zone A in Figure 8.4):

- $d < 0$: in sharp contrast with the 'ordinary' and 'advanced' types of market, higher quality is paradoxically less costly to produce than lower quality.

- $a/c < 1$: as in the 'ordinary' type of market, there are decreasing returns to scale.
- $K \leq 0$: under that condition, the market is not subject to unravelling, whereas it may unravel with $K \geq 0$.[59]

This whole set of features mixes up quite usual aspects, like decreasing returns to scale, with quite unusual aspects, like decreasing costs with respect to quality. The chance of locating a 'paradox' is endangered by the risk of finding an inconsistency: how could it be that all producers do not jump to the best possible level of quality, if it is also the least expensive?[60]

Our hypothesis is that the 'paradox' markets are founded on the 'domestic' quality convention.[61] This order of quality is constituted by conformity to an authentified pedigree. Quality of a product depends on how embedded it is in an issue of products originating from a common matrix. 'Domestic quality' is defined outside the market, like 'industrial' market, but the former differs from the latter, in the same way as procedural rationality differs from substantive rationality, according to Simon (1978). That form of quality is not so much a property of the product itself as of the sequence of operations implied in its production, with a predetermined starting point. Of course a substantive element remains inside the procedural content: the judgment about quality assumes a relative grading between starting points. The best instance is given by traditional products, for example cheese made with milk collected from old-fashioned farms, still practising ancient methods.[62] In that case, quality springs from the integrity of the whole process (the starting point plus the sequence of operations). Another example is the trademark, when it is associated with a reputation for expertise or ability, rather than an image built by advertising outlays: in that case, quality springs primarily from the starting point. Still another example is the field of those sports (such as football) or arts (such as theatre) where performance is highly dependent on motivation, especially collective motivation: a younger and eager group will often get better results than more established ones. In that case, quality springs primarily from that part of the process which consists in the sequence of operations. In any case, producers can never simply handle quality, although quality is always associated with production, viewed as a temporal and spatial process.

The 'model of firm' coherent with the 'domestic' quality is centred upon immaterial investments and specific assets, which warrant the character of the product: its peculiarity with regard to other products through space, its continuity through time with preceding products of the same family. But we have to specify more explicitly the nature of those resources (immaterial, specific) which allow a higher level of quality to be matched by a lower level of costs. The most plausible explanation is to be found in the hidden presence of an important factor of production not totally compensated. We will give three pieces of evidence, corresponding to the three cases above.[63] The first is *tradition.* When a firm has devised an exactly appropriate technology (rather than an all-purpose equipment),[64] thanks to a long familiarity with the sector which accounts also for the popularity of the product, there are no wasted inputs, contrarily to the other less experienced firms. The second is *reputation.* When a company has a strongly established name for know-how, it does not need to incur any advertising expenses; therefore its less renowned competitors display higher costs (they need advertising) and lower quality (by hypothesis). Finally, there is *motivation.* Sometimes a new theatre company, a football team without stars, a passionate, little-known orchestra, an ambitious research centre and so on may offer higher performances in spite of, not to say because of, salaries lower than those of more established rivals: productivity is superior, wages are inferior. Except in pathological cases, that should not be too quickly dismissed as 'exploitation'. A deeper explanation could be devised with the help of the theory of compensating differentials. The gap between wages and productivity may be filled by a non pecuniary source of utility, which, by chance, is also an input in the process of production:[65] can we not consider motivation as such?[66]

Our conventionalist reading of the first feature $d < 0$ is surprisingly well suited to the interpretation of the last feature $K \leq 0$: within that order of quality, producers should not hope to see (something like) their fixed costs covered by their receipts. To produce in that field implies first making some irreversible advances, perhaps in the form of a necessary but not marketable input, as though the 'domestic' quality, with its extraordinary property of being inexpensive, has to be deserved, before being obtained.[67] No doubt, it limits the number of candidates! So we conclude there is no inconsistency behind the paradox.

Non-viable markets

We can gain a fuller understanding of viable markets and their quality conventions by reconsidering what happens with quality in the three cases of non viable markets (already introduced but only through their technical aspect, above).

First, $d < 0$ and $a/c > 1$ (see Zone B in Figure 8.5): no value of the constant of integration K can be found which satisfies the two main constraints (**pos**: non-negative profit, **max**: existence of a maximum). If $K > 0$, firms will minimize, rather than maximize, their profits; if $K < 0$, firms are unable to make positive profits.[68] What does that mean about quality? Quality should not be too easy: otherwise, is it still quality? Indeed, in that case, constraints, far from being too heavy, are too light,[69] since there are, at the same time, increasing returns to scale and increasing returns to quality. The personal computer industry may be a paradigm for this case.

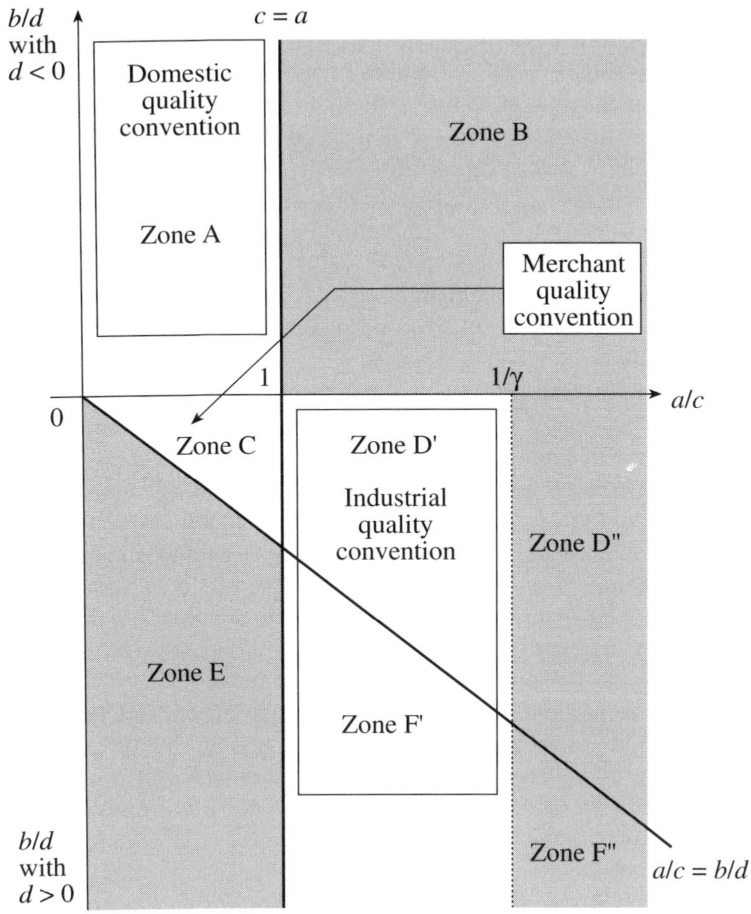

Figure 8.5 Viable markets and quality conventions

Second, $d > 0$, $b/d > a/c$ and $a/c < 1$ (see Zone E in Figure 8.5): the market is subject to unravelling, because of corner optima. This case is, in a sense, the opposite of the previous one: quality should not be too difficult and suffer too many constraints. It should be somewhat fostered by the environment. There are decreasing returns to scale and decreasing returns to quality. Moreover, we first have $a < c$ and $b < d$, which implies that costs grow faster than satisfaction, with respect to quantities and qualities; then the relation reverses for qualities ($b/d > 1$) but the constraint on costs through $a/c < 1$ is all the more severe: too many firms are concentrated on the lower levels of quality which become the Achilles heel of the market, like a ladder broken step by step, starting from the bottom. Road transport is a clear-cut illustration.[70]

Third, $d > 0$ and $a/c > 1/\gamma$ (see Zones D″ and F″ in Figure 8.5): the decreasing returns to quality are no longer sufficient to block the increasing returns to scale, which are now strong enough to make any change in n induce an unlimited growth of *W*, *V* and *S*. By contrast with the second case, the higher levels of quality become the new Achilles heel of the market, but by contrast with the first case, firms earn positive profits and maximize them. The problem is that any new entrant with a higher quality will be warm-heartedly welcome by consumers and the size of the market will never cease growing. A new industry (like cellular telephones of first and second generations) in an expanding economy[71] may be evoked for this case.

To conclude this section, let us think about the common nature of these three cases of non-viable markets. It will give us the third and last explanation – the most psychological or cognitive one – for the absence of *n* from the market schedule *W*(*y*), although *n* is the fuel necessary for the social engine which produces a viable market. In the first and second cases, *n* is unable to produce a schedule *W*(*y*) independent of *n* and/or sustainable, that is satisfying the set of constraints; in the third case, the schedule is sustainable but not stable with respect to a change in *n*. So, in all three cases, 'market failure' is linked with the persistent dependence (for better or worse) of the macro structure on the micro behaviour. The viability of markets is one instance of a general class of problems where a system has to appear independent of its elements, in spite of their giving rise to it. As a matter of fact, conventions belong to that very class, according to the 'economics of convention': 'a convention must be taken account of both as the result of individual actions and as a framework constraining the agents' (Dupuy et al., 1989, p. 143).

Apart from mathematical reasons (already quoted above), this point was the only one, alluded to by White, commenting the exclusion of *n* from *W*(*y*). As early as 1982, he wrote: 'It [*W*(*y*)] cannot depend on *n* because it is perceived by every firm as the frame of possibilities available to it, the possibilities being the set of observations over all firms' (1982, p. 6). And more recently, he has been a little more explicit: 'Since (. . .) every producer sees itself as facing the same menu of alternatives, the same market profile *W*(*y*), the index for quality *n* cannot directly influence the shapes of market profile derived for any given context. But in the other functions describing context for the observer, *n* does appear and thus it also must appear in the derivation of the profile, as well as of the terms of trade' (1997, p. 46). The argument is less evident than it seems. Why, after all, is it necessary for all firms to see the same ecosystem as it were from the outside, if each firm is to succeed in finding its own niche, inside it?

Our answer will start from the proposition that the market schedule *W*(*y*) actually works like a 'focal point', along the lines of Schelling: 'when a man loses his wife in a department store without any prior understanding on where to meet if they get separated (. . .) it is likely that each will think of some obvious place to meet, so obvious that each will be sure that the other is sure that it is "obvious" to both of them' (1980, p. 54). What about applying the metaphor to the market place? To tell the truth, the likeness does not seem to resist too close a scrutiny. First, coordination between firms is more difficult (because of their indeterminate number) than between two persons as proximate to one another as a man and his wife; second, it is rather quaint to deal with competing firms through a coordination game! On second thoughts, the apparent differences should be commuted into deep convergence. Firms have to choose a market and a niche on the chosen market. They need the most objective characterization of the world they want to enter or where they want to stay – which means a rigorously collective description, that no single firm can manipulate, even if (from the observer's point of view) it can be established that all firms elaborate it jointly. So there is a level of observation where all firms have a paradoxical common interest, and that is precisely the level where the market is a collective object, subject to a collective description. $W(y)$ corresponds exactly to what we are looking for: the 'common world'[72] between all competing firms, before they fight against one another by searching for their best separate niches, without knowing that their common fight will create their common world.

Our explanation, founded on the notion of a 'focal point' (but revisited in terms of a 'common world'), is in line with the recent theoretical development of that notion offered by Sugden (1995). Schelling underlined 'the intrinsic magnetism of particular outcomes'[73] which will help the agents to adopt an external object as a coordinating device. That peculiar property will put us definitely on the right track: a focal point owes its role of focal point to some property of 'prominence' or 'salience'. Therefore, 'to understand focal points, we need to consider the players' own descriptions of their options'.[74] This remark by Sugden confirms the result of our inquiry: $W(y)$ is precisely the description (by means of public figures) of the 'common world' between competing firms. So the areas of non-viable markets may be gathered under the same heading: the rules of adaptation materialized in the elasticities a, c, b, d, do not happen to be legitimated by any quality convention; they are unable to generate a 'common world' with its shared description.[75]

Our excursus through this third explanation, which led us from the notion of 'focal point' to that of 'common world', can now elucidate the strange property of conventions[76] we have just recalled: 'a convention must be taken account of both as the result of individual actions and as a framework constraining the agents' (1989, p. 143). The reader may think the apparent contradiction could be easily dismissed by having recourse to different temporal horizons: in the short period, the agents are forced to comply with institutional forms, but, in a longer period, the same agents could manage to change them,[77] by means of appropriate collective action. The problem with that solution is not that it is mistaken – it is not at all mistaken but it underscores what may be the most original aspect of a non-standard approach to coordination: it is in fact within the same time period that the conventions prove their dual nature, simultaneously (and not only successively) constraint upon the (individual) choices and result of the (aggregate) choices. Dupuy (1992, chs 1, 8, 10; see also his paper with Koppel and Atlan, 1987) offers a penetrating analysis of coordination on the fictitious Walrasian markets, by establishing its association with an 'endogenous fixed point' – a modern mathematical translation of Adam Ferguson's insight: 'result of human action but not of human design'. As we have seen, his analysis can now be extended to a non-standard (conventionalist) view of coordination of actual markets.

What then are the remaining problems on our way to building an alternative theory of markets and competing firms?

Robustness

Semantic

The 'family resemblance' between the economics of conventions and White's model, on a semantic level, is so striking that the sceptical reader is entitled to suspect we are playing with words. What substantive matters can make it plausible that an economic (and mathematical) inquiry about quality will be reasonably derived from a philosophical (and speculative) investigation of justice?[78] We just hinted at the subject above.[79] It is high time to answer this objection with the seriousness it deserves.

The core of our answer can be enunciated in a nutshell: quality is to manufactured objects what is justice to human beings – or, more precisely, quality concerns interrelations between human beings with respect to manufactured objects, whereas justice concerns direct interrelations between human beings.[80] Of course, human beings live in a socialized world, full of socialized 'things' and if those 'things' play an important role, as an element of proof, in the debate between human beings, the interrelations are at most mediated by those things. In the case of quality, we have something more. The interrelations are literally supported by the things under scrutiny; that makes a difference, but not so great after all: a difference of degree, rather than a difference of nature. Therefore we must not be too surprised by the capacity of a theory of justice to serve as a foundation for a theory of quality. We should be even less surprised by the reluctance of standard economic theory to integrate quality in the analysis of markets, since that implies an enlargement of economic rationality, from computation abilities to interpretation skills, which are obviously required for discussions about justice. And we should be not at all surprised when Harrison White insists that each area of viable markets should be understood as a 'subculture':[81] indeed justice – and therefore its little sister, quality – speaks several languages and each area is devoted to one of its languages.

So much for the general link between quality and justice.[82] Its strength does not go without charges: three pure models of quality/justice have been specified. Why not four or ten? Where could they be located in White's topology (it seems as if there is no room left for a new conception of justice/quality[83])? More simply, but not less sharply, how could we analyse mixed models of justice/quality, the frequency of which is probably higher than for pure models?[84]

These are difficult questions. Let us only sketch possible strategies for future answers. First, White's topology does not exhibit really mixed models, according to our conventionalist interpretation; neither is it restricted to rigorously pure models, since a model close to a borderline is expected to show some common features with a model belonging to the other side of the borderline. Second, a quite appealing model of justice, besides the three we made use of, is the 'civic' one, founded on a principle of conformity to 'general will' (Boltanski and Thévenot, 1991, pp. 137–49, 231–40). It would be easy to build a model of quality upon this foundation, but the type of product subject to this criterion of quality clearly characterizes the public sector. White's model of the market should be limited to the private sector. That does not mean it could not be used *a contrario* to a better understanding of what must/can not be supplied by private firms. Third, as for a network model of justice/quality, it seems to us that at least part of this model is encapsulated in the 'domestic' model, as we have specified it. Our provisional conclusion would be that White's model has succeeded in identifying the three basic components of quality, as the emergent effect of a system of interactions between firms offering products and consumers accepting or rejecting them.

Syntactic

The first technical limit of White's model is the implicit hypothesis of mono-product firms: one point on the schedule $W(y)$ corresponds to one firm, as if all the products offered by the firm could be sensibly aggregated in one figure for proceeds (W), which is natural, and one figure for volume (y), which is more demanding. To deal with multiproduct firms, in the framework of the model, is not altogether impossible: either the index n, instead of denoting the quality of a single product, denotes the whole package of products manufactured under the same trademark, or as many indices are allocated to the multi-product firm as there are lines of product. The former solution implies it is meaningful to give a definite and unitary level of quality to a trademark, excluding the case where it covers a large range of products; the latter solution can take account of this case but by assumption does away with any problem of coherence between the various departments of the multiproduct firm.

The second technical limit of White's model is the absence of explicit dynamics. It is indisputable that a fixed point is not the most convenient tool to study dynamics (except if the variables are rates of growth, which is not the case). Nevertheless, once more, we must bring to the fore the peculiarities of the fixed point on which White's model is founded. The existence of the function $W(y)$ is intrinsically linked with the existence of the ordering on n. The fixed point logically implies a distribution of niches in a space of qualities: White is then entitled to write that in the $W(y)$ models, as in the size-distribution models (for example, Ijiri and Simon, 1977), 'dynamics (. . .) are not studied directly but inferred from distributions in equilibrium' (2002, p. 225).

Let us try to follow the point for a while. Firms are faced with two decisions, one on y, the other on n. The two decisions are not on a par. The decision on y must be taken after the decision on n. The model is explicit on the former, only implicit, if not silent, on the latter. The decision about y is reversible and its time horizon is a short period; since n is a summary of all previous organizational learning (relative to technology – see function C – and demand – see function S), the decision about n has a strong flavour of irreversibility or path-dependency and its time horizon is long-period. That intertemporal hierarchy of decisions cannot but remind an economist of the essential distinction (albeit seldom emphasized) introduced by Keynes,[85] between the 'state of short-term expectation', governing decisions of employment and production, and the 'state of long-term expectation', governing decisions of investment. In spite of its implicitness, what the network sociologist suggests about the decision relative to n should be welcomed by the Keynesian economist because it supplements what he is able to say explicitly about the decision of investment and that is excessively unspecific.[86] The appropriate choice of n must be backed by a perception of an unoccupied niche, in the space of qualities:[87] the rightly inspired firm in White's non-standard model sees what is lacking, that is, what does not (yet) exist, whereas the well-informed firm in the standard rational expectations model only sees what exists. Possible worlds are perceived through the gaps of the actual world.

Although it is clearly static, White's model, through the structure of its fundamental fixed point, tells an important truth for those, like us, anxious to go to dynamics: it should be twofold and the second one should have little in common with the first one.[88]

We have reached the end of the second section of our chapter and we think the provisional conclusion of the first section may now be strengthened: it seems to us that the two approaches to the producer market, one through networks, the other through conventions, go further and deeper in the analysis of competition when they are combined, as we tried to do in this chapter, than when they were introduced independently and separately, in 1981 and 1989. That result opens new perspectives for research to which we now turn.

CONCLUSION

This chapter should be considered as a resolute farewell to the Walrasian view of markets, at least for manufactured products. This has definite consequences for mainstream microeconomics, even outside the paradigm of general equilibrium, for a simple reason we have developed at length. No one can seriously hope to have a theory of competition without a theory of quality – and no one can seriously hope to have a theory of quality without a theory of interpretive rationality. This is the ultimate ground for acknowledging some convergence between conventionalist and structuralist (network) programmes of research.[89] Let us spend a little more time extending those propositions, which are less provoking than they might initially seem.

Quality is a much more complex notion than Walrasian economists were ready to admit.[90] There is quality 'in the eyes of producers' (what we called quality factor α), but there is also quality 'in the eyes of consumers' (what we called quality factor ω). Coordination implies that producers and consumers succeed in speaking a common language. Whereas production flow y results from a computation, quality index n results from an interpretation. Indeed, evaluating the quality of a product looks like elucidating the meaning of a text. So quality conventions $\{n\}$ are the interpretive basis of the market schedules $\{W(y)\}$. We explained then, by means of three different arguments (philosophical, p. 225, mechanical, p. 231 and psychological, p. 238) why the subsumption of calculative rationality into interpretive rationality makes it necessary for the variable n to disappear from the fixed point defined on the function $W(y)$.

As a consequence, markets are no longer a place of aggregation, as in Walras's general equilibrium, but of differentiation, with two converging approaches: one in terms of the interaction structure[91] making that differentiation possible, that is networks, as White emphasized so strongly;[92] the other in terms of social representations[93] making the same differentiation legitimate, that is conventions, as we tried to argue in this chapter. Our joint view of goods markets[94] is also critical of present contractual models of market equilibria, with imperfect and asymmetrical information, the importance of which has been overemphasized. The core of competition around quality does not come so much from uncertainty as from interdependency: 'markets are argued here to be matters of ecology across populations rather than threat and bluster among actors'. The reader will now have understood that the three authors of this chapter want to add psychosociology to ecology, as mentioned here by White (2002, p. 705).

Of course, we spoke only about producer markets. That does not mean we have nothing to say about other kinds of market (labour markets, financial markets and so on) or that all markets should be moulded after the same print – that is the 'Walrasian vice'[95] we want to avoid. Our programme would simply require that we apply the same method to the other markets; that is, we carefully define quality on these markets and then go from networks to conventions and vice versa. As for the producer markets themselves, we had better conclude that the job is not completely over. White, after resuming his 1981 work, endeavoured to generalize it by integrating intermediate products, excluded, as every economist knows, from the system of national accounts – but always heavily present in business accounts. He showed that the downstream model, which we only studied briefly here, has a dual or a symmetrical form, with an upstream model. There is insufficient space here to explore this dual model. It suffices to underline the relevance of the metaphor, because it implies irreversibility of production – and not circulating funds, as thought by classical writers up to Sraffa, or reversibility of the neoclassical production function.[96]

At the very end of this chapter, fairness commands us to return to the mathematical model without which we could not have written a single line of this chapter: Spence's model, so skilfully transformed into White's model. We owe this ironical last comment on our own work to the reader still astonished by the tight, albeit unintended, connection between conventionalist individualism (with its focus upon mental representations) and network approach (and its spontaneous structuralism). White was attracted by Spence's model for its mathematical flexibility. Now, Spence's model is the most extreme representationalist model of all modern economic theory (announcing sunspot models) and, for that reason, is a useful vehicle for a first reading of conventions.[97] So our conventionalist answer to White's question, and the resultant project of combining individualist and structuralist programmes of research,[98] are just another 'ruse de l'histoire'.

NOTES

1. See Scott (1991), Degenne and Forsé (1999) and Lazega (1996) for details.
2. The vocabulary used to provide this short definition of 'convention' should make it clear that the two pillars of this research programme are (1) the economics of bounded rationality ('satisficing') and (2) the interpretive, or hermeneutical, component of some human sciences ('arguing'): sociology, psychology, cognitive sciences, political philosophy, law, and so on.
3. This chapter, as a collective enterprise, has an unusually long story: the preliminary steps were Eymard-Duvernay and Bony (1982), Favereau (1982, 1989) and Biencourt (1995); the first co-authored working paper was Eymard-Duvernay and Favereau (1990), the second was Biencourt, Eymard-Duvernay and Favereau (1994). We gratefully acknowledge Harrison White's extremely positive comments on our work in progress, in May 1996 and in July 1998.

4. For more mathematical references, see White (1981b, p. 522, n. 2).
5. We will quickly drop the symbol*, since we spend most of the time on the fixed point equilibrium.
6. We do not make any distinction between 'bounded rationality' and 'procedural rationality': we agree with Simon (1976) that each notion can be deduced from the other one. We select the first one as a label, because of its more common use.
7. See Rabinow and Sullivan (1987).
8. All these points are stressed by Leifer and White (1988, p. 86) and White (1995, pp. 61–2). We may also recall Keynes's second thought, one year after the 'General Theory': 'I now feel that if I were writing the book again I should begin by setting forth my theory on the assumption that short-period assumptions were always fulfilled . . . The main point is to distinguish the forces determining the position of equilibrium from the techniques of trial and error by means of which the entrepreneur discovers where the position is' (1973, pp. 181–2).
9. The phrase was coined by Demsetz (1969).
10. We borrow this metaphor from White's original paper (1981b, p. 522).
11. See White (1988, pp. 250–52), Biencourt (1995, pp. 408–12) and Wächter (1999, pp. 160–61). White (2002, ch. 6) prefers to use $\tau = \mathbf{V/W}$, which generalizes θ, by integrating the weight of the market under scrutiny relative to all other markets, and reduces to θ when $\gamma = 1$ (no saturation effects).
12. See Simon (1955).
13. We are grateful to Christian Bidard for this remark and a convincing illustration. See also Wächter (1999, p. 149).
14. Strangely enough, the analytical importance of market size was stressed by Adam Smith (1776, ch. 3: 'The division of labour is limited by the extent of the market') before getting lost from sight by all his successors, either classical or neoclassical, with the notable exception of Stigler (1951), moreover rejected by Becker and Murphy (1992)!
15. See note 10.
16. The orderings are the same but they can be 'stretched, shrunk or even reversed. This means that either: (1) the producer whose product commands the highest value has the highest costs, the second highest value highest costs, etc., or (2) the producer who commands the highest value has the lowest costs, the second highest has the second lowest, etc.' (Leifer and White, 1988, p. 93).
17. For an example, see White's, 2002, ch. 2, pp. 30–33.
18. It is not altogether certain, since we could imagine a lower price compensating the overestimated quality (not a common case according to usual business practices!): the assumption on n excludes this uncommon case.
19. Leifer and White (1988, p. 93) foreshadowed our comments in a less emphatic tone: 'we see this as a reasonable hypothesis about real world economics: a sustainable market cannot be built among a set of products whose valuations are unrelated to their costs'.
20. We adopt this convenient but loose writing to denote the set of values of n.
21. From now on, in order to spare mathematical symbols, n designates either one typical value of the index of quality or the cardinal of the set of indices; the context should make clear which is the appropriate meaning.
22. We are grateful to Xavier Ragot for showing us the analytical depth of this seemingly technical peculiarity.
23. That will be formally established below, but it is obvious for any observer that a market is first characterized by data of the form $W(y)$. Only on closer examination will data on n be fetched, necessarily at a micro level, firm after firm. The case for θ is strikingly different: it will appear in the mathematical resolution of the macrofunction $W(y)$, although it is less visible than n, at a micro level.
24. Title of the book by Harrison White (2002).
25. That means that solving White's model must not be reduced to the problem of finding a fixed point $W(y)$, since it is not independent of the problem of finding the linear order $\{n\}$.
26. Harrison White refers to the explicit form of function C (Cobb-Douglas), the introduction of which we chose to delay until the second part of our chapter.

27. Our y*[*n*].
28. It could also be partially reworded according to a theory of action perspective (Argyris and Schön 1978, ch. 1, pp. 10–11): 'in situation S, if you want to achieve consequence C, under assumptions a, . . ., n, do A, . . .'.
29. See Hart (1948–9) and the comment by Ricoeur (1971).
30. We closely follow Taylor (1971) and Ricoeur (1971). Modern archaeology supports our view (Bruneau and Balut, 1997). White (1995) was not far from our reading with his stress on the 'personality' of a market and White (2002, ch. 15) is quite near (more on this below). The sceptical reader should be reminded of White's warning (2002, pp. 152–3): 'usually no explicit index of quality is observable'. So where does quality comes from?
31. To understand at once how much Keynes used the word 'convention' to grasp a phenomenon close to, but distinct from, Lewis's use, the reader should consider, in each case, (1) whether behaviours should be similar (surely not on the financial markets!); (2) whether it is necessary to go beyond mutual expectations and imagine a truly collective entity (think of trifling notions like the 'sentiment of the public' or 'the state of confidence').
32. The distinction between convention_1 and convention_2 was first introduced in Favereau (1986).
33. The reference to the possibility of arguing is our main reason for focusing on the interpretive capacities of economic agents, when dealing with quality. Corcuff (1995, p. 111) rightly emphasizes that coordination according to 'economics of convention' is not restricted to behaviours, as in mainstream economics, but has to be extended to *statements* about behaviours. More on quality and justice below.
34. The role of equal θ is all the more important as it outweighs the partially subjective nature of the judgment about *n*, especially in the case of a dispute which would be submitted to a court.
35. McCormick (1989) equivalently discriminates between 'rule-text' and 'rule-content'. Ricoeur (1986, pp. 161–82)) would add: the meaning of a text is not part of the text; the meaning of an action is not part of the action. The sceptical reader is invited to think about a world where this theorem would be false: what would be the literary value of a book whose meaning had not to be understood but simply read like an exhaustive set of operating instructions? That world would be properly inhuman.
36. This road runs two ways: first, rules do not determine actions directly (Hart, 1961); second, we could never be sure that an action really complies with the rule (Kripke, 1982).
37. See White (2002, p. 40).
38. This is the appropriate place to recall that White (1976) first borrowed these specifications from Spence's model of labour market and, indeed, spent much time exploring generalizations of his model not only on the consumer side, as did Spence himself, but also on the producer side, by reinterpreting it 'in terms applicable to negotiation of subcontract payments between a set of big firms in an industry and the population of smaller firms regularly supplying them with parts or services of a particular kind' (pp. 1–2). On the conversion of Spence's model into White's model, see Biencourt (1995, ch. 5 § 1) and also White (1979, p. 45; 2002, ch. 5 and p. 297).
39. Asymptotic analysis is required, which shows that products are perfectly homogeneous: $b = 0$ and $a = 1$; see White (1981a, p. 19; 1988, pp. 236, 241–2).
40. This feature is so emphatically stressed by Lewis as for him to assert: 'It is redundant to speak of an arbitrary convention' (1969, p. 70). Lewis sometimes seemed to restrict arbitrariness to a syntactic condition of multiple equilibria, but a more sympathetic reading of his book would show he actually focused on a semantic condition: self-suspension of reason in order to find a way out of indetermination.
41. Path dependency is another valuable aspect for our conventionalist interpretation, but less specific.
42. See Wächter (1999, p. 156) or White (2002, p. 45). The reader should remember that a , b, c, q, r, $\theta > 0$ but d may be > 0 or < 0.
43. If the mathematical substance of 'unravelling' is the fact that the general solution of the differential equation misses corner optima, the empirical content is the idea of 'free-loading' (White, 1981b, pp. 528–9; and 2002, p. 82).

44. For details see White (2002, ch. 3, Table 3.2, pp. 54–5).
45. See White (1979, pp. 26–30; 1981a, pp. 22–3; 1988, pp. 250–52), Biencourt (1995, pp. 408–13) and Wächter (1999, pp. 160–1).
46. For that reason, White (2002, p. 140) calls those varieties of markets 'crowded'.
47. For that reason, according to White (2002, p. 144), that region deserves the joint label 'explosive/collusive'.
48. Another difference is the display of non-viable markets on a par with viable ones. Coordination failures are defined simultaneously with coordination successes.
49. 'Constructivism (. . .) insists that we should postulate entities (numbers, etc.) only if we know how to construct them, i.e. how to specify them systematically in terms of things we already accept' (Lacey, 1976, p. 114).
50. See Shoven and Walley (1992, p. 13).
51. The same criticism would be unfair against computable general equilibrium models (see Shoven and Walley, 1992), but an important difference would remain: those models rely on fixed point algorithms to find equilibrium solutions (one pair of price/quantity for each market), whereas White is looking for a market function (several pairs of price/quantity on a single market).
52. Macrovariables are straightforwardly translated into microvariables, and macroeconomics is just microeconomics with a new scale: see Malinvaud (1998, vol. A).
53. See Wächter (1999, note 9, p. 157).
54. We could have written 'justified'. We follow the way opened by Eymard-Duvernay (1989) to refer to 'quality' as the result of an interpretive judgment, grounded on one of the principles of justice, axiomatized by Boltanski and Thévenot (1991): here the 'merchant' one. More on this below.
55. 'Merchant' quality is summarized by the correspondence between a high level of n and a high level of y: everybody wishes to buy the product bought by everybody. The market is the place of mimesis 'par excellence', as Keynes (1936, ch. 12) saw so clearly, when analysing speculation on the financial markets.
56. White (1988, p. 250) remarks that, when $K > 0$, $W(y)$ 'appears to be the businessman's familiar cost-plus-mark-up pricing, although there is the oddity that K is a fixed mark-up and not a percentage'.
57. White initially called this market 'grind', rather than 'ordinary', 'because producers grind their teeth: buyers' evaluations of goods go up less rapidly with increase in quality than do the costs of producing them' (1981a, p. 31).
58. Eymard-Duvernay (1987, 1989).
59. See White (2002, Ch. .5, p. 97).
60. The symmetrical statement that rising production costs accompany declining quality is less risky, but, we think, less fruitful, notwithstanding White's comment (2002, p. 154).
61. Eymard-Duvernay (1987, 1989).
62. See Boisard and Letablier (1987); since this pioneering study, the exponential growth of 'green' products proves the relevance of 'domestic' judgments for our times: far from being an archaism, they are becoming up to date (cf. the notion of 'traceability' in food security).
63. It seems as if the three cases could be subsumed under the heading 'produit-maison'.
64. See the debate on 'appropriate technology' in Marsden (1971) and Sen (1975), and the analysis of flexibility by Stigler (1939).
65. Then labour looks underpaid (in terms of money) – but it is not undercompensated (in terms of utility).
66. This would not be an orthodox account of the paradox, quite the contrary: labour becomes a direct source of utility, which hinders the construction of the labour supply. One of its building blocks is the disutility of labour (symmetrically the utility of leisure, of which the wage rate measures the opportunity cost): without it, the mainstream framework of market cannot apply to labour.
67. White (1981a, p. 26) takes some steps in that direction.
68. See White (1981a, p. 29; 1981b, p. 528).
69. Note the proximity to Schumpeter's most famous argument (1942, ch. 8) on the efficiency of monopoly practices: a car runs more quickly with its brakes in order, than without!

70. See Biencourt (1996) and the chapter by Biencourt and Urrutiaguer, in the present volume.
71. We borrow this remark from Wächter (1999 , p. 158).
72. We borrow this phrase from Hannah Arendt's writings in political philosophy (especially 1958, ch. 2), to which the most thorough introduction is Tassin (1999). See also Boltanski and Thévenot (1991, 3rd part) and Esposito (2000) for supplementary views on what it means to be 'common'.
73. See Schelling (1980, p. 70; also p. 111).
74. Sugden (1995, p. 535) is extending an insight of Gauthier (1975). Note that, by referring to 'descriptions', we are now entitled to find another confirmation of the drift from rationality-as-computation to rationality-as-interpretation.
75. 'Shared' knowledge is enough in a justified world. Lewis needed 'common' knowledge (not to be confused with the meaning of 'common' in 'common world'), because of his focus upon arbitrariness.
76. It is probably a general property of social representations, which must appear as completely objective and independent of individual behaviour and representations, in order to be efficient, although its efficiency proceeds from the individual capacity of interpretation. Nevertheless it must be noticed that the efficiency of $W(y)$ does not depend, in any essential way, on its role being unperceived by agents.
77. Boyer (see his book with Saillard, 2002, p. 3 and p. 332) suggests calling this methodology 'holindividualism', which, he thinks, is the mark of his own model of 'Regulation'; Defalvard 1992 in a similar vein, argues that the true methodology of the 'economics of conventions' is 'morphogenetic holism', rather than simple individualism.
78. Boltanski and Thévenot (1991).
79. See note 54.
80. Our argument is, we think, quite close to the views of Boltanski and Thévenot (1991, pp. 164–8).
81. White (2002, p. 20 and ch. 15).
82. We have just argued from justice to quality. The other way round would also be useful, in stressing the efficiency component (obviously present in quality), of which justice cannot be totally deprived.
83. Such as the emerging network-like model of justice studied by Boltanski and Chiappello (1999).
84. See Boltanski and Thévenot (1991, chs. 9 and 10), Thévenot (1990) and Eymard-Duvernay (1989, pp 340–56) for arguments on the ubiquity of compromise between pure models.
85. See Keynes (1936, chs. 3, 11 and 12).
86. It reduces to the rule: invest as long as the cost of investment is inferior to the sum of present values of expected cashflows (or the interest rate inferior to the marginal efficiency of capital).
87. The 'missing link' between the Whitean decision relative to n and the Keynesian decision of investment may be Burt's theory of 'structural holes' (1992).
88. '(. . .) after giving full weight to the importance of the influence of short-period changes in the state of long-term expectation' as Keynes wrote (1936, p. 164) in a sentence which could have been written for White's model.
89. A similar project is defined by Callon (1998, introduction).
90. A striking exception is the work of Benetti and Cartelier (1980).
91. Not a sum, as in Walras, but a function: $W(y)$.
92. 'Markets work through and by dispersions: this is the key claim, from which the other derives' (2002, p. 152).
93. Not a sum, once more, as in Walras, but an ordering: $\{n\}$.
94. Condensed in the formula: $M = \{W(y), \{n\}\} = M_N = \{\text{resources, niches}\} = M_C = \{\text{convention}_2, \text{convention}_1\}$.
95. The application of severely simplified abstractions to the solution of practical problems was defined by Schumpeter as the 'Ricardian vice', in his 'History of economic analysis'.
96. The fundamental reference here is Georgescu-Roegen (1971, 1976), whose work has foreseen modern ecology (and, moreover, an acute analyst of quality, as 'non-reducible to number'). Not so surprising after all: White's model of market is openly inspired by ecological patterns (see his notion of niche).

97. As pointed out by Poulain (2001) in a recent paper.
98. Heir to Ricoeur's project 'to treat structuralism and hermeneutics as complements ' (1986, p. 154).

REFERENCES

Arendt, Hannah (1958), *The human condition*, Chicago: University of Chicago Press.

Argyris, Chris and Donald A. Schön (1978), *Organizational learning: a theory of action perspective*, Reading, MA.: Addison-Wesley.

Becker, Gary S. and Kevin M. Murphy (1992) 'The division of labor, coordination costs and knowledge', *Quarterly Journal of Economics*, 107 (4), November, 1138–60.

Benetti, Carlo and Jean Cartelier (1980), *Marchands, salariat et capitalistes*, Paris: Maspero.

Biencourt, Olivier (1995), 'Théorie de l'entreprise, pluralité des gestions de la qualité et fonctionnement des marchés internes du travail', University of Paris X dissertation, Paris.

Biencourt, Olivier (1996), 'Concurrence par la qualité dans le transport routier de marchandises: normes ou réseaux', *Revue d'économie industrielle*, 75, 1st quarter, 211–22.

Biencourt, Olivier and Thierry Jolivet (2000), 'Quand le marché interne devient conversationnel: conception des produits et modification des règles', *Revue d'économie industrielle*, 93, 4th quarter, 51–72.

Biencourt, Olivier, François Eymard-Duvernay and Olivier Favereau (1994), 'L'économie doit définir le marché à partir de l'entreprise, plutôt que l'inverse: une relecture du modèle de White en termes de conventions', paper prepared for the international colloquium of the Society for the Advancement of Socio-Economics, Jouy-en-Josas, July.

Blin, Jean-Marie (1977), 'Fuzzy sets in multiple criteria decision-making', in Martin Starr and Milan Zeleny (eds), *Multiple criteria decision-making*, Amsterdam: North-Holland, pp. 129–46.

Boisard, Pierre and Marie-Thérèse Letablier (1987), 'Le camembert: normand ou normé. Deux modèles de production dans l'industrie fromagère', in François Eymard-Duvernay (ed.), *Entreprises et produits*, Cahiers du centre d'études de l'emploi, no. 30, Paris: PUF, pp. 1–30.

Boltanski, Luc and Eve Chiappello (1999), *Le nouvel esprit du capitalisme*, Paris: Gallimard.

Boltanski, Luc and Laurent Thévenot (1991), *De la justification: les économies de la grandeur*, Paris: Gallimard.

Boyer, Robert and Yves Saillard (eds) (2002), *Régulation Theory: The State of the Art*, London: Routledge.

Bruneau, Philippe and Pierre-Yves Balut (1997), *Artistique et archéologie*, Paris: Presses de l'Université Paris-Sorbonne.

Burt, Ronald (1992), *Structural holes: the social structure of competition*, Cambridge, MA: Harvard University Press.

Callon, Michel (ed.) (1998), *The laws of the markets*, Blackwell: Oxford.

Corcuff, Philippe (1995), *Les nouvelles sociologies: constructions de la réalité sociale*, Paris: Nathan.

Defalvard, Hervé (1992), 'Critique de l'individualisme méthodologique revu par l'économie des conventions', *Revue économique*, 43, January, 127–43.
Degenne, Alain and Michel Forsé (1999), *Social networks*, Beverly Hills: Sage.
Demsetz, Harold (1969), 'Information and efficiency: another viewpoint', *Journal of law and economics*, 12, 1–22.
Dupuy, Jean-Pierre, François Eymard-Duvernay, Olivier Favereau, André Orléan, Robert Salais and Laurent Thévenot (1989), 'Introduction', *Revue Economique*, 40(2), 141–5.
Dupuy, Jean-Pierre (1992), *Le sacrifice et l'envie: le libéralisme aux prises avec la justice sociale*, Paris: Calmann-Lévy.
Esposito, Roberto (2000), *Communitas: origine et destin de la communauté*, Paris: PUF.
Eymard-Duvernay, François (1987), 'Les entreprises et leurs modèles', introduction to: *Entreprises et produits*, Cahiers du centre d'Etudes de l'Emploi, no. 30, Paris: PUF, pp. V–XXII.
Eymard-Duvernay, François (1989), 'Conventions de qualité et formes de coordination', *Revue économique*, 40(2), 329–59.
Eymard-Duvernay, François and Daniel Bony (1982), 'Cohérence de la branche et diversité des entreprises: étude d'un cas', *Economie et statistique*, 144, 13–23.
Eymard-Duvernay, François and Olivier Favereau (1990), 'Marchés internes, modèles d'entreprise et conventions de qualité', paper prepared for the 7th 'Journées de microéconomie appliquée', Montréal, 25–6 May.
Favereau, Olivier (1982), 'Le niveau de l'emploi dans une économie en croissance', University of Paris I dissertation, Paris.
Favereau, Olivier (1986), 'La formalisation du rôle des conventions dans l'allocation des ressources', in Robert Salais and Laurent Thévenot (eds), *Le travail: marchés, règles, conventions*, Paris: INSEE-Economica, pp. 249–67.
Favereau, Olivier (1989), 'Marchés internes, marchés externes', *Revue économique*, 40(2), 273–328.
Gauthier, David (1975), 'Coordination', *Dialogue*, 14, 195–221.
Georgescu-Roegen, Nicholas (1971), *The entropy law and the economic process*, Cambridge, MA.: Harvard University Press.
Georgescu-Roegen, Nicholas (1976), *Energy and economic myths*, New York: Pergamon.
Hart, Herbert L.A. (1948–9), 'The ascription of responsibility and rights', *Proceedings of the Aristotelian society*, 171–94, reprinted in A.G.N. Flew (ed.) (1963), *Logic and language*, first series, 5th impression, Oxford: Basil Blackwell, pp. 145–66.
Hart, Herbert L.A.(1961), *The concept of law*, Oxford: Oxford University Press.
Ijiri, Yuji and Herbert A. Simon (1977), *Skew distributions and the sizes of business firms*, Amsterdam: North-Holland.
Keynes, John M. (1936), *The general theory of employment, interest and money*, London: Macmillan.
Keynes, John M. (1973), 'Notes from the 1937 lectures: ex post and ex ante', in *The General Theory and after. Part II: defence and development*, The Collected Writings of John Maynard Keynes, vol. XIV, London: Macmillan, pp. 179–83.
Koppel, Moshe, Henri Atlan and Jean-Pierre Dupuy (1987), 'Von Foerster's conjecture: trivial machines and alienation in living systems', *International Journal of General Systems*, 13, 257–64.
Kripke, Saul A. (1982), *Wittgenstein on rules and private language: an elementary exposition*, Cambridge, MA: Harvard University Press.

Lacey, A.R. (1976), *A dictionary of philosophy*, London: Routledge & Kegan Paul.
Lazega, Emmanuel (1996), 'Arrangements contractuels et structures relationnelles', *Revue Française de Sociologie*, 37 , 439–56.
Leifer, Eric M. and Harrison C. White (1988), 'A structural approach to markets', in Mark S. Mizruchi and Michael Schwartz (eds), *Intercorporate relations: the structural analysis of business*, New York: Cambridge University Press, pp. 85–108.
Lewis, David K. (1969), *Convention: a philosophical study*, Cambridge, MA: Harvard University Press.
MacCormick, Neil (1989), 'On open texture in law', in Neil MacCormick and Paul Amselek (eds), *Controversies about law's ontology*, Edinburgh: Edinburgh University Press, pp. 72–83.
Malinvaud, Edmond (1998), *Macroeconomic theory: a textbook on macroeconomic knowledge and analysis*, Amsterdam: North-Holland.
Marsden, Keith (1971), 'Progressive technologies for developing countries', *International Labour Review*, 101.
Piore, Michaël, Richard K. Lester, Fred M. Kofman and Kamal M. Malek (1994), 'The organization of product development', *Industrial and Corporate Change*, 3(2), 405–34.
Poulain, Edouard (2001), 'Le capital humain, d'une conception substantielle à un modèle représentationnel', *Revue économique*, 52(1), 91–116.
Rabinow, Paul and William M. Sullivan (eds) (1987), *Interpretive social science: a second look*, Berkeley: University of California Press.
Ricoeur, Paul (1971), 'The model of the text: meaningful action considered as a text', *Social Research*, 38(3), 529–62.
Ricoeur, Paul (1986), 'Expliquer et comprendre', in *Du texte à l'action: essais d'herméneutique II*, Paris: Editions du Seuil, pp. 161–82.
Schelling, Thomas C. (1960), *The strategy of conflict*, 1980, Cambridge, MA: Harvard University Press.
Schön, Donald A. (1983), *The reflective practitioner: how professionals think in action*, New York: Basic Books.
Schumpeter, Joseph A.(1942), *Capitalism, socialism and democracy*, London: George Allen & Unwin.
Scott, John (1991), *Social network analysis: a handbook*, London: Sage.
Sen, Amartya (1975), *Employment, technology and development*, Oxford: Clarendon Press.
Shoven, John B. and John Whalley (1992), *Applying general equilibrium*, Cambridge surveys of economic literature, Cambridge: Cambridge University Press.
Simon, Herbert A. (1955), 'A behavioural model of rational choice', *Quarterly Journal of Economics*, 69, 99–118.
Simon, Herbert A. (1976), 'From substantive to procedural rationality', in Spiro Latsis (ed.), *Method and appraisal in economics*, Cambridge: Cambridge University Press, pp. 129–48.
Smith, Adam (1776), *An inquiry into the nature and causes of the wealth of nations*, London: W. Strahan and T. Cadell.
Spence, A. Michael (1975), *Market signalling*, Cambridge: Harvard University Press.
Stigler, George J. (1939), 'Production and the distribution in the short run', *Journal of Political Economy*, XLVII, June, 305–27.
Stigler, George J. (1951), 'The division of labor is limited by the extent of the market', *Journal of Political Economy*, LIX, June, 185–93.

Sugden, Robert (1995), 'A theory of focal points', *Economic Journal*, 105 (May), 533–50.

Tassin, Etienne (1999), *Le trésor perdu: Hannah Arendt, l'intelligence de l'action politique*, Paris: Payot.

Taylor, Charles (1971), 'Interpretation and the sciences of man', *The Review of Metaphysics*, 25(1); reprinted in: Paul Rabinow and William M. Sullivan (eds) (1987), *Interpretive social science: a second look*: Berkeley: University of California Press, pp. 33–81.

Thévenot, Laurent (1990), 'Les entreprises entre plusieurs formes de coordination', in Jean-Daniel Reynaud et al. (eds), *Les systèmes de relations professionnelles*, Paris: Editions du CNRS, pp. 347–70.

Wächter, Matthias (1999), 'Rational choice and social networks in ecological economics', dissertation ETH no. 13244, Zurich.

White, Harrison C. (1976), 'Subcontracting with an oligopoly: Spence revisited', Harvard RIAS project, working paper no. 1, September.

White, Harrison, C. (1979), 'On markets', Harvard RIAS project, working paper no. 16, April.

White, Harrison C. (1981a), 'Production markets as induced role structures', in S.L. Leinhardt (ed.), *Sociological Methodology*, San Francisco: Jossey-Bass, pp. 1–57.

White, Harrison C. (1981b), 'Where do markets come from?', *American Journal of Sociology*, 87(3), 517–47.

White, Harrison C. (1982), 'Markets as an interface defining product', Department of Sociology working paper, Harvard University, April.

White, Harrison C. (1988), 'Varieties of markets', in Barry Wellman and Stephen Berkowitz (eds), *Social structures: a network approach*, Cambridge: Cambridge University Press, pp. 226–60.

White, Harrison C. (1995), 'Social networks can resolve actor paradoxes in economics and in psychology', *Journal of institutional and theoretical economics*, 151(1), March, 58–74.

White, Harrison, C. (2002), *Markets from networks: socio-economic models of production*, Princeton, NJ: Princeton University Press.

9. Market profiles: a tool suited to quality orders? An empirical analysis of road haulage and the theatre

Olivier Biencourt and Daniel Urrutiaguer

INTRODUCTION

If there is an object that has retained economists' attention it is certainly the market. Walras established its importance in his lengthy and detailed description and formalization of the stock exchange. It is almost as if this mode of coordination, a subject of controversy among classical authors, had not already been at the centre of Adam Smith's reflection. In any event, the organizational dimension was totally overlooked since it was only in the 1970s that other mechanisms of coordination emerged alongside the market. Since then there has been a strong focus on organization studies in economics: rules replace prices, whether these are contract rules (as in the theory of contracts) or convention rules.

Although the market is always there, it is not necessarily a meeting place but perhaps rather an area of competition between firms trying to distinguish themselves. That is the case, in particular, of the goods market, which Favereau (1989) qualifies as the organizations market. A new variable therefore has to be taken into account: the quality of products. As early as 1943, Schumpeter highlighted the impact of quality on forms of competition.

More recently, understanding of the product market has been enhanced by studies from sociology and, more precisely, the sociology of economics. The aim of this discipline is to elucidate the objects of economics – of which the market is one – by means of sociological tools. The work of White (1981) is an example. White presents the market as a social construction which may (or may not) result from individuals' actions. Two points in particular in this model seem to us particularly significant.

Networks and Markets

White formalizes a market as a particular form of network structured by an interface between consumers and producers. Firms in a market are compared to a small clique (with between six and 12 members) whose reproduction is based on knowledge of one another's strategies and results. Firms thus choose the volume that will maximize their profits, based on reliable information of sales potential, a condition for market stability. The concept of a firm is therefore essential and, from there, the market can be analysed.

Niches and Quality

Consumers distinguish firms in terms of their perception of the quality of the product offering. They accept or reject producers' offers, each of which is in a specialized niche. The ecological concept of a niche corresponds, for a population, to all the resources that it exploits better than others (Hannan and Freeman, 1977). Thus the niche identifies the organizational competencies at play in the production and distribution of a product of a given quality. Quality therefore plays a key role in the coherence of the market by generating an order so that production costs can be adjusted to buyers' value scales (Leifer, 1985) – even if White compares quality to an exogenous social fact that confronts producers with buyers' judgments. His representation of quality by an index implies a vertical differentiation of products, that is, a consensual evaluation of their level of quality.

On the basis of these elements, and with prime importance granted to elasticity of consumer satisfaction and elasticity of production costs in relation to two variables (volume of production and quality index),[1] White constructed a typology of markets. He thus showed that certain market profiles are not necessarily sustainable. For example, White shows that that is the case when consumers are never satisfied with the quality/price ratio proposed by producers. They will always be tempted by new firms in the market which have significantly lower prices, even if the quality of their products is lower. These new firms behave like freeloaders, entering from the bottom of the quality scale in a market where buyers do not attach enough importance to quality and snatching market shares from incumbent firms.[2] In this way the market disintegrates with the successive entry of new firms and the constant deterioration of quality: 'firms (. . .) are in the wings seeking possible entrance to the market' (White, 1981, p. 529). This market configuration is called 'freeloading' (White, 1981).

In our view this model provides a suitable framework of analysis for two apparently totally unrelated fields of investigation: theatrical institutions and road haulage.

THE CONTRIBUTION OF WHITE'S MODEL TO THEATRICAL INSTITUTIONS

The main advantage of White's model concerns the interdependence of the market structure and individual decisions, through niches. Theatrical organizations base their construction of niches on the competencies of their administrative, technical and artistic teams, the public's former experiences and the programming policy that orients choices of repertories and directors.

The concept of a niche is suited to the uniqueness of performances. Their quality is the result of a combination of the quality of actors' and technicians' individual work on a project, under the control of the director. The same applies to each performance, shaped by the collective energy, the actors' individual inspiration and the reactions of an audience that are never the same.

This model therefore affords a convenient framework for a quantitative empirical study of organizations' performance. The comparison of the reactions of consumers' tastes and producers' costs to changes in the volume and quality of products makes it possible to classify markets according to the level of producers' success or failure.

THE CONTRIBUTION OF WHITE'S MODEL TO THE ANALYSIS OF ROAD HAULAGE

Deregulation of road haulage in 1986[3] constituted a legislative break, although in many cases it officialized former dispensatory practices of both a formal and informal nature. The immediate effects were a proliferation in the number of firms (the number of licences rose from 28 000 in 1979 to over 82 000 in 1993[4]) and an increase in the corporate mortality rate (the number of bankruptcies tripled between 1986 and 1991[5]). The new system of free rates had the effect of shifting fraud towards the evasion of social and road legislation,[6] for the purpose of reducing transport time and consequently prices.

In short, three facts illustrate the effects of deregulation: a substantial drop in transport prices, constant deterioration of quality and a challenge to the market through the intolerable increase in the number of firms. More precisely, these three features correspond to one of the non-viable market configurations put into evidence by White: the freeloading zone. Since deregulation, road haulage has been characterized by three elements. First, quality is expensive to produce. The different laws and regulations have repercussions in terms of production costs. That is the case, for example, with rules concerning long-distance truck drivers' working hours, which make resting periods or the use of two drivers for long distances compulsory. They are justified by safety requirements[7] (the safety of the drivers themselves, of their goods and of all users of the road). If they are complied with, they result in a better-quality service – freight is transported in better conditions as regards time and safety – and in higher production costs. 'This regulation has a major impact on the shaping of costs in the sector, which explains why it is the source of a substantial amount of fraud' (Detchessahar, 1997, p. 61).

Second, quantity is expensive to produce, but is of less importance to consumers. Producing more means covering more kilometres. The repercussion in terms of cost is therefore twofold. First, cost increases in relation to distance. Secondly, in a context where freight is on the decrease and the number of firms is growing, the risk of 'returning empty' increases – and with it transport costs. Now, owing to over-capacity and atomization of the sector, shippers, dominant actors in the haulage business, take it for granted that road hauliers should foot the bill. Thus, although they care about the quantity produced – it is their goods that are concerned – their satisfaction will be less sensitive to variations in quantity than will be road hauliers' costs.

Third, when there is a variation in the quantity transported, the consumer's evaluation of changes in quality, in terms of utility, is less than that of the road haulier, in terms of cost.

Because of the complexity of regulations, in which measures of a social nature add to those concerning road safety, road hauliers know their impact in terms of costs. In fact they are the only ones who do know it. Thus, if they want to guarantee a certain quality in their service, they immediately know what the repercussions will be. Consumers see that their goods have every chance of arriving at their destination (accidents may be spectacular but they are relatively rare). Thus, if they care about quality, their satisfaction will react less than producers' costs to changes in the quality of the service.

We can reinterpret these elements, using different elasticities identified by White.

1. Given the form chosen for the function of cost, saying that quality is expensive to produce amounts to stating that *the variable d is negative*.
2. Elasticities a and c are presumed to be positive. To indicate that satisfaction is less sensitive to a variation in quantity than is cost, we write $a < c$, or the ratio a/c is less than 1 (we therefore necessarily have $0 < a/c < 1$).
3. Producers' cost sensitivity to a quality variation, expressed in relation to a quantity variation, is greater than that of consumer satisfaction, that is to say: $-d/c > b/a$. This inequality can also be written as: $a/c > b/-d$.

We find here the conditions defining the risks of freeloader behaviour. Thus it seems that, in haulage, the effects of the 1986 deregulation can be analysed through the dynamic that is destructive to markets. In order to do so, it is legitimate, using White's typology of markets, to look in viable zones for other forms of competition that might stabilize the haulage sector. This was the theoretical background on which was based the empirical research in Biencourt *et al.*, (1994).

Empirical investigations based on White's market profile will enable us to define some of its advantages and limits. The first part of this paper is devoted to a qualitative study of producers' and consumers' reactions to deregulation of the haulage sector. The second part proposes an operational method for classifying degrees of adaptation of theatrical institutions to quality requirements in the sector.

MODELLING THE HAULAGE MARKET

Our study consisted of field research on road hauliers.[8] The limits of this work are the result of our approach which was of a qualitative rather than quantitative nature, concerning sellers (that is, road hauliers) and not buyers (that is, shippers).

This apparently paradoxical choice, given the extremely formalized nature of White's work,[9] is justified by his characterization of quality which, unlike quantity, is 'in the eyes of buyers'(White, 1981, p. 520). Since the population of buyers (shippers) is both vast and extremely heterogeneous, we focused on the more homogeneous population of road hauliers who, to meet their customers' needs, have to know and evaluate their concern for quality. In other words, our interviews were conducted with those who constantly monitor 'buyers' eyes'. In any event, it is clear that our research could be taken further by switching the focus to the demand side of this market.

From Prices to Networks: a New Form of Competition in the Road Haulage Sector

The mode of coordination at work in the haulage sector seems, historically, to be of a domestic nature in the sense of 'economies of worth' (Boltanski and Thévenot, 1991). There are many indications of this. Most of the firms visited still bear the name of the founding family. Typically, the manager is a former truck driver who took over the family business. Customers are very often situated close by and relations with them are stable and longstanding.[10] This loyalty is also found in relations with employees, where length of service makes regular and objective evaluation of drivers unnecessary. Recruitment often takes place through contacts, on the basis of criteria which rarely match pre-established rules. Staff are trained on the job[11] and learn the customary rules in the process. We could therefore say that the profession is imbued with an 'oral culture'.

Because the relationship between hauliers and suppliers is based essentially on a moral commitment, its viability depends on trust. The haulage sector provides an illustration of a situation in which 'personal relations can be a non-institutionalized way of guaranteeing interaction' Geographical proximity is justified by the need to 'solidify' personal contacts. A haulier's local establishment is a determining asset, as the importance of informal agreements on goods' exchanges between 'locally established' hauliers shows.

Detchessahar (1997, p.67) notes that 'these inter-regional relations certainly warrant an analysis in terms of social interaction'. He describes a mechanism in which the 'gift' of freight by one haulier to another implies, for the latter, a 'counter-gift', 'at a later stage and not strictly specified *ex ante*'. This analysis corresponds to our own earlier observations (Biencourt, 1996) on personal contact between small hauliers whose largely informal networks often resemble a 'gang of friends'.

Paradoxically, this organization in informal networks was not called into question after deregulation in 1986. While liberalization led to a reorganization of interaction around essentially market criteria, many hauliers, both large and small, have tried to protect themselves by reinforcing the role of personal relations. By granting such importance to interpersonal contacts, not only with other hauliers but also with their customers, they have facilitated the emergence of another form of judgment on the quality of their products, a domestic type of judgment, as defined by Boltanski and Thévenot (1991).

The example of a firm in our sample is particularly meaningful. In parallel with its partnership with 'some haulier friends', a comparable strategy was applied with customers. The idea was for the company to differentiate its product by placing itself very high upstream from the actual business of transporting goods from A to B. Given that transport as such is easy to do, the challenge consists of banking primarily on a more specific product based on equipment ('the truck') totally suited to the shippers' needs, and on a full range of logistic services (storage, stock management, preparation of orders and so on). This strategic orientation was accompanied by an informative approach. Customers tend to look for a good price rather than good quality. It is therefore necessary to explain to them that the price of transport is a very relative indicator and that, with good packaging, up to 40 per cent more freight can be fitted into the same vehicle. Shippers are thus made aware of the importance of packaging and the quality guarantees offered by professional hauliers. This form of diversification is possible owing to the good relationship the firm maintains with its customers. The longer they have been using a firm the more easily they will be able to appreciate the quality of the service. When a new company sets up, this network of customers will inform the entrant of the quality of the incumbent's services. These recommendations are a way for the incumbent firm to consolidate its 'breeding ground' of customers. For shippers they provide a guarantee that the haulier will honour the confidence it enjoys. In these practices we see the spin-off of a long-standing 'investment' in personal relations.

The coexistence of a network of hauliers and one of customers, combined with diversification of the product, seems to be a way of replacing an essentially market-based mode of coordination with one that is primarily domestic.

The question is whether this evolution will make the haulage market more viable. We shall try to answer it by matching the above elements with the framework of analysis proposed by White.

The relationship between the quality and the cost of a product raises the question of 'investments' made by hauliers who have banked on domestic forms of quality evaluation. There are two such strategies: (a) the acquisition of specific and obviously expensive equipment, and (b) the strengthening of personal relationships. Yet the latter investment, which may seem anecdotal, generates the first. Hauliers rely on relationships of trust with shippers to be able to offer them customized transport services. This may imply adjustments to the hauliers' existing equipment – and hence adjustments to costs – which they accept because they are assured of a lasting relationship with their customer. Thus the main investment is in the longevity of interpersonal relations. It is the basis of a new way of judging quality and the emergence of a new form of competition of a domestic nature. At the same time, it is often pointed out that such investments are difficult to quantify and evaluate in financial terms. That is where the paradox lies: an approach that is extremely expensive in terms of time defies, to a large extent, all monetary calculation. Anyone observing the situation at one point in time, *t*, even if they were to gather all available information in figures, would conclude that domestic quality does not involve heavy expenses for the firm. Of course this is not true.

In this particular context, where the specific quality of haulage services has been recognized, efforts in terms of quantity are, to an extent, pushed into the background. While these may prove costly for haulage firms, they are taken for granted by shippers. To summarize: (a) available monetary elements suggest that *quality is not expensive to produce*, that is to say, if we take White's parameters, *the variable d is positive*; (b) a shipper's satisfaction will be more inelastic to a variation in quantity than a haulier's costs; that is to say $a < c$.

White shows that these elements define a viable market zone, which he qualifies as paradoxical because of this *a priori* counterintuitive relationship between quality and cost. The adoption of a domestic logic would then be a way of stabilizing a population of firms in the haulage sector. Can these informal networks at the base of this form of competition last? It is by examining another form of competition, closer to an industrial logic, that elements of an answer can be found.

From the Informal to the Organized Network: Emergence of an Industrial Logic

In the haulage sector the growing complexity of service delivery is a major trend. For the economist, the explanation for this stylized fact cannot be limited to the predominance of a domestic logic since these changes are also experienced by big companies – in fact they are the main beneficiaries. 'The evolution of the structure of freight has initiated a new demand for haulage services consisting of a more complex and extensive service (. . .) It therefore seems that deregulation has favoured a shift of dominant positions from intermediaries (transport agencies) towards major hauliers' (Detchessahar, 1997, p. 80).

Interpersonal agreements characteristic of a domestic logic stumble against a 'threshold effect'. To be fully effective, especially in the movement of freight, the network has to cover an extensive geographical area.[12] This requirement often implies a more structured network which will consequently become formal. The network thus moves further afield than the 'gang of friends'. Endowed with a status and internal rules, the network is transformed into a formal association of hauliers, based on a quality charter. What was formerly transmitted orally is written down in communication and coordination procedures. Even the truck drivers' know-how is synthesized in a 28 page document. There has thus been a switch to a logic of norms, similar to a form of industrial judgment in the sense that Boltanski and Thévenot (1991) give the term. Detchessahar (1997, p. 80) makes the same point when he states that 'informal agreements of correspondence between dominant hauliers are threatened by the network policy implemented by some of them'. This is a new management of haulage, related to quality and quality approval policies and often imposed by shippers who themselves have a quality label. The aim is to reduce costs to a minimum, for example by optimizing trips.

The financial cost of these new procedures can explain hauliers' lack of enthusiasm as regards quality labels. Yet, at the same time, relations with shippers have changed. Firstly, each customer inquiry is answered by a quotation on which the customer's requirements in terms of equipment are listed. It is becoming easier to define the cost price of haulage. Secondly, the number of disputes has declined.[13] As a result, cost–benefit analysis has become more complex.

The generalization of calls for tenders puts pressure on the reduction of cost prices allowed by hauliers' commitments to quality standards. The mobilization of quality standards determined elsewhere reflects the adoption of an industrial quality convention as defined by Eymard-Duvernay (1989). Here again, White's model enables us to analyse these developments to ascertain whether they contribute towards the viability of the haulage market.

On the organization of structured networks and the formulation of quality standards, we wish to make two comments. First, in an industrial logic, quality is expensive to produce. When a firm opts for quality approval there is an entry cost due essentially to audits. Above we developed various arguments showing that the system of quality standards can generate returns to investments that are favourable to hauliers. It would be wrong to deduce that industrial quality is not expensive to produce. In our view, that is not the case at all. Intuitively, it can be taken for granted that stricter quality standards will, in concrete terms, imply additional constraints on the firm. These constraints will, in turn, imply higher costs. Apart from this intuition, interviews enabled us to identify the following perceptions among hauliers:

1. Greater profits, owing to revenue that increases proportionally more than costs following the adoption of an industrial model, mask the rise in costs.
2. Some hauliers that are 'in the process of obtaining a quality label', in order to meet shippers' requirements, admit that for them this apparently temporary status is satisfactory. By thus indicating that they care about quality, they reassure their customers. However, they actually hope they will not be forced to accept quality approval. Behind this reasoning there is a monetary evaluation of the additional costs generated by quality.
3. We think that haulage companies' emphasis on the positive spin-offs of quality approval is precisely a sign that they are not that obvious. In this, we methodologically follow the analysis of Boltanski and Thévenot (1991) in terms of justification regimes.

Secondly, since quality is guaranteed by the existence of standards, the shipper is highly sensitive to quantity. In the firm under study the quality approval policy led to better control of production costs and prompted it to calculate an accurate cost price for each trip, as the drawing up of a quotation for each service attests. Thus, if the increase in quantity has an effect on the cost and therefore the price of haulage, this development will be controlled. At the same time shippers, whose goods are transported in compliance with 'quality standards', will be sensitive to changes in quantity. Often themselves engaged in a process of quality approval in their own market, shippers are forced to reduce the number of hauliers with whom they deal and to give more tonnage to fewer of them (those who have a quality label). Moreover, since the organization of just-in-time production implies delivery on appointment at a fixed time, the shipper–consumer depends crucially on quantity. Its satisfaction will be more elastic to a variation in quantity than the cost of a haulier–producer.

Formally, these two comments can be reinterpreted as follows: (a) saying that quality is expensive to produce amounts to stating that *variable d is negative*; (b) to indicate that satisfaction is more sensitive to a variation in quantity than is cost, we write $a > c$, or that *the ratio a/c is greater than 1*. White has shown that the conjunction of these two elements places us in an area (called 'crowded') in which there is market viability.[14] In this, we understand that hauliers might have seen the adoption of a competitive logic as leading to competition with destructive prices. However, for this area White (1981,

p. 530) states that 'Such markets are viable because buyers have no means to realize or organize to exploit the realization that they are better served the fewer the firms there are.' Given that quality approval is often imposed on the haulier by the shipper, it would be legitimate to wonder if it is not a way for shippers to control and thus to reduce the number of hauliers. In a dynamic perspective, this domination by shippers could well challenge the viability of a market even if it is engaged in an industrial mode of coordination. White's essentially static model does not enable us to answer this question. That is perhaps one of its limitations.

MODELLING THEATRICAL INSTITUTIONS

Amendments to the model required to analyse the production of theatrical organizations with a public service mission (and therefore public funding)[15] will first be presented. The method of quantitative evaluation of elasticity of satisfaction and cost, with a quality index determined by judgment variables, will then be outlined. Finally, the main results obtained will be indicated.

Necessary Amendments

The constraint of a balanced budget

The directors of theatrical institutions try, above all, to maximize their productive capacity within the constraints of a balanced budget monitored by public authorities. These authorities control the adjustment of costs in relation to own income and subsidies. A large deficit usually results in underproduction in the following season, sometimes accompanied by reduced fixed costs.

The theatrical institution compared to a market

The director managing a theatrical institution has two main functions:

- producing shows by coordinating a network of technicians and artists employed on a temporary basis. Labour relations in this case can be defined as precarious jobs with stable employer/employee relationships (Degenne, 2002, ch. 7). Contracts are limited to the duration of a single show (preparation and exploitation) but are renewed with a view to cultivating artistic loyalty, a source of a common aesthetic language;
- planning hosted shows. Their selection is based on a market logic organized by an intermediary, the director of the institution whose choices determine its image. This market consists of an average of 15 selected companies and theatrical institutions. Competition for access is stiff, with hundreds of candidates.

The analysis of the market institution is focused on the creation and exploitation of plays for all age groups and for children. The boundaries with other artistic disciplines have become more fluid with the emergence of new forms that combine dramatic art and music, dance, mime or circus arts. The main idea has been to select those shows which seem to be based on dramatic art.

Endogenous quality

Theatrical products cannot be evaluated by a representative consumer. Their differentiation is horizontal and based on an organized combination of stimuli from characteristics, both artistic (text, casting, production, place of performance) and cultural (contact with locals, social event), which are judged in very different ways. In the world of theatre,[16] judgments on the quality of shows involve two types of actor. Audiences are biased in their anticipation of the quality of a show, firstly, by hearsay and the degree of satisfaction of preceding experiences (Lévy-Garboua and Montmarquette, 1996). Secondly, they may be influenced by the opinions of experts, drama critics and programme planners who judge from an aesthetic viewpoint, and public authorities whose political evaluation may be based on aesthetic criteria. The need for mediation in the aesthetic experience has already been emphasized by David Hume (1974), for whom only people with sensitive taste, having developed a critical mind through practising the arts and comparing types of beauty, can discern the aesthetic quality of artistic objects.

Aggregation of satisfaction and costs in the institution market

The institution market can be conceived as an adequate source of homogenization of shows to enable us to estimate consumer satisfaction and the total variable cost in relation to the overall level of the volume and quality of shows performed in the theatre. The place of performance creates an interface between hosted shows, which have to adapt to the space of the stage, and the audience, which is attracted partly by the reputation of the theatre, the comfort of the hall and the conviviality of the place.

Analytical accounting done annually for the civil year has required the addition of data established on an annual basis rather than data corresponding to the theatrical season.

By posing for a number h of producers who present their shows on the institution's stage:

$$Y = \sum_{i=1}^{h} y_i$$

where y_i is the volume of the show of producer i and N the perceived global quality of the h shows, we deduce the functions of aggregated satisfaction and cost:

$$S = r \cdot Y^a \cdot N^b \tag{9.1}$$

$$C = qY^cN^{-d} \tag{9.2}$$

The Choice of Variables

The volume of production *Y*

Throsby and Withers (1979, p. 11) prefer the number of tickets sold as an indicator of the volume of production *Y*. The determination of *S* would then require one to know the degree of audience satisfaction after each performance, something that is impossible. Because variations of *Y* are confronted in the model by tastes and costs, it is more coherent to estimate it by means of an overall supply indicator. It was not possible to select as a variable the number of seats available in the theatre for each show, owing to a lack of data on the capacity, especially for regional theatres. That is why volume *Y* is estimated by the number of performances listed in the theatres' annual reports.

The satisfaction of consumers *S*

The number of paid visitors to the institution market is an acceptable indicator of satisfaction *S* of consumers. The only national survey on theatre audiences' habits and representations carried out in 1987 indicates that 85 per cent of the people concerned, over the preceding 12 months, were satisfied with their last performance and that 83 per cent considered that they did not go to the theatre enough (Guy and Mironer, 1988, p. 49). Moreover, the total number of paying visitors to the theatre fluctuated, depending on the initial degree of audience satisfaction made known by word of mouth. The 1987 survey established that the two main factors of choice in the most recent show were the presence of well-liked actors in the cast and the opinions of other people (friends, colleagues, family) (ibid., p.38). The rule applied was the counting of audiences in the theatre in which the show was performed.[17]

The aim was to compare visits satisfaction as if the structure of the repertory was the same in the different theatrical institutions. Four categories were distinguished: 'classical' (Cl) for plays whose authors died before the 20th century; '20th century' (20th) for plays whose authors died in the 20th century and had written them before 1980; 'contemporary French' (Fr) for the plays which were written in French by an author still alive and those written in French by an author now dead but published after 1980; 'contemporary foreign' (Fo) for the plays which were written after 1980 in a foreign language by an author belonging to the contemporary category (usually translated). A total of 11 158 performances attracted 2 814 264 paying visitors to theatrical institutions in 1995, compared to 10 860 and 2 603 303 in 1996.[18] Their

Table 9.1 Breakdown of performances (P) and number of visits (V), according to structure of repertory

	P Cl	V Cl	P 20th	V20th	P Fr	V Fr	P Fo	V Fo
1995	24.74	33.65	22.22	26.63	37.98	30.32	15.06	9.40
1996	30.53	44.94	17.50	19.33	38.30	26.89	13.67	8.84

breakdown into percentages according to categories of repertory is given in Table 9.1.

The repertory effect can be corrected by multiplying the number of paying visitors observed in each of the four categories by the average ratio $\bar{x}_i$ between the share of performances and that of the number of visitors in a given genre i for all the institution markets.[19] If $\tilde{P}_i$ represents the number of performances and $\tilde{V}_i$ the number of paying visitors to all the theatrical institutions in category i of the repertory, it is defined by

$$\bar{x}_i = \frac{\tilde{P}_i / \Sigma_{i=1}^{4} \tilde{P}_i}{\tilde{V}_i / \Sigma_{i=1}^{4} \tilde{V}_i} \tag{9.3}$$

If v_i denotes the number of paying visitors in category i of the repertory, obtained by an institution market, the estimation of satisfaction of its public will be given by

$$S = \Sigma_{i=1}^{4} \bar{x}_i v_i \tag{9.4}$$

The aggregated variable cost *C*

The variable cost C of the institution market is obtained by adding up theatrical artistic expenses.[20] Their differentiation from fixed costs poses a problem of nomenclature, although it is limited by the absence of changes in accounting requirements by supervisory authorities between 1995 and 1996. We can presume that the administrators of institutions maintained their framework of reference.

The absence of necessary analytical data limited the calculation of elasticities to 76 institutions (5 TN, 21 CDN, 6 CDR, 4 CDNEJ and 40 regional theatres).

Scales *r*, *q*

Scale r of the function of satisfaction S was chosen to be equal to the inverse of the average price of seats $\bar{p}$ in all theatres in 1995 prices. Scale q of the function of costs C was considered equal to 1. This choice is justified by the need for the ratio between scales to correspond to the size of the structural deficit of theatrical performances, while units of C are millions of francs in 1995 prices and of S thousands of paying visitors.

Calculation of the average price of seats requires us to focus on the number of visits to the institution's home theatre, for the selling price of performances on tour is substantially higher than their local takings. It is obtained by dividing the box office revenues by the number of paying attendees at the institution's home. Its evaluation can only be approximate, for occasional subsidies granted to shows are integrated into own income in the accounts without always being distinguished from takings. It was estimated at 63.41 francs in 1995 and 63.76 1995 francs in 1996.

Judgments of drama critics N_1

Exploratory interviews with professionals and the 1987 survey on theatre audiences revealed consensus on the fact that the newspapers *Le Monde* and *Libération* and the magazine *Télérama* could be considered as opinion leaders among drama critics. The method therefore consisted first of recording all reviews of shows scheduled in theatres, published in 1995 and 1996 in the three publications. The critics' comments were converted into a score between 1 and 10, depending on how the critic rated the show.[21]

The main difficulty calculating the average score of reviews attributed to a show is how to deal with the frequent case of its partial coverage by one or two reviews. The method of calculating this score, to then estimate the variable N_1 of the judgment of drama critics on the theatrical production of an institution, is however too long to explain for the purpose of this chapter.

Judgments of programme planners N_2

Through their choice of programme, the directors of theatrical institutions participate actively in judgments on the quality of production. They discriminate between directors by controlling access to artistic legitimacy in the theatrical world.

Annual reports on the activities of theatres and national drama centres, and analytical budgets of regional theatres' shows, enable us to construct a matrix of performances of shows produced by each theatrical institution and presented by others.[22]

Interorganizational relations also concern co-productions. They were included only if the share contributed by each institution was detailed in the budget allocated to preparation of the show. In general, this information is provided only in the annual reports of CDNs, CDRs and CDNEJs. In these cases, the number of performances on tour in the institutional network was distributed as far as possible between the different co-producers, in proportion to their participation in the budget allocated to preparation of the show. This taking into account of co-productions has made it possible to increase the density[23] of the matrix of interorganizational exchange from 0.1 to 0.23, but it remains low. Theatrical institutions are therefore not structured in segmented interorganizational networks.

Centrality of degree represents the number of connections of an individual with others (Degenne and Forsé, 1994). These may be internal (coming from others) or external (towards others). The chosen variable N_2 is the centrality of the normed internal degree, that is, the number of performances of shows produced by other theatrical institutions, scheduled by the theatre, divided by the maximum centrality of the network. It is used to measure the public's sensitivity to institutional quality assurance.

Judgment of the public authorities N_3

The public authorities' judgment on the quality of theatrical institutions' production plays an essential economic role, since subsidies account for approximately 70 per cent of their income. Variable N_3 chosen to represent it is the amount of state subsidies in 1995 francs. This choice is justified by the weight of the state, which is greater than that of local authorities in the political recognition of an institution's artistic reputation.

Influence of previous consumption N_4

Owing to a lack of survey data on satisfaction with shows in theatrical institutions, the impact of past experience can be measured only by the number of paying visitors in the preceding period. The number of paying visitors per performance in the previous year was taken for variable N_4 in order to measure the influence of the institution's image in the expected judgment by audiences of its programme schedule.

Function of Quality Approval

Principles of construction

The overall quality perceived by the public is constructed by aggregating the four variables of judgment in the form of a Cobb–Douglas function that White used to model *S* and *C* (equations (9.1), (9.2)). This type of appropriate function for expressing the substitutability of variables can reveal conflicts of influence, among audiences, between the different sources of aesthetic judgment. It is written for a year *l* in the form:

$$N_l^{b_l} = N_{1l}^{b_{1l}} N_{2l}^{b_{2l}} N_{3l}^{b_{3l}} N_{4l}^{b_{4l}} \qquad (9.5)$$

The weight of each quality variable can be estimated by means of the hedonistic method where the number of paying visitors corrected by the repertory effect (multiplied by the overall average price) each year l, is explained by variables N_1, N_2, N_3 and N_4.

The selected variable to explain was the *number of paying visitors per performance*, corrected by the repertory effect and multiplied by the average price of the whole. The use of a deflator can lessen the risks of heteroskedasticity relating to the gap between the dimensions of the variables (entries in tens of thousands, number of performances and centrality of internal degree in tens, critics scores from 1 to 10, and subsidies in millions of francs).

From (9.1), $r = 1/\bar{p}$ and (9.5), we deduce that the following can be estimated:

$$[S\bar{p}/Y]_l = Y_l^{\hat{a}_l} N_l^{\hat{b}_l} \varepsilon_l = Y_l^{\hat{a}_l} N_{1l}^{\hat{b}_{1l}} N_{2l}^{\hat{b}_{2l}} N_{3l}^{\hat{b}_{3l}} N_{4l}^{\hat{b}_{4l}} \varepsilon_l, \tag{9.6}$$

where $\hat{a}_l$ and $\hat{b}_{jl}$ represent estimations of parameters a_l and b_{jl} of variables Y_l and N_{jl} for the year l, and ε_l the random component which is partly associated with the other quality characteristics.

The weight of the parameters is therefore evaluated by the following multiple linear regression:

$$\log([S\bar{p}/Y]_l) = \hat{a}_l \log Y_l + \hat{b}_{1l} \log N_{1l} + \hat{b}_{2l} \log N_{2l} + \hat{b}_{3l} \log N_{3l} + \hat{b}_{4l} \log N_{4l} + \hat{\varepsilon}_l \tag{9.7}$$

without a constant if the variables are centred and reduced. We deduce that

$$\log N_l = \hat{b}_{1l} \log N_{1l} + \hat{b}_{2l} \log N_{2l} + \hat{b}_{3l} \log N_{3l} + \hat{b}_{4l} \log N_{4l} + e_l \hat{\varepsilon}_l \tag{9.8}$$

with $0 \leq e_l\ 1 \leq 1$ assuming $\hat{b}_l = 1$.

The sharing of the residue among variables of volume and quality poses a tricky problem of choice. The starting hypothesis chosen was:

$$e_l = \frac{\hat{b}_{1l} + \hat{b}_{2l} + \hat{b}_{3l} + \hat{b}_4}{|\hat{a}_l| + \hat{b}_{1l} + \hat{b}_{2l} + \hat{b}_{3l} + \hat{b}_{4l}}. \tag{9.9}$$

These proportions were first corrected on certain institutions so that the sign of elasticity of number of entries to quality b remains positive at all times. This adjustment was necessary in almost 20 per cent of the cases. Thereafter adjustments were made on the extent of variations of b so that elasticity is, as a rule, roughly between 0.5 and 2.

Typology of functions of quality

The drama critic variable N_1, *a priori* the least important on the scale of all theatrical institutions, is in fact the most discriminatory. To attract attention,

Parisian drama critics have to defend a theatrical taste. This leads them to alternate enthusiasm and vengeful rejection, depending on how well the show corresponds to their aesthetics principles. They also favour institutions that are seen as proposing an innovative programme.

The critics' value scale therefore results in a contrasted evaluation of theatrical production, a source of clear differentiation of institutions, depending on whether the local theatre-going public's taste follows the critics' choices or opposes them. Two groups were formed each year, based on the differentiated impact of the two variables N_1 and N_2 on the number of paid entries per performance, corrected with the repertory effect. This typology enabled us to reveal an unexpected opposition in the sign of these two coefficients, and hence a contrasted adherence to the judgments of programme planners and drama critics.

In Group 1, the coefficient of the drama critic variable is positive, while that of the centrality of internal degree is negative. This reflects support of paying audiences for the judgments of drama critics and their mistrust of the programme bought from other institutions. In Group 2, the signs are inverted, as if audiences support the institutional quality assurance of the programmers and oppose the views of critics published in the national press.

The classifications thus obtained must of course be relativized by the existence of a few extreme cases that were found either in both groups or in neither group. The table in the appendix gives the results of tests and the coefficients of reduced centred variables of volume and quality for each group in 1995 and 1996.[24]

From relations (9.8) and (9.9) and from the attached table, by removing the non-significant variable of state subsidies on the threshold of $P = 0.05$ in Group 2 in 1995 and 1996, we deduce the expression of the variable of aggregated quality:

$$N = N_1^{0.214}\, N_2^{-0.277}\, N_3^{0.32}\, N_4^{0.806}\, \varepsilon^{0.787h_i} \quad \text{in Group 1 in 1995}$$
$$N = N_1^{-0.289}\, N_2^{0.287}\, N_4^{0.804}\, \varepsilon^{0.728h_i} \quad \text{in Group 2 in 1995}$$
$$N = N_1^{0.392}\, N_2^{-0.36}\, N_3^{0.47}\, N_4^{0.629}\, \varepsilon^{0.784h_i} \quad \text{in Group 1 in 1996}$$
$$N = N_1^{-0.213}\, N_2^{0.289}\, N_4^{0.726}\, \varepsilon^{0.797h_i} \quad \text{in Group 2 in 1996,}$$

h_i being the parameter of correction of residue ε for each institution i.

We can distinguish four groups of theatrical institution markets according to their type of aggregated quality function in 1995 and 1996. Group 1.1 consists of 31 institutions, whose aggregated quality function has retained the characteristics of Group 1 in 1995 and 1996. Group 2.2 has 51 institutions which have retained characteristics of Group 2.

Transformations in the quality function were rare. In Group 1.2, four institutions moved from the first type in 1995 to the second in 1996. The reverse trajectory concerned one theatre in Group 2.1.

Results of the Adjusted Model

Definition of market profiles based on elasticities

Since the number of paying visitors corrected with the repertory effect S, theatrical artistic expenditure C, the number of performances Y, the quality index N and the scale r were estimated in 1995 and 1996, we can deduce from (9.1) and (9.2) the expression of elasticities a, b, c and d as solutions of a system of two equations to two unknowns. By posing $\Delta = \log Y_{95} \cdot \log N_{96} - \log Y_{96} \cdot \log N_{95}$, we obtain:

$$a = \frac{\log([S\bar{p}]_{95}) \cdot \log N_{96} - \log([S\bar{p}]_{96}) \cdot \log N_{95}}{\Delta},$$

$$b = \frac{\log([S\bar{p}]_{96}) \cdot \log Y_{95} - \log([S\bar{p}]_{95}) \cdot \log Y_{96}}{\Delta},$$

$$c = \frac{\log C_{95} \cdot \log N_{96} - \log C_{96} \cdot \log N_{95}}{\Delta},$$

$$d = \frac{\log C_{95} \cdot \log Y_{96} - \log C_{96} \cdot \log Y_{95}}{\Delta} \qquad (9.10)$$

To simplify the scores, we pose

$$S^o = \frac{\log([S\bar{p}]_{96})}{\log([S\bar{p}]_{95})};\ Y^o = \frac{\log Y_{96}}{\log Y_{95}};\ N^o = \frac{\log N_{96}}{\log N_{95}};\ Co = \frac{\log C_{96}}{\log C_{95}};$$

$$(C/S)^o = \frac{\log[C/S\bar{p}]_{96}}{\log[C/S\bar{p}]_{95}};\ (C \cdot S)^o = \frac{\log[CS\bar{p}]_{96}}{\log[CS\bar{p}]_{95}} \qquad (9.11)$$

The following figures situate the theatrical institution markets on axes a/c and b/d. Since the variation of the volume is the most discriminating factor, Figure 9.1 places the institutions for which volume increased and Figure 9.2 the ones for which volume decreased. The institutions which belong to group 1 are underlined in both figures.

Table 9.2 summarizes the direction of variations in volume Y of production, in quality N, in the cost per performance,[25] in the cost per visitor and the conditions met by relations of elasticities a/c and b/d for each market profile. These deductions are obtained from the equations of (9.10) applied to the criteria that delimit the extent of these profiles and are expressed by (9.11).

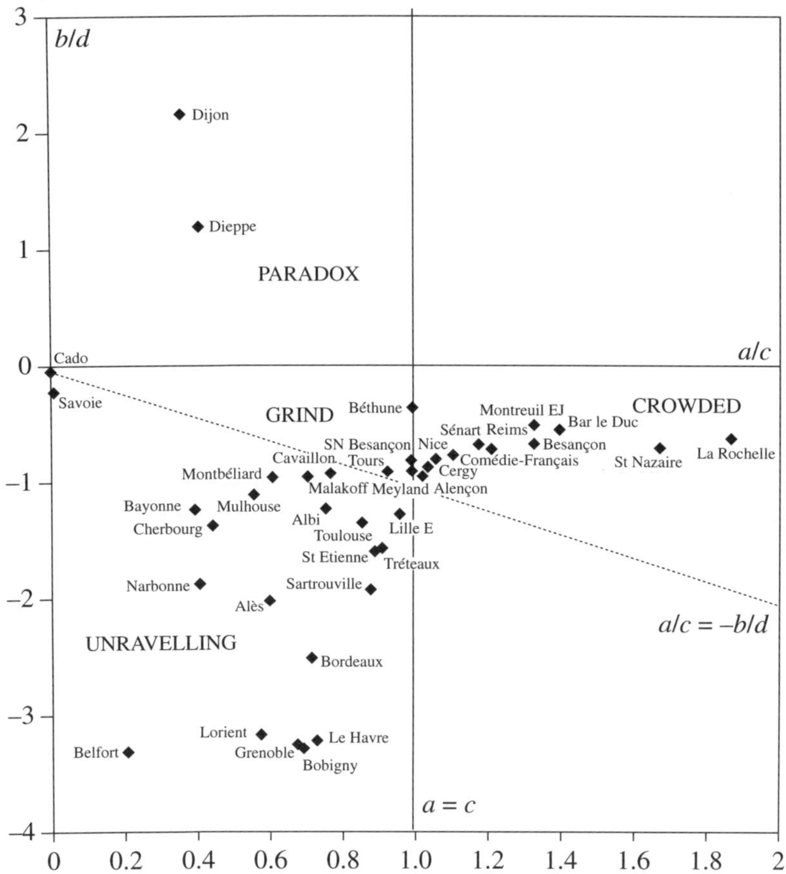

Figure 9.1 Trade-off volume/quality when volume increased

We can check that the variation of production is in fact the most discriminating factor, since the performance of theatrical institutions situated in the same area is totally different, depending on whether the volume has increased or decreased.

Apart from the paradoxical zone, institutions which improved the quality of their production between 1995 and 1996 are almost all those who have reduced their volume. Recession in the public theatrical sector has been marked by a 7.5 per cent decrease in the number of paying visitors and 2.7 per cent in the number of performances between those two years. In this context, the most effective adjustment strategy consisted of reducing the programme

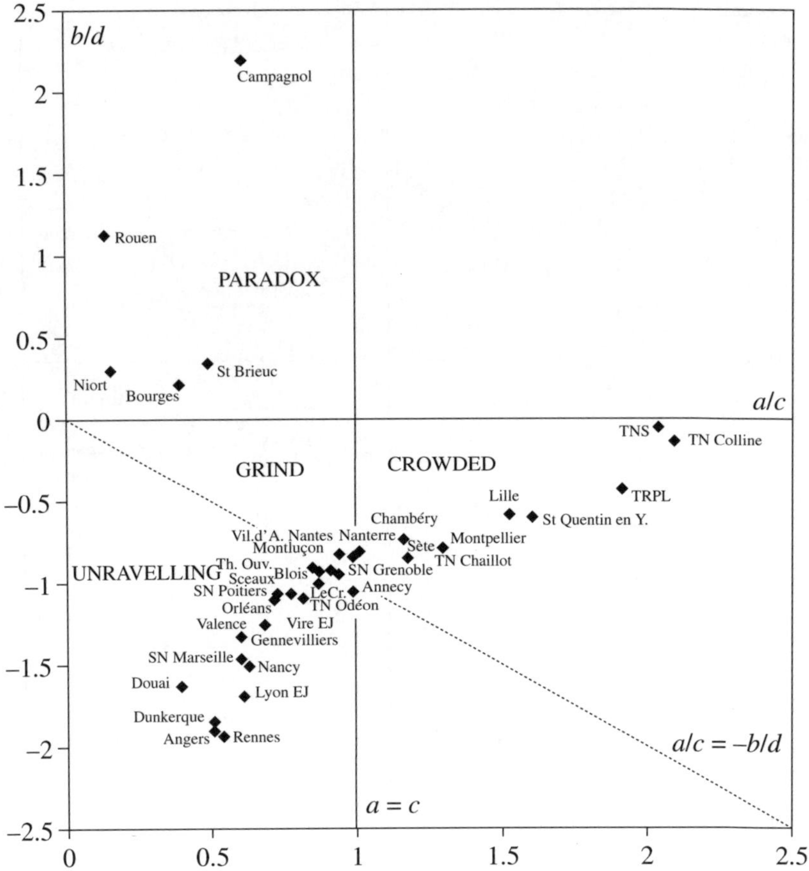

Figure 9.2 Trade-off volume/quality when volume decreased

with a view to promoting an increase in the number of visits to shows put on by the institution.

Paradoxical and unravelling profiles of a market institution

The origin of performance is totally different for these two profiles. The increase in the number of performances is reflected in improved quality for 'paradoxical' institutions and its deterioration for 'unravelling' institutions. Inversely, the drop in volume is accompanied by a deterioration of quality in the first case and by its improvement in the second. The common point between them is their small size, with a budget of 13 635KF for the paradoxical profile

Table 9.2 *The characteristics of market profiles*

	Volume Y	Quality N	C^o/Y^o	C^o/S^o	Conditions on b/d	Conditions on a/c
Paradox		$N^o > Y^o$	<1	<1	$b/d > 1 \Rightarrow Y^o < (C \cdot S)^o$ or $0 < b/d < 1 \Rightarrow Y^o > (C \cdot S)^o$	$a/c < 1$: $\nearrow N$ and $\searrow C/S$
	or					
		$N^o < Y^o$	>1	>1	$b/d > 1 \Rightarrow Y^o > (C \cdot S)^o$ or $0 < b/d < 1 \Rightarrow \searrow Y > \searrow C \cdot S)$	$a/c < 1$: $\searrow N$ and $\nearrow C/S$
Unravelling	$\nearrow$	$\searrow$	<1	>1	$0 > b/d > -1 \Rightarrow Y^o > (C/S)^o$ or $0 > b/d < -1 \Rightarrow \nearrow Y < \nearrow C/S$	$a/c < 1 \Rightarrow N^o < (C/S)^o$
	or					
	$\searrow$	$\nearrow$	>1	<1	$0 > b/d > -1$ $Y^o < (C/S)^o$ or $0 > b/d < -1 \Rightarrow Y^o > (C/S)^o$	$a/c < 1 \Rightarrow N^o > (C/S)^o$
Grind	$\nearrow$	$\searrow$	<1	<1	$-1 < b/d < 0 \Rightarrow Y^o > (C/S)^o$	$a/c < 1 \Rightarrow N^o < (C/S)^o$
	or					
	$\searrow$	$\nearrow$	>1	>1	$-1 < b/d < 0 \Rightarrow \searrow Y, \nearrow C/S$	$a/c < 1 \Rightarrow \nearrow N > \nearrow C/S$
Crowded	$\nearrow$	$\searrow$	<1	<1	$-1 < b/d < 0 \Rightarrow \nearrow Y, \searrow C/S$	$a/c > 1 \Rightarrow \searrow N < \searrow C/S$
	or					
	$\searrow$	$\nearrow$	>1	>1	$-1 < b/d < 0 \Rightarrow \searrow Y, \nearrow C/S$	$a/c > 1 \Rightarrow \nearrow N < \nearrow C/S$

and 17 129KF for the unravelling profile, as opposed to an average budget of 21 101KF for all in 1996.

In the case of the 'paradoxical' profile, the two conditions for d to be positive can be $N^o > Y^o$ and $Y^o > C^o$ or $N^o < Y^o$ and $Y^o < C^o$. The first case reflects an apparent increase in the number of better appreciated and less expensive performances but in fact no institution was successful to that extent. The number and the quality of the performances of three institutions were more or less stable. The only institution for which Y increased met the condition $N^o < Y^o$ of the second case, so that its cost per performance increased.

For three institutions, the second case means that they have slightly reduced their production in situations of failure, for a reduction in quality was more pronounced than that in volume. Theatrical artistic spending per visitor increased ($N^o < (C/S)^o$).

In 'unravelling' institutions the increase in the volume of production resulted in a decline in quality ($N^o < Y^o$, first condition for d to be negative) so that theatrical spending per visitor increased (meaning here of the condition $N^o < (C/S)^o$ so that $a/c < 1$). The second condition for d to be negative ($Y^o > C^o$) is ambivalent here.

The variable cost per performance has decreased in 12 cases, which reflects a depreciation of more economical programming, with scaled-down presentations or more limited casts. White's interpretation in terms of freeloaders cannot apply here because cheaper, lower quality is rejected. In 10 other cases theatrical spending per performance has increased, which indicates an increase in the scale of productions. The public has not responded enough to this, though, as shown for example by the fact that a tour was less successful than programme planners had anticipated. Moreover, Tabulation[26] indicates that the programming of this institution profile was open mainly to authors who are still alive.

In the case of a decrease in volume, 'unravelling' institutions improved quality (meaning of $Y^o < N^o$) so that theatrical artistic spending per visitor decreased (meaning here of $N^o > (C/S)^o$, the condition so that $a/c < 1$). The ambivalence of the second condition of the negative sign of d ($Y^o < C^o$) is a little less pronounced. The variable cost per performance increased in 15 cases and decreased in five.

This logic amounts, to a large extent, to rectifying a former situation of overproduction that generated a financial deficit. Compliance with budgetary constraints then alters the artistic project, and a return to a balance will involve a shorter programme to adapt it to the potential public.

Grind and crowded profiles of market institution

The common point of these two profiles is the negative sign of elasticity quality of cost d. The 'grind' market profile corresponds to institutions whose coordinates match inequalities $-b/d < a/c < 1$ and the 'crowded' profile to zones where $a/c > 1$ and $d < 0$. Since no institution of the latter type has an ordinate b/d smaller than -1, the comparison can be centred on the relationship between elasticities volume of visits and cost a/c, depending on whether the production has increased or declined.

In the case of an increase in volume, the common points between 'crowded' and 'grind' institutions are a decrease in the quality (meaning of $Y^o > N^o$, the first condition for d to be negative), of the variable cost per performance ($Y^o > C^o$) and a drop in theatrical artistic spending per visitor (meaning of the condition $Y^o > (C/S)^o$ so that $b/d > -1$).

Differentiation of the two regions is defined by the compared evolution of quality and cost per visitor. The 'grind' profile is characterized by the condition $N^o < (C/S)^o$ so that $a/c < 1$, which means *a priori* a greater decline in quality than in the variable cost per paying visitor (in four cases), whereas the decline was more moderate for the 'crowded' profile. In fact this decline can be more important for the 'crowded' profile because of a 9 per cent decrease of the average cost per performance as opposed to a 3 per cent increase for the 'grind' profile. The ambiguity of the logarithmic scale is also reflected by a smaller decline in quality than that of theatrical artistic spending per paying visitor in five cases but a greater decline in six institutions. Moreover, the decrease in the number of paying visitors per show was greater for the 'crowded' than for the 'grind' profile.

For 'crowded' and 'grind' profiles the reduction in volume is accompanied by an increase in quality (meaning here of $Y^o < N^o$, first condition for $d < 0$), which is more expensive ($Y^o < C^o$, second condition for $d < 0$), and in theatrical spending per visitor (meaning here of the condition $Y^o < (C/S)^o$ so that $b/d > -1$).

The two 'grind' institutions experienced an increase in quality that is greater than the increase in variable costs per paying visitor ($N^o > (C/S)^o$ so that $a/c < 1$) but the condition $N^o < (C/S)^o$ when $a/c > 1$ has an ambivalent meaning, since the increase in N is less than C/S for six 'crowded' institutions but greater in four other cases.

The greater stability in the quality of 'crowded' institutions when volume decreased is supported by their size, which is the largest of the profiles. Their average budget in 1996 was 32 997 KF, while the cost per performance was the highest (61.2 KF as compared to an overall average of 53.3 KF). Their programme was more classical than the average in 1995 but a little less so in 1996. Yet 'grind' institutions are in third place in terms of size; their average budget in 1996 was 15 986 KF.

Success of a more reduced programme, with more expensive performances, is less sensitive in 'grind' and 'crowded' institutions than in most of 'unravelling' institutions. Their increase in theatrical artistic spending per visitor results most often in a decline in the number of visits which is less than that of the volume, while the variable cost has increased for seven institutions and decreased in five other cases.

The failure of an extended programme on the basis of reduced artistic costs per performance is less pronounced in 'grind' and 'crowded' institutions than in most of 'unravelling' institutions. Their decrease in theatrical artistic spending per visitor reflects an increase in the number of paying visitors that is lower than that of the volume but greater than that of costs.

Instability of the central zone ($a/c < 1$ and $|b/d| \leq 1$)

We have seen that fluctuations in quality are more pronounced in 'grind' than in 'crowded' profiles. Variations in volume and thus in its positive or negative effects have been greater for 'paradoxical' and 'unravelling' institutions when $|b/d| \leq 1$.

In the 'paradoxical' profile, the ordinate b/d smaller than 1 corresponds to the condition $Y^o > (C \cdot S)^o$ in the event of an increase in volume, that is, an increase in the number of performances greater than the product of the variable cost (decreasing) by the number of paying visitors (increasing). Failure is also more pronounced because the condition for b/d to be less than 1 becomes $Y^o < (C \cdot S)^o$ when the volume has decreased, that is, a decline in production that is greater than the preceding product.

In the 'unravelling' profile the condition for $b/d > -1$ is $Y^o > (C/S)^o$ when production has increased. It reflects an increase in the number of performances that is greater than that of artistic spending per paying visitor. Similarly, the decline is more pronounced when the volume decreases, for the condition for $b/d > -1$ becomes $Y^o < (C/S)^o$. Hence the top part of this profile experienced the greatest economic success or failure.

This instability cannot be reduced to a market logic where products with little differentiation are exposed to strong competition. The central zone combines amplified fluctuations of volume between 'paradoxical' and 'unravelling' profiles, vertically, and of quality between 'grind' and 'crowded' institution, horizontally.

In the case of the 'grind' profile, the cost per performance (47.1 KF in 1996) was close to the 'unravelling' profile but their structure of programming shifted towards classical plays in 1996. 'Unravelling' institutions for which $b/d > -1$ are smaller than those where $b/d < -1$ (average budget of 12 790 KF as compared to 18 668 KF in 1996). On the other hand, their cost per performance was higher (54.1 KF as compared to 47.1 KF). Unlike the 'grind' profile, their programme was the most open to living authors, but it was a bit closer to the average structure in 1996.

CONCLUSION

The application of White's model to theatrical institutions could not use the hypothesis of the representative consumer underlying the consensual quality index *n*. Econometric estimations of the model that aggregate the judgments of the different types of actor have shown that the order of theatrical quality is marked by an opposition of influence between media renown and institutional quality assurance. On the other hand, the conceptual framework of market profiles offered a sufficiently operational grid for the qualitative study of modes of adjustment of road haulage to deregulation. Without being an obstacle *a priori*, the limits of a model of vertical differentiation of products have become a problem only for understanding the real process of quality creation. This process engages hauliers and shippers in conversation from which agreement on judgment criteria emerges. Apart from the fact that individuals talk to one another, what is essential is the process of construction of quality which, like a conversation, does not have a predetermined objective and is not entirely aimed at its realization. Adjustments take place between the interpretations of the parties, since what links them 'is nothing more than a space, *a priori* empty but potentially a provider of solutions to construct. The challenge now is to make these spaces live, through processes of continuous discussion, so that productive solutions emerge and agreement is reached' (Detchessahar, 1997, p. 30). To sum up, quality – or at least judgment on quality – is constructed in social interaction between hauliers and shippers. This process defies the framework proposed by White. His model tries to account for the social construction of the market, but as it takes the quality index as exogenous, it is therefore forced to reject the fact that quality is based on a totally comparable logic.

The absence of intermediaries in White's model where producers and consumers meet through a direct interface is consistent with a view of exogenous and consensual quality. But the analysis of quality as the result of an endogenous process implies that the role of intermediaries will be taken into account in the model. In theatrical activity the state and local authorities are the main sponsors. Drama critics and programme planners evaluate shows and can accelerate their end or make them into hits. In road haulage the state must guarantee adherence to social agreements limiting the effects of deregulation. Associations of local hauliers that share freight are a way of opposing a market-based order of quality in the form of intermediaries between hauliers and shippers.

Yet White's model helps to fill in the gaps in our understanding of logics on which production quality is based. The main axis consists of comparing elasticities of the function of consumer satisfaction and of cost, to volume and quality. Interviews with hauliers enabled us to reveal the relevance of this formalization of volume/quality exchange. The constitution of local networks for exchanging freight enhances hauliers' power of negotiation, while industrial quality assurance improves customers' positions.

The method of quantitative evaluation has proved to be sufficiently operational to classify successes and failures of theatrical institution markets in terms of the evolution of volume, judgments on quality and theatrical artistic expenses per performance or per visitor between 1995 and 1996. Differences of behaviour between producers and consumers are, to a large extent, articulated around the size of fluctuations in production. Of course the comparison of two years is not enough to define structural characteristics and needs to be completed by a longitudinal analysis and qualitative studies of representative cases.

NOTES

1. According to White, there is (a) elasticity of satisfaction in relation to the quantity produced (y), (b) elasticity of satisfaction in relation to the quality index (n), (c) elasticity of the production cost in relation to the quantity produced (y), and (d) elasticity of production costs in relation to the quality index (n).
2. In so doing, it also becomes a potential victim of new freeloaders.
3. The system of licence quotas set up in 1949 was abrogated on 14 March 1986. The system of compulsory road tariffs (TRO, *tarification routière obligatoire*), which set both the maximum and minimum rates, was similarly abrogated on 1 December 1986. This left contracting parties with some room for manoeuvre.
4. Source: OEST (Observatoire Economique et Statistique des Transports), 1993.
5. Source: OEST, 1993.
6. To compensate for lower rates, it was necessary constantly to increase the number of kilometres covered. Cf. Biencourt (1996, diagram 1, p. 212).
7. The physical limits of individuals make them incapable of exceeding a certain number of hours' driving without a safety hazard.
8. In the Sarthe (administrative) department in France.
9. Swedberg (1990, p. 38) refers to the abstruseness of White's thesis because of his intensive and complex use of mathematics.
10. Relationships which last up to 15, 20 or even 30 years.
11. Initially, newly recruited drivers accompany more experienced drivers on their rounds. In that way they are immersed in the firm's ways of doing things. Very few written instructions exist.
12. The whole country and even further afield, so that a haulier can go anywhere with the hope of obtaining freight from another member of the network.
13. Innovations such as bar codes have made it easier to meet deadlines and ensure the safety of freight. These new techniques have also solved the problem of theft within the company.
14. Provided the ratio a/c remains below a certain threshold which would make the dynamic explosive.
15. In 1996 there were five national theatres (*théâtres nationaux*, totally subsidized by the state), 27 national drama centres (CDN), nine regional drama centres (CDR), six national drama centres for children and young people (CDNEJ) and 58 regional theatres (*scènes nationales*, subsidized mainly by local communities).
16. Howard Becker (1983) defines a world of art as a network of cooperation which associates creators, actors, equipment providers, publishers, financiers and concerned audiences in artistic production. Their coordination is based on shared conventions which orient working procedures and the attribution of value to high-quality work.

17. Statements on producers' tours were therefore corrected by cancelling performances and their audiences in other theatrical institutions.
18. Owing to a lack of detailed data on number of visits, 16 regional theatres were excluded from the study. As a result, the figures presented do not cover all theatrical institutions.
19. If $\bar{x}_i$ is smaller than 1, it measures the degree of overrepresentation of the overall theatre audience (that is, for all theatrical institutions) in the category of the repertory, and if it is greater than 1 it measures the extent of its underrepresentation.
20. The exclusion for an institution of performances and audiences on tour, in other theatrical institutions, requires the withdrawal of artistic spending.
21. With this operation there is of course a questionable reduction. Someone else may have allocated different scores in the interpretation of the same comments, and slight differences are levelled out by a cardinal evaluation.
22. The institutional network was extended to include organizations that actively participated in the circulation of shows. These include Swiss and Belgian theatrical institutions, Parisian municipal theatres, whether subsidized or private, several municipal theatres (that is *théâtres missionnés* which received an additional subsidy, with a mission of increasing audiences) and the Avignon festival.
23. For a valued graph the density of the matrix of relations between actors is given by the total of all values divided by the number of cells.
24. One CDN and one CDR are excluded from the test because of their exceptional changes in their scale of production from 1995 to 1996.
25. As the number of performances is expressed in tens and the variable cost in millions of francs, the logarithmic scale complicates the interpretation of the ratio C^o/Y^o. We can observe the inequality Log $C96$/Log $C95$ < Log $Y96$/Log $Y95$, whereas the increase in variable costs was greater than that of the number of performances. The same applies when $C^o > Y^o$. Variable costs were able to decrease faster than the volume. As a result, the comparison of growth rates of volume and cost, based on logarithms, leads to *a priori* deductions that have to be inverted in certain cases. The interpretation of the ratio C^o/S^o is also sometimes equivocal, and the deductions are rather unexpected in the paradoxical profile for three cases for which Y^o and N^o are close to 1.
26. The share of performances devoted to classical shows and 20th-century shows in the programme is given below in percentages for each market profile.

	Paradox	Grind	Unravelling	Unr. $b/d < -1$	Unr. $b/d > -1$	Crowded	Mean
1995	62.4	48.3	40.4	43.0	26.7	52.8	46.8
1996	46.6	64.0	47.3	47.8	44.6	49.2	48.9

REFERENCES

Becker, Howard S. (1983), 'Mondes de l'art et types sociaux' *Sociologie du travail*, 4, 404–17.

Biencourt, Olivier (1996), 'Concurrence par la qualité dans le transport routier de marchandises: normes ou réseaux?, *Revue d'économie industrielle*, 75, 211–22.

Biencourt Olivier, François Eymard-Duvernay and Olivier Favereau (1994), 'Concurrence par la qualité et viabilité d'un marché. Le cas du transport routier de marchandises', Rapport pour le Commissariat Général du Plan, Paris, November.

Boltanski, Luc and Laurent Thévenot (1991), *De la justification – Les économies de la grandeur*, Paris: Gallimard.

Degenne, Alain (2002), 'Employer/employee relationship regulation and lessons from school/work transition in France' in Oliver Favereau and Emmanuel Lazega (eds).

Conventions and Structures in Economic Organization: markets, networks and hierarchies, Cheltenham, UK and Northampton, MA, USA: Edward Elgar.

Degenne, Alain and Michel Forsé (1994), *Les réseaux sociaux*, Paris: Armand Colin.

Detchessahar, M. (1997), 'Eléments pour une théorie de l'espace de discussion en situation de gestion. Réflexion à partir du cas des entreprises de transport routier de marchandises (1980–1995)', Thèse de doctorat en Sciences de Gestion, Université de Rennes 1.

Eymard-Duvernay, François (1989), 'Conventions de qualité et formes de coordination', *Revue économique*, 40 (2), March, 329–59.

Favereau, Olivier (1989), 'Marchés internes, marchés externes. Conventions de qualité et formes de coordination', *Revue économique*, 40 (2), March, 273–328.

Guy, Jean-Michel and Lucien Mironer (1988), *Les publics du théâtre. Fréquentation et image du théâtre dans la population française âgée de 15 ans et plus*, Département des Etudes et de la Prospective – Ministère de la Culture et de la Communication, Paris: La Documentation Française.

Hannan, Michael T. and John Freeman (1977), 'The population ecology of organizations', *American Journal of Sociology*, 82 (5), March, 929–64.

Hume, David (1974), 'De la norme de goût', *Les essais esthétiques. 2ème partie : Art et psychologie*, 1st edn 1757, translated from the English by Renée Bouveresse, Paris: Librairie philosophique J. Vrin, pp. 79–104.

Leifer, Eric M.(1985), 'Markets as mechanisms: using a role structure', *Social Forces*, 64 (2), December, 442–71.

Lévy-Garboua, Louis and Claude Montmarquette (1996), 'A microecoeconomic study of theatre demand', *Journal of Cultural Economics*, 20 (1), 25–50.

Swedberg, R. (1990), *Economics and Sociology. Redefining their Boundaries: Conversations with Economists and Sociologists*, Princeton, NJ: Princeton University Press.

Throsby, C. David and G.A. Withers (1979), *The Economics of Performing Arts*, London: Edward Arnold.

White, Harrison C. (1981), 'Where do markets come from?', *American Journal of Sociology*, 87 (3), 517–47.

APPENDIX

Table 9A.1 Estimated coefficients with the equation (9.7) and t*–statistics between brackets*

	Group 1 1995		Group 2 1995		Group 1 1996		Group 2 1996	
Number of obs.	35		52		32		55	
Adjusted R^2	0.778		0.691		0.797		0.655	
R^2	0.811		0.716		0.829		0.681	
Statistics F	24.84		28.97		25.28		26.64	
$\hat{a}$	–0.287	(–2.06)	–0.3	(–3.22)*	–0.312	(–2.46)	–0.204	(–2.05)
$\hat{b}_1$	0.214	(2.31)	–0.28	(–3.36)*	0.392	(3.87)*	–0.213	(–2.3)
$\hat{b}_2$	–0.277	(–2.38)	0.287	(2.91)*	–0.36	(–2.37)	0.289	(2.86)*
$\hat{b}_3$	0.32	(2.31)	+	(0.3)	0.47	(3.69)*	+	(0.44)
$\hat{b}_4$	0.806	(8.98)*	0.804	(10.06)*	0.629	(7.35)*	0.726	(8.77)*

Note: *statistically significant at level 1%.

10. Solidarity, its microfoundations and macrodependence: a framing approach

Siegwart Lindenberg

INTRODUCTION

I get by with a little help from my friends (de Graaf and Flap, 1988). Having friends in important places is surely a useful thing, and one of the important changes in network analysis is the attention to the fact that people do not just have networks but actively build networks (Kaplan, 1984; Grieco, 1987). Ties are social resources, a network is social capital (Ben-Porath, 1980; Flap, 1988; Coleman, 1990; Burt, 1992). My social capital will provide me with important information, help me in need, get me favourable treatment and so on. Stories abound about how businessmen invite each other to expensive dinners, keep track of social events, like birthdays, and quite generally invest in befriending those business partners whose trust they need most. Casson (1991, p. 20) speaks of 'the engineering of trust'. Heimer (1992, p. 143) even argues that organizational life is much about helping your friends and that relations in organizations are among named individuals who know one another as particular others.

Attention to this active side of people's pursuit of social ties connects nicely with sociology's most revered topic: solidarity. What it adds to this traditional topic is the possibility that solidary relations are not only 'naturally' grown but also strategically created or maintained. In this way, it seems that traditional sociology is brought together with rational choice sociology in a very congenial way. The term 'social capital' suggests that both sides have been covered: the social and the rational side. If this is correct, it would constitute a major advance because, as Hechter (1987, p. 30) argues at length, there is a severe problem with traditional sociology. Although much of the work in sociology is based on the concept of solidarity, neither normative, functional nor structural explanations provide adequate accounts of when solidarity is likely to occur and how it is brought about. Hechter (ibid., p. 31) goes on to argue that a satisfactory theory should be based on microfoundations and that the best elaborated theory of action in the social sciences is that of rational choice.

Thus, if theories of social capital indeed provide us with the missing microfoundations of a theory of solidarity, we will have advanced a great deal.

I would like to argue here that rational choice theories of solidarity (including theories of social capital) do not offer these microfoundations, and that also the 'classical' attempts which offer some microfoundations are seriously wanting. In this chapter, I would like to make an attempt to furnish such microfoundations.[1] Before I get into the microfoundations themselves, I would like to do three things. First, I will turn to the question what kind of behaviour patterns constitute solidarity. It is this kind of behaviour that needs to be explained. Then I will briefly discuss why I think even the most sophisticated traditional sociological accounts of solidarity are wanting. Finally, I will try to show that the three kinds of rational choice theories developed to overcome problems with the traditional explanations have by and large not succeeded in doing so.

SOLIDARITY BEHAVIOUR: EXAMPLES

What is solidarity? How can it be defined in such a way that it covers the most important intuitive conceptions of the phenomenon? Hechter contrasts two basic ways to define solidarity:[2] through behaviour or through sentiment (Hechter, 1987, p. 18f). The behaviour refers to contributing private resources to collectively determined ends. The sentiment refers to love, fellow-feeling or the feeling of brotherhood. He argues that the sentiments are much more difficult to measure than the proportion of an individual's private resources contributed to collective ends, and that therefore the behavioural definition should be used. It is perfectly legitimate to proceed as Hechter did, but it is theoretically unsatisfactory to rest matters of conceptualization on the ease of measurement.[3] There is no discussion on the importance or unimportance of sentiment for solidarity, nor is there a distinction between kinds of solidary behaviour that differ in other respects (for example in the rules) from the individual's contribution to a collective end. For these reasons, I will proceed differently. I will begin with examples of what to me are instances of solidary behaviour; I will then define solidarity more systematically in terms of five kinds of behaviours, with the claim that somebody who acts solidarily in some of the five situations but not in the others is not considered to act solidarily at all. Solidarity is thus a behavioural pattern *across* these five situations. Later on I will try to show why a definition of solidarity on the basis of sentiment is theoretically unsatisfactory. Pragmatic issues of measurement do not enter this argument.

For convenience of the exposition, the examples that I will present are dyadic. This should not imply that there are no groups involved. The issue of groups will be dealt with later on. At this point, the reader might imagine Alter to be the representative of a group, and Ego to be a member of a group, but it is also possible to simply take them as two individuals.

First example: Ego and Alter are sisters, both very busy in their professional lives. Their old mother is ill. Alter goes first to help her. Ego volunteers to take turns caring for the mother.

Second example: Alter is looking for a rare second-hand book and is willing to pay up to a hundred dollars for it. Ego knows this. He happens to find this book in a rummage sale for ten dollars. He buys it and will let Alter have it for the cost price: ten dollars.

Third example: Alter's house has been flooded by a rainstorm. Ego helps him clean it up. There is no direct payment and even consideration of payment would be felt to be inappropriate.

Fourth example: Ego and Alter had agreed to pool their resources and start a restaurant together. They have worked out all the details of how they would do it. A third person turns up and proposes a different deal to Ego. At the moment, this new deal looks more attractive to Ego than the agreement with Alter but Alter would be disadvantaged if the agreement did not go through. Ego will stick to this agreement with Alter and not enter a deal with the third person, even though he thereby passes up a deal that looked better to him than the one he kept.

Fifth example: Ego has promised Alter to help clean up the mess from the rainstorm but he does not show up. Later in the day, Ego calls Alter to say that he is sorry and explains why he was unable to come and even unable to notify Alter earlier.

In general terms, in each example, Ego contributes private resources without compensation, so all of them fall under Hechter's definition of solidarity. But in addition, each example stands for a type of situation in which Ego displays solidary behaviour:

Common good situation: Ego and Alter both belong to a group that produces a common good. Ego will contribute to the common good even if he could free-ride (the minimal amount of contribution in terms of money, effort, time and so on expected for solidary behaviour varies).[4]

Sharing situation: if there are joint divisible benefits and costs and if Ego is the one who can divide them, he will not seek to maximize what he gets from the benefit and minimize what he gets from the costs but take his 'fair share' of both (what the 'fair share' is varies).

Need situation: Ego will help Alter in times of need (what constitutes need and how much help is minimally expected for solidary behaviour varies).

Breach temptation: Ego will refrain from hurting Alter even at a cost to himself (the minimal amount of cost expected for solidary behaviour varies).

Mishap situation: acts can be intendedly solidary but factually turn out to go against the expectation of solidary behaviour. In that case, Ego will show that he meant to act differently, that he feels sorry that it turned out that way, and he will make amends if the mishap has caused damage to others. Also, if Ego knows in advance that he will not be able to keep to the agreement, he will warn others in advance, so that they can mitigate the damage.

The claim is that these five situations cover all aspects of what one would intuitively call 'solidary' behaviour. Notice that solidary behaviour is much more than just being cooperative behaviour (that is, behaviour in common good situations). A theory of solidarity would have to explain why solidarity is not just cooperative behaviour in common good situations and why it covers the other four situations as well. Each of the five situations asks for a sacrifice by Ego and there are trying times when the sacrifice may be expected to be particularly high: for example, when each member has to put in extra time to work on the common good, or when a number of members are struck by disaster and they need help. The *strength* of solidarity in a particular group can now be defined as the sum of the legitimately expected sacrifices (in terms of time, money and effort) in trying times (over all five solidarity situations). Let us call this sum *solidarity costs*. A theory of solidarity would also have to explain ordinal differences in the strength of solidarity.[5]

WHAT IS WRONG WITH DURKHEIM?

Everybody agrees that Durkheim is the major sociological theorist on solidarity. There is probably less consensus about elaborations after Durkheim and their relationship to what 'the master' had done. I would like to maintain that Durkheim's theory of mechanical solidarity is still the most sophisticated theory of that phenomenon within traditional sociology, and elsewhere I have devoted considerable effort to reconstructing Durkheim's contribution in detail (see Lindenberg, 1975). In this chapter, there is only room to mention a few highlights of this complex theory.

The standard view, one that some of Durkheim's own formulations have helped to foster, is that mechanical solidarity is brought about by similarity, as if similarity by itself would somehow make people stick together. This is somewhat unfortunate because it leaves out the mechanism that connects similarity to the production of solidarity, and it is exactly in this point that Durkheim's theory is so interesting. The major point about the mechanism that brings about solidarity in Durkheim's theory is the dependence of the individual on the sentiments of others. The individual has one overriding goal: the coordination of energy of various physiological centres (Durkheim [1893], 1933, p. 97, mentions cortical centres, motor centres, sensorial centres and vegetative functions). Durkheim calls this coordinated energy 'vitality'.

A sentiment is a belief with an affective (right/wrong) component. The stronger a sentiment the more it coordinates the energy of our various physiological centres. The individual is thus searching for strong sentiments that are congruent with the sentiment he or she already has. Because in interaction the strength of individual sentiments can fuse, collective sentiments (or what has come to be called 'morality') are generally stronger than individual sentiments and individuals will seek out either exposure to these collective sentiments or exposure to a process in which individual sentiments can fuse. Sentiments contrary to our own weaken our vitality, and the stronger they are, the more they weaken it. Therefore, individuals will tend to avoid exposure to contrary sentiments and, if they have been exposed to such sentiments, they will make extra efforts to strengthen their threatened vitality by interaction with others of similar sentiments. This can only be done by coming together face-to-face and expressing one to the other the adherence to the collective sentiments. This expressive behaviour Durkheim called 'ritual'.

Ritual interaction is the major vehicle of maintaining solidarity in the face of exposure to contrary sentiments. The more vitality individuals receive from collective sentiments, the more they value them and want to protect them from contrary sentiments. They become 'sacred' and the rituals that protect them become more elaborate (Durkheim mentions alimentary communion, ritual sacrifice, dances, hymns and so on). This, then, is the heart of mechanical solidarity. In more recent times, Collins (1985) has followed this line of reasoning.[6]

There are three important points that come out of this reconstruction of mechanical solidarity. First, mechanical and organic solidarity come much closer together than they seemed to be in traditional constructions of 'similarity' (mechanical) versus 'interdependence' (organic). Now it can be seen that, in both forms of solidarity, it is interdependence that creates the solidarity. In one case, it is the interdependence regarding the strength of sentiments and, in the second, it is the interdependence through the division of labour. Second, mechanical solidarity is so important because the very organization of energy and motivation for the individual depends on the joint production of collective conscience. Third, because of the importance of joint production, solidarity is not a matter of dyads but of groups. Why would we need still another theory of solidarity, if Durkheim's theory is so powerful?

The answer to this question is that Durkheim had two major problems. First, his theory of action did not allow him to detect, let alone explain, problems of solidarity that come from inside the group. Second, his theory of action did not allow him to elaborate the relationship between mechanical and organic solidarity (that is, the relation of internal and external threats to solidarity). The reason that a theory of solidarity has to be able to deal with threats to solidarity is that only then will it be able to explain the major puzzle: the behaviour in solidary groups that is aimed at maintaining solidarity, that is, at mitigating these dangers. Let me briefly elaborate.

One can see right away that Durkheim's theory is not related to solidary *behaviour*. There is no part of the theory that relates directly to the types of situations detailed above. This is serious because the action of maintaining solidarity (rituals) is not related to everyday actions. This lack might be repaired by adding assumptions on the link between solidarity and liking and then between liking and the various sorts of solidary behaviour, but if one does that then solidarity is assumed to create a stable cooperative disposition. There is then no precariousness of cooperation. To me, a great admirer of the theory, the major flaw is exactly in this point. The theory is all about the benefits and contains nothing about the costs of solidarity. Therefore the theory is very weak when it comes to the description of the dynamics and precariousness of solidarity.

Durkheim does not assume that solidarity is simply self-maintaining, because he had the anthropological evidence on periodic assemblies of tribes and the historical evidence of declining mechanical solidarity. But he has no clue where the built-in problems of solidarity lie. For him, the major threat to solidarity comes from the outside through contrary sentiments. Basically, as long as you stick to your own group, there should be no problem, but what to do about the fact that tribes would assemble periodically for ritual activity? Durkheim's answer is as simple as it is unsatisfactory: everyday life, with its 'utilitarian and individual avocations', is contrary to sentiments surrounding the sacred; and thus everyday life will slowly reduce the vitality coming from these sentiments (Durkheim [1912], 1965, p. 390), providing the impetus for periodic assembly. There is nothing in Durkheim's theory that would enable us to trace this impact of 'utilitarian and individual avocations' of everyday life. It is completely ad hoc.

The division of labour comes in as the major external threat to mechanical solidarity and, at the same time, as its replacement. But here Durkheim lacks a theory that could help him explain what problems arise within organic solidarity and how people deal with them. The theory of action (concerning the role of the collective conscience) that served him well with mechanical solidarity could not be applied to organic solidarity. Division of labour brings out individual autonomy: 'the individual becomes more of an independent factor in his own conduct . . . the progress of individual personality and that of the division of labor depend upon one and the same cause. It is thus impossible to desire one without desiring the other'. However, he has no theory for the individual as independent factor, and, as if to reclaim the entire matter for mechanical solidarity, he added to the sentence just quoted: 'But no one today contests the obligatory character of the rule which orders us to be more and more of a person' (Durkheim, 1933, pp. 404f). Of course, even if society expects individuals to show autonomy, that does not explain what they will do, and certainly not what they will do in interdependence situations.

In the end, Durkheim can deal with neither internal nor external threats to solidarity. This problem also shows up in the way he deals with sanctions. He assumes that there are very strong sanctions for deviating against the collective sentiments and he even uses these sanctions as an indicator for a society in which mechanical solidarity is strong. But why would anybody deviate from the collective sentiments? They gain nothing and lose everything from doing so. Thus sanctions can only be levelled at people who have contrary collective sentiments and they *must* be members of another group. So why are there such strong sanctions against group members?

Hechter has also observed the lack of theory on sanctions in the normative explanations of solidarity (see Hechter, 1987, p. 23). The theory of 'internalization' which works with stable behavioural dispositions has a systematic problem of dealing with obligations and sanctions at the same time. It creates what has been called 'the sociologist's dilemma'. Durkheim's (and thus the 'classical sociological') view on behaviour is that, through an elaborate process of socialization, the individual learns to *want* to do what he *has* to do. There are moral rules (norms) and they are 'internalized' by the individual so that he feels *obliged* to follow the rules. There is no weighing of costs and benefits regarding the moral course of action; conformity to moral rules is thus not a matter of *expedient* choice. Yet, according to the same orthodoxy, moral rules are *always* stabilized by 'sanctions', that is, by costs for deviance and benefits for conformity. The absence of sanctions is a tell-tale sign that the rule is not a moral rule. How can sanctions have any effect on conformity with moral rules if consideration of costs and benefits of this conformity is said to be absent? The dilemma is this: either the sociologist drops the assumption that cost–benefit considerations are absent from conformity to moral rules or he drops the assumption that moral rules are always stabilized by sanctions. In the first case, he would make conformity to moral rules a matter of expedient choice, negating what is said to be *the* central insight of traditional sociology. In the second case, he would negate the empirical foundation of sociology, forcing him back to the purely idealistic position. Clearly, both horns of the dilemma are unacceptable and a solid microfoundation of solidary behaviour would have to deal with this dilemma. Did rational choice theories of solidarity solve it? Can these theories deal with internal and external threats to solidarity?

RATIONAL CHOICE VIEWS ON THE EMERGENCE OF SOLIDARITY

Rational choice theorists have dealt with solidarity either as social capital or as the result of dependency. Of the former, I can find two kinds, both of them focusing on ties rather than groups.[7] I will briefly review all of these theories.

The Investment Theory

Ties come about because people invest in other people. The tie-forming mechanism itself has been gleaned from Marcel Mauss. It is the idea that gifts (investments) create obligations to be used later on. Prominent social capital authors who make use of this idea are Flap (1988) and Coleman (1990). Coleman asks: why do rational actors create obligations? His answer rests on the assumptions that obligations must be seen as 'credit slips' which one can accumulate as a kind of insurance. According to him such credit slips work for goods that at any given time have different value to the actors. 'When I do a favor for you, this ordinarily occurs at a time when you have a need and involves no great cost to me. If I am rational and self-interested, I see that the importance to you of this favor is sufficiently great that you will be ready to repay me with a favor in my time of need that will benefit me more than this favor costs me' (Coleman, 1990, p. 309).

At this point, three observations must be made. First, the point that the goods can have different value to the helper and the helped and thus create an incentive to invest in low cost/high gain exchanges is a very interesting version of the gift idea quite different from the one presented by Mauss. For Mauss, this difference in value was decidedly not the issue of gift giving. Often, the opposite would be true. The gift might be a real sacrifice to the giver and only of symbolic relevance to the receiver. Second, why are obligations repaid? Coleman only points to the high value of the favour received now that would make me repay (at low cost) later. But there is no hint that the temporal gap between receiving and repaying may cause a problem. Most likely, Coleman tacitly assumes a preference change stable enough to last over longer periods of time. Against this idea, it is interesting to note that in the analysis of 'archaic' societies, Mauss finds this temporal gap bridged by severe sanctions.[8] Third, it is possible that low cost/high gain situations are created by specialization. But then the goods (that is, the results of specialized skills) can be traded and no obligation will evolve except if there are barriers to quid pro quo exchanges, as in high tax situations. What is at the heart of Coleman's low cost/high gain exchange *with* the creation of obligations is the fact that people can experience situations of need, that is, of unpredicted increase in the value of certain goods, say through sickness or disaster, events for which they are not otherwise insured. His theory then only applies to need situations but does not cover breach temptations, common good, sharing and mishap situations. The importance of solidarity is thus limited to unpredictable need, and internal and external sources of precariousness are not addressed at all.

By-Product Theory

A second way in which some social capital theorists see solidarity ties emerge could be called the 'by-product theory' of solidarity. People meet and either on the basis of increasing familiarity alone or on the basis of some attributes (such as similarity) they find each other attractive. There is good company for this assumption: interpersonal attraction has been a corner stone of theories of social cohesion in social psychology for a long time.[9] In contrast to the investment theory of solidarity, gift giving here is not meant to rationally create indebtedness in the other but meant as token gesture that indicates liking. Homans (1958) has given prominence to this view and he had found plenty of empirical evidence for it. Take, for example, his famous cash posters: 'Girls who sat near one another then had many chances to interact and tended to become friends, and the friendships once made were apt to persist even after seating arrangements were changed' (Homans, 1954, p. 729). Rationality does not come in in the emergence of the tie or in its maintenance. Rather, it is assumed that attraction changes somebody's preferences and as a consequence the rational pursuit of one's own preferences includes attention to the other's well-being. Thus liking affects the utility function: the other's utility has become one of the arguments in Ego's utility function ('altruism through liking'). Examples of prominent authors of social capital working with this by-product theory of solidarity are Feld (1981) and Burt (Burt, 1992; Burt and Knez, 1995). Related work is done by Lawler (see Lawler and Yoon, 1993; Markovsky and Lawler, 1994).[10]

The by-product theory does not address any particular situation of solidary behaviour but, with the appropriate auxiliary assumptions on what increases and decreases Alter's utility, one can make a case for need, common good and sharing situations. The theory also allows purposeful manipulation of liking (and thus of solidary behaviour) by the influence on interaction frequencies. In that it seems to be the most general of the three. One big problem, however is that, similar to Durkheim's theory, the theory works with the assumption of stable solidarity preferences which exclude the internal and external precariousness of solidarity and this leaves out mishap situations and breach temptations. As we will see, these two neglected aspects are vital with regard to the way solidarity is socially embedded in and with other groups and instrumentally embedded in opportunism-reducing arrangements.

Among the evidence contrary to the stable preference assumptions, the studies of categorization experiments seem to point to a situational influence (Tajfel, 1970; Tajfel *et al.*, 1971). Solidary behaviour in sharing situations is sensitive to experimenter-induced categorization even against pre-existing individual relations. There seems to be a situational sensitivity to solidary behaviour that is incompatible with the assumption of transsituational preference effects. Another piece of evidence against the by-product theory is the fact that, when individuals are confronted with two legitimate ways of showing solidary behaviour vis-à-vis members of their own group, one being much more advantageous to themselves than the other, they tend to choose the one that is more advantageous to themselves, irrespective of the effect on the group (see De Vries, 1991). This does not point in the direction of altruistic motivations. Lastly, the fact that by all accounts sanctions are necessary for stable solidary behaviour does not make altruism through liking a theoretically stable basis for the explanation of solidary behaviour. The by-product theory may thus seem more general than the investment theory. But it is also the more troublesome.

Group Solidarity

Next to these two dyadic theories of social capital, there is Hechter's theory of group solidarity, also based on rational choice.[11] Here, social norms specify individual contributions to collective goods in groups, but in contrast to the normative theories of traditional sociology, conformity to norms is here related to expediency rather than morality. Rational individuals will be willing to follow these norms if there are effective sanctions against not following them. Hechter distinguishes between accepting a normative obligation to contribute to a collective good and complying with it. If Ego can get the same collective good with smaller obligations in another group, he will leave. But if he stays, he may still try to evade the obligations. 'The more dependent a member on the group (that is, the more costly it is to leave the group in terms of opportunities forgone), the greater the tax that the member will be prepared to bear for a given joint good. However compliance requires formal *controls*' (Hechter, 1987, pp. 10f). Without control and sanctions, the individual will try to free-ride. Thus one has to look at both control and exit effects. To the degree that observability of conformity diminishes (for example through increasing size), or to the degree that exit costs decrease (for example through new alternatives for the collective good), solidary behaviour will diminish as well, *ceteris paribus*.

This dependence/control theory of solidarity does deal with groups and the importance of solidarity is clearly linked to common good situations. This is clearly an advance. But Hechter does not work out the aspect of joint production, he only concentrates on dependency. A positive point is also that there is some attention to internal (free-riding and control) and external (exit temptations) precariousness. But the theory views solidarity as solely a matter of a single group[12] and within that group solely a matter of cooperative behaviour (common good situations), without specifying joint responsibility. It does not cover any of the other situations of solidary behaviour. Mishap situations are not covered, even though mishaps can happen right under the eye of the guardian who has to decide whether he's dealing with a mishap or motivated disobedience.

Help in need situations is also ignored. Breach temptations are presumably no problem because they are curbed by observability and control so that there is no need for a member to sacrifice voluntarily in order not to breach. In sum, imagining that there is a prison with open doors and hell outside, even that would fit Hechter's view of solidarity. In fact, in Hechter's theory, solidarity only works if people have no alternative outside and nothing escapes the eye of the watchful guardian inside. Yet this is against common experience. In solidarity groups, people are expected and encouraged to cooperate even if nobody is watching, and the suspicion that somebody only cooperates when observed will in all likelihood lead to exclusion from the group.[13] No wonder that Hechter laments that his theory 'does not seem capable of accounting for the kind of solidarity that is so often celebrated in our own experience' (ibid. p. 183).

USEFULNESS AND PRECARIOUSNESS OF SOLIDARITY

Where do these developments leave us? I suggest that it is useful to have a closer look at the context in which solidarity arises and is maintained in order to get a grasp on the question when and why people would like to keep it going, what problems people have to overcome in order to succeed in keeping solidarity going, and finally how people attempt to keep solidarity going. There are two theoretical pillars for this effort: sharing group theory (on joint production and use) and a theory of bounded rationality (myopia and framing). Both build on work done in a more concise language in the *Journal of Mathematical Sociology* (Lindenberg, 1980, 1982). In contrast, the purpose of this chapter is to add complexity in order to bring out the detailed preconditions (such as precariousness, self-signalling and formation of rules) as clearly as possible. Other theories are often only seemingly simpler in this regard because they leave important mechanisms implicit for the sake of simplification.

Sharing Groups

Solidary behaviour will evolve where it is useful for people and where there are no major obstacles for its realization. If any kind of behaviour is recognized as being useful by a number of interacting people and if that usefulness is fairly stable over time, its occurrence will lead to regular expectations which, in turn, are governed by rules. The major interest here is with solidary behaviour that is non-incidental and thus the first task is to look for an answer to the questions under what conditions solidary behaviour will be predictably useful, what rules are created to maintain this behaviour, and under what conditions the rules are observed.

The prime context of usefulness for solidary behaviour is where people are face to face to share in production and/or use of some goods. I have called these groups 'sharing groups' (see Lindenberg, 1982).[14] For example, farmers may share the production and maintenance of a dike around their fields and they may share a combine which each can use on his own field. They need each other (for production and for cost sharing) but they also exert negative externalities on each other. If someone does not show up for the joint work on the dike, others may be greatly inconvenienced, and while one farmer uses the combine, the other cannot use it although rain may be coming soon and the wheat has to be brought in dry.

In such situations of combined positive and negative externalities, solidary behaviour is useful for the establishment of the rules for joint production and sharing and for the mitigation of the negative externalities. The more there is being shared (that is, the higher the total value of what is jointly produced or consumed), the more positive the externalities – the less attractive the exit options. Also, the more is being shared, the higher the damage if negative externalities are not mitigated. Non-cooperative behaviour thus engenders the more damage, the more is being shared. Thus the usefulness of solidary behaviour of each for all, at least as one solution among others to prevent non-cooperative behaviour, will increase with the amount and value of goods being shared.

Because of this combination of positive and negative externalities, all kinds of sharing groups have one feature in common: the group *as group* is responsible for maintaining the conditions that are necessary for joint production or use. This feature of sharing groups can be simply called *joint responsibility*. This is different from a situation where an owner of capital hires (and pays) people to perform certain activities which jointly produce a marketable good. In the latter case, the owner is responsible for maintaining the conditions of cooperation.

One of the important issues that the group has joint responsibility for is regulating the joint production and/or use and the sharing of joint costs and benefits by means of rules. The process of negotiating these rules may be quite difficult and conflict-ridden, as the interests may not be homogeneous and there may be distributional disagreements.[15] The content of rules to these ends can be quite practical, depending on the goods jointly produced or consumed, such as division of labour for building the dike or regulating timeshares for the use of the combine, or delineating common property and allotting private property. Once the rules have evolved, non-cooperative behaviour refers first and foremost to failure to conform to (the spirit) of these rules. The substantive claim I make at this point is that the question whether solidarity or some other solution to prevent non-cooperative behaviour will be used depends on what we assume to be the sources of possible uncooperativeness. For example, if that source is the tendency to free-ride, as Hechter assumes, a group does not need solidarity (in the sense used in this chapter) but control and effective sanctions.

Internal Sources of Precariousness in Sharing Groups

No set of sharing rules can anticipate all contingencies, and the joint agreement on these rules as well as the handling of them post hoc will be subject to solutions to the precariousness of cooperation. In the very heart of a sharing group, the interests of an individual and the group are partially non-aligned because the individual could contribute less if others contributed more. Since the sharing groups we are talking about are face-to-face groups, Olson's logic of collective action for large groups (Olson, 1965) does not apply. But there is asymmetric information in the sense that surveillance (including surveillance of intentions) will be systematically limited. In sharing groups, most of the relevant contributions to a collective good consist of actions rather than money or material goods. There are typically many situations where failure to contribute (in terms of effort) or to comply with rules (in terms of intentions) cannot be determined unambiguously. If somebody is sick with a headache and does not show up for the joint work on the dike, what is going on? There are also many moments when a farmer is unobserved with the communal combine on his field. How careful is he in avoiding the bumpy rocks? In general, there is likely to be a considerable regulatory interest in sharing groups but also the realization that monitoring is limited. Thus the *regulatory interest* will prominently include the wish that individuals would effectively monitor themselves. However, there are two systematic problems: myopia and decay of solidarity motivation, both related to bounded rationality (framing). These points will turn out to be very central to the microfoundations of solidarity and I will go into somewhat more detail than warranted for the flow of the chapter.

Myopic versus Far-sighted Rationality

If a human being really were the far-sighted rational creature she is made out to be in neoclassical microeconomics then cooperative behaviour by Ego vis-à-vis certain others would pay and thus be just another instance of maximizing behaviour for certain need situations (insurance!) or it would be without object because breach temptations and mishap situations have been taken care of ex ante (through credible commitments[16]) or breach would be advantageous to both parties. This point is forcefully made by Williamson (1993) who does assume far-sighted rationality and who chides Coleman and others for using the word 'trust' (which leans on solidarity imagery) where what is really meant is 'calculated risk'. For example, if I lend a substantial amount of money to a friend without a formal contract then I calculate the risk that he will pay me back, considering that he is also far-sightedly rational, that the friendship is worth much to him and that he would lose it if he defaulted on the debt. To say that I trust the friend does not add anything to the explanation.[17] Coleman's investment view of helping fits perfectly into this calculated risk view of dealing with needy situations of certain others (that is, when the calculated risk of default is small enough to make the investment attractive). Given the assumptions of far-sighted rationality and continued interaction, this suggestion seems perfectly reasonable and it also applies to game theorists using the term 'trust'. The jargon of solidaristic imagery is thus really quite superfluous, at least for repeated need situations and breach temptations.

For the explanation of cooperative behaviour in common good situations we can do with Hechter's point that even far-sighted rational people will not free-ride if they have no alternative group for the production of the collective good and if there is observability with sufficient sanctions. What about solidary behaviour in one-shot situations of need and sharing situations in general? The most far-reaching additions to rationality (in game theory) are being made for these kinds of situations in order to square solidary behaviour with far-sighted rationality. I just mention the introduction of emotions (Frank, 1988), fairness (Kahneman *et al.*, 1986), altruism (Margolis, 1982) and empathy (Binmore, 1994). All these additions are considered to be theoretically 'harmless' as long as they do not call into question far-sighted rationality. For example, after introducing empathy, Binmore quickly adds that 'this view can be defended without going outside the traditional optimizing paradigm of neoclassical economics' (ibid., p. 57). Still, the additions thus bring in solidarity in the form of sentiments and, once they are admitted, they might as well be applied to the other situations. This reintroduces a meaningful solidaristic language (like trust) into situations in which Williamson wanted to ban this language as being superfluous. The further elaboration of these theoretical efforts clearly pulls in the direction of specifying the conditions under which emotions, fairness and altruism operate, and we can expect a lot more research in this area.

All this would be very nice and an important lesson to sociologists were it not for the fact that there is overwhelming evidence that people are by and large not far-sighted maximizers. Rather, *people are mostly myopic* (see, for example, Loewenstein and Elster, 1992). There are probably various reasons for this, but in our context here one reason sticks out: the importance that goods have for an individual changes situationally, even if that individual had stable underlying preferences. The reason for this is that attention is necessarily selective, some goals are focal, others are pushed into the background. Unless the value of goods related to background goals is quite high or very vivid, their importance momentarily escapes our attention. For example, a student had an important exam on 10 January, and on 1 January he received an invitation to a party to be held on 4 January. He remained officially undecided but for himself he was sure he would not go to the party, in order not to lose valuable time for preparation for the exam. A good party lasts late into the night and wastes the following day. On 4 January in the afternoon, the situation looked different. Now, the party looked more desirable and he told himself that he could leave early so as not to waste the following day. He decided to go the party. At midnight, he decided to stay on for a little bit because, just at that time, the party began to be really fun. Finally, he went home at four-thirty, went to sleep and got up at one o'clock with a terrible headache and a feeling of low self-esteem.

Action plans are often reversed without change in underlying preferences. Learning from such experience is limited by the fact that the next action plans feel very secure. 'We always plan to be more farsighted in our future behavior than we are in the present' (Loewenstein, 1992, p. 30). In the following section, a process that can generate such myopic behaviour, called *framing*, will be described in more detail.

For solidarity, this has one very crucial consequence: people may breach agreements, although this is against their long-term interest. They may fail to fulfil obligations, although this is against their long-term interest. What threatens solidary behaviour most is *myopic opportunism*, the tendency to give in to short-term temptations at the expense of long-term advantages. In a way, this is also rational, but it renders credible commitments much more limited than Williamson and others are willing to assume, and reciprocity over time becomes a theoretical puzzle. A long shadow of the future may help to curb myopic opportunism (for example through reputation effects: see Ostrom, 1990; Raub and Weesie, 1990), but, contrary to what is assumed on the basis of far-sightedness, it will never eliminate non-cooperative behaviour.

As Durkheim described, there is danger to solidarity lurking from the outside of the group. But that danger does the biggest damage when it feeds on what is produced inside: myopic opportunism. In this light, it is not an exaggeration to say that the main reason solidarity is an important topic in its own right is that human beings are myopic.

Framing, Rules and Decay of Saliences

We are cognitively so limited that only some situational aspects will have our full attention while others only operate peripherally. This is called *framing* (see Lindenberg, 1993).[18] The focal aspects that capture the attention are related to the definition of the situation and the major goal in that situation. One defines a situation as a reaction to the action of others and part of that definition is the goal one will pursue in that situation, that is, the definition of the situation drives the selection of the major goal; or one sets the goal to be pursued beforehand and lets the goal drive the definition. For example, you desperately need money and go to your colleague Fritz and ask him for some. For you, the goal is getting money and, as you considered Fritz to be not just a colleague but also a friend, you define the (potential) situation as one in which a friend in need asks a friend for money. This goal-related definition mobilizes in you the expectation that Fritz will help if he can, because that is what a friend does, if indeed Fritz still considers himself your friend. In any case, it is your goal that drives your definition of the situation as you confront Fritz.[19]

For Fritz, by contrast, the definition drives the goal. He sees you asking for money and, screening and rejecting the possibility that the purpose is frivolous, comes to the conclusion that this situation is 'a friend in need'. This definition mobilizes the goal 'to help a friend in need' or, more precisely, 'to act appropriately given a friend is in need, observing the situational constraints'.[20]

With regard to the definition of the situation, this view is not much different from that advocated by Goffman (1974). What is different is the relation to rational choice theory, especially with regard to the structuring process, the evaluative process and the choice process. Maybe the easiest way to summarize what is going on is to say that individuals are generally intelligent about pursuing one goal in any given action situation but that other potential goals in that situation are pushed into the background and only affect the strength with which the focal goal (frame) guides structuring, evaluation and choice processes. Rationality is thus strongly bounded by the fact that the various goals are not equally taken into consideration.

Specifically, the situationally focal goal together with the definition of the situation will govern the mobilization of knowledge chunks and expectations, the screening of further information and the selection, evaluation and ordering of alternatives. Other goals in that situation do not vanish but affect the salience of the goal. Take the example above. Fritz defines the situation as 'a friend in need'. Thus other goals, such as 'not losing valuable resources (such as money, time or effort)', will be in the background. Money in Fritz's pocket is at that moment worth much less to him than if the focal goal had been 'not to lose valuable resources'. *This situationally variable marginal utility of goods is the crucial framing effect*. The strength of this situational effect of marginal utility depends on the weight of the focal goal relative to the background goals. If Fritz had just lost $100 before he encountered you, the goal 'not to lose valuable resources', though in the background, would be stronger and weigh more heavily on the salience of 'helping a friend in need'. This would translate itself in a higher probability for giving you less than you asked for. In the extreme, the background goal could become so strong that it displaces the focal goal. Imagine Fritz had already given you money two days in a row. In that case, the definition of the situation might be driven by the goal 'not to lose valuable resources' and Fritz might now see the situation as 'Ralph, the colleague, using friendship to get money out of me'.

We can now answer the question how opportunism, and *a fortiori* myopic opportunism, can be checked. The crucial point for checking opportunism is the fact that framing lowers opportunity costs of acting 'appropriately' according to some rule by pushing some aspects into the background. The important difference from the standard theory of rational behaviour is thus that the opportunity costs of, say, helping the friend are greatly reduced through the fact that the alternative uses for your money, your time and your effort pertain to the background goals and they affect the frame only indirectly through the salience. Potential temptations to deviate from the friendship norms on account of not wanting to spend the money or time or effort are thus considerably weakened and the ability to conform to rules is strengthened. In this sense one can say that there is no rational calculation of costs and benefits of norm conformity that includes both the frame and the background goals. On this point, traditional sociologists did have it right when they considered morality to be something that is outside the context of expediency. Still, the costs of deviance (sanctions from others for your not helping your friend) will increase the salience of the frame, and the costs of conformity (in terms of money, time and effort) will lower the salience. In the first case, the probability of conformity is pushed up, in the second, it is pushed down even though the costs were not directly taken into account. *Sanction thus does matter, even when expediency does not.*

The sociologist's dilemma described above can thus be solved by the theory of framing and solidarity frames in particular. The explanatory burden, then, is shifted to the question, what (de)stabilizes such a solidarity frame? Or, what amounts to the same thing: what (de)stabilizes the marginal utility of cooperation across situations? One answer has already been given: prominent short-term advantages can lower the salience of the frame to such an extent that it changes, leading to myopic opportunism. But there are still other dangers to the stability of a solidarity frame, such as frame decay and competition.

In many cases, the salience of the solidarity frame is the result of conflicting influences from the background, positive and negative ones. Let us say your frame is conformity to solidarity norms and you help a friend in need move. During your activity of putting books into boxes, you receive periodic encouraging approval from your friend as he comes by to see what you have achieved. This approval increases the salience of your frame. At the same time, the effort of putting the books in the box goes against the background goal to avoid effort, which lowers the salience. What will be the net effect?

When there are fairly high costs involved in executing solidary behaviour and when the situations are repetitive, we are likely to observe, *ceteris paribus*, a *decay* in the overall salience of the solidarity frame. The reason for this lies in the different timing of costs and rewards which are both related to the background but still act on the salience of the frame. In repetitive solidary behaviour, approval from others is likely to be much more intermittent than the costs made to execute the behaviour. The higher the costs are, the more this difference in timing will pull down the salience over time. If you keep helping, or you keep resisting lucrative outside offers, or you keep contributing to the common good, or you keep dividing resources fairly, then, at every single turn, you experience the cost of conforming to the solidarity expectations. When your behaviour accords with expectations, it does not attract special attention. Although there will be some positive feedback, it will be only on certain occasions while the costs are quite continuous, lowering the salience. This decay phenomenon is well documented for collective good contributions (see, for example, Andreoni, 1988).

It is also possible that the stability of the solidarity frame is endangered by *competition* or other conflicting interests internal to the group (see Ostrom, 1995). For example, positions in joint production may differ in attractiveness and members compete for these positions while cooperating with regard to the common goal. This competition may even help productivity in achieving the common goal, but then it may also interfere with cooperation (see Abell, 1996). Because competition is no inherent feature of sharing groups, I will only deal with it in passing (in the next section).

HOW SOLIDARITY GROUPS DEAL WITH PRECARIOUSNESS

The basic point here is that the cognitive limitation that creates myopic opportunism and decay also drives the solutions to these dangers. There is a strong resemblance between, on the one hand, Durkheim's theory of vitality and collective conscience and, on the other hand, the theory of framing, except that the latter also specifies myopic opportunism and decay of salience whereas the former does not. Collective conscience can be interpreted as consisting of normative frames (situational goals tied to the intelligent conformity to rules), and the high salience of a frame is equal to vitality in the sense that a high salience makes a person very sure about the 'right' course of action and sending all energies in the same direction.

With myopic opportunism and decay of salience as a threatening possibility, we can suspect virtually a universal interest among members of sharing groups in the stabilization of solidarity frames and in signals of that stability, that is, signals that convey the continued disposition to behave solidarily. Members are interested, not only in the stability of other people's frames, but also in the stability of their own frames, and this is due to the effect of *loss* on framing. There is a well-known preponderance of losses over gains (see Kahneman *et al.*, 1991). If a person experiences a loss, due, say, to uncooperative behaviour of another, then the fact that losses quickly produce strong emotional reactions makes it likely that, whatever frame a person is in, it will be replaced by a loss frame in which eradication of the loss is the focal goal. If nothing can be done to restore the loss, then 'getting even' would be one way, although not a productive one, to balance the loss. For example, Uzzi (1997, p. 59) in investigating inter-firm networks in the apparel industry found that 'if the strong assumptions of trust and cooperation are exploited in embedded ties, vendettas and endless feuds can arise'. Behaviour in loss frames is rational only in a very limited sense and it can be very destructive. Uzzi reports a CEO as saying, 'If you screw a guy like that [a close tie] he'll stay in business just long enough to get even' (ibid.). Members would like to avoid bringing another person into a loss frame when they have to confront the consequences. Thus they are interested in not 'slipping' into uncooperative behaviour via myopic opportunism and decay.[21] *They are interested in their own frame stability*. In this sense, there is nothing altruistic about solidary behaviour or, rather, altruism is beside the point.

Sharing groups must be seen as social processes in which solutions to problems of frame stabilization are evolving over time in a collective learning process. Results crystallize in rules which can be taught to newcomers (including children), can be changed, refined and adapted. But the substantive claim here is that this process will be driven by problems which all sharing groups have in common: getting people to cooperate in reaching the joint goal, sharing the joint costs and benefits and taking joint responsibility for the conditions of maintaining joint production/use. Because there is limited observability of behaviour and intentions, control and sanctions cannot solve problems that arise with regard to cooperation and sharing. Thus solidary behaviour will always cover cooperative behaviour and fair sharing. Because of joint responsibility in sharing groups, a situation which endangers a member's ability to contribute to the common goal is everybody's responsibility. Need situations are recognized as such in the group if they address themselves to this responsibility. Solidary behaviour will thus also always cover need situations (not just any kind of need). Because of myopic opportunism and decay of salience and because people's behaviour (and intentions) cannot be observed at all or not all the time, two extra problems arise universally in sharing groups: breach temptations and the ambiguity of mishaps. For this reason, solidarity will also always cover these two situations.

Thus, although concrete rules may differ in different groups, the underlying problems will be the same in all sharing groups, as will be the range of solutions which have to address simultaneously the five solidarity situations listed above.

The Stabilization of Frames

Because of the close resemblance of solidarity frames and collective conscience, I look to Durkheim first for a theory of the stabilization of frames. As mentioned above, he had shown that collective rituals have the ability to reinforce the collective conscience and thus rituals must also stabilize frames. But Durkheim had not considered the relation of functional interdependence to the stabilization of the collective conscience and, therefore, his rituals do not relate explicitly to sharing groups. For example, in an industrialized country, he recognized only a need for collective conscience of professions, not within and between organizations. Other work on rituals refers mainly to dyads (as, for example, Goffman's and Collin's work). Work done on intergroup relations (Sherif, 1966; Turner and Giles, 1981), on 'collective identity' in the social movement literature (for example, Pizzorno, 1978; Melucci, 1989) and on 'purposing' in organizations (see Vaill, 1986) may be more closely related to frame stabilization in sharing groups even if they do not analyse processes in these terms.

The most obvious and well recognized focus of a frame-stabilizing ritual in a sharing group is the identification of the group as group, making membership easily recognizable,[22] and the celebration of a common goal that is abstract enough to cover all joint lower-level goals. For this purpose, symbols and periodic collective face-to-face gatherings are necessary. But equally important is the link to the outside of the group. Groups gain unity, that is, the solidarity frames of their members gain stability, by defining themselves in relation to other groups and thereby increasing the salience of the solidarity frame. Remember, sustained cooperation is made possible by sustained low weights for its opportunity costs. The very point of framing was that a salient frame would greatly diminish the opportunity costs which are related to goals that have been pushed into the background of the frame.[23] How is this achieved?

The rites and rituals work directly on the salience of the frame by increasing the value of the focal goal, decreasing the value of conflicting background goals, increasing confidence in the efficacy of the joint effort and making members alert to possible dangers. Quite typically, the worthiness of the group goal is enhanced by its relation to the realization of a still higher goal (the sharing group as unit being part of a larger sharing group). The group's ability to achieve the worthy goal is brought into relief by its relative superiority to other groups. The insignificance of internal divisions (that is, the importance of not letting background goals become unduly important) is stressed by a collective definition of the dangers to cooperation, especially those stemming from certain other groups. Because of the decay of salience, these relations to other groups must be reflected in the daily activities of the group itself. This last point will be discussed again below when I talk about relational signals.

The *minimum number of groups* needed for the stabilization of a solidarity frame within a group is thus three if the groups of points two and three are identical, and four otherwise. This contrasts sharply with Durkheim's theory which would predict that a highly cohesive group does best without any other group in its environment.

Another instrument for the stabilization of frames in sharing groups is purely internal. It consists of rules which govern the way the negative sides of joint production or use (the negative externalities) are dealt with. These externalities frustrate either the joint production or the individual use. In either case, they create dissatisfaction with the cooperative arrangement and lower the salience of the solidarity frame.

There are mainly three kinds of *externality rules*: those dealing with identification of sources of disturbance, those dealing with the recognition of externalities and those dealing with the size of externalities. Take an example regarding the first kind of rule. If my cattle grazes on your land, did I not watch my cattle or did you fail to fence your field? Clearly, if this question is unsettled, there will be escalation of conflict rather than amelioration. The classical question of tort already posed by Coase (1960) belongs here. Rules identifying the source of disturbance greatly reduce agreement costs on this point and thereby make it possible to deal with negative externalities more efficiently.[24]

Rules concerning the recognition of negative externalities are exemplified by the adage 'fish and guests stink after three days'. It conveys to those who might not know that one can easily overstay one's welcome. Sometimes this is also expressed in terms of putting yourself in the shoes of the other, or, even more general, as the golden rule. Of course, recognizing potential negative externalities before they have occurred greatly enhances the likelihood that their effects and thus their negative influence on framing are small.

For making up in mishap situations, there must be rules that roughly *measure the amount of damage* that arises from externalities. These rules will also be needed for control measures if making up did not work (see below).

Here much collective learning is likely to take place before there are informal estimates of externalities which represent the damage to the joint effort. The reason for this is that framing makes either for individual underestimation of damage (if it is in the background) or for an individual overestimation (if a person is in a loss frame). Leadership (or what may be called wisdom) is likely to play an important role in arriving at equivalences over time when there cannot be a market price for externalities.

Relational Signals

Because reliable cooperation depends on a solidarity frame and because this frame is precarious, individuals in a sharing group all have an interest in seeing whether the others still have a solidarity frame and in showing to others that they still have a solidarity frame. This is to say that the precariousness of framing engenders a process of mutual signalling with regard to solidarity frames. This process has been called relational signalling.[25]

There is indeed much monitoring going on in solidary groups but it is a different kind of monitoring from the one assumed in the dependency/control theories.

What kinds of signals are being used? Goffman had aptly observed that when signals are important in interaction they tend to include prominently what he called 'expressions given off' (Goffman, 1959, pp. 2f). These are expressions which are seemingly involuntary (like blushing). They are less open to manipulation and therefore are used to interpret the signals that are purposefully given by the interaction partner. Frank (1988) made use of these signals in order to show that emotions have an important role within rational behaviour for creating credible commitments.[26]

Most ordinary everyday behaviour acquires relational signal functions, including solidary behaviour. For example, if the very first offer in bargaining is very low, this may be useful in getting a low price, but it is also likely to be interpreted as a quick sign of lack of interest in the relationship. The offer you make in another context may signal right away your relational interest because you offer a 'fair share'.[27] People judge not only the outcome but also the intention. A bad outcome may become more acceptable if it does not also signal relational lack of interest. A good outcome may be worth much less if it is known that the intended outcome was much worse. There is also experimental evidence for these effects. For example, Kramer *et al.*, (1995) showed that, in an experimental situation, people were very willing to accept a highly unequal offer when they knew that the intended offer was equal and that 'bad luck' had made the offer unequal. Conversely, many people were dissatisfied with an equal offer when they knew that the intended offer was highly unequal. Results in exchanges in which relational concerns matter are thus *judged simultaneously both for outcome and for the relational signal.* Any theory that negates this double judgment (as often happens in game theory) will be seriously off the mark in explaining cooperation.

This argument also tells us why people would signal their 'real' intention in *mishap situations*. If you meant to display solidary behaviour but for some reason you did not succeed, it is important that you avoid the impression that you are not interested in the relationship between you and the others. You will go to the trouble of sending a relational mishap signal.

Self-signalling

Because, as Goffman suggested, purposeful relational signals are likely to be judged against the background of more or less involuntary signals, people learn about the importance of such signals and how to handle them. Duplicity will very likely be betrayed by involuntary signals. For this reason, people will tend to avoid a situation in which they signal relational interest to Alter while they interpret their action as relational lack of interest about Alter. In that case, the action would inform the actor that he or she is somebody who deceives another person who considers himself a friend. Such discrepancy will in many cases show up in the involuntary signals, in pitch or tremble of voice, things said or forgotten to notice and so on.

Keeping the signals to Alter and to yourself compatible has a crucial consequence in the way you treat situations with asymmetric information. For example, Ligthart (1995) could show that, when Alter was Ego's friend (in a scenario experiment), he would offer Ego a fair share even if Ego had no way of knowing whether what Alter offered was indeed a fair share. Thus, for solidarity relations (including acquaintances), the standard neoclassical assumption that asymmetric information would be exploited does not generally hold.[28] Only if the criteria for solidary behaviour are ambiguous will the individual choose the one more compatible with self-interest (see De Vries, 1991). Of course, as stakes get higher, the goal in the background (to increase your wealth) will increasingly lower the salience of the solidarity frame, lower the probability of cooperation to the vicinity of 0.5 and then abruptly switch to a different frame (in our example: to increasing your wealth) with a very small probability of cooperative behaviour. If we were to include framing in general and self-signalling behaviour in particular in game theory, we would end up with very different experimental designs for behaviour in non-cooperative games, even one-shot games among people who are likely to perceive each other as belonging to some common sharing group.

People who have no relational concern can and probably will try to exploit relational signalling. This was found to be the case by Murnighan and Pillutla (1995). For example, subjects strategically created the impression of fairness. People can also create consonance between the signals by lying to themselves (see Goleman, 1985). Frank (1988, p. 131) suggested that, if there are too many people who can lie to themselves, cooperative behaviour will grind to a halt. However, the strategic creation of solidary ties, say through relational signals such as inviting business partners to dinner, inquiring about their family and so on, will work only under exceptional circumstances as an asymmetric relationship in which Ego simply exploits Alter's solidary behaviour. The reason for this is that the very situations that are meant to rope in Alter also tend to rope in Ego, even if Ego lies to himself. Ego will fall into his own trap because of the way framing works: it pushes certain goals into the background and that can happen to the manipulator just as much as to the manipulated, especially if the manipulator tries to avoid giving off signals that would expose his plan. A confidence man must have considerable framing skills to avoid this trap.

The most powerful relational signals are those which (a) combine the signal with a direct contribution to the joint production and/or use, (b) are expensive to fake, and (c) cover the major ex ante and ex post problems of (re)alignment, as for example in rule change and the interpretation of ambiguous information.

These signals relate to the solidary behaviour in the five situations described above. In all five cases (need situations, common good situations, breach temptations, sharing situations and mishap situations), sending the signal contributes at the same time to the cooperative effort and is costly to the sender. In ex ante situations of making sharing agreements, the behaviour relating to need, common good, and sharing aspects signals the spirit within which the agreements are made. Once the agreements are in place, each one of these situations will come up post hoc again and again as agreements or even joint products need to be adjusted and incomplete agreements made to apply to unforeseen situations. There will also be various occasions to breach the agreement and even to breach the cooperative spirit about incomplete or lacking agreements, and each one offers the opportunity to signal cooperativeness (including making a plausible case for exceptions in a need or a mishap situation). 'Good standing' in a sharing group refers to the history of a member's relational signalling. Members in good standing will be given the benefit of the doubt in mishap situations. By the same token, it is clear that the range of solidary behaviour is always the full five situations. It is not possible to be extra solidary in one situation and little or not at all solidary in another. This is solely due to the fact that lack of solidary behaviour in one situation signals to the other members that in all likelihood the conforming behaviour was strategic rather than really solidary (really within a solidary frame). A 'dear Abby' letter to a newspaper illustrates this point.[29]

> *Dear Abby*. After nearly 20 years of marriage, my husband has asked me for a divorce. . . . Two years ago, in the middle of a heated argument I told my husband that his love-making did nothing for me – that I had only been putting on an act.

> Abby, it wasn't exactly the truth. I only said it to hurt him. He hasn't touched me or kissed me since that day. I would do anything to have my husband back the way he was.

In short, because of myopic opportunism and decay, relational signalling will be concentrated around these five situations and lack of positive signals in any one of these situations occasions a reinterpretation of behaviour in the others. For example, as an illustration of the five situations, we can take an inter-firm network such as the one described by Uzzi (1997) for the better dress sector of the apparel industry in New York. Uzzi makes a distinction between 'arm's-length ties' (market relationships) and 'embedded ties' (close or special relationships). The apparel industry contains simultaneously market and embedded relations, the former being a majority, the latter being the relations of special importance. Individuals (contractors, manufacturers, production managers and so on) would behave blatantly with self-interest in the market and cooperatively in the embedded relationships. The latter developed over a long time and showed typically solidary behaviour in the five situations. The profitability for each was seen as a *common good*. 'We are all in the same boat,' Uzzi reports a contractor as saying. Uzzi found that extra effort was voluntarily given and reciprocated, there was joint problem solving, much communication and a very quick understanding of what adjustments had to be made.

Signalling in *sharing situations* was also part of the routine interaction. Uzzi found a belief among partners of embedded ties that the other would not act in self-interest at another's expense; this showed up in concrete action such as resource pooling among partners and, when transactions had to be done fast, post hoc pricing. As one CEO put it, 'we do first and fix price after'; or another CEO would say 'the contractors know that they will not lose'. Help in *need situations* was taken for granted: 'If there was a problem you knew you'd work it out and they'd help you,' said a manufacturer of 30 years' experience. A production manager even reports creating work for the contracting partners when there is a lull in the market. 'We will put a dress into work to keep the contractor going. We'll then store the dress in the warehouse.' By contrast, in arm's-length relationships the other would 'push the price down when the contractor tells his production problems'.

Restraint vis-à-vis *breach temptations* was very evident in Uzzi's study. He reports that there is non-defection where defection clearly would serve the self-interest of a business partner. But then, there is also a watchful eye. Too frequent need situations are under suspicion of being covert breaches, putting the partner on the alert. Clear breaches are not forgiven. 'If he switches to a new contractor then I won't work with that manufacturer again.' This is in contrast to *mishap situations*. A manufacturer expressed it thus: 'When you deal with a guy you don't have a close relationship with, it can be a big problem. Things go wrong and there's no telling what will happen. With my guys [his key contractors], if something goes wrong, I know we'll be able to work it out.' One partner also warns the other about expected problems so the other can adjust in time. A production manager explains: 'I tell them [key contractors] that in two weeks I won't have much work. You better start to find other work.'

If the five solidarity situations come up routinely in the course of the daily activities of joint production and/or use, and if they are within the range of legitimate solidarity costs for Ego, then more and clearer signalling will be possible than if they happen rarely. For example, if there are regularly need situations which hit all members (but at different times) such that the other members can show their ability and willingness to help, the solidarity frame is more often reinforced and monitored, leading to a higher probability that the solidary behaviour will be continued in the future. This deviates from the view that a solidary group does best if there are no problems. What makes some teams so solidary is exactly this combination of daily activities of joint production and the opportunity to signal cooperativeness. Regularly recurring minor crises and uncertain environments of the sharing group serve the same purpose and can at times even be manipulated by group leaders to this end. In this sense, frame stability should not be confused with stability of the circumstances of cooperation. On the other hand, even though the range of legitimate solidarity costs may increase in crisis situations, the need may be too high, the mishaps too often, the breach temptations too large, the windfall gains or unexpected joint losses too large to be handled by the signalling rules. I will come back to this point when talking about weak solidarity below.

Competition

There is a possibility that competition furnishes regular occasions for strong relational signalling and as such may even be beneficial for the stabilization of a solidarity frame. As mentioned above, Abell (1996) has recently suggested a model in which a productive balance between cooperation and competition could be achieved through the development of a team spirit which involves generalized reciprocity (the willingness to do something for someone in the expectation of getting something back *from somebody* at some other time). The problem is that, for this to function, solidarity costs (the costs one is expected to incur in the five solidarity situations) must be quite high or the attractiveness of the prize for which one competes quite low. This may restrict the possibility of such a team spirit to situations of strong solidarity (see below) which in turn creates problems of cooperation with other groups. Abell had not considered this problem. It is more likely that competition and cooperation have to be governed by very clear relational signals. If that is possible, they can be combined; if not, they will constantly disturb each other. Arrangements for clear relational signals in such situations prominently include solutions to the question who can legitimately exert social control (see below).

Auxiliary rules

The bulk of the rules concerning relational signals will be pegged to the five situations. However, there must be accompanying rules that fine-tune relational signalling to the specific context. One may call these *auxiliary solidarity rules*. There must be some rules of a social grammar, specifying what range of actions is considered to be a relational signal for certain classes of situations. For example, in many situations, relational signals allow quite a range of personal variance, as long as the signal is clear and unambiguous. If Fritz's cow eats Ralph's flowers, Fritz can help Ralph replant or bring him a present or help him dig a ditch around the flower bed. Paying money in mishap situations is often outside the range. 'Shasta County landowners regard a monetary settlement as an arms'-length transaction that symbolizes an unneighborly relationship,' says Ellickson (1991, p. 61) in his landmark study of order without law. The reason for this is probably that, unless the payment is very generous, it would symbolize a market transaction that leaves out all the costs of inconvenience, and thus be considered too little; and if it is very generous, it creates reverse indebtedness, symbolically also confusing the roles of the situation about who should feel sorry.

There are situations where signalling behaviour would always be ambiguous unless there were clear conventions without much personal variance. For example, when people share small living quarters, it is quite important that the joint living room is relatively free to move about in. What is the cooperative thing to do when one of the group members has a guest (which inevitably causes negative externalities)? Should everybody join in, or should he take him upstairs, or should he sit in a corner and whisper? No matter what he does, he might be giving the wrong signal. In such a case it is in his and everybody else's interest in a group that shares living quarters to agree on a preferred way of dealing with guests.

The more important it is that people act solidarily, that is, the more there is being shared in the group, the more likely that there will be additional rules about the importance of having and showing a cooperative attitude (signals), of keeping promises and of sticking to rules. Above these, there are likely to be common values that stress the importance of common goals. These are the social norms and values in the traditional sense. They function here as *meta rules*. Notice, however, that these norms and values are built on sharing rules and rules for relational signalling, not the other way around. As I will stress later on, if the productive context that brings about sharing changes, so will norms and values.

Sharing rules, relational signal rules, norms and values: all these point to a common culture that creates the grammar for relational signalling. This culture is also important for providing events, symbols and activities for the maintenance of frames. In this point, the framing approach to solidarity is very much in accordance with Durkheim's view of embeddedness. However, we can predict important features of this common culture because its generation over time is subject to recognizable and recurring problems which emerge from contexts of joint production and use in the face of myopic opportunism and decay. This cultural aspect of solidarity is another indication that it is only of very limited use to look at solidarity as a phenomenon between dyads or within single groups. I will come back to this point time and again in this chapter.

Social Control

As mentioned above, sharing groups create internally a regulatory interest in every member because of the externalities. Thus, when things go wrong and they are not solved by mishap signals, the regulatory interest will turn into an interest of exercising social control. It should be clear by now that social control, like any behaviour inside the group, will be subject to constraints set by relational signalling.

If Fritz takes Ralph to court, Fritz signals that he has no particular relational interest (any more). Ellickson (1991) in his study of Shasta County found this very much to be true: 'Being good neighbors means no lawsuits' (ibid., p. 251). Litigation is only expected for parties 'who lack the prospect of a continuing relationship' (ibid., p. 274). There is likely to be a control hierarchy in which the more severe means progressively indicate lack of relational interest (see Ellickson, 1991; Lindenberg, 1994).

At first the deviant will be informed that the act had been discovered, giving him a chance to take remedial steps and explain why the mishap signal had not been given or in which way it could be made more believable. If this does not help, negative gossip may be circulated about the uncooperative member. If this still does not help, the member may be shunned. Then physical intervention may be the appropriate fourth step. If this is still not enough, third parties (organizations or the law) and/or forced exit may be brought in.

Relational signalling thus governs the kind and calibration of social control efforts. It also influences *who does the controlling*. Whenever social control cannot be unambiguously distinguished from a negative relational signal between A and B, control is likely to be indirect and it will be exercised by somebody for whom control is not associated with a negative relational signal. For example, colleagues in a law firm earn joint income. They will of course also exert negative externalities on each other and even be in competition for positions in the firm. Say that the slowness with which partner Fritz works on a case interferes with a case of partner Ralph. What will Ralph do? Because the legal work is very complex and it is difficult to prove lack of effort or even uncooperative intentions, there are few if any clear-cut cases. Ralph is convinced that Fritz is not pulling his weight, but he is in a bad position to complain to Fritz because in such a complex situation complaining by a direct colleague is ambiguous: it may be legitimate or a strategic effort to get Fritz to earn more for the joint pot so Ralph might put in less effort or even an attempt to get ahead of Fritz (both negative relational signals). In a situation like that, the control efforts would in the longer run cease to be direct and run instead via persons in the firm who have a neutral position, so that their control could not be interpreted as a negative relational signal, and/or via persons who earn so much for the firm that their control efforts would be beyond strategic suspicion (see Lazega, 1995, for a case in point).

The substantive claim is thus that the clarity of relational signals will strongly influence all other arrangements in sharing groups, including social control.[30]

STRONG AND WEAK SOLIDARITY

The biggest difference in the way solidarity functions in a society depends on whether solidarity is weak or strong. While there are gradations within these categories, they are qualitatively quite different.[31] Let us first look at weak solidarity.

Weak Solidarity

Take a sharing group that has been around for enough time to have had the chance for individual and collective learning in terms of knowledge necessary for the sharing arrangements and in terms of the formation of rules. When the members of this sharing group are also members of various other sharing groups and the value to an individual of the good(s) jointly produced or used in this particular sharing group is low relative to the total value (to that individual) produced in all sharing groups in which the individual participates, then solidarity will be weak in the sense that the solidarity costs are relatively low and in the sense that the sharing group as group will influence but not dominate the framing of the individual. Examples of such weak solidarity groups are colleagues in a university department, an inter-firm network, a tennis club and people sharing neighbourhood space.[32] For *need*, *common good* and *mishap* situations, this means that the amount of money, time or effort Ego may legitimately be expected to sacrifice for others is quite limited.

In addition, the standards of evidence required for indicating need and for legitimate mishaps are also relatively easy to meet.

For *breach temptations*, solidarity costs will always be much higher than for the other situations because the regulation of these temptations is the basis for cooperative arrangements of the joint production or use. Still there are limits here, too, which play an important role in the mutual expectations concerning breach and, as I will discuss below, concerning the safeguards used against breach.

For *sharing situations* there is a special feature of weak solidarity that is very different from strong solidarity. In a weak solidarity situation, the group as group is not strong enough to override differences in investment in the joint production or use. A *fair share* in weak solidarity will thus be linked to the size of the input (equity). The group is not strong enough to suppress 'gain' as a focal goal. One can do business in a weakly solidary group, one can make a profit from the other members of the group, one can become richer or acquire more status than the others in the group, given that input to the joint production or use can be measured, that this gain is related to differences in input and that it is accompanied by solidary behaviour. From a framing point of view, it is most easily modelled as a seesaw balance between two goals which keep replacing each other as frame: gain and solidarity. Imagine a person is in a solidarity frame. There are solidarity costs attached to solidary behaviour. As the costs of being cooperative go up (that is, as personal gain goes down as a result of solidary behaviour) the salience of the solidarity frame will drop to a level where gain abruptly becomes the new frame. As the costs of increasing one's gain go up (as cooperative behaviour decreases owing to the pursuit of personal gain), the salience of the gain frame will drop to a level where the cooperation will abruptly become the new frame, and so on.

Because equity (rather than equality) is the basis for fairness in weakly solidary groups, solidarity will suffer less in such groups on the basis of a *division of labour* for the joint production than strongly solidary groups (see below). Division of labour introduces differences in input and, unless these differences are legitimate, they will not be linked to output and thus will have no motivational basis for being sustained as a group-related activity. Authority in such groups must be legitimized in terms of the contribution to the common goal, and status differences are likely to develop on this basis (see Ridgeway and Walker, 1995). But it is clear that such an authority structure can only function if solidary behaviour is maintained even across hierarchical levels. The reason is not one of human relations per se and of being nice to one another, but of dealing with the precariousness of cooperation due to myopic opportunism and decay of the salience of a frame that ensures the motivation and flexible adjustments necessary for the joint production.

We come now to the *embedding of solidarity*. Because the group does not have a strong grasp on the framing of the individual, the range within which it can contain myopic opportunism and decay of the salience of the solidarity frame is also narrow. For some sharing groups of weak solidarity, this will not do because the curtailment of breach temptation is too important for its functioning and they have to be confident of a broader range within which breaches are unlikely to occur. In general, this will involve sharing groups in which economic transactions play an important role. The solution in these cases is to use other means than framing to reduce myopic opportunism, so that the temptation that is left is small enough to be governed by solidarity frames. Such means lower the real pay-off for non-cooperative behaviour, not just the perceived pay-off through framing. Standard examples of such means are reputation, selection, credible commitment devices and legal instruments (see Williamson, 1993; Raub and Weesie, 1996).

For this embedding to function, certain preconditions must be met. There is *reputation*, in the sense of a good standing in the sharing group. This has everything to do with relational signalling and internal exchange of information. However, reputation effects in a wider circle will not work unless the environment of the sharing group (a) has some incentive to pass on negative and positive information, and (b) shares the standards of judging misconduct. For example, Uzzi (1997, p. 55) relates that in the apparel industry in New York 'generalized reputations are surprisingly weak control devices'. In this case, the market is large enough for firms to escape bad reputations and – this is the important point here – positive information is hoarded and shared only very selectively in order to keep down the competition. Thus, in this inter-firm network, the reputational effects are mainly restricted to privileged expansions of the sharing group via 'go-betweens' who transfer 'the expectations and opportunities of an existing embedded social structure to a newly formed one' (ibid., p. 48). These three forms of reputation effects are often not distinguished in the literature.

Related to the last two forms of reputation effects is *selection* as an instrument for flanking solidarity. For selection to work, it is not necessary to assume that there are stable personality traits in terms of virtues (such as trustworthiness). Selection is more likely to work on aspects which indicate greater ease for the stabilization of a solidarity frame, akin to the way Spence (1974) has looked at education as a signal in the selection process on the labour market. This ease may come from various sources. For example, a person who has talents and attitudes which fit well into the arrangements of joint production of the group would acquire more (less) social and self-(dis)approval in the group than a person without such talents or attitudes. As a result, outside opportunities would be smaller by comparison and the person would have less decay in the solidarity frame, offering less of a chance to myopic opportunism. Other aspects may indicate the alternative sharing groups a person has due to easily identifiable and stable characteristics, such as ethnic or racial characteristics. The fewer alternative sharing groups somebody has, the smaller the chance of myopic opportunism.

Credible commitments within the sharing group depend on the nature of the joint production or use. For example, two firms in an inter-firm network may jointly pay for a machine which creates a hostage for each. In addition, credible commitments depend on differences in the (market) power of members. As Gál (1997) has shown, it is the strong party that will have to show credible commitments rather than the weak one because the weak partner has more to lose by defecting and is thus more reliable. If the judicial system works in such a way that its verdicts cannot be predicted on the basis of non-juridical characteristics (such as the relative market power of a contractual partner) and if the standards of evidence are in principle tied to those of science, then general *laws and regulations* can reduce myopic opportunism and dyadic relationships can be embedded in explicit contracts, even if they are necessarily incomplete. For example, Blumberg (1997) finds that network embedding is no substitute for contracts. Even if these contracts are never used, the very possibility that they could be used and tie up both parties in costly litigation serves to reduce myopic opportunism on the level of the sharing group. The dyadic nature of these contracts should not distract from the fact that long-term relations are in all likelihood part of a larger sharing group or groups and the contracts are likely to refer explicitly or implicitly to practices and standards of that sharing group or collection of sharing groups.

The point I am trying to make is that, even if we concentrate on long-term relations, it seems wrong to assume that the various means for the reduction of myopic opportunism must be substitutes. Often they are complements. Either the stakes are low enough to allow a narrow range of protection against breach temptations, so that weak solidarity (with its own informal means) will be sufficient and the alternative use of non-solidary means would be counterproductive because of their lower flexibility post hoc, or the stakes are too high for weak solidarity to handle alone, so that non-solidary means are used to reduce the myopic opportunism enough for solidarity to do the rest. There is then nothing that can replace weak solidarity as a means of making long-term cooperative relationships possible, both in ex ante arrangements and in ex post adaptations. However, when stakes are high, other means must flank weak solidarity; the weaker the solidarity, the more help from other means there must be, and only in this sense is there substitutability. For example, Blumberg (1997) found for inter-firm R&D cooperations that good experience with the same partner in the past led to less formal flanking of the cooperation.[33]

The fact that the flanking of solidarity is often not used is no sign that it is not necessary. As I elaborated above, social control is itself restricted by relational signalling. For this reason, escalation is stepwise and there is always the danger that it will rip the relational fabric as it approaches litigation. Hostages and the courts are thus actually invoked only when the relationship has already failed.

Strong Solidarity

The more sharing groups overlap, the stronger the hold of the group over the individual member. Imagine that a group of farmers share, not just a piece of equipment, but also neighbourhood space, defence against destructive wild animals, ditches against flooding, construction of houses and barns, the risks of bad harvest and of bad health, child socialization and a way of life. Such a group is strongly solidary. In such groups, it is likely that one of the goods that is being jointly produced is shared risk (such as risk of bad health). This risk sharing will greatly increase the legitimate sacrifice in times of need which will *look like* strongly altruistic behaviour. However, there is no need to make an assumption about altruistic behaviour here. In fact, the theory proposed would definitely argue against the interpretation of helping behaviour in terms of altruism because that would imply stable preference for helping rather than the influence of situational factors (that is, sharing arrangements).

Since by assumption there are no superior alternative ways of production for any of these goods, it is very important for the group members that there be no deviation from the sharing rules. Frame stability is thus itself an important joint product and the tolerance for individual variance will be low.

In comparison to weak solidarity, strong solidarity differs both quantitatively and qualitatively. The quantitative difference lies mainly in the solidarity costs. The amount of money, time and effort people are expected to sacrifice for helping others in need, for reaching the common good and so on is considerably higher than in weak solidarity. The qualitative difference is that there is no duality of frames (gain and solidarity) for group members, but only solidarity, so that a number of expectations are thoroughly different. From a normative point of view, the importance of the individual will be small in comparison to the importance of the group; this is so because the individual's non-conformist wishes would be so loss-producing for the others that the wishes themselves are deemed illegitimate. For this very reason, the basic expectation in strong solidarity is *equality* rather than equity. Difference between group members will be played down and all behaviour that increases these differences discouraged. Need is only legitimate if it is related to the joint responsibility to keep things going. Differences in investment in the joint production or use refer to the ability to contribute, but they are decoupled from the size of the share of the joint result. Authority differences in strongly solidary groups clash with the claim to equality even though they may be functionally necessary for the achievement of the common goal and even though people contribute differently. For this reason, authority differences in such groups can only be legitimated in two ways: symbol of the group or need. Thus there are two such roles: the representation of the whole group and somebody who is able to recognize need (and maybe help) better than others. Legitimate differences in the share of the joint results can only come from differences in legitimate need, and these differences may in turn arise from members' different ability to contribute to the joint production or use (say children versus adults, men versus women, and so on).

Because of the strength of the group, the range within which solidarity can deal with myopic opportunism without flanking arrangements is much larger than with weak solidarity. Indeed, the very wish for flanking arrangements (other than selection) for the reduction of opportunism can only be seen as a negative relational signal in a strongly solidary group. The downside of this strength is that its requirements for the purity of relational signals is very high. Relations to other groups and possibly conflicting loyalties are potential negative relational signals. For this reason, group boundaries will be strict.[34] Strong solidarity will thus automatically imply a possibility for unbridled opportunism between groups without the ability to engage in mutually advantageous exchanges within the group. Weber (1961, pp. 261f) saw this clearly when he described the contrast of the moral code towards the in-group ('Binnenmoral') and lack of any moral code towards the outgroup ('Aussenmoral'). Profitable economic relationships could not grow on the basis of strong solidarity and all the talk about embedding and the importance of trust, cooperation and solidarity for capitalism should make a clear distinction between strong and weak solidarity and pay attention to the different conditions under which they occur (see Lindenberg, 1988).

When the flanking arrangements for weak solidarity become endangered, say because the state apparatus is falling apart, as happened towards the end of the former Soviet Union or Yugoslavia, the range that could be handled by weak solidarity without the flanking is too narrow to support the existing arrangements. If there is no quick flanking alternative, individuals will gravitate to stronger sharing groups, attempting to concentrate joint production and use of as many goods as possible in one strong sharing group. Given the importance of clear group boundaries for strong solidarity, the dimensions that offer themselves for forming the nucleus of strong sharing groups in such situations of weakening flaking arrangements have to answer three criteria: (a) it should be possible to say with a high degree of certainty who belongs and who does not, (b) it should be a criterion that cannot easily be manipulated; (c) it should be a criterion that is assumed to have worked for strong solidarity in the past.

The first criterion puts an extra premium on selection and symbols of identity. Ethnicity and practised religion are often the criteria that answer all three requirements, helped by sharing group entrepreneurs who have their own goals in the process (see Hardin, 1995). In fact, these entrepreneurs are likely to use the frame-stabilizing techniques discussed above, except that becoming part of a larger sharing group is less likely when the strong solidarity comes about though failing support outside the group. In addition, a group that has many joint goals would gain frame stability if the goals were seen as interdependent. For these two reasons, a strongly solidary group is likely to turn to abstract unifying goals embedded in *ideology* and stress more strongly its own superiority to other groups. Because of the ideological embedding and of the importance of conformity (and therefore of meta rules), it looks like a strongly solidary group is (re)turning to fundamental values and clear norms. This is not without consequence for the size of a strongly solidary group. Whereas the importance of strong group boundaries favours a small size, the ideological support and also the talents needed inside the group to jointly produce many goods favour a large group. Although there might be a size that optimizes both (see Lindenberg, 1982), it is likely that such a group is subject to conflicting 'policies', expanding in order to increase ideological support and internal diversity of talents and then contracting again as the expansion endangers the purity of the group boundaries.

Thus, like weakly solidary groups, strongly solidary groups are likely to be locked onto other groups. However, the reasons for and the way of interlocking are very different.

From Strong to Weak Solidarity

On the basis of the arguments just given, strong solidarity is the result of the breakdown of weak solidarity when stakes are high and flanking arrangements fail. Then solidarity muffles distinctions within groups, and between groups unbridled opportunism reigns supreme. Of course, the development can also go the other way around, and that is closer to the traditional story told by sociologists: from *Gemeinschaft* to *Gesellschaft*, from mechanical to organic solidarity, from status to contract. However, the story told in the context of the arguments above would look different from these traditional accounts in some important aspects.

The major difference comes from the two pillars of the solidarity theory: the precariousness of solidarity and the productive context in which all solidarity arises. All forces that change production and use patterns are likely to affect solidarity. When a good is offered via the market or the state, sharing groups which formerly produced it for themselves are likely to turn to the market or the state if the price is lower for these new alternatives (which it often is). For example, when health insurance is offered via market or state, health risks will soon no longer be shared in community-like arrangements. In addition, when individual or family income goes up on a wide scale (as it would in consequence of the changes in production), sharing groups for joint consumption will become smaller and smaller, with fewer joint goods per group. For example, as farmers who share a combine and health risks become richer, they purchase health insurance and split into smaller combine sharing groups, eventually each owning his own combine. The reason for this is that sharing creates negative externalities which are mitigated more effectively by making the sharing group smaller than by regulating the externalities in the larger group.

At the same time, some sharing groups will grow into large, anonymous associations with no face-to-face interaction and little or no solidarity. For example, sharing group entrepreneurs sell shares in a sharing group on the market, such as mutual insurance companies.[35] In short, increasing production by market and state and increasing income will create less sharing in production and use. What does this mean for solidarity? Clearly, where there was strong solidarity, it will diminish and individualism in the midst of large producing or sharing units will develop. Coleman (1982) called this 'the asymmetric society'. As conformity becomes less important to each group, the solidarity costs will turn towards zero, social control will greatly diminish and rules, including social norms and values, will feel vague. Note that there may have also been weak solidarity before and that even weak solidarity will be affected by this development. There is no movement from strong to weak solidarity here, but from solidarity strong or weak to (atomistic) individualism with arm's-length relationships and opportunism. But the important point is that this is only half of the story.

There are goods which cannot be produced by the market or the state and which are still vital for individuals. These goods prominently include a sense of purpose, of being important, of being appreciated, and a sense of stability in acting, thinking and expecting. These goods have been by-products of functioning sharing groups in which the jointness of production and use created the foil for purpose, and the frame-stabilizing mechanisms of group identity, symbols, rituals, comparisons and external flanking created a sense of cognitive and motivational stability. In fact the 'sense of belonging' which makes group membership so attractive is likely to be the result not just of help in need but also of these by-products of functioning sharing groups.

In addition, during this phase of atomistic individualism, it turns out that the more complex the production for the market and by the state, the less it can function adequately without solidarity in face-to-face groups. The reason for this has already been mentioned above: the need for networks of patterned long-term relationships which, in turn, necessitate ex ante and ex post solidary behaviour for quick coordination and flexible adjustments. Technological changes strengthen this need for flexibility and thus the need for weak solidarity (see Piore and Sabel, 1984).

There are, then, two developments, where the second is not simply the complement of the first. First there is a change in production and use. This brings individualism and large production and sharing units with arm's-length relationships among them. The second development deals with the changes brought about by the first. Above all, what used to be by-products of sharing groups must now be purposefully produced. In part, this will lead to changes in the role of work and home (with pressure for work as a provider of meaningful activity and importance especially for women, and home *ownership* providing a sense of stability and meaningful activity) and an increase in purely social sharing groups (hobbies, vacations and sports with others). And what seemed like a new order with arm's length relations and individualism (*Gesellschaft*) in business develops new forms of solidarity. It is in these two contexts that weak solidarity appears on a grand scale in modern societies and where lapses of weak solidarity produce episodes both of strong solidarity (say in ethnic groups) and of atomistic individualism.

There is still an important addition to this story. We know by now that weak solidarity needs to be flanked when stakes are high. That means that there is a crucial role for the state to aid that flanking by offering instruments for credible commitments and legal arrangements with the right criteria for evidence in courts and arbitration. But this is not enough. The state must also stand for a policy that reduces the chance for the development of strong solidarity. This is to say that the state must help prevent a failure of weak solidarity. Weak solidarity will only function if strong solidarity is kept in check. For example, great social inequalities in income, political rights, labour market chances and so on are likely to create subgroups of strong solidarity, first among the permanent minorities who have to fend for themselves by whatever means they have (including violence) and then among the better-off who have to fend for themselves against the permanent minorities.

Blatantly strategic behaviour by the state vis-à-vis citizens will encourage atomistic individualism. It is part of the standard wisdom in the social sciences that, in order to function, the state and its laws should have legitimacy. In this context, gaining legitimacy means that the state has to see to it that society as a whole is also seen as a sharing group with weak solidarity (turning to strong solidarity in times of disaster and external threat). Although society is so large that, as a group, it does not allow face-to-face interaction, it is present in all public and official face-to-face interactions and it contains nested sharing groups such as provinces and communities. Legitimacy of the state translates directly into the use of relational signals in public and official face-to-face interactions. For example, there are many breach temptations regarding taxes, public assistance and so on. Monitoring and legal measures by the state will reduce but not eliminate these breach temptations, so that some solidarity will always be needed to achieve conformity to the laws that concern common goods, sharing situations and help for the needy. Can Ralph brag to his friends about having cheated in getting payments from the state meant for the needy? Will Ralph be susceptible to the opinion expressed in a debate among his colleagues about the importance of going against the misuse of public assistance money? Will Ralph support an initiative to reduce public assistance to the needy in favour of an increase of unemployment benefits for his own occupational group?

The state clearly has to fight the view that society is a strongly solidary group (except in emergencies) because otherwise the solidarity costs would be too high, the breach temptations too great, or the ideological and selective needs for the suppression of individualism too severe. However, there is still a burden of relational signalling to be carried by the state. All signs of strategic action by the state vis-à-vis the citizen, and all signs of corruption involving public money, will send negative relational signals from the state to the citizen, lowering the salience of the solidarity frame and increasing the citizen's willingness to cheat. There has been no cost accounting on this point so far, but it stands to reason that negative relational signals by the state are very costly in terms of reduced tax income, waste of public assistance money, costs of increased monitoring and so on. The important point for weak solidarity in general, however, is not the individual free ride on taxes and public programmes, but the impact that legitimacy has on the workings of flanking support for private sharing groups. This support consists of adequate legal instruments, of generating adequate political support for measures that keep strong solidarity at bay, and of providing planning stability for long-term relations, creating a general atmosphere of gain from cooperativeness. In short, solidarity and its forms have everything to do with the state because it needs the state's flanking support to enlarge the range within which myopic opportunism can be held at bay by solidarity on the lowest level.

SUMMARY AND CONCLUSION

There is no topic that has captured the sociological imagination more than solidarity. Society would fall apart without it. Despite this prominent position of solidarity, there has been surprisingly little attention given to the question what kind of behaviur constitutes solidarity. Maybe as a result of this lack of behavioural anchorage of theories of solidarity, it is also not clear at all under what conditions solidarity is supposed to arise and why. Worse, there is no theory of the precariousness of solidarity and consequently also no theory of the solutions to this precariousness. Rational choice theories of solidarity and the related social capital theories have not got much further on these points.

In this chapter, I have attempted to show these gaps and then to close them as best I can. Even though the story is complex, the most important points can be summarized quite succinctly. Solidarity comprises a definite set of behaviours; it arises in situations where groups attempt to reach common goals; and it is always precarious but cannot be replaced by something else. Because it is precarious, it needs mechanisms that support it and they always involve other groups and, in modern societies, also the state. The study of solidarity of dyads and even of single groups is therefore only of very limited usefulness.

More specifically, this chapter makes the following points. Solidarity is defined in terms of *behaviour* that involves a certain sacrifice for the actor in five problematic situations: contribution to common good situations, sharing joint costs and benefits, help in need, resisting breach temptations and making up in mishap situations.

Solidarity arises in sharing groups. These are face-to-face groups that jointly produce and/or use one or more goods and that have joint responsibility for the maintenance of the conditions of sharing. These sharing groups create positive and negative externalities from each member to all other members. Thus there is mutual dependency, with good and bad consequences. This creates potential conflict between individual and group interests. Sharing groups will create rules about the joint production and/or use and rules about sharing of costs and benefits arising from production and/or use. It is the potential non-conformity to the (spirit) of these sharing rules and the potential non-acceptance of joint responsibility due to conflicting interests that creates the problem of cooperation.

There are three prominent solutions in sociology to this problem. Individual *preferences change* in the direction of cooperation (say, through gifts or other investments, socialization or interpersonal attraction). Or transaction *partners bind themselves* (say, through hostages) in such a way that it would be against their own interest to defect from cooperation. Or individuals will cooperate because they are dependent and at the same time *closely watched and sanctioned* if they free-ride on the efforts of others. All three positions are criticized. Neither preference change nor self-binding nor conformity due to dependency and control can explain solidary behaviour across the five problem situations and/or are compatible with the evidence. Another micro-foundation is needed.

The new micro-foundation begins with the empirically well-supported claim that individuals are not far-sighted maximizers but only boundedly rational in the sense that their attention is selective; it is guided by their goals (that is, they perceive a situation in terms of a goal of action); and it is most frequently guided by short-term goals. People are thus by and large myopic and therefore prone to being tempted by short-term advantages. This makes people *myopic opportunists* and it makes cooperation and sharing precarious, particularly behaviour in breach temptation, mishap and need situations.

Because individuals frame, the opportunity costs (the alternative ways of spending their resources) are mostly outside the frame (outside the direct attention). They will influence behaviour the less, the stronger the frame is. Therefore, if the goal is solidary behaviour and it is strong, the sacrifices required for this kind of behaviour are only vaguely perceived and do not discourage cooperative behaviour. The question then for cooperation is how such a frame of action can be and factually is sustained.

There is an extra danger for the stability of a cooperative frame because the strength of a frame *decays* over time unless there is special effort to prevent such decay. Myopic opportunism and decay of frames render the self-binding and other explanations based on far-sightedness untenable. Experiments about the sensitivity of cooperativeness to situational cues render the preference change explanations (such as the investment and by-product theories) untenable. Theories that explain cooperativeness by dependency and control (such as Hechter's theory of solidarity) neglect the fact that surveillance is always imperfect, especially surveillance of intentions, which leaves such theories without explanation for mishap situations and resistance to unobserved breach temptations.

Instead, it is argued that a solidarity frame is stabilized through mechanisms of building *group identity* including common symbols and rituals and – this is very important here – positive and negative comparisons with other groups. These points have often been stressed in sociology, but they have not been linked to precariousness and to the need for flanking arrangements. Unless the aggregate value of the goods being jointly produced or used is very high, solidarity frames will be also stabilized by an *embedding in external means* for the reduction of opportunism: reputation, credible commitments and legal means. Such means factually reduce the pay-off from giving in to breach temptations, thereby rendering the breach temptations small enough to be handled by framing effects (which reduce the perception of opportunity costs). In terms of the logic of the explanation, this is a very important point because it shows that solidarity and other means of reducing opportunism are in this important sense not substitutes but complements and it shows that solidarity should not be treated as a matter between dyads or even as a matter of single groups.

Solidary behaviour will ultimately always depend on the stability of the frame and this stability is always precarious. For this reason, every behaviour relating to the group in some way acquires a signalling function: is the other still in a solidarity frame or is he beginning to slip? Such *relational signals* latch on first and foremost to the recurring situations in which solidarity could go wrong: common good, sharing, need and mishap situations, as well as breach temptations. For this reason, solidary behaviour cannot be compensated by much conformity in some situations and little in others. If you contribute to the common good but refuse to make amends when you have done something wrong, your intentions are under suspicion and the cooperative behaviour is reinterpreted as strategic rather than solidary. It is thus relational signalling that gives solidarity this broad range of behaviour.

Framing also suggests an important difference between weak and strong solidarity. This difference is not always well appreciated. *Weak solidarity* allows for the importance of the individual member of the group, for individual gain. The distributional principle recognizes individual investments and is therefore equity. The amount of time, money and effort individuals are expected to sacrifice for the group is modest or low, except with regard to breach temptations. Ideological requirements are medium or low. In *strong solidarity* (that is, solidarity in sharing groups with a very high aggregate value of the goods being jointly produced or used), individual interests are negligible in comparison with group interests; vis-à-vis other group members only the solidarity frame is legitimate; and vis-à-vis members of outside groups there are no restraints. And the distributional principle is equality, rather than equity. The amount of time, money and effort individuals are expected to sacrifice for the group is high or very high. Group boundaries are sharp, to maintain clear identifiability and group identity, and ideological embedding of group goals is strong in order to create interdependence of goals and thereby stabilization of the frame (which may lead to conflicting direction in development: enlargement for ideological support, compacting for sharpness of group boundaries). When compared to weak solidarity, strong solidarity is bad for business within and between groups.

Lastly, the traditional idea is being rejected that the historical movement is *from strong to weak solidarity*. Rather, owning to technological developments in production and to increasing wealth, strong and weak solidarities have been giving way to a stronger (atomized) individualism with a widespread incidence of arm's-length relationships and opportunism. Only as a reaction against this kind of individualism did we get a widespread development of weak solidarity and its embedding in flanking measures in policies of the state (including income policies). At times, when the flanking measures fail, strong solidarity reappears with sharp group boundaries, inter-group conflict and declining social product, as does atomistic individualism.

All in all, solidarity turns out to be much more anchored in the macro structures than often assumed *because* it is so precarious in its micro foundations.

NOTES

1. In this, I will draw on a variety of work I have done in this area, but the chapter is meant to be more than a summary of my own previous thoughts on the matter.
2. Hechter talks about 'group solidarity' in order to capture what sociologists have implied all along: that groups influence their members' behaviour (more or less).

3. This point has also been made by Fararo and Doreian (1998).
4. A prisoner's dilemma could be seen as either a common good situation or as a breach temptation, depending on the particular interpretation given to the story.
5. Observe that strength of solidarity is not defined by the factual 'average proportion of a member's private resources contributed to collective ends' (as in Hechter) but by the (legitimately) *expected* sacrifice in trying situations. Whether these costs are factually incurred depends on the frequency with which trying situations occur.
6. My critique of Durkheim's approach also holds for Collins's elaboration of that approach.
7. This does not mean that they would exclude groups. Rather, for them groups are either just the aggregate result of concatenated ties or the locus in which the formation of solidarity ties takes place. As Homans said: 'Small groups are not what we study but where we study it' (1961, p. 7).
8. In this context, Hollis' (1992) article on honour among thieves is instructive. Hollis shows that within the framework of game theory there can be no such thing as honour among thieves.
9. See Hogg and Abrams (1988) and Lindenberg (1997) for a critique of the interpersonal attraction theories of social cohesion.
10. A variant of the by-product theory is the idea that there are cooperative personality types (Liebrand, 1983). Here cooperation would be a question of selective processes.
11. There is an interesting attempt to deal with group solidarity by Markovsky and Chaffee (1995). They work with the assumptions of preference change (interpersonal attraction, here tied to emotional reactions, see Markovsky and Lawler, 1994), but they add structural aspects (reachability) and cognitive aspects (the cognition of the group as group). While this seems an advance in many ways, it still contains no notion of solidary behaviour, no theory of the importance of solidarity and no theory of its precariousness.
12. It is, of course, progress to view solidarity as a phenomenon of groups rather than of dyads. But as we will see later, it is necessary to look at systems of groups and other kinds of embedding of solidarity.
13. Close supervision is even likely to crowd out the motivation to be cooperative; see Frey (1997).
14. The economist Buchanan (1965) had before me developed a theory of 'clubs' on the basis of which I had built the sharing group theory which took a more sociological direction. It should also be mentioned that early on in group dynamics (Lewin, Deutsch), the group had also been defined in terms of the pursuit of a common goal. Only later did this view gave way to interpersonal attraction (see Lindenberg, 1997, for an account of this development).
15. For an interesting description and analysis of such a process, see Ostrom (1995).
16. Raub and Weesie (1993) add legal or extralegal ex ante commitments, a basis for ' "precontractual solidarity" à la Durkheim'. They also add conditions that make certain credible threats feasible, such as network effects that induce concern for one's reputation. Williamson (1993) himself mentions these things under the heading of 'institutional trust' (see next note).
17. Williamson suggests reserving the term 'trust' for situations where calculation and monitoring are purposefully suppressed (as in very special relations) and for institutional environments that provide strong safeguards. How, from the perspective of a rational choice theory, it is possible to 'suppress' calculation is not answered by Williamson. Again, if one allows suppression of calculation one should have a theory that explains how this is possible and why it can be ignored.
18. The term 'framing' is being used in different ways in the literature. Observe that 'framing' here refers specifically to the definition of the situation and not to any subjective distortion of objective reality, as Kahneman and Tversky (1984) often use the term. The framing theory presented here is based on the discrimination model of stochastic choice (see Lindenberg, 1980).
19. Of course, it is also possible that all interaction partners come into the situation with a preconceived goal, in which case the definition of the situation will be negotiated (see Goffman, 1969).
20. I do not assume any general human desire to act appropriately. This assumption is sometimes made by advocates of a 'logic of appropriateness' (for example, March and Olsen, 1995,

pp. 30ff). Rather, the importance of 'acting appropriately' comes from the importance of social (dis)approval (including self-(dis)approval). The anticipated (dis)approval for acting (in)appropriately, rather than appropriateness itself, is the relevant motivator in such a situation.

21. This point has been worked out in more detail in Lindenberg (1994).
22. See Carr and Landa (1983).
23. Sherif (1966) had clearly identified the framing aspect of these processes by showing that individuals act differently towards members of other groups, depending on whether they act as members or as individuals.
24. The basis for such rules is again solidarity rather than the principle of welfare maximization of the group (see Ellickson, 1991). For example, the rule would have to follow sharing conventions and need considerations used in this group, and these differ in weak and strong solidarity (see below).
25. See Lindenberg (1993) and Wielers (1993) for more detailed information on the relational signalling theory.
26. In this context, Tannen's popular book on the power of meta messages that accompany ordinary conversation is very much to the point (see Tannen, 1990).
27. For example, this has been empirically shown to be the case with long-term baby-sitters, where solidary behaviour from both sides play an important role (see Wielers, 1993). Murnighan and Pillutla (1995) found in ultimatum games that unfair offers elicited negative emotional responses and rejection.
28. This is one reason why solidarity plays an important role in networks of long-term business relations (see, for example, Uzzi, 1997).
29. It is quoted in Goffman (1974, p. 462).
30. Whereas clarity of relational signal can be interpreted as low transaction costs, this only shows that Williamson's theory (1985) can be related in some way to this theory of solidarity. It does not indicate that Williamson's theory could have generated anything in this theory of solidarity.
31. This difference has been discussed in more detail in Lindenberg (1988, 1992).
32. A sharing group may also have a very loose organization, as in neighbours sharing common space, and therefore also some risks without any conscious effort at rule formation. Another example of such a loose sharing group is what Harrison White (1993) has called an 'interface' (group of producers who produce the same good and share the creation of an intelligible front vis-à-vis the buyers). White, however, has not taken up the relational signalling within such an interface.
33. See also Raub (1996).
34. Contrary to balance theory, the claim here is that the group is not closed because strong individual ties create a pressure for transitivity. Rather, dyadic solidary ties are part of the sharing group and the latter is not the result of concatenation of dyads. If a friend of a friend is added to the group, then a larger group size is useful for the joint production or the cost sharing. Beyond that size, if there is at all a friend of a friend outside the group, there will be no transitive closure (see Lindenberg, 1982).
35. For more detail on these arguments, see Lindenberg (1986).

REFERENCES

Abell, P. (1996), 'A model of the informal structure (culture) of organizations: help, trust, rivalry and team spirit', *Rationality and Society*, 8 (4), 433–52.

Andreoni, J. (1988), 'Why free ride? Strategies and learning in public goods experiments', *Journal of Public Economics*, 37, 291–304.

Ben-Porath, Y. (1980), 'The F-connection: families, friends and firms in the organization of exchange', *Population and Development Review*, 6 (1),1–30.

Binmore, K. (1994), *Game Theory and the Social Contract Volume I: Playing Fair*, Cambridge, MA: MIT Press.

Blumberg, B. (1997), *Das Management von Technologiekooperationen*, Amsterdam: Thesis.

Buchanan, J. (1965), 'An economic theory of clubs', *Econometrica*, 32, new series, 1–14.

Burt, R.S. (1992), *Structural Holes. The Social Structure of Competition*, Cambridge, MA: Harvard University Press.

Burt, R.S. and M. Knez (1995), 'Kinds of third-party effects on trust', *Rationality and Society*, 7 (3), 255–92.

Carr, J.L. and Janet T. Landa (1983), 'The economics of symbols, clan names and religion', *Journal of Legal Studies*, 12 (1), 135–56.

Casson, M. (1991), *The Economics of Business Culture*, Oxford: Clarendon Press.

Coase, R. (1960), 'The problem of social cost', *Journal of Law and Economics*, 3, 1–44.

Coleman, J.S. (1982), *The Asymmetric Society*, Syracuse, NY: Syracuse University Press.

Coleman, J.S. (1990), *Foundation of Social Theory*, Cambridge, MA: Harvard University Press.

Collins, R. (1985), *Three Sociological Traditions*, Oxford and New York: Oxford University Press.

De Graaf, N.D. and H. Flap (1988), 'With a little help from my friends. Social resources as an explanation of occupational status and income in the Netherlands, the United States and West Germany', *Social Forces*, 67, 43–72.

De Vries, S. (1991), *Egoism, Altruism, and Social Justice*, Amsterdam: Thesis.

Durkheim, E. ([1893] 1933), *The Division of Labor in Society*, New York: Macmillan.

Durkheim, E. ([1912] 1965), *The Elementary Forms of Religious Life*, New York: Free Press.

Ellickson, R.C. (1991), *Order Without Law. How Neighbors Settle Disputes*, Cambridge, MA: Harvard University Press

Fararo, T. and P. Doreian (1998), 'The Theory of Solidarity: An agenda of problems', in P. Doreian and T. Fararo (eds), *The Problem of Solidarity: Theories and Models*, Amsterdam: Gordon and Breach Publishers.

Feld, S. (1981), 'The focused organization of social ties', *American Journal of Sociology*, 85 (5), 1015–35.

Flap, H. (1988), *Conflict, Loyalty and Violence*, Frankfurt: Peter Lang.

Frank, Robert H. (1988), *Passions within Reason. The Strategic Role of the Emotions*, New York: Norton.

Frey, Bruno S. (1997), *Not Just For the Money. An Economic Theory of Personal Motivation*, Cheltenham, UK and Lyme, US: Edward Elgar.

Gál, R. (1997), *Unreliability: Contract Discipline and Contract Governance Under Economic Transition*, Amsterdam: Thesis.

Goffman, E. (1959), *The Presentation of Self in Everyday Life*, Garden City, NY: Doubleday Anchor Books.

Goffman, E. (1969), *Strategic Interaction*, Philadelphia: University of Philadelphia Press.

Goffman, E. (1974), *Frame Analysis. An Essay on the Organization of Experience*, Cambridge, MA: Harvard University Press.

Goleman, D. (1985), *Vital Lies, Simple Truths*, New York: Simon & Schuster.

Grieco, M. (1987), *Keeping it in the Family. Social Networks and Employment Chance*, London & New York: Tavistock Publications.

Hardin, R. (1995), *One for All: The Logic of Group Conflict,* Princeton, NJ: Princeton University Press.
Hechter, M. (1987), *Principles of Group Solidarity*, Berkeley: University of California Press.
Heimer, Carol (1992), 'Doing your job *and* helping your friends: universalistic norms about obligations to particular others in networks', in N. Nohria and R. Eccles (eds), *Networks and Organization. Structure, Form and Action,* Boston: Harvard Business School Press, pp. 143–64.
Hogg, M.A. and D. Abrams (1988), *Social Identifications: A Psychology of Intergroup Relations and Group Processes*, London & New York: Routledge
Hollis, M. (1992), 'Honour among thieves', in M. Hollis and W. Vossenkuhl (eds), *Moralische Entscheidung und rationale Wahl*, Munich: Scientia Nova, Oldenbourg Verlag, pp. 115–30.
Homans, G.C. (1954), 'The cash posters', *American Sociological Review*, 19, 724–33.
Homans, G.C. (1958), 'Social behavior as exchange', *American Journal of Sociology*, 63 (6), 597–606.
Homans, G.C. (1961), *Social Behavior: Its Elementary Forms*, New York: Harcourt, Brace & World.
Kahneman, D. and A. Tversky (1984), 'Choices, values and frames', *American Psychologist*, 39 (4), 341–50.
Kahneman, D., J.L. Knetsch and R.H. Thaler (1986), 'Fairness as constraint on profit seeking: entitlements in the market', *American Economic Review*, 76 (September), 728–41.
Kahneman, D., J.L. Knetsch and R.H. Thaler (1991), 'Anomalies: the endowment effect, loss aversion, and status quo bias', *Journal of Economic Perspectives*, 5, 193–206.
Kaplan, R.E. (1984), 'Trade routes: the manager's network of relationships', *Organizational Dynamics* (spring), 37–52.
Kramer, R.M., P.P. Shah and S. Woerner (1995), 'Why ultimatums fail. Social identity and moralistic aggression in coercive bargaining', in R.M. Kramer and D. Messick (eds), *Negotiation as Social Process,* Thousand Oaks, London & New Delhi: Sage Publications, pp. 285–308.
Lawler, E. and M. Yoon (1993), 'Power and the emergence of commitment behavior in negotiated exchange', *American Sociological Review*, 58, 465–81.
Lazega, E. (1995), 'Protecting the common good among equals: a lateral control regime of partners in a law firm', LASMAS Preprint 96/1.
Liebrand, W.B.G. (1983), 'A classification of social dilemma games', *Simulation & Games*, 14, 123–38.
Ligthart, P.A.M. (1995), *Solidarity in Economics Transactions: An Experimental Study of Framing Effects in Bargaining and Contracting*, Amsterdam: Thesis.
Lindenberg, S. (1975), 'Three psychological theories of a classical sociologist', *Mens en Maatschappij,* 50 (2), 133–53.
Lindenberg, S. (1980), 'Marginal utility and restraints on gain maximization: the discrimination model of rational, repetitive choice', *Journal of Mathematical Sociology*, 7 (2), 289–316.
Lindenberg, S. (1982), 'Sharing groups: theory and suggested applications', *Journal of Mathematical Sociology*, 9, 33–62.
Lindenberg, S. (1986), 'The paradox of privatization in consumption', in A. Diekmann and P. Mitter (eds), *Paradoxical Effects of Social Behavior. Essays in Honor of Anatol Rapoport,* Heidelberg & Vienna: Physica–Verlag, pp. 297–310.

Lindenberg, S. (1988), 'Contractual relations and weak solidarity: the behavioral basis of restraints on gain-maximization', *Journal of Institutional and Theoretical Economics*, 144, 39–58.

Lindenberg, S. (1992), 'An extended theory of institutions and contractual discipline', *Journal of Institutional and Theoretical Economics*, 148 (2), 125–54

Lindenberg, S. (1993), 'Framing, empirical evidence and applications', *Jahrbuch für Neue Politische Ökonomie*, Tübingen: Mohr (Siebeck), pp. 11–38.

Lindenberg, S. (1994), 'Norms and the power of loss: Ellickson's theory and beyond', in E.G. Furubotn and R. Richter (eds), *The New Institutional Economics. Bounded Rationality and the Analysis of State and Society*, special issue of the *Journal of Institutional and Theoretical Economics*, 150 (1), 101–13.

Lindenberg, S. (1997), 'Grounding groups n theory: functional, cognitive and structural interdependencies', *Advances in Group Processes*, 14, 281–331.

Loewenstein, G.F. (1992), 'The fall and rise of psychological explanations in the economics of intertemporal choice', in G.F. Loewenstein and J. Elster (eds), *Choice over Time*, New York: Russell, pp. 3–34.

Loewenstein, G.F. and J. Elster (eds) (1992), *Choice over Time*, New York: Russell Sage.

March, J.G. and J.P. Olsen (1995), *Democratic Governance*, New York: Free Press.

Margolis, H. (1982), *Selfishness, Altruism and Rationality: A Theory of Social Choice*, Cambridge: Cambridge University Press.

Markovsky, B. and M. Chaffee (1995), 'Social identification and solidarity', *Advances in Group Processes*, 12, 249–70.

Markovsky, B. and E.J. Lawler (1994), 'A new theory of group solidarity', *Advances in Group Processes*, 11, 113–37.

Melucci, A. (1989), *Nomads of the Present: Social Movements and Individual Needs in Contemporary Society*, ed. by J. Keane and P. Mier, Philadelphia: Temple University Press.

Murnighan, J.K. and M.M. Pillutla (1995), 'Fairness versus self-interest', in R.M. Kramer and D. Messick (eds), *Negotiation as Social Process*, Thousand Oaks, London & New Delhi: Sage Publications, pp. 240–67.

Olson, M. (1965), *The Logic of Collective Action*, Cambridge, MA: Harvard University Press.

Ostrom, E. (1990), *Governing the Commons: The Evolution of Institutions for Collective Action*, Cambridge: Cambridge University Press.

Ostrom, E. (1995), 'Constituting social capital and collective action', in R.O. Keohane and E. Ostrom (eds), *Local Commons and Global Interdependence*, London: Sage, pp. 125–60.

Piore, M. and C. Sabel (1984), *The Second Industrial Divide*, New York: Basic Books.

Pizzorno, A. (1978), 'Political exchange and collective identity in industrial conflict', in C. Crouch and A. Pizzorno (eds), *The Resurgence of Class Conflict in Western Europe since 1968*, London: Macmillan, pp. 277–98.

Raub, W. (1996), 'Effects of temporal embeddedness on *ex ante* planning under incomplete information', Iscore-Paper no. 87, University of Utrecht, mimeo.

Raub, W. and J. Weesie (1990), 'Reputation and efficiency in social interactions: an example of network effects', *American Journal of Sociology*, 96.

Raub, W. and J. Weesie (1993), 'Symbiotic arrangements: a sociological perspective', *Journal of Institutional and Theoretical Economics*, 149 (4), 716–24.

Raub, W. and J. Weesie (1996), 'The Management of Matches. Decentralized Mechanisms for Cooperative Relations with Applications to Organizations and

Households', Progress Report 1993–1995. Iscore-Paper no. 62, University of Utrecht, mimeo.
Ridgeway, C.L. and H.A. Walker (1995), 'Status structures', in K.S. Kook, G.A. Fine and J.S. House (eds), *Sociological Perspectives on Social Psychology*, Boston: Allen and Bacon, pp. 281–310.
Sherif, M. (1966), *In Common Predicament: Social Psychology of Intergroup Conflict and Cooperation*, Boston: Houghton-Mifflin.
Spence, M. (1974), *Market Signaling*, Cambridge, MA: Harvard University Press.
Tajfel., H. (1970), 'Experiments in intergroup discrimination', *Scientific American*, 223, 96–102.
Tajfel, H., C. Flament, M.G. Billig and R.P. Bundy (1971), 'Social categorization and intergroup behaviour', *European Journal of Social Psychology*, 1, 1459–78.
Tannen, D. (1990), *You Just Don't Understand: Women and Men in Conversation*, New York: William Morrow.
Turner, J.C. and H. Giles (eds) (1981), *Intergroup Behaviour*, Oxford: Blackwell.
Uzzi, B. (1997), 'Social structure and competition in interfirm networks: the paradox of embeddedness', *Administrative Science Quarterly,* 42 (1), 35–67.
Vaill, P.B. (1986), 'The purposing of high-performance systems', in T.J. Sergiovanni, and J.E. Corbally (eds), *Leadership and Organizational Culture*, Urbana and Chicago: University of Illinois Press, pp. 85–104.
Weber, M. (1961), *General Economic History*, New York: Collier Books.
White, H.C. (1993), 'Markets, networks and control', in S. Lindenberg and H. Schreuder (eds), *Interdisciplinary Perspectives on Organization Studies*, Oxford: Pergamon Press.
Wielers, R. (1993), 'On trust in employment relationships: the case of child-minders', *Netherlands Journal of Social Sciences*, 29, 43–63.
Williamson, O. E. (1985), *The Economic Institutions of Capitalism*, New York: Free Press.
Williamson, O.E. (1993), 'Calculativeness, trust and economic organization', *Journal of Law and Economics*, XXXVI, 453–86.

Conclusion: quality is a system property. Downstream

Harrison C. White

In 1996 in Paris, goaded by Favereau and Lazega, I began working towards the book, *Markets from Networks* issued in 2002 from Princeton University Press. The manuscript that I presented in 1999 in Paris is now much revised under the impetus of the many discussions there and since. It extends my original model of 'the market' to systems of markets such as concern the 'economics of convention', with its explicit attention to culture. Intricacy and subtlety mark the reality and thus the argument.

What has most fascinated me is the simultaneous *closeness* and *distance* between my market approach and that of the Convention School. Eymard-Duvernay sketches the latter (drawing on earlier pieces joint with Thévenot, Favereau and others) in his chapter. That, plus my book, provide the basis for my first section. I next turn to network and decision within organization, referring to Lazega and Mounier's chapter. Only then do I bring to bear the brilliant further light shed by the chapter that was written last, that by Favereau and Biencourt with Eymard-Duvernay. My title is justified there.

The editors asked me to situate my market book in earlier theory of mine. They also gave me licence to probe in this chapter some other commonalities among these very diverse analyses from two years ago in Paris that they have now shepherded into a book of great scope and diversity. I shall fit these brief comments within the general flow. As conclusion I speculate about research on a new phenomenon.

INSTITUTION AND STYLE

There are striking similarities between Eymard-Duvernay's and my accounts of markets. Production dominates consumption. Market terms, such as contract or profile, are shaped by *local* balances in information. There are zones of indeterminacy around such market terms. Procedural matters are central. One can predict market failure from context. Uncertainty is the underlying driving force. Taming it induces ordering by perceived quality. Seven similarities!

Let us begin with the market plane of mine (see illustrations in the Biencourt–Urrutiager chapter above). This market plane maps out the varieties of market interface that are feasible, along with what latitudes of membership and path of formation for market they exhibit. So that market plane should map into the varieties of convention that Eymard-Duvernay has proposed.

The initial spark for my *Markets from Networks* came from a *journée* organized in 1995 by Favereau. The spark was mapping distinct conventions onto major regions of this plane, which had been derived independently. And, in chapter 7 (White, 1992), I sketch what has seemed an effective such matching since even the first draft of the book. That, indeed, is the *closeness*.

Such a market plane (see the chapters by Biencourt and Urrutiaguer, and by Favereau *et al.*) can, however, be seen in two very different lights, which can explain the *distance*. A comprehensive theoretical framing is helpful here. For that I turn to my earlier *Identity and Control* (1992). The insight is that the Convention School argues about what I had defined in my chapter 4 as 'institutions', whereas my market manuscript concerns the 'styles' of my chapter 5 of 1992. Conventions are rule- and value-centred. Thus conventions are amorphous on the ground as to pattern in network terms, and indeed even as to number and provenance of member firms and markets. Markets in networks, by contrast, are seen (chapters 8–10 of the new book) as decoupled from particular substantive value terms to the benefit of a determinate style of interaction on the ground.

My 1992 theory of social action endogenizes identities along with control. Networks among actors (chapter 3) and disciplines constituting actors (chapter 2) together provide the foundation structures. Choosing an order for chapters was a puzzle in this book. *Networks presuppose disciplines which presuppose networks*. They are incomparable yet on the same level of generality. The same puzzle recurred with institutions, which presuppose styles, which presuppose institutions. Each of these 'larger' constructs, from chapters 3 and 4 *Identity and Control*, folds in both disciplines and networks as building materials.

Yet style is akin to network whereas institution is akin to discipline, with respect to the uncertainties that drive all social action towards identity and control. Uncertainty in respect to physical objects (*à la* Callon, 1986) comes accompanied by interpretive or cultural uncertainty, which I termed 'ambiguity', and in addition by vagueness in concrete social pattern, termed 'ambage'. Style and network take on ambiguity in reducing ambage, whereas the reverse is true for institution and discipline.

We now bring down the level of abstractness. Markets, in my approach, but also, I think, in that of the Convention School, are production or processing markets rather than markets of exchange. Producers seek niches in an array by quality as perceived downstream by buyers: this corresponds to just one of my 'disciplines', the interface (White, 1992, ch. 2). But one production market can only evolve among many others. It accommodates itself somehow in chains of relations across some network population of markets in that production economy.

A given relation downstream from a production market may be perceived very differently on reception and sending ends. In making commitments, producers bracket actors downstream, who may, however, look to individual firms upstream. Decoupling that allows choice thus must accompany the embedding of producers into that market interface.

Convention as Institution or as Style?

My analysis of the market system has the constituent interface disciplines as the nub of both facets, of institution but also of style. But only particular markets, as individual interfaces, are mapped into this market plane. The argument in chapters 8–10 of my new market book takes production market *systems* as examples of styles, which (from White, 1992, ch. 5) structure network flow patterns despite and around differences in interpretive moments of the various markets.

To characterize such a system with many market interfaces is complex, except in one very special case, *homogeneity*. Imposing such homogeneity on a system of production markets would, of course, run against its underlying specialization in *kinds* of labour, expertise, equipment, location and so on. But this is *the only case in which institution and style may dovetail.*

Let me turn to an analogy, the classificatory kinship system in which each clan (and thus every ego of given gender) has the same set of role relations prescribed for marriage. In Australia this is common.[1]

Classificatory Kinship Analogy

The analogy is drawn to the generalized exchange of spouses in classificatory kinship systems, with clans being analogous to markets and lineages of one sort or another being analogous to producer firms: This analogy sets up just the contrast in emphases that I see between the convention and my approaches to production market systems.

Very strong 'conventions' in the form of prescriptions of partners for marriage characterize a system of classificatory kinship. They are its interpretive facet and thus constitute what I call an institution. Among the Kariera, for example, a male must marry his Mother's Brother's Daughter (where, however, the capital letters signify that the references of these terms, in a consistently functioning classificatory system, are to a much broader array of persons than in our own kinship). Some array of lineages by attractiveness in marriage could, like convention, be analogized to determinant of market terms.

Must is not *is*, in aboriginal social formations as much as in our own. Bearman, in his analysis of exhaustive kinship data on the Groote Eylandt tribe, follows many anthropologists in seeking pattern in tangible tracks of actual marriages (Bearman, 1997). He thus is, in my terms, seeking style rather than institution. Of course, in some world without demographic and other chance forces, a given style could prove to be just the dynamic playing out of a particular institution that presupposed just such a pattern of flows. (In such a world we social scientists would be much less bamboozled by complexity – but what need would there be for social science?). Should then we resort to institution or to style in portrayal of markets?

Institution

Portrayal of market system as institution would require at least specifying a distribution of the markets across the market plane. The final version of my market book in fact drew on Barron's presentation in Paris (his chapter, this volume) to guide my portrayal in chapters 11 and 13 of such distributions.[2]

But this will do little to characterize the process aspect, the intercalations of flows, of the way commitments to production are made and get interdigitated. Choosing institution as vehicle of portrayal, as I think the Convention School does, makes sense, then, not for a system but rather for some subset of markets similar as to materials, customers and so on. That is to say, convention as institution (in my usage of that term) makes more sense just for markets which lie in parallel, not to say structurally equivalent, locations, rather than scattered upstream and down.

Allowing for substitutability among such a parallel cluster brings in a full market space with a third dimension, substitutability, adjoined to the market plane. And indeed it is only in the corresponding seventh chapter of the new book that I map Eymard-Duvernay's conventions types into my market space. So in my eyes these conventions correspond to market sectors, such as Biencourt's road hauling or Urrutiaguer's theatre productions in France (their chapter, this volume).

I regret that Biencourt and Urrutiaguer had for their chapter only the earlier version to guide their rich analyses of transport and theatre markets. Much of what each calls for is now outlined: respectively, feedback loops (chapters 4, 5 and 12) and interpretive shadowing (chapters 6, 9,and 15). But then research practice requires feedback loops from theory to field investigation just as business practices revolve around the feedback loops for which Biencourt seeks analytic tools.

Style as Core Issue

The map of interfaces onto market plane is certainly instructive. And it is pleasing to find a match between my predictions and the Convention School's empirical findings on market rationales or subcultures for market sectors. But this may not address the core issue.

I take the core issue for my new book to be process or social dynamics, as interface structure was for my initial 1981 article on markets. The interface mechanism is modelled and the essentials of market plane is already laid out by the end of my chapter 3 of the new book (with some extension of phenomenology through the following three chapters). How decoupling and embedding are jointly effected, upstream and downstream, across a network population of markets, is the central issue which dominates the rest of the book. *An understanding as style, rather than itself coming from the market plane* or market space, permits deriving (in the first section of chapter 8 – see the end of the present chapter) the parameters which identify dimensions of, and locations, in market space. *The parameters of market space are endogenized to these mutual nestings of decoupling and embedding into each other within a style.*

Put in terms used by Favereau (1998), the point is that distinct levels necessarily are invoked in articulating decisions (here commitments made within market system). And as Favereau goes on to point out, this is but a transposition of the problem of moving from macro to micro. More generally, it makes clear how mechanistic and thus inadequate is a Lego set view of social organization such as tends to accompany billiard ball views of social actors.

Yet the very lack of match between style and institution formulations generated from market interface models can be exploited. Because there is no one-to-one matching (as in principle there is for homogeneous classificatory kinship) each institutional 'take' in convention terms must correspond partially to each of *several* 'takes' as to style in the sense of my 1992 book – and conversely. Eymard-Duvernay chronically argues for just that, a mixture of conventions to be observable in a given system (in a style in my terms). And conversely, the vision in my later chapters of market as molecule in self-consistent Field of decoupled molecules – embedded only stochastically in flow patterns – this vision invokes and uses an array of sectors, of Eymard-Duvernay's conventions as varieties.

RELATIONS AND AGENCY AND ORGANIZATION

Much these same lines of argument can be transposed to very different scopes of system and organization. To me the most puzzling aspect of Eymard-Duvernay's chapter is his tendency to confound organizations of various sorts with markets. In this he parallels approaches in new institutional economics and transaction cost economics, such as are laid out in the chapter by Chabaud and Saussier, whereas I argue, here and again below, that the organization of a producer firm is, in analytic terms, more comparable to one or another *system* of markets – and much the same view seems implicit in another chapter by Favereau, with Quiers-Valette (1998): see especially their 'typologie des incitations', p. 249.

Let us turn to Lazega (2002) for further guidance. In this book, previewed in the joint chapter here with Mounier, he is one of the few to make a serious modelling study of a particular formal organization. This empirical work helps set a new standard for scope, rigour and thoroughness. His law firm, though in one sense of only moderate size, is in a theoretical sense large. Lazega's work shows formal organization as a genus into which are folded many other constructs, including interfaces, institution and style, as well as, of course, the networks and cliques which he operationalizes explicitly. His work shows that theorizing a firm is more complex than theorizing a market.

We may bring out the complexity through comparison with my analysis of the market system. Lazega resorts to dual analyses of the firm. Relations, when seen as lateral among peers, shape into networks sufficient to monitor and contain free-loading through invocation of ties differentially according to calculi of seniority and attributional identities. Visualize the firm as a tribe of clans structured by classificatory kinship, clans analogous to the blocks Lazega and Mounier map from reported networks. Such discipline, in tribe or firm, is akin to market interface, but in this first analysis Lazega treats the firm as its own locality; so enforcement must be endogenous rather than by terminations from downstream external to the firm. This treatment diverges from Eymard-Duvernay's.

This first analysis aims to account for work assignment patterns and their stability. Lazega offers a second analysis, of clientelistic power relations for which there is no analogue in my market system model. Clientelism within the firm derives from inequality between members in obtaining business, in 'rainmaking', and Lazega's book works hard to account for control over rainmakers together with their 'shadow' in dependency relations within the firm, control which can only come from higher-order cumulation of structure. Lazega confounds the two analyses in invoking 'politicization'; his real task is accounting for his wonderful data on actual rewards, incomes and their evolution over time, subject to both analyses. Perhaps he must, in order to complete this, build on three-role unit processes rather than the two roles in decisions of exchange markets, where stocks rather than flows are at issue; his three roles evoke the tripartite layering in the market of upstream, producer and downstream. Agency is rife.

For sensible views on agency, see the compendium edited by Pratt and Zeckhauser (1985). It has an explicit empirical focus, American business, and further it pairs each academic author with a practitioner as author/commentator. Agency analyses in these hands clearly do have pragmatic force, but there are signs even in the editors' introduction of theoretical limitations. From the first page the editors insist that multiple principals are integral to agency, which makes the agent an intermediary, which raises the questions of how this theory differs from general social network theory and of just how agency comes to be bounded. Similarly, and also on their first page, the editors appeal to embeddings as reputations in larger structures – as a major way to make agency effective. So agency is derivative; on page 7 the editors emphasize the unavoidable miring of agency in entanglements. This concedes the value of structural analysis and network modelling for agency problems.

First, Structural Analysis

Supportive context is necessary to agency relation, or indeed to any other network relation, kinship or other. Consider the emergences, painfully over time, of the employment relationships that Degenne uncovers and dissects in his chapter. His basis is empirical studies both intensive and extensive. He, a pre-eminent network analyst (Degenne and Forsé, 1999), is coming to insist on how complex and extensive (both in time and in space) is the gestation of ties. Analysts too frequently take ties for granted as unproblematic indicators of a relation that is seen as being between two billiard balls, here employer and employee, principal and agent. Degenne is calling for, rather than yet proposing, explicit models so that one cannot yet say whether 'institution' and/or 'style' must be invoked already here, in self-similar logic, for characterizing the employment ties being presupposed in labour market models.

Agency is Degenne's key, with the exact role of formal organizations not yet clear. Degenne is calling for much more intensive confrontation with actual interpretive practices, on elucidation of relations as constructs. These are practices followed by actors that seem to be quite additional to the subcultural common beliefs propounded by the Convention School. This projects still another analytic depth onto Favereau's levels.

Formalization of organization is an interpretive practice, and recent work by Stinchcombe (2001) can contribute here. Degenne and Stinchcombe agree on the indispensability of an intervening layer or parties (mediator for the former and communicability for the latter). Both are recognizing distinct levels, now of discourse versus formal interpretation, and both are insisting that the two aspects interpenetrate (reminiscent of institutions and styles in the previous section).

Stinchcombe chooses five empirical cases where smooth match is common and so he is unabashedly functionalist in seeing the informal network and mediation facet as completing the formal practice, whereas, in contrast, Degenne is wrestling with settings with searing levels of disconnection, specifically of unemployment, and in particular of stubbornly large subsets of long-term 'stayers' not embedding into these 'ties', or relations of agency which are easier to postulate than to institute. Here is another illustration of the way analysis of structure cannot be disentangled from context of dynamics.

One way to capture the distinction between the problematics Degenne and Stinchcombe face is in the required shapes of stories (known to go with ties in general – see chapter 3 of *Identity and Control*). It appears to me that Stinchcombe's context calls forth justifications in the sense explained by Boltanski and Thévenot (1999), whereas surely the context Degenne is studying will remain a crippled one until it generates history out of its myriad stories, in the way proposed by Bearman *et al.* (1999).

Network Modelling

Now let us dig deeper, reaching beyond agency, market and firm to seek a broader common basis in network mobilization. That was the goal of my 1992 book already invoked in the first section. We may begin from the mapping of varieties of markets resulting from my model, which we call MAP.

There is one area of contexts in MAP where viable markets are not feasible, and one further expects wholesale dissolution of markets rather than one-by-one unravelling of firms. The two lines splitting the plane at unity ratio mathematically cross at the centre point (1,1) in MAP. But this crossing should be left blank in (for example White 2002, Fig. 3.5). Performances predicted for a market are extreme for either ratio being unity, but in opposite ways, so that the predictions break down when they intersect.

Just around the central point is a *black hole* of contexts which will not support a market: there is neither enough contrast between the two sides of the market interface, nor enough contrast between volume trade-offs and quality trade-offs to support the balancing act. The viable market profile plays off matchings of variability. This is just as we should expect, since the market interface equilibrates itself by trading off variation in volume valuation with variation in quality valuation. This becomes difficult as sensitivities on the two sides tend towards equality.

What happens as and after markets fall apart by unravelling or other dissolution? Business is observably getting done even with factual contexts corresponding to MAP locations not viable for production markets. But there is no polarization there, not enough guidance from any tentative spread in quality among producers. One is returning to a putting-out system of pre-industrialization or moving into a morass of network organization. Understanding emergence of a market is tied up with evocation of constituent firms, among continuing production activity and flows. How can networks come together in such complex coevolutions?[3]

Some species of mechanism other than market interface, perhaps seen as enlargement of the internal organization of a firm, may supervene. I survey two other species in my 1992 book (council and arena, chapter 2). But the prior question is what situations intervene immediately after some dissolution and provide the seedbed for any new construction, of market or other species.

One needs to see what sorts of network configuration can come to be subsumed into a production market. We focus on networking in some fringe of an already established sector of a production economy with proto-firms around, and sophistication about role systems of more traditional sorts; so mores and cultural routines are available as building blocks for participants negotiating emergence. Such firms are 'proto' in that, only with full establishment of their market, do full articulation and scope in authority structures appear (see White, 2002, chapter 11; White, 1992).

The results, whether for dissolution or for emergence, lead me to question the diagnosis of 'network organization' as being a superior new form towards which the economy is moving (Piore and Sabel, 1983; Zeitlin, 2002). We should think instead of network organizations as interim forms, neither from the future nor from the past of some evolutionary history of species, but rather as constituting a standard fall-back mode of operation.

PHENOMENOLOGY OF NETWORK EMBEDDING

The particular goal here is the etiology of the trade-off ratios used in MAP to characterize how firms are embedded in a market. What was the network configuration out of which firms and production markets coalesced in some instance? How, and how effectively did it function as a matrix for specialized production? Let us simplify to just the actors (proto-firms or whatever) and the pair ties in networks of continuing flows.

Each actor in such a pair assesses how much time or talk transpires in that tie according to some schedule of valuation of its own, the two schedules usually different. We may approximate each valuation schedule using a single parameter, say an exponential growth rate of value with degree of commitment. So the two parameters will differ, with asymmetry from the two ends.

No tie stands by itself and, typically, it is but one in a set of existing ties that inform one another within some social setting. And the setting will tend to evoke a status ordering among the actors. Let a second parameter be an exponential measure of how much the valuation of a tie increases with the status seen for the actor at the other end. This is highly abstract. We develop it further in the context of a homely situation.

Networks and Cliquing across Boys and Girls: Teenager Caricatures

Let the set of ties be between girls and boys in some locale. Typically (Coleman 1959; Bearman *et al.* 1999) girls fall into an acknowledged order of attractiveness, and similarly for the boys. And the set can be polarized, with, say, left ends thought of as girls and right as boys.

Teenage girls are terrified of and yet also fascinated by relations to boys, and so on. The stakes in embarrassment and status seem high. On this supposition, the girl values a given level of involvement more highly than does the boy at the other end. So the first parameter will exceed unity from the left end, the girl. The second parameter may, however, be less than unity from the left end, if girls are swayed less in their assessment of intimacy than are boys by the public standing.

If the girls' trepidation is great, they may wish so much to lower the terrible uncertainty that they start taking their cues from each other's commitments – signalled by comments as well as actual dates – rather than worrying so much about reactions from particular boys. In short, a clique will form among the girls, a clique that straitjackets how much these girls put out to the array of boys paying attention to them, responding to their profile of demeanour towards girls of varying status in cuteness.

Although this is of course a caricature, it opens up on a very different scale a mechanism partly analogous to that for firms in a production market. *The clique is a mechanism in which your observation of your peers' various outcomes shapes how much you commit.* The girls are embedded into an interface like a market profile. But there is a crucial difference – where here is the upstream and the downstream?

Asymmetry from Specialization: Generalized Exchange

The girl–boy situation we caricature has actually a more subtle mechanism than that in production markets because there is direct exchange, so that benefits and costs get piled in together at a given end of a given tie. Unlike girl–boy talk, production flows are not their own reward, once specialization emerges. Instead, each flow is rewarded by fungible counterflow, notably of money.

Uncertainty and anxiety remain huge, as Frank Knight (1921) made vivid long ago. So producers, like girls, huddle together in cliques, called industries or markets, but not with respect to a counterpart species, of boys. The chances are that they are not offering cabbages grown on their own but rather goods manufactured out of streams of procurement from other firms in markets upstream. It is a distinct range of still other firms and customers downstream from them, from whom they turn to huddle in a clique, a market. The payments they are making, out of their revenue from downstream, are their costs, which are flows upstream to entirely different partners than they found downstream with purchasers. The producers' rewards are not intrinsic pleasure but a payment flow.

Only a single status ordering, that of producers by quality, is evoked in a given step along the stream – not an ordering for boys by status and another one for girls. There is no longer a matching as of boys to girls, just transactions in products. This is a deep, structural asymmetry from embedding in network, rather than the superficial asymmetry from a mere attribute, gender. A correlative change is that now the *minimal* unit of decision invokes *three* layers of actor: the producers, their suppliers upstream and the purchasers downstream. But a similarity is that the producers continue to be the ones committing for the next period, like the girls signalling via their clique interfaces in choosing what the intimacy regime is to be.

These changes all derive from having a regime of generalized exchange (Bearman, 1997) in contrast with a regime of direct exchange as for adolescents. Producers are orienting to benefit from their downstream, but only as framed by negative benefit, cost, expected from their transactions with upstream. Thence comes their guidance, the number for profit as difference between revenue and cost. The market mechanism is thus the more complex and sophisticated as social organization.

Yet the boy–girl mechanism is subtler in cultural and emotional–cognitive terms, in that both negative and positive evaluations enter, separately and distinctly, into each tie as viewed both from one end and from the other. Producers send only goods to, and receive only money from, their downstream side; producers send only money to, and receive only goods from, their upstream side. The producers are making self-centred decisions based directly on quantity of money without direct regard to quality for its own sake as standing.

Like the hypothetical girls' clique, the producers are so uncertain of response from their 'boys' (their downstream) as to base their judgments on how well the various members of their clique are doing. That is the root similarity. The root difference is the polarization of flows from generalized exchange for markets. The boys and girls engage in conversation (Gibson, 1999; Mische and White, 1998) in which participants, adolescents or not, necessarily take turns with each other listening as well as talking.

The similarity and difference together enable us to motivate the embedding parameters for the market. If we return to the MAP from my mathematical model of a mechanism for a market profile, the first dimension is found indeed to concern exponentials for valuation versus commitment volume, as for the first parameter in this section. But it is, because of generalized exchange, a ratio. The numerator derives from valuations by downstream from the given industry, and the denominator derives from negative valuation, cost, seen by the given industry with respect to procurement flows from upstream. The second dimension again contrasts valuation, but with respect to quality not flow. Each dimension comes as a ratio, not a multiplication, since cost is the negative of revenue.

The third dimension is now easier to motivate. It, the involution, describes the degree of substitutability, on an exponential basis, between flows from the given industry and others, which are cross-stream from it rather than either downstream or upstream. This involution parameter, gamma, is kept in the background of my model of these production markets precisely because degree of involution is taken for granted, that is to say hegemonic, in the perceptions of participants across these production markets.

ENDOGENIZING VALUATION: QUALITY IS A SYSTEM PROPERTY

This section will redevelop the substantive theme of the first section to view it in the different light offered by the Favereau chapter, but it picks up from the preceding discussion of networks.

Dissecting out network constructs in Lazega's study helps to clarify the new institutional economics along with those aspects of the Convention School with which it overlaps. The common idiom in the new institutional economics is building up views of organizations in terms of agency and contract relations. I argue that this confounds coherency in theory by overlooking the contextual and interactive field relations that precede and structure, rather than grow from, agency and contract relations. The litmus test is accounting for the way valuations emerge.

Henk Flap's chapter addresses many of these overlookings. Indeed he enriches his account of social capital approaches with a thoughtful overview of more structural approaches. In his hands they seem quite parallel. Flap assimilates the views of Siegwart Lindenberg (see his chapter in this volume) as a foundation for structural approaches. These views also are invoked by social capital analysts and account for their split of actor goals, as reported by Flap, into government, political and symbolic. The thematic of unintended consequences in social capital theories (which itself can be seen as a sort of embedding in time) surely corresponds to the interpretive moment, which Flap has as the third characteristic of the structuralist stance. I take 'path dependency' to be technical jargon corresponding to interpretive moment.

More generally, Mark Granovetter's embedding arguments appear parallel to the emphasis in social capital analyses on contexts as resources and constraints. Lazega insists on both endogenized and exogenous 'resources', and these are interpretive as often as physical, and so his approach seems consistent with the broad overview of a 'social capital' approach offered by Flap. Flap is in more danger of missing the effects of structural equivalence played out in network process because of his focus on immediate locality in network, with longer-range effects ceded to a concept of 'resources' of one sort and another. Similarly, Flap treats identities in rather mechanistic fashion, whereas Lazega can tease out the emergent construction of some aspects of identity from his rich and concentrated data of a case study that is as much ethnography as field study.[4]

The main open problem for the social capital school, in my opinion, is supplying some explicit mechanism to account for valuations. Valuations are central, at least in Flap's account. But where do they come from? Valuations should be endogenized.

We turn for this purpose to the chapter by Favereau, Biencourt and Eymard-Duvernay, who show how my mechanism for market necessarily calls forth and invokes their conventions of market sector. I will elaborate on their elegant account as to just one point. What makes the market price profile manageable for producers as for modellers is continuity as a continuous schedule, rather than the set of discrete points for member producers. That suggested thinking in terms of a representative firm of some unspecified quality as sufficient basis for the analysis, even though an arbitrary set of firms has in the end to be accounted for in niches. When one thinks further this can be seen as but another way to say that a consistent ordering on quality is all that is needed to support a viable profile in general. Given the ordering, any set of numerical qualities in numerical form can be accommodated.

This is proved in White (2002): the first section of chapter 8 recovers the set of quality values *n* from the observed set of firm niches lying along their market profile. The sheer ordering on quality is sufficient to underwrite a market profile, so long as this quality ordering is the same on the cost side from upstream as on the demand side from downstream.

The same market price profile can hold across the most various sets of producers. All that is needed to specify this profile is (exponential) sensitivities, towards upstream and toward downstream, in valuations with respect to quality and volume. This is a sign that culture stands on an equal footing as determinant with social structure, which is, after all, the burden of the chapter by Favereau *et al.*

But a challenge for the Convention School comes from the dual view implicit in my model of mechanism for market. My theory of markets, formulated as a style in the 2002 book, contains within itself dual forms. The talk above was of interfaces pointed downstream towards crucial uncertainties found there. But an interface can also orient upstream. The model for it is dual, not a simple converse to that for downstream, so that the market plane/space has a quite different pattern (White 2002, chapter 9). This is a pattern which, for example, precludes any stable approximation to pure competition (chapter 11). Distinct markets are decoupled enough (chapter 10) for their orientation not to be preset by embedding with other markets.

Orientation of market, upstream or down, has not heretofore been recognized as such, to my knowledge. This raises issues as to the meaning and interpretation of quality. The model for upstream orientation raises no mathematical problems whatever. But the substantive difference in the market profile is huge. Now the producers are eyeing each other to estimate how much to pay out to entice an amount of factor of production optimal for them given the observed profile. Ordering is again the key, but ordering on relative unattractiveness. Should not conventions emerge for this orientation too, depending on its persistence and sectoral spread?

CONCLUSION: UPSTREAM OR DOWN?

What we should be attempting to provide, Swedberg (2000) suggests, is insights towards viable arrangements never seen before. Theory of agency, with its incomplete contracts and the like, should not be propounded as a rhetorical escape from the subtle and high-stacked intricacies of sociocultural structure/process. Instead, agency theory should be shaped to suggest, along lines found in many chapters of this volume, unheard-of ways of putting us together.[5]

The upshot is to focus our attention on how one can get action (White, 1992, ch. 6). Getting action comes only through figuring out and manoeuvering among the endless blockings of action that are the chief sign of social order and process. This is the venue in which Pratt and Zeckhauser's robust views of agency, realized in Lazega's study along with the blocking patterns, can hold sway.

Consider just one possible line for engineering innovation in social structures deriving from my market model: switch of orientation for the market interface between upstream and down. Switch of orientation invokes decisions, several and joint. White (2002, Figures 9.7, 9.6) offers predictions of which orientation is more attractive to producers, with particular focus on profitability. Matthew Bothner has developed this theme much further with simulation studies (Bothner and White, 2001). But there is no basis in present folk knowledge, or its variant as microeconomic theory, for recognizing the possibility of such a switch in orientation. Surely there is room here for development of social innovation. It is, after all, just where one can expect on theoretical grounds to find decision making, which is to say getting action in my sense, rising out of, and despite, the paradoxes of choice within social determinism.

And just here we must recognize and deal with the fact that 'decision' itself, rather than just invoking some principal and agents, comes into being only in a process spread across different levels. Decision intercalates with situation, much as network was seen earlier to intercalate with structure. One should try to predict when it is Favereau's situation inducing Boltanski's justification and when, rather, it is the historical 'casing' of Bearman, et al. (1999) which is being called for. One should educe, that is, some grammar of warranty and entailment as narrative for Lazega's resource and constraint.

Let me end by considering the underlying strategies of method for dissecting social constructions here. There are three: parameterize, endogenize and exploit duality. When modelling calls on more than a few parameters, results are too obscure to support theorizing. Social constructions build themselves within embedded orbits of reference which permit endogeneity. And, as Favereau has so elegantly demonstrated, mechanism and convention are the two equal hands needed for social clapping.

NOTES

1. But it need not be so with kinship crossed with invidious social stratification, as in some South Asian systems (Leach, 1954).
2. And this also clarifies its relations to work of organizational ecologists of the Hannan school (Hannan and Carroll, 1992).
3. In recent work, Zuckerman (1999, 2000) has established that professional observers, market analysts in investment banks, exert tacit, yet heeded, pressure on firms to assimilate themselves within a definite production market.
4. Flap is well aware of the virtues of the latter and brings in the 1960s English anthropology school for well-deserved attention in this book.
5. Natural scientists are providing liquid crystal for the hardware enabling our convenient new keyboards and calculators. It seems only fair that we bring the same subtlety to the analyses we write using their technology that they offer concerning these amazing materials (Walbe *et al.*, 2000; Pratibha *et al.*, 2000). They flow like liquids and yet diffract like crystals, and thereby can be engineered to be enormously responsive to signals through teasing them into ferromagnetic arrangements down at nanometric scales unheard of until recent decades.

REFERENCES

Bearman, Peter (1997), 'Generalized Exchange', *American Journal of Sociology*, 102, 1383–1415.

Bearman, Peter, Robert Faris and James Moody (1999), 'Blocking the Future', *Social Science History*, 23: 501–33.

Boltanski, Luc and Laurent Thévenot (1999), 'The Sociology of Critical Capacity', *European Journal of Social Theory*, 2, 359–77.
Bothner, Matthew S. and Harrison C. White (2001), 'Market Orientation and Monopoly Power', in Alessandro Lomi and Erik Larsen (eds), *Simulating Organizational Societies*, Cambridge, MA: MIT Press.
Callon, M. (1986), 'Eléments pour une sociologie de la traduction'. *L'Année Sociologique* 6, 169–208.
Coleman, James S. (1959), *The Adolescent Society*, Glencoe, IL: Free Press.
Degenne, Alan and Michel Forsé (1999), *Social Networks*, Beverly Hills: Sage.
Favereau, Olivier (1998), 'Decisions, situations, institutions', in Annie Vinokur (ed.), *Décisions Economiques*. Paris: Economica, pp. 153–169.
Favereau, Olivier and Suzanne Quiers-Valette (1998), 'Tous les problèmes d'incitation sont des problèmes d'interdépendance des niveaux de décision', in Annie Vinokur (ed.), *Décisions Economiques*, Paris: Economica, pp. 245–55.
Gibson, David (1999), 'Taking Turns in Business Talk', Preprint 225, Center for the Social Sciences, Columbia University, NY.
Hannan, Michael T. and Glenn R. Carroll (1992), *Dynamics of Organizational Populations: Density, Legitimation and Competition,* New York: Oxford University Press.
Knight, Frank ([1921] 1977), *Risk, Uncertainty and Profit*, Cambridge, MA: Houghton Mifflin.
Lazega, Emmanuel (2002), *The Collegial Phenomenon: The Social Mechanisms of Cooperation among Peers in a Corporate Law Partnership*, Oxford: Oxford University Press.
Leach, Edmund (1954), *The Political Systems of Highland Burma*, Boston, MA: Beacon.
Mische, Ann and Harrison C. White (1998), 'Between Conversation and Situation: Public Switching Dynamics across Network Domains', *Social Research*, 65, 695–724.
Piore, Michael J. and Charles F. Sabel (1983), *The Second Industrial Divide: Possibilities for Prosperity*, New York: Basic Books.
Pratibha, R., N.V. Madhusudana and B.K. Sadashiva (2000), 'An Orientational Transition of Bent-Core Molecules in an Anisotropic Matrix', *Science*, 288, 2184–7.
Pratt, John W. and Richard J. Zeckhauser (1985), Principals and Agents: An Overview', in J. W. Pratt and R. J., Zeckhauser (eds), *Principals and Agents: The Structure of Business*, Boston, MA: Harvard Business School Press.
Stinchcombe, Arthur (2001), *Thinking about Formality in Law and Organizations*, Chicago: University of Chicago Press.
Swedberg, Richard (2000), 'Economic Sociology', Department of Sociology, University of Stockholm.
Walbe, David M., Eva Korblova, Renfan Shao, Joseph E. Maclennan, Darren R. Lind, Matthew A. Glaser and Noel A. Clark (2000), 'A Ferroelectric Liquid Crystal Conglomerate Composed of Racemic Molecules', *Science*, 288, 2181–4.
White, Harrison C. (1992), *Identity and Control: A Structural Theory of Social Action*, Princeton, NJ: Princeton University Press.
White, Harrison C. (2002) *Markets from Networks*, Princeton, NJ: Princeton University Press.
Zeitlin, Jonathan. (2002), 'Production Alternatives: Flexibility, Governance and Strategic Change in Industrial History', in Franco Amatori and Geoffrey Jones

(eds), *Business History around the World*, New York: Cambridge University Press.
Zuckerman, Ezra W. (1999), 'The Categorical Imperative: Securities Analysts and the Illegitimacy Discount', *American Journal of Sociology*, 104, 1398–1438.
Zuckerman, Ezra W. (2000), 'Focusing the Corporate Product: Securities Analysts and De-Diversification', *Administrative Science Quarterly*, 45, 591–619.

Index